WALKING BY FAITH

Also by Angus Buchan

WALKING
BY
FAITH

Angus Buchan

MONARCH
BOOKS
Oxford UK, and Grand Rapids, USA

First published in South Africa by Maranatha

Published by Monarch Books
an imprint of
Lion Hudson plc
Wilkinson House, Jordan Hill Road,
Oxford OX2 8DR, England
Email: monarch@lionhudson.com
www.lionhudson.com/monarch

ISBN 978 0 85721 659 5
e-ISBN 978 0 85721 660 1

First edition 2015

Acknowledgments
Unless otherwise stated, Scripture quotations are taken from the New King James Version. Copyright © 1982 by Thomas Nelson, Inc. Used by permission. All rights reserved.
Scripture quotations marked KJV are taken from The Authorised (King James) Version. Rights in the Authorised Version are vested in the Crown. Reproduced by permission of the Crown's patentee, Cambridge University Press.
Scripture marked NASB is taken from the New American Standard Bible®, Copyright © 1960, 1962, 1963, 1968, 1971, 1972, 1973, 1975, 1977, 1995 by The Lockman Foundation. Used by permission.
Scripture quotation marked NIRV is taken from the Holy Bible, New International Reader's Version®. Copyright © 1996, 1998 Biblica. All rights reserved throughout the world. Used by permission of Biblica.
Scripture quotation marked NIV is taken from the Holy Bible, New International Version, copyright © 1973, 1978, 1984 International Bible Society. Used by permission of Hodder & Stoughton, a member of the Hodder Headline Group. All rights reserved. 'NIV' is a trademark of International Bible Society. UK trademark number 1448790.
Scripture quotations marked NLT are taken from the Holy Bible, New Living Translation, copyright © 1996, 2004, 2007 by Tyndale House Foundation. Used by permission of Tyndale House Publishers, Inc., Carol Stream, Illinois 60188. All rights reserved.
Scripture quotation marked NRSV is taken from The New Revised Standard Version of the Bible copyright © 1989 by the Division of Christian Education of the National Council of Churches in the USA. Used by permission. All Rights Reserved.
Scripture marked The Living Bible is taken from The Living Bible copyright © 1971 by Tyndale House Foundation. Used by permission of Tyndale House Publishers Inc., Carol Stream, Illinois 60188. All rights reserved.
Scriptures marked The Message are taken from The Message Bible. Copyright © 1993, 1994, 1995, 1996, 2000, 2001, 2002. Used by permission of NavPress Publishing Group.

A catalogue record for this book is available from the British Library

Printed and bound in Malta, May 2015, LH28

This book is dedicated to all new believers in Jesus Christ. Believing in Jesus is undoubtedly the best decision that you have ever made in your life. It is our Lord's desire that all of us should be "good finishers". We must complete the race, and as Paul the apostle said, "I press on to reach the end of the race and receive the heavenly prize for which God, through Christ Jesus, is calling us."

(Philippians 3:14, NLT)

Each of our lives is a journey and we must walk it by "faith in God" (Mark 11:22). Quite simply, if we do not walk by faith, we will not finish the course. I have tried many times to do things my way and it has never worked for me. There is only one way and that is God's way. Both Martin Luther and John Wesley endeavoured to earn their way to eternal life, but both failed miserably. Luther tried to put down his flesh by starving himself – he punished his flesh in many different ways, but none of it worked; he still did not gain the victory. John Wesley thought that travelling to America, and preaching the gospel to the American Indians, would help him find the way to Jesus, peace, and everlasting life. He returned to England completely disillusioned. It was only after they each discovered Romans 1:17: "The just shall live by faith" that they were set free. This explosive little piece of Scripture changed those two very average theologians into giants of the faith. If we declare as they both did – "for we walk by faith, not by sight" (2 Corinthians 5:7) – we will finish strong for Jesus!

Angus Buchan

WALKING BY FAITH

Choosing to walk by faith

1. Walk by faith
2. A mighty man of God
3. Counting the cost
4. The just shall live by faith
5. A new creation
6. Jesus never changes
7. A persistent faith
8. Living water
9. A desperate faith
10. Jesus rewards persistence
11. Come just as you are
12. Turn your eyes upon Jesus
13. Commit your ways to the Lord
14. Jesus will carry you through
15. Wait patiently for the Lord
16. Will the Son of Man find faith?
17. The substance of faith
18. God's way or your way?
19. Without faith you cannot please God
20. Be still and know...
21. Let not your heart be afraid
22. A mind stayed upon Jesus
23. Time in God's presence
24. Have faith in God
25. Faith as a mustard seed
26. The prayer of faith
27. Praying according to God's will
28. The just shall live by faith
29. Your Light and your Salvation
30. A hymn of faith
31. The sleep of faith

WALK BY FAITH

Read 2 Corinthians 5

FOR WE WALK BY FAITH, NOT BY SIGHT.

2 Corinthians 5:7

Down through the ages, from the beginning of time up to the present day, men of faith have walked with God. Each of them have walked different, unique paths. Their assignments have been diverse. God chose each of them to play a role in fulfilling His purposes. They all had a God-given task to fulfil in establishing His Kingdom here on earth. At the end of the day, though, they all have one thing in common – they have chosen to walk by faith and to obey God no matter what the sacrifices or consequences.

We stand on the brink of a new year. It is a year that will bring new opportunities as well as challenges. We cannot see into the future. The choice you have to make as you step into this new year is – will you walk by faith or by sight? Paul, in his letter to the Corinthians, exhorted them: "for we walk by faith, not by sight". If you want to be a mighty man of God your only option is to walk by faith. It is the road of faith that will lead you to fulfil your destiny and purpose. This road of faith will bring you closer to your Heavenly Father. It is the road of faith that will one day cause Him to say to you: "Well done, good and faithful servant; you were faithful over a few things, I will make you ruler over many things. Enter into the joy of your lord" (Matthew 25:23).

This year, we will embark upon a faith journey together. We will trust God to speak to us through His Word. Together we will examine the lives and faith walks of men of God throughout history. Every man of God, no matter which century or era he lived in, has known successes as well as failures in his life. Each of them were human and they all had struggles as well as challenges to overcome. In many ways they were no different from us. My question to you is: will you walk by sight or by faith?

Prayer

My Father God, it is such a privilege to come into Your presence at the beginning of this new year. Lord, I want to walk by faith and not by sight this year. I place my life in Your hands. I want to walk in Your ways and do Your will. Amen.

Read 2 Samuel 23:1–17

THESE ARE THE NAMES OF THE MIGHTY MEN WHOM DAVID HAD…

2 Samuel 23:8a

I want to talk to you about being a mighty man of God. The name "mighty men" comes from 2 Samuel 23 where the Bible speaks about the mighty men of David. These men did great exploits for God and for David, their king. They were not mighty men in their own eyes, but rather they were mighty men for God. You know, I got hammered when people first heard that we had called our men's conference, which was to become an annual event, the "Mighty Men Conference". A theologian wrote to me querying how I could call it by the name "mighty" men, when, as Christians, we are supposed to be humble people.

That theologian had it all wrong, my friends. We are not mighty men in our own eyes; we are mighty men in God's eyes. David's mighty men lived for him. We have just read about how one day David was thirsty. He longed for water from the well in Bethlehem. Immediately, with no thought for their own safety, three of David's mighty men went down to fetch water for him. They passed right through the Philistines' camp, went to the well, drew water, and brought it back to David. He was so overwhelmed by their love that he took the water and poured it out to the Lord: "And he said, 'Far be it from me, O Lord, that I should do this! Is this not the blood of the men who went in jeopardy of their lives?'" (verse 17a).

The men listed in today's passage did great exploits for their king. As men, we are to do great exploits for our King Jesus. How do we do this? By looking after our wives; loving and encouraging them to become the wonderful women God created them to be. We do it when we protect, discipline, and put food on the table for our children. So, mighty men, stand up for what you believe in. You are an ambassador for Jesus Christ. A mighty man of God chooses to walk by faith and not by sight. A mighty man of God knows that: "I can do all things through Christ who strengthens me" (Philippians 4:13).

Prayer

My Father God, You have called me to be a mighty man for You. Help me to be willing to do whatever it is that You ask of me without hesitation. Give me the grace to be all that You want me to be to my family. Amen.

Read Luke 9:57–62

> BUT JESUS SAID TO HIM, "NO ONE, HAVING PUT HIS HAND TO THE PLOUGH,
> AND LOOKING BACK, IS FIT FOR THE KINGDOM OF GOD."
>
> Luke 9:62

My friends, it is time to get serious about following Jesus. As you stand at the beginning of a new year it is a good time to examine your heart. It is important to stop for a moment and count the cost of the commitment you have made to Jesus. I want to ask you a question: Did you count the cost before you said, "Lord, I am going to serve You with all of my heart?" We have to count the cost. Take a moment to reflect on what you are doing with what God has given to you.

Each of us is going to stand accountable when we get to Heaven one day. Before I go any further with this topic I want to make sure that you understand where I am coming from. I don't believe that you have to earn your way to Heaven. That would be impossible, because no one can earn their Salvation. We will get to Heaven because we believe in Jesus Christ. Ephesians 2:8–9 tells us: "For by grace you have been saved through faith, and that not of yourselves; it is the gift of God, not of works, lest anyone should boast."

Having said this, today's Scripture reading gives us a strong exhortation about counting the cost of following Jesus. It is not to be taken lightly. God is looking for mighty men who will walk by faith and not by sight. He is looking for ordinary men like you and me who will do extraordinary exploits for Him. We have a choice before us: we can either live this year going about our business as usual, or we can choose to make it a year where we will put our hand to the plough and not look back. Take some time to examine your heart before God, your Father. Ask the Holy Spirit to illuminate the areas that you need to recommit to Jesus. The time has come to get serious with God. Don't delay thinking tomorrow is another day – do it today!

Prayer

My Father God, You have spoken directly to my heart. Thank You for Your amazing grace to me. I am grateful that You love me. Help me, as I sit in Your presence, to make the decision to place my hand on the plough and move forward with You. Amen.

Read Romans 1:1–17

> FOR IN IT THE RIGHTEOUSNESS OF GOD IS REVEALED FROM FAITH TO FAITH; AS
> IT IS WRITTEN, "THE JUST SHALL LIVE BY FAITH."
>
> Romans 1:17

Isn't this a wonderful verse of Scripture? I want to share with you about some of the mighty men of God and their journey to understanding what it means to live by faith. George Whitefield was one of the greatest preachers and evangelists of all time. He lived during the eighteenth century, at the same time as John and Charles Wesley who founded the Methodist movement. These young men, who were all students together at the University of Oxford in England, formed what was known as the "Holy Club". They, just like other God-fearing men who came after them – such as James Hudson Taylor (1832–1905), the founder of the China Inland Mission – would gather together to seek the face of the Lord. They prayed, "Lord, we will do whatever You want."

Now when those men gathered together at the Holy Club they lay on their faces before God. They would pray and beat their bodies – fasting and praying they would go without sleep until they almost collapsed. Similarly James Hudson Taylor, who came from a fairly wealthy family but who gave all his food money to the poor in the East End of London, had a diet that seemed to consist of half a loaf of bread and an apple a day. He believed he was toughening his body for the work that he was going to do in China. Each of these men tried to put down the flesh, but they failed miserably. They were counting the cost, but in the wrong way.

In fact, one day George Whitefield did collapse and he was confined to bed for seven weeks to recover from his self-inflicted suffering. It was while he was recovering that he realized the truth of the words in Romans 1:17: "The just shall live by faith." This is the same biblical verse that changed both Martin Luther and John Wesley's lives. After this experience George Whitefield said that trying to earn your way to Heaven through good works is as futile as trying to climb a rope of sand to the moon. Isn't that beautiful? Can you imagine climbing to the moon on a rope of sand? It is impossible. It is also impossible to get to Heaven by good works. We get to Heaven by faith. My friend, are you living by faith today?

Prayer

My Heavenly Father, I come to You in Jesus' Name. I thank You from the bottom of my heart that I am saved by grace. Thank You for Your Word that tells me that "the just shall live by faith". There is no other way for me to please You; there is no other way for me to get to Heaven. Amen.

Read 2 Corinthians 5

> THEREFORE, IF ANYONE IS IN CHRIST, HE IS A NEW CREATION; OLD THINGS HAVE PASSED AWAY; BEHOLD, ALL THINGS HAVE BECOME NEW.
>
> 2 Corinthians 5:17

What wonderfully encouraging words these are: "Therefore, if anyone is in Christ, he is a new creation; old things have passed away; behold, all things have become new." These are God's Words to you today. They are meant to give you strength, firming your resolve to walk by faith and not by sight. With the new life that we enjoy comes responsibility. We still need to count the cost. Our Scripture from a couple of days ago exhorted us: "No one, having put his hand to the plough, and looking back, is fit for the kingdom of God" (Luke 9:62).

So often we are no different from those who are in the world. At the beginning of a new year people everywhere make New Year's resolutions. They undertake to do certain things that they haven't done before, or in some cases to stop doing things that they have been doing. For most people these resolutions do not last very long. Usually, shortly into the new year, they forget the promises they made to themselves and they revert back to their old ways.

This is not how it is meant to be in the life of a Christian. The reason that we can live victoriously is because of what God has done for us through Jesus Christ: "For He made Him who knew no sin to be sin for us, that we might become the righteousness of God in Him" (verse 21). Live as the new creation that Jesus has saved you to be. Walk by faith and not by sight. Don't fall into the trap of works – because that is a dead end, doomed to failure. You will never know victory through your own efforts. Live and walk each day in the Spirit. Have your hand firmly upon the plough and do not look back. This is not a decision you make once at the beginning of a new year. It is a decision that you make daily. Each day you have to choose to follow Jesus and not your own way.

Prayer

My Father God, You have spoken to me once again today. I realize that too often I try to do things in my own strength. I want to be totally dependent upon You. I realize that there is no other way to serve You. Help me to live as Your new creation. Amen.

Read Hebrews 13

JESUS CHRIST IS THE SAME YESTERDAY, TODAY, AND FOREVER.

Hebrews 13:8

Are you struggling with your faith as you begin this new year? We are almost through the first week of the year. Maybe you have been reading these devotionals with a heavy heart. You want to be a man who lives by faith and not by sight, but you are overwhelmed by your circumstances. Over the next few days I want to talk to you about the persistence of faith. However, I believe that you will not be able to embrace what I have to say regarding perseverance until you have established in your heart that you can trust Jesus. Our verse tells us: "Jesus Christ is the same yesterday, today, and forever." Do you really, deep down in your heart, believe this? More importantly, is this how you experience Jesus?

"For He Himself has said, 'I will never leave you nor forsake you.' So we may boldly say: 'The Lord is my helper; I will not fear. What can man do to me?'" (verses 5b–6). This is the crux of the matter, my friend. Walking by faith will only be possible if you believe that Jesus is who He says He is. Faith is about a Person – Jesus Christ. Faith is not a philosophy or a resolution that you make. Faith is not a decision. Faith is born out of a relationship with Jesus Christ. So if you are feeling overwhelmed, this is where you must start. Re-establish your relationship with Him.

If you do not have a vibrant, growing relationship with Jesus, your Christian walk will always be a struggle. You will be like the young men who belonged to the Wesleys' "Holy Club". You will exhaust yourself with your efforts to serve God. Allow Jesus to illuminate your heart, soul, and spirit with His love and power right now. Let His grace wash over you. Revel in the fact that it is by grace and grace alone that you are saved. Then walk in this grace each day, firmly holding on to Jesus' hand. Then, no matter what life tosses your way, you will never be defeated.

Prayer

My Father in Heaven, I come before You with a grateful heart. I realize that I have tried to walk this faith road in my own strength. It has worn me out. I once again surrender to You. Thank You for Your grace, love, and mercy toward me. Thank You that Jesus is the same yesterday, today, and forever. Amen.

Read John 7:25–39

> ON THE LAST DAY, THAT GREAT DAY OF THE FEAST, JESUS STOOD AND CRIED
> OUT, SAYING, "IF ANYONE THIRSTS, LET HIM COME TO ME AND DRINK. HE
> WHO BELIEVES IN ME, AS THE SCRIPTURE HAS SAID, OUT OF HIS HEART WILL
> FLOW RIVERS OF LIVING WATER."
>
> John 7:37–38

Yesterday we established that faith is grounded in a relationship with Jesus Christ. A result of a deepening relationship with Jesus Christ is perseverance. You will begin to have a faith that perseveres through difficulties. In Mark 10:46–52 we read the story of blind Bartimaeus. If asked to sum up his story in one word, I would say: persistence.

Bartimaeus was a desperate man. As you sit reading this you might say to me, "Angus, I am also desperate. I am really, really battling because things aren't going well and I feel God is not coming through for me." I want to tell you that this is a lie from the pit of hell, my friend! God is never early and He is never late. He is always exactly on time. He is here for you right now and He wants to remind you that, as we learned yesterday, He is exactly the same as He was yesterday, and He will remain the same tomorrow (Hebrews 13:8, paraphrased). So if He healed the sick when He walked on this earth, you can rest assured He still heals the sick today and He will continue to heal the sick tomorrow. He uses people like you and me as His instruments of healing.

Today we read the beautiful Scripture: "He who believes in Me, as the Scripture has said, out of his heart will flow rivers of living water." This is a wonderful promise, isn't it? If you believe in Jesus, then living water will flow from your heart! If you aren't receiving any living water at the moment, it is because you are not giving any. You see, God only gives you His power in order for you to share it with others. Freely you have received; freely give. Like blind Bartimaeus, do not give up – be persistent. Make your relationship with Jesus everything in your life. Then living by faith and not by sight will be a natural choice for you. Reach out to Him, allowing Him to flow through you and out toward others. This is the path to blessing, fulfilment, and joy.

Prayer
My Father God, it is with joy that I come before You. I know that so often I become bogged down by the cares of life. You have reminded me again of what is important. I place my trust in You. I look to You. I want to experience the rivers of living water flowing from my heart. Amen.

Read John 4:1–42

> JESUS ANSWERED AND SAID TO HER, "WHOEVER DRINKS OF THIS WATER WILL
> THIRST AGAIN, BUT WHOEVER DRINKS OF THE WATER THAT I SHALL GIVE HIM
> WILL NEVER THIRST. BUT THE WATER THAT I SHALL GIVE HIM WILL BECOME IN
> HIM A FOUNTAIN OF WATER SPRINGING UP INTO EVERLASTING LIFE."
>
> John 4:13–14

You might say to me, "I am trying! Angus, I am asking the Holy Spirit to fill me." What is the reason you want to be filled? Is it for personal gain? If this is the case, there is a good chance you will not receive anything. If your desire is to bless others then without a doubt God will fill you up. When the woman at the well accepted Jesus' offer of living water she immediately shared what she had experienced with others (verses 28–30). She didn't keep the living water for herself only.

In my talks I often make mention of the two lakes in Israel. As you know, the lifeblood of Israel is the River Jordan. It starts at the top and flows all the way down through Israel right to the bottom. As you enter Israel the River Jordan flows into the Sea of Galilee. It is a beautiful freshwater lake teeming with life. The water flows in at the top and out at the bottom, continually moving. Receiving and giving. It is fresh and full of fish. Fishermen have been fishing on that lake for over 3,000 years. While visiting there I sat down and ate the same kind of fish that the Master ate when He walked by the Sea of Galilee all those years ago. Isn't that amazing?

As the River Jordan leaves the Sea of Galilee it eventually flows into another sea called the Dead Sea. It is also a lake, but there is a big difference between the two lakes. The water flows into the Dead Sea but it doesn't flow out. It stops there. It is so dense that you can lie on top of the water and you do not sink. You cannot drink it. There is no life there. There are no fish. It is just a big, salty lake. Which are you: the Sea of Galilee or the Dead Sea? Choosing to live by faith and not by sight means that you will be the Sea of Galilee. From your "heart will flow rivers of living water" (John 7:38).

Prayer
Lord, I choose to live by faith and not by sight. I do not want to live a selfish life where it is all about me. I want to have Your rivers of living water flow from my heart, reaching out to others and blessing them. My Father, bless me so that I can be a blessing, I pray. Amen.

Read Mark 10:46–52

> So Jesus answered and said to him, "What do you want Me to do for you?" The blind man said to Him, "Rabboni, that I may receive my sight."
>
> Mark 10:51

What does a desperate faith look like? Bartimaeus was blind, he was desperate, and he had nothing left to lose. So he put everything that he had into believing in God – and God came through for him. Bartimaeus was sitting on the side of the road when he heard the crowds saying that Jesus was approaching. He began shouting: "Jesus, Son of David, have mercy on me!" (verse 47c). The crowd became irritated and told him to keep quiet and not to trouble the Master. Bartimaeus ignored them; he was not going to be put off. This was his one chance to reach out to Jesus and he wasn't going to miss out on it.

Isn't it interesting that the people did not care about blind Bartimaeus? They didn't want him to be a nuisance and embarrass them in front of the Visitor. They totally missed the point of what Jesus was about. We are often no different from the crowd around Bartimaeus. As we go about our business of looking after number one we often overlook the opportunities that God puts in our path to be a blessing to others. The irony is that the more we share the living water, the more we will receive; it can never run out. There is an abundance of water available to us.

Bartimaeus was determined to attract Jesus' attention. He knew that he wanted an encounter with Jesus. As I say, he was a desperate man. Do you think that the problem is that we are so self-sufficient that we get into a position where we are not desperate enough for God? Or, alternatively, that we are in dire circumstances, but we are too proud to surrender to God? We want His blessing, but on our own terms. This will never work. God doesn't operate on our terms. If you are desperate right now, how are you handling it? Are you still trying to call the shots, are you negotiating with God, or are you sitting on the side of the road, calling out: "Jesus, Son of David, have mercy on me!"?

Prayer

My Father, I proclaim that I am desperate for You. I come with empty hands outstretched to You. I am not interested in bargaining, dictating, or working out my own plans. I surrender to You. Fill me with Your living water so that it can flow through me and outwards to others. Amen.

Read Mark 10:35–52

> Then Jesus said to him, "Go your way; your faith has made you well." And immediately he received his sight and followed Jesus on the road.
>
> Mark 10:52

It is interesting that in the verses preceding the story of Bartimaeus, Jesus had been speaking to His disciples about what it means to serve. He wanted them to understand that all that they received from Him was not for their benefit alone, but for the benefit of others as well. This fits right in with what we have been talking about over the past few days. Despite the people trying to quieten Bartimaeus, Jesus heard him. This is so amazing. You too can know, my friend, that when you call out to Jesus He will hear you. It doesn't matter how much noise there is around you – He hears the faintest whisper.

Jesus immediately instructed the people to bring Bartimaeus to Him. We see the attitude of the crowd change: "Then they called the blind man, saying to him, 'Be of good cheer. Rise, He is calling you'" (verse 49b). Doesn't this ring with the tones of hypocrisy? A few minutes before they had been telling Bartimaeus to keep quiet; now, when Jesus took notice of him, they all wanted to be his friend. Then Jesus asked Bartimaeus what he wanted. Do you think Jesus didn't know what his need was? Of course He did! However, He wanted Bartimaeus to verbalize his need. Jesus rewarded Bartimaeus' faith.

Whatever your need is, Jesus wants you to verbalize it. Ask Him, talk to Him. God's Word tells us: "If you abide in Me, and My words abide in you, you will ask what you desire, and it shall be done for you" (John 15:7). Jesus rewards persistence. He is the same Jesus who healed blind Bartimaeus, who heard him call in the midst of the crowd. He will do the same for you. Choose to live by faith and not by sight. Reach out to Jesus and when He blesses you go and bless others in turn. Be a free-flowing river of blessing, touching the lives of those around you and you will never run dry. Bartimaeus' response was to follow Jesus on the road – what is your response?

Prayer

My Father God, thank You for Your Word that has spoken so clearly to me. I am so grateful that You hear me when I call to You. Thank You that You reward persistence. Help me never to give up. Fill me so that I can reach out and touch the lives of others. Amen.

Read Mark 10:46–52

> AND WHEN HE HEARD THAT IT WAS JESUS OF NAZARETH, HE BEGAN TO CRY
> OUT AND SAY, "JESUS, SON OF DAVID, HAVE MERCY ON ME!"
>
> Mark 10:47

The other day I asked you the following questions: If you are desperate, how are you handling it? Are you still trying to call the shots? Are you negotiating with God, or are you sitting on the side of the road, calling out: "Jesus, Son of David, have mercy on me!"? Bartimaeus was a beggar; he didn't have a reputation. Our problem is often our pride. They say the last sin you have to deal with before you die is foolish pride. My dear friend, we need to lay our pride down. Pride was the cause of Lucifer being thrown out of Heaven along with a third of the angels. He was the most beautiful angel in Heaven, but he began thinking that he was better than God. God will not tolerate that from anybody. It is pride that keeps us from moving on with God.

Bartimaeus had no pride. He had nothing to lose. Therefore he wasn't going to let the opportunity pass him by. If you take a moment to think about it, we are in the same boat as Bartimaeus. What do we have to lose? Nothing. What do we have to gain? Eternal life. Be persistent. Keep on keeping on. Cry out to God! Continue believing Him for a miracle. Keep trusting that your family will be restored. Come to Jesus just as you are and be persistent. Maybe you are a sportsman and you believe you are going to play professionally. Keep believing. You never know how close you are to a breakthrough.

Sir, maybe you are a pastor who has fallen by the way. Possibly you've been caught in adultery or you have embezzled money. On the other hand, maybe you are simply discouraged and burned out. You are reading this devotional wondering if there is any hope for you. Oh yes, there is, my friend! Go and read 1 John 1:9. Repent of your pride and your sin. Stop negotiating with God. Whatever your need, learn a lesson from Bartimaeus – be persistent; don't give up. Come just as you are.

Prayer

My Father God, I come to You just as I am. I repent of my sin. I repent of my pride. I bow at Your feet and thank You for Your Word that says, if I confess my sins, You are faithful and just to forgive me of all my sin and to cleanse me from all unrighteousness. Thank You, Lord. Amen.

Read Mark 10:46–52

So Jesus answered and said to him, "What do you want Me to do for you?" The blind man said to Him, "Rabboni, that I may receive my sight."

Mark 10:51

We will spend one more day learning lessons from the story of Bartimaeus. As long as you are fearful of man, you will never be able to consistently walk by faith and not by sight. God will not be able to use you. The only way to deal with your fear of man is to focus on Jesus, and then the fear of the world will simply dissipate. Remember the beautiful old song by Helen H. Lemmel:

Turn your eyes upon Jesus,
Look full in His wonderful face,
And the things of earth will grow strangely dim,
In the light of His glory and grace.

I had a terrible fear of man, but God took it away from me. Now I fear God more than I fear man. This gives me great liberty. Not that I am brave, I hasten to add – not at all. I simply love Jesus so much that He is the only One whom I want to please. As long as I keep my eyes fixed upon Him I don't fear any man. It doesn't really matter what you think of me. All that matters is what Jesus thinks of me. The exact same thing is true for you.

Whatever your need is, God wants to meet it. Jesus is right there with you. Be persistent; call out to Him. Reach out and touch Him. Tell Him your need, then believe Him for the answer. Do you want to be healed? Yes, Lord! Do you want to be restored? Yes, Lord! Do you want to have a new start? Yes, Lord! Well then, ask Him. "Ask, and it will be given to you; seek, and you will find; knock, and it will be opened to you. For everyone who asks receives, and he who seeks finds, and to him who knocks it will be opened" (Matthew 7:7–8). Isn't this a beautiful promise from God? It doesn't matter what you have done. God still loves you, my friend. He loved you so much that He died on the Cross of Calvary for you.

Prayer
My Father in Heaven, today I turn my eyes upon Jesus. I look full in His wonderful face. As I look to You, Jesus, take away my fear. Touch me, heal me, and restore me, I pray. Fill me with Your Spirit. Lord, I want to be persistent. I want to live by faith and not by sight. Amen.

Read Psalm 37:1–6

COMMIT YOUR WAY TO THE LORD, TRUST ALSO IN HIM, AND HE SHALL
BRING IT TO PASS.

Psalm 37:5

Who does our Scripture say will bring it to pass? Not you, no, but the Lord – He will bring it to pass. I have been farming for close on forty years and I want to tell you, it is the Lord Jesus Christ who brings us through, every single time. What about you? In whom are you placing your trust?

I want to share the story of Doctor David Livingstone with you over the next few days. You know by now that I love the stories of the mighty men of God from history: those men who held nothing back as they committed their lives to serving Jesus. David Livingstone was a great missionary, evangelist, explorer, linguist, and astronomer of the nineteenth century. He is one of my heroes of the faith. Not because he comes from the bonny Scotland of my ancestors, but because he trusted God. The Scripture verse we highlighted just now was used by Livingstone to sustain him when journeying through the dense African jungle.

From the age of ten up until he was twenty-six Livingstone worked in a cotton mill in the little village of Blantyre, just outside Glasgow in Scotland. Unlike the other children of his day, who often grew up illiterate, the young David set his books up in front of his spinning loom and he educated himself while he worked. At the age of sixteen he completed his schooling. Later he studied medicine and theology and graduated as a medical missionary. (So don't keep complaining about your past. Put your past behind you and let God make a difference in your life today.) Eventually Livingstone felt called by God to go to Africa, and so it was that he came to my beloved continent, this continent that I too love so much. He began his journey in 1841, in Cape Town, and he walked from there up into Central Africa. You heard me! He walked, my friend. Can you imagine? Along the way Livingstone was ravaged by a lion who broke his shoulder. If it were not for his Scottish tweed jacket, the lion would have killed him – the beast couldn't get its teeth through the thick material. Like the psalmist David, Livingstone was protected from wild animals. I ask you again: in whom are you placing your trust today?

Prayer

My Father God, I thank You for Your Word and Your promise to me. Like all Your promises it comes with a command. Lord, help me to commit my ways to You anew this day and every day. I want to have a persistent faith. I want to walk by faith and not by sight. Amen.

Read Psalm 37:1–8

Trust in the Lord, and do good; dwell in the land, and feed on His faithfulness.

Psalm 37:3

Don't let anyone tell you that when you come to Jesus all your problems will be over. That is a lie. There is no Scriptural evidence to support this statement. No, my friend, what He says is this: "Commit your way to the Lord, trust also in Him, and He shall bring it to pass. He shall bring forth your righteousness as the light, and your justice as the noonday" (verses 5–6).

Getting back to David Livingstone, of whom we spoke yesterday. After his skirmish with the lion he bound up his broken arm and continued his journey. (By the way, if you go to the Livingstone Museum in Zambia you will see a plaster cast of Livingstone's shoulder bone where the lion attacked him.) When he died, Livingstone's faithful men carried his remains some 1,500 miles, on their shoulders, back to the coast, and from there he was shipped back to England. When he arrived home he was identified by his broken shoulder bone. In Africa, Livingstone was known as "the good man". God had given him a heart for Africa, and he committed his ways to the Lord.

Livingstone walked up to the Victoria Falls and from there right across to the west coast of Africa. It took him four years to do this. After that he walked back to the Victoria Falls and then on to the east coast of Africa. He did not allow anything to deter him. Not malaria nor the sleeping sickness he contracted that was caused by the tsetse fly. The fear of death didn't deter him. Starvation didn't stop him. He continued walking because he had committed his ways to the Lord. Livingstone trusted in God and He brought it to pass.

My friend, I don't know what the challenges are that you are facing in your life. I can assure you, though, that you serve the same God as Livingstone. What He did for Livingstone, He can do for you. If you put your trust in Him, if you choose to walk by faith and not by sight, if you are willing to persevere, God, your Father, will undertake for you. He will see you through. You can "trust in the Lord… and feed on His faithfulness" today. He will not let you down.

Prayer

My Father in Heaven, I bow before You with a grateful heart. Forgive my unbelief. When things don't go my way I am so easily tempted to turn away from You. Thank You for Your faithfulness toward me. Help me to feed on Your faithfulness today. Amen.

Read Psalm 37:1–11

> REST IN THE LORD, AND WAIT PATIENTLY FOR HIM… BUT THOSE WHO WAIT
> ON THE LORD, THEY SHALL INHERIT THE EARTH.
>
> Psalm 37:7a, 9b

Livingstone came on three expeditions to Africa. He loved the African people and his great desire was to see Africa set free from the curse of the slave trade. Livingstone's life ended, in 1873, in a little grass shack in his beloved continent. He died alone, riddled with malaria, kneeling beside his cot in the heart of Africa. He committed his ways to the Lord Jesus Christ right up to his last breath.

Looking from the outside in, one might think Livingstone failed at his mission. He didn't find the source of the Nile. Nobody seemed to listen to him. The London Missionary Society (LMS) struck him off their books because they considered him a failure. He buried his wife beneath a baobab tree at the mouth of the Zambezi River. His children didn't know him. Yet, after he died the whole world sat up and realized that the slave trade could not continue. People began reading the letters that he had faithfully written and sent back to Britain, as well as over to America. Yet, just weeks after Livingstone's death in 1873, Britain realized that the Arab slave trade in East Africa – the horrors of which Livingstone had highlighted in letters home – could not continue. Finally the slave market in Zanzibar was closed, ending the eastern trade in slaves, and subsequently thousands of young university students went into the East African mission field preaching the gospel.

"Commit your way to the Lord, trust also in Him, and He shall bring it to pass" (verse 5). As you read this, are you thinking that it was all very well for someone like David Livingstone to serve God with such fervour and commitment? You feel that you cannot serve God wholeheartedly because you have too many problems, too many things that are holding you back. My friend, no one who has done great exploits for God has had it easy. I can mention name upon name to you of people whom God has used mightily down through history; every one of them has known hardship and difficulty. Psalm 37 goes on to promise: "He shall bring forth your righteousness as the light, and your justice as the noonday" (verse 6). Wait patiently for Him; trust in your God – commit your ways to Him and He will bring it to pass in His own time.

Prayer

My God, You are a great, merciful and faithful God. There is none like You. I realize once again as I contemplate your Word that Your ways are not my ways. You do not work in the same way that humans do. Help me to wait, trust, and commit my ways to You – not only today, but every day. Amen.

Read Luke 18:1–8

THEN HE SPOKE A PARABLE TO THEM, THAT MEN ALWAYS OUGHT TO PRAY
AND NOT LOSE HEART...

Luke 18:1

Our theme this year is *walking by faith and not by sight*. In order to do this you have to develop perseverance. We spent a few days discussing Bartimaeus' persistence. He would not be deflected from his goal of catching Jesus' attention. When he did, Jesus asked him what he wanted. Bartimaeus was very clear and very specific about what he wanted Jesus to do for him. In our Scripture reading Jesus once again tells a parable that illustrates the need for persistence. You cannot have persistence and perseverance without faith. I suppose another way of putting it is that you must not lose heart. You must keep on believing.

There is no Christian on this earth who is exempt from experiencing problems. We live in this world. It is an important part of our testimony for the world to see how we handle our problems. If you do not experience problems the world can easily say, "These guys don't know what they are talking about. They cannot identify with us because they don't know what we are going through." Of course we have problems – the question is, how do we handle them? We handle them by taking them to Jesus. He told the parable in today's reading specifically so that we can be encouraged to come to Him. He says that "men *always ought to pray and not lose heart*".

Are you losing heart? I hope not, my friend. You have everything to hope for – you have Jesus. A book I once read said that we must burden Jesus with our problems. You can burden Him because He can carry your load. Acquaint Jesus with your problems. What does this mean? It means telling Him what your problems are. Often you tell everybody else except Jesus. Go, sit down and have a good chat with Him. Say, "Listen, Lord, I can't go on any more. I need help." Then trust Him to meet your needs. Jesus asks you the following question: "when the Son of Man comes, will He really find faith on the earth?" (verse 8b).

Prayer

My Father God, I come to You in the Name of Jesus, my Saviour and Lord. As I sit in Your presence I have to tell You that I cannot cope with my situation any more. Forgive me that I so often turn to everyone else before I turn to You. Lord, give me faith; give me perseverance, I pray. Amen.

Read Hebrews 11:1–16

NOW FAITH IS THE SUBSTANCE OF THINGS HOPED FOR, THE EVIDENCE OF
THINGS NOT SEEN.

Hebrews 11:1

You might remember that the UK went through the most horrific foot and mouth epidemic it had ever experienced some years ago. None of the European countries bought their milk, meat, and livestock. The farmers went through hell, folks, absolute hell. They had to shoot their own cattle. Many of them didn't know Jesus and they couldn't handle it so they ended up shooting themselves. Suicide is never the answer, my friend. It is a selfish course of action leaving your loved ones behind to deal with the consequences of your actions. I want to share with you how the Lord Jesus Christ undertook for some of those farmers.

I was invited to go over to England by a farmer named Nigel Butler, who farms in the Newbury area, to encourage the farmers there. He hired the town's Corn Exchange for the rally. It is a beautiful upmarket theatre with all the modern conveniences. The rental on this theatre was the equivalent of R30,000 per night. Now Nigel didn't have that sort of money lying around. However, he believed that it was what God wanted him to do, so he went ahead and booked the venue, paying for it from his savings. It seated 1,000 people and he gave the tickets away to non-Christians in the area.

All the tickets were taken. If you have done any preaching in Britain or even Europe you will know that to get a crowd together there is almost impossible. Nigel heard God speak to him and he obeyed God, not knowing how he would recoup his savings. Shortly after returning to his farm, a motor vehicle with the British telephone company's logo on the side drew up. They confirmed with him that he had ten of their telephone poles running through his farm. Then they informed him that the company owed him R3,000 per telephone pole. Yes, my friend, a total of R30,000 – exactly the amount he had paid for the theatre. What is God telling you to do – and what are you going to do about it?

Prayer

My Father, I am so encouraged when I read stories such as this one. You are indeed a faithful God! Help me to trust You. I know that You are talking to me about doing certain things. I realize that faith and obedience go hand in hand. I know that I can trust You to do what You say You will do. Amen.

Read Psalm 37:1–17

COMMIT YOUR WAY TO THE LORD, TRUST ALSO IN HIM, AND HE SHALL BRING
IT TO PASS.

Psalm 37:5

I hope as you read one of David Livingstone's favourite psalms one more time that God's Holy Spirit spoke to your heart. I hope that the truths we have shared so far this month have shown you that you are not dependent upon the things that are happening around you. It is not about what is happening in the agricultural sector. It is not about the global economic situation. It is not about what is happening with your family. It is about what is happening with God. You see, when you start to focus on the "Problem-Solver", the problem diminishes as Jesus grows bigger. Our problem is that we run to everyone but God. Then at the eleventh hour when no one can help us – not the doctors, not the bank manager, nor the counsellor – we finally run to God. Sometimes it is too late by then, so don't delay any longer.

The result of Nigel Butler committing his ways to the Lord and trusting Him was that a revival took place at the Corn Exchange on 18 February that year. It was extra special to me because 18 February was also the day that I made a commitment to Jesus Christ. On top of that in South Africa, Anna Anderson, a lady for whom we had prayed to fall pregnant, gave birth that night. She had said to her husband that she would like their baby to be born on the anniversary of when I came to know Jesus. So there were many celebrations happening that night.

My friend, you serve an awesome God. Let Him be God in your life. Is Jesus in the driver's seat or are you still sitting there? Allow God to make the decisions in your life. Every man of God down through history has faced the choice: will it be God's way or my way? You face the same decision as you stand halfway through the first month of this new year, my friend. What will it be: God's way or your way?

Prayer

My Father God, I stand before You with a heart filled with praise. Thank You for Your faithfulness and Your patience with me. You never leave me; You never forsake me. You are always there. Today, I choose Your way instead of my way before it is too late. Amen.

Read Hebrews 11:1–6

> BUT WITHOUT FAITH IT IS IMPOSSIBLE TO PLEASE HIM, FOR HE WHO COMES TO GOD MUST BELIEVE THAT HE IS, AND THAT HE IS A REWARDER OF THOSE WHO DILIGENTLY SEEK HIM.

> Hebrews 11:6

I don't know how many times drought has struck this farm and I have thought we are finished. I have put my whole production loan and my savings into the crop. There has been no rain and I've been desperate, looking up into a sky that is like brass. There are no clouds, so there is no rain. A situation like this, my friend, is the time to put your faith in God.

I am telling you, folks, I don't know how God does it, but He does. I've seen those wilted plants somehow stand up straight every morning. Then the Lord sends His gentle rain of grace upon that crop. As a result of the drought the roots have gone down deep, therefore they take up the moisture, and we end up with a bumper crop. We have gone from disaster to victory. Now this can be your experience too. What do you have to do? You have to have faith – "believe that He is, and that He is a rewarder of those who diligently seek Him."

Some years ago now, Frans Cronjé, a producer and director, received a vision from God to make a feature film of our lives. Maybe some of you have seen the movie *Faith Like Potatoes*. When they had finished production they came and screened the premiere on our farm. That night I was so busy with all the arrangements that I couldn't really appreciate the movie properly. Early the next morning I went into my prayer closet and I opened the Word of God. It was as if the whole movie played before my eyes. God replayed my whole life, right back to when I was six years old. I began weeping. Not because of the tragedies in the movie, not because of the tests, but because of the goodness of God. The Holy Spirit showed me through that movie how Jesus has never once forsaken or let me down. This can be true for you too. Place your trust in Him. Remember: "without faith it is impossible to please Him".

Prayer

My Father God, Your grace is sufficient for my every need. I come before You and I ask You to undertake for me. All I see is disaster, but I know that You see beyond the natural. I place my trust in You. I believe in You and Your Word. I know that You will do what is best for me. Amen.

Read Psalm 46

BE STILL, AND KNOW THAT I AM GOD; I WILL BE EXALTED AMONG THE
NATIONS, I WILL BE EXALTED IN THE EARTH!

Psalm 46:10

On my farm I have an orchard and around it I have planted beautiful beefwood trees. I have not done this simply because they are lovely trees. They serve a purpose and that is to shelter the fruit trees from the prevailing north wind. God has a message for you today: He wants to be like a beefwood tree to you. He wants to shelter you, my dear friend, from the storms of life. Our Scripture says: "Be still and know that I am God".

The Lord says to us: "God *is our refuge and strength, a very present help in trouble*" (verse 1). Isn't it a wonderful thing to know with certainty that, no matter what this year holds, God is in control of your life and the lives of your loved ones? There is no greater security to be had than this. It is in being still that we can come to know God. It is in the quiet that He can speak to us.

We live in a world that is filled with stress and noise. I think a lot of our medical problems are brought on by the tremendous pressure under which we are living. A few years ago there were no cellular phones. We had a party line here on the farm – the older folks will know what I am talking about. All the surrounding homes shared the same line. Each home had their own ring. Our ring was two shorts and one long. When we heard the phone go beep-beep, b-e-e-p we knew the call was for us. When we answered we knew that everyone could hear our conversation. We were not governed by cellular phones in those days. Don't get me wrong; they are wonderful inventions – I have one myself. All the technology we have ties us down, though. We become stressed out and then we cannot hear God. He wants us to come to Him and be still in His presence. Sit at His feet, allowing Him to surround you and shelter you. Feel the security that only He can give you.

Prayer
Lord, help me to take the time to regularly step away from all the noise and activity that invades my life. I want to spend time with You. Lord, I need You to surround me and protect me. I want to shelter in Your arms. Help me to be still in Your presence and hear Your voice. Amen.

Read John 14:25–31

> PEACE I LEAVE WITH YOU, MY PEACE I GIVE TO YOU; NOT AS THE WORLD GIVES DO I GIVE TO YOU. LET NOT YOUR HEART BE TROUBLED, NEITHER LET IT BE AFRAID.

John 14:27

We live in a world where people are fearful. A lack of peace makes you a fearful person. People go to great lengths to obtain peace. Some go on pilgrimages, follow after gurus, and meditate or isolate themselves from the world. There are those who try to lose themselves in drugs and alcohol all in an effort to forget or escape their reality. People spend huge amounts of time and money trying to attain peace. Yet for many people inner peace remains an elusive quest. Sadly, mental institutions are filled with those who are broken as a result of not finding peace.

So why does Jesus make the statement, "Peace I leave with you, My peace I give to you; not as the world gives do I give to you. Let not your heart be troubled, neither let it be afraid"? He makes it because He is the source of peace. If you put your trust in the Lord it doesn't matter what you are going through or what your situation is; He can give you inner peace so that, when the world is going crazy around you, your heart is absolutely peaceful.

I am told that at the centre of a hurricane there is absolute peace and stillness. The hurricane screams and swirls around the centre, but in the midst of the turmoil there is quiet. Does this describe the state of your heart at this moment? As a child of God you cannot allow yourself to be governed by your circumstances. Your birthright in Jesus is inner peace. Jesus didn't promise you outer peace – only inner peace. My friend, peace is not a feeling or a situation – no, it is a Person, Jesus Christ. So, irrespective of what your condition is, you can still have that peace if you put your trust in Jesus. He made you another promise: "But the Helper, the Holy Spirit, whom the Father will send in My name, He will teach you all things, and bring to your remembrance all things that I said to you" (verse 26).

Prayer

My Father in Heaven, thank You for the peace that is my birthright in Jesus. I pray that Your Spirit would fill me with Jesus' peace right now. Holy Spirit, help me to remember all that Jesus spoke to me in Your Word. Let me remember and be encouraged. I take hold of Your peace. Amen.

Read Isaiah 26:1–12

YOU WILL KEEP HIM IN PERFECT PEACE, WHOSE MIND IS STAYED ON YOU, BECAUSE HE TRUSTS IN YOU. TRUST IN THE LORD FOREVER, FOR IN YAH, THE LORD, IS EVERLASTING STRENGTH.

Isaiah 26:3–4

Our Scripture tells us that if we want peace we have to trust in the Lord Jesus Christ. In order to experience His peace your mind needs to be fixed upon Him. You have to put yourself in the place where you can hear God speaking to you. I believe it is one of the devil's ploys in these last days to keep people in a state of perpetual motion, especially young parents. Dad is working all the hours in a day, often holding down two jobs; Mom is out working as well, and the children are placed in a day care centre. I know that you probably don't want to be living like this. Some of you say that you cannot manage unless both of you work. You have to pay the mortgage or the rent and put food on the table.

The sad thing about this is that when your days are spent running from one commitment to another without any respite it is hard to hear the voice of the Lord. He says, "Be still, and know that I am God" (Psalm 46:10a). George Matheson, a mighty man of God, was a nineteenth-century blind Scottish preacher from the Highlands. He said that God's voice demands the silence of the soul. You cannot hear from God if you never take the time to stop and spend time being quiet, listening to His voice.

If your response to me is that you are too busy, then I must draw your attention to Jesus. None of us are as busy as Jesus was at the height of His ministry. He was healing the sick, setting the captives free, feeding the hungry, and bringing the Word of the Lord to the people. Yet, very often, when the disciples looked for Him, where was Jesus? He was up a mountain. He had drawn aside to be quiet and to spend time in His Father's presence, listening to His voice. If you want peace then the answer is to spend more time in your Father's presence. Take the time to hear His voice and receive from Him.

Prayer

My Father God, in the midst of the chaos of life help me to take the time to draw aside to listen to You. I know that You are always with me. You are always there. It is me who so often becomes sidetracked. I realize that You are speaking to me in this moment. Lord, I want Your peace. Amen.

Read Isaiah 26:1–12

> YOU WILL KEEP HIM IN PERFECT PEACE, WHOSE MIND IS STAYED ON YOU, BECAUSE HE TRUSTS IN YOU. TRUST IN THE LORD FOREVER, FOR IN YAH, THE LORD, IS EVERLASTING STRENGTH.
>
> Isaiah 26:3–4

One of the best resolutions you can make at the beginning of this year is to commit to spending regular time in God's presence. I am not speaking about your daily quiet time; I am suggesting that you take the time to withdraw at regular intervals to hear from God. This will be the best investment you will ever make, believe me. We have it back to front when we think that we do not have time to spend with God. We spend endless hours frantically trying to find solutions to our problems; we worry and fret about what to do. Instead, spend time with God; concentrate your mind upon Him. Trust in Him; listen to Him. He will give you His perfect peace and His plan. Then the fretting and the stress will end. Instead of spending time trying to sort out your problems on your own, spend the time with Jesus and receive His peace.

I want to say to those men who are in leadership positions in the church: "First the mountain, then the ministry". As I say, so often we have it back to front: first the ministry, and then the mountain. You can hear by the way a man preaches whether he has spent time on the mountain or not. He becomes stressed and dry, because instead of giving out of an overflow, he gives from his very substance. From there it is a short step to burn-out. You cannot give until you have received. If you are feeling dry and ineffective, go up the mountain. Don't come down until you have met with Jesus and received His peace. For many the mountain will not be a physical one. Find a spiritual mountain – a place where you can be quiet and meet with God.

I regularly spend time on the mountain. I sit and allow God to renew my soul. I hear from God and I receive from Him. Then I am able to return to the ministry with new vigour and fervour. Commit to spending regular time in God's presence throughout this year.

Prayer

My Father, it is so true that I spend much of my time trying to keep all the plates that make up my life spinning in the air. I so long to stop and just be. Lord, I am making a commitment to spend regular time with You. I want to know Your peace, no matter what is going on around me or in my life. Amen.

Read Mark 11:12–24

> So Jesus answered and said to them, "Have faith in God. For assuredly, I say to you, whoever says to this mountain, "Be removed and be cast into the sea,' and does not doubt in his heart, but believes that those things he says will be done, he will have whatever he says."
>
> Mark 11:22–23

Jesus went on to say: "Therefore I say to you, whatever things you ask when you pray, believe that you receive them, and you will have them" (verse 24). You might be going through a spiritual drought at the moment. You are trying to pray, you are having your quiet times with the Lord, but your prayers are bouncing off the ceiling. The ceiling is like brass and you are not seeing a breakthrough. My message to you is that you must press on, my friend. Press on by faith and you will experience a breakthrough. Continue to spend time with God.

Read again what Jesus said to His disciples in verses 22–23: "Have faith in God. For assuredly, I say to you, whoever says to this mountain, "Be removed and be cast into the sea,' and does not doubt in his heart, but believes that those things he says will be done, he will have whatever he says." Jesus said this after He cursed the fig tree. A couple of days later they passed that way again and the disciples couldn't believe that the fig tree was dead. Jesus gently rebuked them, saying that all things are possible for those who believe.

At the end of the day, my dear friend, it is not good works and good habits that will get you to Heaven – it is the fruit of faith. It is trusting in God. The greatest sin in the Bible is the sin of unbelief. Lord, I don't believe that You can heal my child. Lord, I really cannot believe that You can heal cancer. Lord, I don't see how You can save my business. My friend, this is the one time that the Lord really gets angry. You have a choice to make: will you live by faith or will you live by sight? We are called to live a life of faith. If you are experiencing a drought in your life don't give up. Your mandate is to persevere with God. Do not doubt in your heart – have faith and God will come through for you.

Prayer

My Father, once again I have been convinced by Your Spirit. Like the disciples I am prone to unbelief. I so easily doubt. Father, forgive me for my sin of unbelief. Fill me with faith. Strengthen me and fill me with perseverance. Lord, I want to be a mighty man of God. I want to walk by faith and not by sight. Amen.

Read Matthew 17:14–21

> So Jesus said to them, "Because of your unbelief; for assuredly, I say to you, if you have faith as a mustard seed, you will say to this mountain, "Move from here to there,' and it will move; and nothing will be impossible for you."
>
> Matthew 17:20

How do we receive faith? Romans 10:17 says: "So then faith comes by hearing, and hearing by the word of God." Some of us need to stop running after this preacher or that prophet. Stop running from one conference to another. There are those who need to stop constantly requesting prayer for more faith. Instead they must begin spending more time in the Word of God. They must begin to take God's Word literally. If they would pray God's Word they would begin to see things happen.

You see faith is contagious. Faith begets faith. The more faith you have, the more faith you will want, and the more faith God will give you. Jesus said you only need to start with faith the size of a mustard seed. It will grow from there. Use it and it will grow. Don't use it and it will wither and die. You will never learn this kind of faith in a Bible college or a university. You learn it by doing. Faith has feet; it is a "doing" word.

St Augustine said: "Faith is to believe what you do not see; the reward of this faith is to see what you believe." I have experienced the reward of seeing what I believed God for like never before. Over the past decade I believed God for the biggest tent in the world until I received the account. My legs turned to jelly when I saw how much it cost. You'd better believe it – God supplied the money. Believing God for the impossible is what we have to begin doing. Don't say you will pray and believe God for something then go right ahead and figure it out for yourself. When you do this you insult God. Having faith means that you trust God and only God. You acknowledge that without God it is impossible, but with Him it is absolutely possible. If you believe Him for nothing, you will receive nothing. If you believe Him for everything then you will receive everything. Will you trust Him today?

Prayer

My Father God, Jesus said that I must have faith like a mustard seed. Right now I bring my mustard seed of faith and I place it before You. Lord, take it and grow it. Multiply it, I pray. I want to do great exploits for You, my God. I want to honour Your Name and glorify You. Amen.

Read Mark 11:12–24

> THEREFORE I SAY TO YOU, WHATEVER THINGS YOU ASK WHEN YOU PRAY, BELIEVE THAT YOU RECEIVE THEM, AND YOU WILL HAVE THEM.
>
> Mark 11:24

God does not honour prayer; He does not respond to prayer – God responds to the prayer of faith. When I say this it upsets certain people, but I say it to make a point. If you look at our Scripture verse, it clearly says: "whatever things you ask when you pray, believe that you receive them, and you will have them." John 14:14 says: "If you ask anything in My name, I will do it." Then it goes on to say in verse 15: "If you love Me, keep My commandments." The result is that when you pray according to God's commandments you will not pray selfish prayers. Your prayers won't consist of "Give me, give me, give me…" Instead you will pray, "Lord, help my mother; she is sick in hospital." "Lord, bring rain to the Eastern Cape because the people there are dying."

Now I want to say something to the younger people, but really it applies to everyone. If you desire more faith, associate with people who are walking by faith. Don't spend your time with negative people; they will only bring you down. If you want to walk by faith and not by sight, walk with those who are living out this truth in their lives on a daily basis.

It is no good praying those repetitive, rote prayers, which, even as you are saying the words, you don't really believe. God doesn't believe them either. He looks upon your heart and He sees what is in it. What God is looking for is a heart filled with faith. A heart that is wholly His. A heart that loves Him and keeps His commandments. It is the prayer prayed from this type of heart that He answers and honours. So, my friend, check your heart. Take stock of your motives. Why are you praying? Do you simply want God to supply your grocery list, or do you want His will to be done in your life and in your circumstances? When you pray according to His will, then He will answer you.

Prayer
My Heavenly Father, I know that You desire to have me speak to You. Thank You that You have promised me in Your Word that if I believe, then You will answer me. Help me to submit to Your will and to pray the prayer of faith. I long to be a man who walks by faith and not by sight. Amen.

Read 1 John 5:1–15

> NOW THIS IS THE CONFIDENCE THAT WE HAVE IN HIM, THAT IF WE ASK
> ANYTHING ACCORDING TO HIS WILL, HE HEARS US.
>
> 1 John 5:14

My friend, you cannot have faith in faith. No, you have faith in a Person, Jesus Christ. John says: "These things I have written to you who believe in the name of the Son of God, that you may know that you have eternal life, and that you may continue to believe in the name of the Son of God" (verse 13). When you pray, you pray in the Name of the Son of God, Jesus Christ. Do you realize what an awesome privilege this is? John goes on to say: "Now this is the confidence that we have in Him, that if we ask anything according to His will, He hears us."

Here is the key question: how do you know what God's will is? We learn to know God's will through His Word. God never acts contrary to His Word. So if you want to know God's will get to know His Word. Verse 15 continues: "And if we know that He hears us, whatever we ask, we know that we have the petitions that we have asked of Him."

If you asked me, "What is the thing that God has impressed upon you more than anything else over the past decade?" I would answer: "Apart from the love of God, which is unconditional, it is that God always honours faith." I want to repeat this: God always honours faith. Not presumption, not "I hope so", not "let's see which way the wind blows". God honours faith. You see, everything works together. You get to know God by spending time in His Word. When you've spent time in God's Word you will understand His will. When you know Him and you understand His will then your faith will increase. The result is that when you pray, you will be praying the prayer of faith, according to God's will. When you pray according to God's will He will answer you and give you what you are asking for. God loves you unconditionally. Approach Him with confidence, because He longs to hear you pray the prayer of faith.

Prayer

My Father, I thank You for Your unconditional love for me. Thank You for Your Word and the clear way that You speak to me through it. Help me to spend more time learning to know You through Your Word. I know that my faith will be built up as I get to know You better. Then I will be able to pray the prayer of faith. Amen.

Read Romans 1:1–17

> FOR I AM NOT ASHAMED OF THE GOSPEL OF CHRIST, FOR IT IS THE POWER OF
> GOD TO SALVATION FOR EVERYONE WHO BELIEVES, FOR THE JEW FIRST AND
> ALSO FOR THE GREEK. FOR IN IT THE RIGHTEOUSNESS OF GOD IS REVEALED
> FROM FAITH TO FAITH; AS IT IS WRITTEN, "THE JUST SHALL LIVE BY FAITH."
>
> Romans 1:16–17

The Bible clearly tells us: "The just shall live by faith." Who are the just? The just are us – the believers in Jesus Christ. This is what Martin Luther came to understand, and the world was changed through his understanding of this one verse. It is what John Wesley discovered, and the world was again changed through his understanding of this Scripture. Both of them were diligent, good men who tried their best to serve God. They went without food and even beat themselves as they endeavoured to bring their flesh into submission. Yet they never knew victory until they realized that "The just shall live by faith."

Ephesians 2:8–10 puts it this way: "For by grace you have been saved through faith, and that not of yourselves; it is the gift of God, not of works, lest anyone should boast. For we are His workmanship, created in Christ Jesus for good works, which God prepared beforehand that we should walk in them." Grace is God's undeserved loving kindness. God saved us for no other reason than that He loves us. He has given us the gift of faith. Our response is to accept His gift and then to live our lives using and exercising our faith.

Lest you think that faith in the Old Testament was only for a select few, Habakkuk 2:4 also speaks about living by faith. "Behold the proud, his soul is not upright in him; but the just shall live by his faith." Are you living by faith – trusting God that your family will be saved and that they will walk a righteous road? The prayer of faith is to be used powerfully so that your children will choose to follow Jesus. The only way that we are going to accomplish this is if we walk by faith and not according to our feelings. The Bible says that the only way for the just to live is by faith. It doesn't matter how you feel; living by faith is a choice that you have to make each and every day.

Prayer
My Father, I realize that, like Martin Luther and John Wesley, I cannot live the Christian life victoriously in my own strength. I am justified by faith and not by works. Thank You for reaffirming to me that You have given me everything I need to live a life of faith through Jesus Christ my Saviour. Amen.

Read Psalm 27

> THE LORD IS MY LIGHT AND MY SALVATION; WHOM SHALL I FEAR? THE LORD
> IS THE STRENGTH OF MY LIFE; OF WHOM SHALL I BE AFRAID?
>
> Psalm 27:1

The opposite of faith is fear. Luke 21:26 says: "Men's hearts failing them from fear and the expectation of those things which are coming on the earth, for the powers of the heavens will be shaken." If we didn't know Jesus there would be much for us to be fearful of. The world appears to be filled with evil and so often it seems as if this evil is overpowering all that is good. What we are experiencing is not unique; the psalmist also felt like this: "When the wicked came against me to eat up my flesh, my enemies and foes, they stumbled and fell. Though an army may encamp against me, my heart shall not fear" (verses 2–3a).

It is exactly in times like these that we need to run to the Lord. In verses 4–5 David says:

> *One thing I have desired of the Lord, that will I seek: that I may dwell in the house of the Lord all the days of my life, to behold the beauty of the Lord, and to inquire in His temple. For in the time of trouble He shall hide me in His pavilion; in the secret place of His tabernacle He shall hide me; He shall set me high upon a rock.*

It is only in His presence that you will know peace. It is there that your faith will be increased.

The devil, our enemy, wants us to turn away from God. He wants us to blame the Lord when things go wrong. It is his plan to make us believe that we can do it alone. Remember that he is the inventor of pride. Don't be fooled by him. There is victory and peace only in Jesus. This is why He said: "Peace I leave with you, My peace I give to you; not as the world gives do I give to you. Let not your heart be troubled, neither let it be afraid" (John 14:27). Take heart and look to Jesus your Light and your Salvation.

Prayer
My Father God, in the midst of difficulty and turmoil I know that there is only one place of solace and safety – it is in Your presence. It is kneeling before You, trusting You and putting my faith in You. Lord, You are my Light and my Salvation. You are my strength. Amen.

Read Habakkuk 3:17–19

THE LORD GOD IS MY STRENGTH; HE WILL MAKE MY FEET LIKE DEER'S FEET,
AND HE WILL MAKE ME WALK ON MY HIGH HILLS.

Habakkuk 3:19

God makes the following promise to you as you walk in His ways: He promises you that if you trust in Him and walk by faith, He will make your feet like deer's feet. You will walk sure-footedly on the high hills. The stones and the rough paths of life will not cause you to stumble, and you will not fall. He will be there to hold you up and give you His strength. How many times have I said to you that anyone who believes coming to Jesus means that all your troubles will be over is believing a lie? God's children experience the same heartache and sorrow that the world experiences, my friend. We are not exempt.

What should make the difference is how we handle our suffering. Habakkuk was no stranger to suffering. Read again his hymn of faith to the Lord:

> *Though the fig tree may not blossom, nor fruit be on the vines; though the labor of the olive may fail, and the fields yield no food; though the flock may be cut off from the fold, and there be no herd in the stalls – yet I will rejoice in the Lord, I will joy in the God of my salvation. The Lord God is my strength; He will make my feet like deer's feet, and He will make me walk on my high hills.*

Habakkuk 3:17–19

This is victory in the midst of disaster. It is not for a few elite Christians. Victory is available to the most humble of God's children. Remember that Jesus said you only need faith the size of a mustard seed. The important thing is that you use your faith. The more you use your faith the more it will grow. Then one day your faith will be a huge mustard tree under which many will be able to take refuge. Will you join Habakkuk and the multitudes of men of faith down through the ages and sing your own hymn of faith to God, your Father and Jesus, your Saviour? "Yet I will rejoice in the Lord, I will joy in the God of my salvation" (verse 18).

Prayer

My Father God, Jesus my Saviour, I join my voice with those of the men of faith who have gone before me. Thank You that because of Your great love and mercy toward me I too can be counted as a man of faith. I want to take my place. I want to live my life in honour of You and to Your glory. Amen.

Read Matthew 8:23–27

> AND SUDDENLY A GREAT TEMPEST AROSE ON THE SEA, SO THAT THE BOAT WAS COVERED WITH THE WAVES. BUT HE WAS ASLEEP.
>
> Matthew 8:24

Jesus slept through the storm. When He was on this earth Jesus was a man just like us. If He cut Himself, He bled. He became hungry, He grew tired, and He experienced emotion. In order to fulfil His calling Jesus needed to receive strength, wisdom, and insight from His Father. This is why He spent so much time alone in His Father's presence. He knew that He could do nothing outside of the Father. When they climbed in the boat Jesus was tired and He went to sleep, knowing that He rested in His Father. Jesus' first thought was always to turn to His Father.

When the storm came up, how did the disciples react? They immediately became fearful. They had Jesus right there with them in the boat. They had seen Him perform miracles, yet their first emotion and reaction was fear. This past month we have spent together discussing what it means to choose to walk by faith and not by sight. We have looked at different aspects of faith. Lessons have been learned from the lives of some of the men of faith from history. I have shared a few of my own experiences with you. Above all, we have looked into God's Word and read some of the wonderful passages of Scripture where God speaks to us about trusting Him and having faith.

I don't know the situation you find yourself in, but I want to encourage you to examine your heart and your life. What does the sea around your boat look like? Maybe it is rough and the waves are rolling in, or it could be that the waters are calm, but there is a storm brewing on the horizon. Whatever your circumstances, take your eyes off the sky and the sea. Look inside your boat. Who is with you in the boat – is it Jesus? If it is then you have nothing to fear. He says to you: "Why are you fearful, O you of little faith?" For "Then He arose and rebuked the winds and the sea, and there was a great calm" (verse 26).

Prayer

My Lord and Saviour, the winds and the waves obey Your voice. The storms around me cannot overpower me as long as You are in my boat with me. I submit my life and the lives of those whom I love to You. Lord, I choose to walk the walk of faith. I choose to honour You with everything that I have at my disposal. I love You, Lord. Amen.

ABRAHAM'S JOURNEY OF FAITH

Abraham's journey of faith began with his first step

1. Who was Abraham?
2. When we are called by God
3. Abram encounters God
4. God calls Abram
5. Faithful Abram
6. Blessed to be a blessing
7. The meaning of the blessing
8. God commands Abram to go
9. The litmus test of faith
10. Your solution, or God's solution?
11. Abram – friend of God
12. Arise, walk in the land
13. Abram builds an altar to the Lord
14. In whom will you trust?
15. Do not be afraid
16. Abram believed
17. God covenants with Abram
18. The meaning of the word "believe"
19. Whose voice are you heeding?
20. The consequences of disobedience
21. The God who sees
22. Abram renamed Abraham
23. The sign of the covenant
24. Is anything too difficult for the Lord?
25. The promised son
26. God tests Abraham
27. Trust and obey Him
28. The Lord will provide
29. Bad choices have consequences

Read Genesis 11:26–32

> THIS IS THE GENEALOGY OF TERAH: TERAH BEGOT ABRAM... AND TERAH
> TOOK HIS SON ABRAM AND HIS GRANDSON LOT, THE SON OF HARAN, AND
> HIS DAUGHTER-IN-LAW SARAI, HIS SON ABRAM'S WIFE, AND THEY WENT OUT
> WITH THEM FROM UR OF THE CHALDEANS TO GO TO THE LAND OF CANAAN;
> AND THEY CAME TO HARAN AND DWELT THERE.
>
> Genesis 11:27a, 31

Abram (or Abraham as God was later to call him) had a godly lineage. His eighth great grandfather was Noah. Genesis 10 and 11 tell us that the genealogy went as follows: Noah, Shem, Arphaxad, Salah, Eber, Peleg, Reu, Serug, Nahor, Terah and then Abram. Can you imagine the stories around the campfire? As he grew up I bet Abram never tired of listening to his father, Terah, talk about great, great, great... grandfather Noah.

It must have been so exciting to hear about how great (x 8) grandfather Noah trusted God when no one else would. Hearing how he built the ark according to God's instructions. How the Noah family, together with the animals, entered the ark. For forty days it rained. Finally God brought them to Mount Ararat, where they disembarked on to dry ground. The first rainbow, a sign of God's covenant with Noah and the generations to follow, was the climax of the story.

Our Scripture reading tells us that Terah, Abram's father, took his family, including his grandson Lot, and moved to Haran in Canaan. There they began farming and over the years they became prosperous. When we are introduced to Abram in Genesis 12 he is doing very well for himself. His family have settled and they are reaping the rewards of their hard work over the years. Abram has everything he could wish for... except a son. The Word tells us (11:30): "But Sarai was barren; she had no child."

A godly heritage is a blessing from God. Looking back over your family tree, are there those who have walked the road of faith before you? If so, thank God for them. The question before us is: are we in turn walking the road of faith, paving the way for those who will come after us? If you don't come from a godly heritage, my friend, you can be the first in your family to begin building a godly legacy. Noah stood out in his generation as a man of faith – he paved the way for Abraham and all those who came after him. You can do the same.

Prayer

My Loving Heavenly Father, how grateful I am for Your Word. You have encouraged me as I look at Abram's lineage. I realize that it doesn't matter who came before me; what matters is how I walk. I want to be known as a man who is obedient and who walks by faith. Amen.

Read 2 Timothy 1

THEREFORE DO NOT BE ASHAMED OF THE TESTIMONY OF OUR
LORD... WHO HAS SAVED US AND CALLED US WITH A HOLY CALLING,
NOT ACCORDING TO OUR WORKS, BUT ACCORDING TO HIS OWN PURPOSE AND
GRACE WHICH WAS GIVEN TO US IN CHRIST JESUS BEFORE TIME BEGAN... .

2 Timothy 1:8a, 9

Have you noticed how every person mentioned in the Bible whom God called to do a particular task had an encounter with the Lord? It began with Adam. God gave him instructions on how he was to care for the Garden of Eden. God told him what he could and could not eat. We mentioned Noah yesterday; he had an encounter with God. God told him to build the ark; He told him exactly how he was to do it. We can name many others who have had encounters with God – each encounter unique according to the individual and God's plans for them. To mention only a few of these people, we have Moses, Samuel, David, Daniel, Jeremiah, the twelve disciples, and Paul.

The circumstances may be different, and the way God goes about extending the call is suited to God's purposes in that particular situation. However, the one consistent outcome for each and every person is that afterwards they are in no doubt that they encountered God. There are no ifs, maybes, or buts; when you have encountered God, you know all about it.

God is still in the business of calling people to accomplish His purposes here on earth. He is still looking for people who will fulfil His plans. He is searching for those who will do their part in building His Kingdom here on earth. Have you had an encounter with God that has led you toward fulfilling your destiny? There is no more worthwhile and satisfying journey, my friend, than the journey of faith. My family and I have been on this faith journey for many years now. We walk the faith walk collectively and individually. Take a few moments today to reflect on what God is saying to you at the beginning of this new year. Is it going to be business as usual or are you going to walk the walk of faith this year? There is only one result that God is looking for when He encounters us – and that is a continuing walk of faith: looking to Jesus.

Prayer
My Father God, I thank You that I can learn so much from the way You have dealt with men of faith throughout the ages. Lord, I have one desire and that is to walk with You. I want to fulfil Your purposes for my life. I want to encounter You so that I too am in no doubt what it is that You are saying to me. Amen.

Read Genesis 12:1–3

I WILL MAKE YOU A GREAT NATION; I WILL BLESS YOU AND MAKE YOUR NAME GREAT; AND YOU SHALL BE A BLESSING.

Genesis 12:2

Abram was a farmer. No doubt on the day Abram encountered God he was going about his business on the farm. He would have been following his daily routine, whatever that might have been. The Bible tells us Abram was prosperous; he was an extremely rich farmer. One day, out of the blue, the Lord came to Abram. God told Abram that He wanted him to pack up his possessions, leave his farm, and travel to an unknown destination.

Abram's day had come; his hour had dawned. If you think of it in the light of his being a descendant of Noah, then it wasn't unheard of for God to ask someone to do something that on the face of it seemed absolutely crazy. If you are a farmer reading this, imagine how you would react if God suddenly told you to up and leave your farm. Not only are you to leave your farm, but God does not clearly tell you exactly where you are going to – He only tells you to leave. What would you do?

On the other hand you may well be a successful businessman – how would you react to being told to walk away from all you have built up over the years? It was no easier for Abram to up and leave his farm than it would be for us to leave our farms or businesses. It would require faith to do this, wouldn't it? A huge amount of faith. It would really be a case of choosing to walk by faith and not by sight. For Abram it was an encounter that would change his life forever – and not only his life, but your life and my life as well. It was a call that came with a promise: "I will make you a great nation; I will bless you and make your name great; and you shall be a blessing. I will bless those who bless you, and I will curse him who curses you; and in you all the families of the earth shall be blessed" (verses 2–3).

Prayer

My Heavenly Father, You asked Abram to do something that was hard, but at the same time You promised him Your presence and blessing. Whatever You ask me to do I know You will be with me. Lord, help me to choose to walk by faith and not by sight. Amen.

Read Genesis 12:1–3

> Now the Lord had said to Abram: "Get out of your country, from your family and from your father's house, to a land that I will show you."
>
> Genesis 12:1

God came to Abram and spoke to him. We don't have any indication of whether God had ever spoken to Abram before this day. God told him to get out of his country. Leave his home. Vacate his farm. We have already said that Abram was a rich farmer. His family was prosperous. I don't know why God couldn't accomplish what He wanted to accomplish through Abram right there in Ur. Maybe God needed to know that Abram was prepared to leave everything behind to follow Him. Abram's faith had to be tested. God had to know if he was willing to take that first step. It was the first step that began Abram's faith journey.

God works in similar ways with us. He needs to know where our faith lies. Is it in Him or is it in our homes, our careers, our professions, our material possessions, or our families? God was specific in His call to Abram: he had to leave his country, his family, and his father's house. In other words, all his security nets and all his infrastructures. In other words, everything he could fall back on and rely upon. God wanted Abram to trust no one but Him. Abram was to have no one to turn to but God. He was about to embark upon a journey of discovery and training. We know that Abram wasn't perfect. He made many mistakes as he travelled toward the fulfilment of the promise God made to him.

My friends, God is not looking for perfection in you. He is looking for a heart that is wholly His. Like Abram He stands before you today, calling you to follow Him wholeheartedly. He is asking you if you will be willing to leave all to follow Him. Maybe God will never call upon you to physically leave your home or family. However, He demands no less from us in terms of our commitment to Him and His purposes for our lives. What will your response be to His call upon Your life today?

Prayer

My Father, I know that You are calling me in the same way that You called Abram. You are asking of me a wholehearted, 100 per cent commitment to You and Your purposes for my life. I say: Yes! I want to serve You, follow You, and love You with all of my heart. Amen.

Read Hebrews 11:1–12

> BY FAITH ABRAHAM OBEYED WHEN HE WAS CALLED TO GO OUT TO THE PLACE
> WHICH HE WOULD RECEIVE AS AN INHERITANCE. AND HE WENT OUT, NOT
> KNOWING WHERE HE WAS GOING.
>
> Hebrews 11:8

Abram (or Abraham as he is known in this passage) is considered to be the father of the faith. The title of Hebrews 11:8–12 is "Faithful Abraham". I have highlighted verse 8 for you to take special note of today. My dear friend, if ever God needed faithful men and women, it is now. You know you can do everything you know how to do. You can spend large sections of time memorizing the Word, or you can endeavour to be as good as you can possibly be. You can feed the hungry or you can fast, but if you don't have faith, you will not please God.

You may ask me, "Angus, can you prove this?" I will answer you, "Yes, I can, my friend." Verse 6 of today's Scripture reading tells us: "But without faith it is impossible to please Him, for he who comes to God must believe that He is, and that He is a rewarder of those who diligently seek Him." There, you have it in black and white, straight from God's Word. Without faith it is impossible to please God. He is not interested in your good deeds or your good works. God is only interested in how much faith you have in Him.

Your good deeds and the good works need to flow from the faith you have in God. If they don't then they are your good works and your good deeds. They emanate from your efforts and your abilities. On the other hand, when they flow out of the faith you have in God then they are His mighty deeds and acts. He and He alone receives the glory. There is nothing of you and nothing of me when we are acting out of faith in God. It is all of Him – the Bible tells us that God doesn't share His glory with anyone.

Prayer
My Father God, forgive me that so often I revert to doing things in my own strength. I turn to You now. Lord, I acknowledge that I am nothing without You. I can accomplish nothing of lasting or real value on my own. I place my faith in You, and in You alone. Amen.

Read Genesis 12:1–9

> I WILL MAKE YOU A GREAT NATION; I WILL BLESS YOU AND MAKE YOUR NAME
> GREAT; AND YOU SHALL BE A BLESSING. I WILL BLESS THOSE WHO BLESS YOU,
> AND I WILL CURSE HIM WHO CURSES YOU; AND IN YOU ALL THE FAMILIES OF
> THE EARTH SHALL BE BLESSED.
>
> Genesis 12:2–3

We do not live our lives for ourselves. Whatever God does in your life it is in order that you in turn will use it first to glorify Him, and then to bless other people. It was no different for Abram. We see in verses 2–3 that God promises to bless Abram and make his name great. God doesn't stop there though, does He? He goes on and says to Abram that he will in turn be a blessing. God said: "and in you all the families of the earth shall be blessed."

We live in a world where so often people live their lives selfishly. They are only interested in themselves and possibly their own families. Sadly, this is often true of Christians as well. God has called us to be salt and light to the world in which we live, as shown in Matthew 5:13–16:

> *You are the salt of the earth; but if the salt loses its flavor, how shall it be seasoned? It is then good for nothing but to be thrown out and trampled underfoot by men. You are the light of the world. A city that is set on a hill cannot be hidden. Nor do they light a lamp and put it under a basket, but on a lampstand, and it gives light to all who are in the house. Let your light so shine before men, that they may see your good works and glorify your Father in heaven.*

Each one of us has to make the decision to walk by faith trusting God for all that we need each day. When we are walking the faith walk then it is not a difficult thing to look beyond ourselves to the needs of others. First and foremost God has called us to share the Good News of Salvation with people, but our commitment should not stop there. Jesus also expects us to meet people's physical needs wherever and whenever we have the opportunity. Through Abram we are blessed spiritually as well as physically. We are to share this blessing with others.

Prayer

My Father God, You have called me to live a life of blessing. I am so grateful for everything that You do for me. You have abundantly blessed me with spiritual as well as physical blessings. Help me to share my bounty with other people every day of my life. Amen.

Read Galatians 3:1–14

> And the Scripture, foreseeing that God would justify the Gentiles by faith, preached the gospel to Abraham beforehand, saying, "In you all the nations shall be blessed." So then those who are of faith are blessed with believing Abraham.
>
> Galatians 3:8–9

Abram (or Abraham here) was the first recipient of the gospel. Our verse says that God preached the gospel to Abram. It was as a result of this that Abram believed God (in a few days we will talk some more about this and what it meant in Abram's life). Today I want us to consider what it means to us. We often speak about "father Abraham". He really is our father, because we are all descendants of his. You might be quick to point out to me that you are not Jewish. Well, that does not matter. If you are a Christian, saved by the blood of the Lord Jesus Christ, then you are a child of Abram.

This means that you have full access to the blessing that God promised to Abram. Far, far more important than the material prosperity that God promised Abram is the spiritual blessing that He promised to him. Ephesians 1:3–6 puts it like this:

> Blessed be the God and Father of our Lord Jesus Christ, who has blessed us with every spiritual blessing in the heavenly places in Christ, just as He chose us in Him before the foundation of the world, that we should be holy and without blame before Him in love, having predestined us to adoption as sons by Jesus Christ to Himself, according to the good pleasure of His will, to the praise of the glory of His grace, by which He made us accepted in the Beloved.

Through Abram you are a child of the King. You are accepted in the Beloved. You have every spiritual blessing in Christ. The key to this blessing is faith in Jesus Christ. If you have accepted Jesus then the blessing is all yours. God cannot do more than He has already done to bless you. The question is: are you living in the fullness of this blessing; are you walking by faith and not by sight? Abraham's journey began with his first step – so does yours. Have you taken it? If not, do it right now.

Prayer

My Father God in Heaven, thank You that I have every spiritual blessing in Christ Jesus. What an amazing statement this is. Help me to live in the fullness of this blessing each and every day of my life. Lord, fill me anew with Your Spirit. Help me to walk as a man who walks by faith and not by sight. Amen.

Read Genesis 12:1–9

> So Abram departed as the Lord had spoken to him, and Lot went
> with him. And Abram was seventy-five years old when he departed
> from Haran. Then Abram took Sarai his wife and Lot his brother's
> son, and all their possessions that they had gathered, and the
> people whom they had acquired in Haran, and they departed to go
> to the land of Canaan. So they came to the land of Canaan.
>
> Genesis 12:4–5

God told Abram to pack up and leave. What would you do if God told you to leave and go to a far country to serve Him? First, you would need to be sure that it is God telling you to go. Then, second, you would have to decide whether to obey Him or not. Down through history God has told people to leave what they are doing and follow Him. Charles T. Studd (1860–1931) was the son of a multimillionaire, a professional cricketer, and at the time one of Britain's most eligible bachelors. After his Christian faith had been reignited both by his questioning of his brother George's serious illnesses and on hearing the American evangelist D. L. Moody speak, the Lord told him to leave Britain and go to China.

Charles arrived in Shanghai in 1885, but some years previous to this his father had died. Edward Studd had stipulated in his will that Charles would not inherit until he reached the age of twenty-five, which he did while he was in China. Without knowing the amount that he was due to inherit, and believing that God would provide, Charles wrote out cheques giving money to – among others – George Müller's orphanages, William Booth's Salvation Army, and James Hudson Taylor's China Inland Mission. Later, in 1913, Studd felt that God wanted him to begin a new mission, and thus the Worldwide Evangelisation Crusade came into being; they still operate all over the world as the WEC International. Charles Studd is one man who, when God told him to go, he went.

My dear friend, where do you stand right now? The Lord is not interested in your good works, nor is He is interested in mine. You might never be called to leave your home and go to a distant land, but that doesn't mean that you are not to walk by faith. In a very real sense He tells us every day to go... and walk by faith. Hebrews 11:1 says: "Now faith is the substance of things hoped for, the evidence of things not seen." Are you a man who is walking by faith, or are you walking by sight? Hebrews 11:6 goes on to say: "But without faith it is impossible to please Him, for he who comes to God must believe that He is, and that He is a rewarder of those who diligently seek Him."

Prayer

My Father, I am so inspired when I read stories of mighty men who have followed You with all their hearts. Lord, touch me in a new and a fresh way so that I will be able to serve You with the abandon that I read about today. Fill me with Your Spirit. Give me Your power, I pray. Amen.

Read Mark 10:17–31

> Then Jesus, looking at him, loved him, and said to him, "One thing you lack: Go your way, sell whatever you have and give to the poor, and you will have treasure in heaven; and come, take up the cross, and follow Me."
>
> Mark 10:21

The account of the rich young ruler must surely be one of the saddest in Scripture. The young man was clearly sincere in his desire to serve God. In verse 17b he asked Jesus, "Good Teacher, what shall I do that I may inherit eternal life?" Jesus replied to him that he should keep the commandments. It is here we see the crack appearing. The young man had clearly been placing his trust in his good works. Notice how quickly He tells Jesus that he had kept the Law since his youth. This is works, not faith. Don't you just love those words in verse 21: "Then Jesus, looking at him, loved him…"? Jesus loves you, my friend; He is filled with compassion toward you.

Then came the test of faith. Jesus told the rich young ruler what it takes to really serve God. How did he react? "But he was sad at this word, and went away sorrowful, for he had great possessions" (verse 22). The disciples were concerned about what had happened and Jesus instructed them:

> *Assuredly, I say to you, there is no one who has left house or brothers or sisters or father or mother or wife or children or lands, for My sake and the gospel's, who shall not receive a hundredfold now in this time – houses and brothers and sisters and mothers and children and lands, with persecutions – and in the age to come, eternal life. But many who are first will be last, and the last first.*
>
> Mark 10:29–31

It is so sad that the rich young ruler didn't realize that Jesus wasn't really asking him to give up anything – instead He was offering him everything. His earthly possessions meant nothing; they in any case were only fleeting. The riches and rewards of Eternal Life would last forever. You can never out-give Jesus, my friend. He will never ask you to give up anything that He cannot restore to you a hundredfold. Don't make the mistake of clinging on to earthly things that are possibly preventing you from experiencing the best that God has for you.

Prayer

My God and Father, this is indeed a sobering story. Lord, I realize that so often I too am guilty of wanting to cling to my possessions. I forget so easily that I can never out-give You. I know that You ask me to surrender all to You so that You can test my heart and the level of my faith. Amen.

Read Genesis 12:7–20

> NOW THERE WAS A FAMINE IN THE LAND, AND ABRAM WENT DOWN TO
> EGYPT TO DWELL THERE, FOR THE FAMINE WAS SEVERE IN THE LAND.
>
> Genesis 12:10

Abram was the father of the faith. He was a mighty man of God. God even referred to him as His friend. However, Abram was human like you and I are human. He took this huge step of obedience: packed up his belongings and left his prosperous farm, his extended family, and all that he knew. That required a great deal of faith. So you would think Abram's first reaction when he ran into a problem would be to turn to God and ask Him what he should do about it – but no, Abram tried to come up with his own plan. Abram had his failings in the same way that we do.

Abram completely forgot that God had promised him that He would bless him. He forgot what God had said to him in verse 3: "I will bless those who bless you, and I will curse him who curses you". He had nothing to fear from the Egyptians. Nevertheless he decided to go down to Egypt to look for food and water. He was worried that the Egyptians would try to kill him, so instead of trusting God he came up with the plan that his wife should pretend to be his sister. There were consequences for everyone concerned because Abram decided to act independently of God.

I would like to invite you to take a few moments to think about this situation that Abram got himself into. Does it speak to you in some way? Are you maybe in a situation where you have to make a choice? Possibly you are facing a challenge in your life and it seems insurmountable. The decision before you is whether you will be like Abram and come up with your own solution or whether you will go to God and ask Him to help you to make a wise decision. My friend, He has the plan, but you have to be prepared to trust Him. You have to come to Him in faith, then you have to be prepared to obey Him and do what He tells you to do.

Prayer

My Heavenly Father, thank You for Your mercy and grace. Thank You that I am saved by grace and not by my own efforts. Like Abram I am nothing without Your grace and mercy. Forgive my independence and help me to run to You before I try to make my own plans. Amen.

Read James 2:14–26

AND THE SCRIPTURE WAS FULFILLED WHICH SAYS, "ABRAHAM BELIEVED GOD, AND IT WAS ACCOUNTED TO HIM FOR RIGHTEOUSNESS." AND HE WAS CALLED THE FRIEND OF GOD.

James 2:23

The behaviour that Abraham exhibited in yesterday's reading was not what one would expect from the father of the faith, is it? No, indeed, my friend, Abraham was not a good man in this act. Would a good man pass off his wife as his sister in order to save his own skin? I am sure you wouldn't do something like that. This was not the only time that Abraham took matters into his own hands. Abraham might have done an awful thing, but isn't it comforting in a way to know that he was human like us? He had weaknesses and failures the same as we do.

So then why is he called "the friend of God"? First, because Abraham served a gracious, faithful God. Second, because, "Abraham believed God, and it was accounted to him for righteousness." Abraham failed. But God didn't; God remained faithful. Paul tells us in 2 Timothy 2:13, "If we are faithless, He remains faithful; He cannot deny Himself." God remains true to His character and His nature no matter how we behave.

You may have heard me say: "Good people don't go to Heaven; Believers go to Heaven." A good person, who does not acknowledge Jesus Christ as their Lord and Saviour, is not going to Heaven. Romans 10:9 reads: "… if you confess with your mouth the Lord Jesus and believe in your heart that God has raised Him from the dead, you will be saved." I will tell you what makes you a Christian: it is when you believe that Jesus Christ is the Son of God. Abraham believed God: he obeyed God and he walked a road of faith with God. Yes, he failed sometimes; yes, he even had moments of doubt, but none of that stopped him from moving forward with God. As you examine your heart, allow the Holy Spirit to speak to you. Let Him show you where you are disbelieving God; where you are organizing your own solutions – then repent and walk by faith and not by sight.

Prayer

My Father God, I thank and praise You for Your graciousness and faithfulness to me. Thank You that You love me so much. Lord, I in turn want to love and serve You wholeheartedly. Help me to walk by faith and not by sight. In Jesus' Name I pray this. Amen.

Read Genesis 13

> AND THE LORD SAID TO ABRAM, AFTER LOT HAD SEPARATED FROM HIM:
> "LIFT YOUR EYES NOW AND LOOK FROM THE PLACE WHERE YOU ARE –
> NORTHWARD, SOUTHWARD, EASTWARD, AND WESTWARD; FOR ALL THE LAND
> WHICH YOU SEE I GIVE TO YOU AND YOUR DESCENDANTS FOREVER."
>
> Genesis 13:14–15

Abram did not want conflict with Lot. Their servants were fighting and it became evident that they needed to part ways. You would have thought that Abram would have been the one to choose the portion of land that he wanted, wouldn't you? After all, it was Abram whom God commanded to go – and it was Abram to whom God gave the promise. Yet we see Abram standing back and allowing Lot to choose the area that he wanted. Lot was greedy and he chose what he thought was the best land. After Lot left with all his servants and possessions God spoke to Abram again.

In the verses above, God reaffirmed His promise to Abram and then, in verse 16, concluded with: "And I will make your descendants as the dust of the earth; so that if a man could number the dust of the earth, then your descendants also could be numbered. Arise, walk in the land through its length and its width, for I give it to you."

What an amazing command – "Arise, walk in the land… for I give it to you." My friend, it doesn't matter what the challenges are that you are facing in your life right now. Maybe you are looking at someone else and it seems as if they have everything going their way. You feel that if only you had what they have you would be successful. I want to urge you not to be envious or bitter about what someone else has. It is a waste of energy and emotion.

Look at Abram. He wasn't upset that Lot took the best land. No, Abram trusted God. He believed God. Are you beginning to see why Abram was called a friend of God? God progressively revealed His plan to Abram. He will do the same for you. You have nothing to worry about because God has a specific plan for your life. Turn your eyes upon Jesus and He will reveal His plan for your life, step by step. He says to you: "Arise, walk in the land… for I give it to you."

Prayer

My Lord and God, in the midst of the battle it is so easy to take my eyes off of You and focus them upon my circumstances. You have spoken to me again and I realize that I do not need to concern myself with what is happening in other people's lives. You will lead me and guide me along my own path. Amen.

Read Genesis 13:14–18

THEN ABRAM MOVED HIS TENT, AND WENT AND DWELT BY THE TEREBINTH
TREES OF MAMRE, WHICH ARE IN HEBRON, AND BUILT AN ALTAR THERE TO
THE LORD.

Genesis 13:18

Throughout the Old Testament, when anything significant happens, we see that people build an altar to the Lord. There are two other occasions when Abram built an altar to the Lord. First, from Genesis 12:7–8:

Then the Lord appeared to Abram and said, "To your descendants I will give this land." And there he built an altar to the Lord, who had appeared to him. And he moved from there to the mountain east of Bethel, and he pitched his tent with Bethel on the west and Ai on the east; there he built an altar to the Lord and called on the name of the Lord.

Second, from Genesis 13:3–4:

And he went on his journey from the South as far as Bethel, to the place where his tent had been at the beginning, between Bethel and Ai, to the place of the altar which he had made there at first. And there Abram called on the name of the Lord.

As we continue through Abram's story I want you to take note each time he builds an altar to the Lord. The reason for building an altar to the Lord was a remembrance of something significant that happened. It helped the person or people to remember. It was a reference that they could look back upon. Sometimes we see people reminding God of what He had done at a particular time. It was also a place at which they worshipped God, bringing glory to His Name. It was a place where they could petition God, but also a place where they could thank and praise Him.

For us, building an altar would be a similar thing to a spiritual marker. Today we wouldn't necessarily build physical altars, but it is a good thing to have those moments when you pause before the Lord and acknowledge Him. You might write the account in your spiritual journal – if you keep one – or in your Bible. It is a faith-building exercise to be able to look back and recall what God has done. If He did it before, He can do it again.

Prayer
My Father God, I come into Your presence and I bow at Your feet. Lord, I build an altar to You today and I call upon Your Name. I come to You in faith, believing that You will hear me and that You will answer me. Lord, I am looking to You to do great and wonderful things for me. In Jesus' Name. Amen.

Read Genesis 14

> BUT ABRAM SAID TO THE KING OF SODOM, "I HAVE RAISED MY HAND TO THE
> LORD, GOD MOST HIGH, THE POSSESSOR OF HEAVEN AND EARTH, THAT I
> WILL TAKE NOTHING, FROM A THREAD TO A SANDAL STRAP, AND THAT I WILL
> NOT TAKE ANYTHING THAT IS YOURS, LEST YOU SHOULD SAY, "I HAVE MADE
> ABRAM RICH.'"

Genesis 14:22–23

There was a war – Abram was not involved in it, but Lot, his brother's son, was, and he, together with all his possessions, was captured. When Abram heard about it he went off to save Lot. God was with Abram and he was victorious. Melchizedek, king of Salem, the priest of God Most High, brought out bread and wine: "And he blessed him and said: 'Blessed be Abram of God Most High, possessor of heaven and earth; and blessed be God Most High, who has delivered your enemies into your hand.' And he gave him a tithe of all" (verses 19–20).

The king of Sodom who met up with Abram after the victory wanted Abram to take all the goods and give him the people who had been taken captive. However, Abram didn't want anything. He didn't want it to be said that anyone other than the Lord God had made him rich. You see, my friend, God had made Abram a promise. He promised to give Abram the whole earth – so why would he sell himself short and take a few paltry spoils of war? He would not be corrupted by greed.

In the world in which we live it is so easy to fall into the trap of cutting corners and going for the quick fix. Every day we read of businessmen giving and receiving bribes in order to be awarded contracts. Sports stars are caught taking steroids or other drugs to improve their performance. Students cheat on their examinations. Ministers are caught embezzling the church funds. Why do we do these things? We do them because we do not trust God to provide for us. We do not believe His promises to us. We are not prepared to exercise the perseverance of faith. We want the quick fix – so we make our own plans – and they fail each and every time. In the face of temptation Abram had to make his decision – in whom would he trust? Right now you too have to make a decision – in whom will you trust?

Prayer

My Father, You have spoken directly to my heart. I know that all too often I fall into the temptation of making my own plans. Forgive me, I pray. I have learned a lesson from Abraham about his faithfulness to You, and Your calling upon his life. Help me to be faithful to my calling too, I pray. Amen.

Read Psalm 27

> THE LORD IS MY LIGHT AND MY SALVATION; WHOM SHALL I FEAR?
> THE LORD IS THE STRENGTH OF MY LIFE; OF WHOM SHALL I BE AFRAID?
>
> Psalm 27:1

In Genesis 15:1 it is reported how God came to Abram and told him not to be afraid. God promised him that He would be his shield: "the word of the Lord came to Abram in a vision, saying, 'Do not be afraid, Abram. I am your shield, your exceedingly great reward.'" God has been protecting His people down through the ages. This does not mean that bad things don't happen to God's people – we all know that they do. The fact of the matter is, my friend, that no one can touch your soul. You are placed on this earth for a purpose and you will stay here until that purpose is accomplished.

I can honestly say that I do not fear any man. What can man do to me? He can only touch my earthly shell. The part of me that matters will live for eternity with Jesus. This is what David was talking about when he asked, "of whom shall I be afraid?" in the psalm above. David learned to trust God as a young man. He learned that his life was in God's hands and that he had nothing to fear from man or beast. Coming back to Abram, God is about to lead him a step further in understanding His purposes for his life. God is calling for a deeper commitment from Abram and He is preparing him for this step.

As you look back over your life, can you see the way God has led you? Are you able to see that the things you have experienced have all led you to the place where you find yourself now? I hope that you are excited about the next stage in your life. Don't let fear hold you back. Take the step of faith. Choose the road of obedience. Like Abram, be prepared to go when God says go. On the other hand, if you feel caught in a rut and you are desperate to hear from God, the psalmist says in verse 14: "Wait on the Lord; be of good courage, and He shall strengthen your heart; wait, I say, on the Lord!"

Prayer

Lord God, You have spoken clearly to me. I have nothing to fear from any man. You alone are my strength and my shield. You are my place of safety; in You I hide from the storms of life. Thank You that I can walk confidently with You because I know that You go before me. Amen.

Read Genesis 15:1–6

AND HE BELIEVED IN THE LORD, AND HE ACCOUNTED IT TO HIM FOR RIGHTEOUSNESS.

Genesis 15:6

God rewards faith – it is as simple, and in a sense as complicated, as that. God has never been, and never will be, interested in what we do for Him. Abram didn't have to do anything in order to be righteous. He only had to believe, have faith, and walk in obedience. You see, my friend, you cannot obey God if you do not believe in Him. Obedience is the outworking of faith. Only when you trust God, knowing without a shadow of a doubt that He will always do what is best for you, will you then be able to obey Him.

When God says go, you will be able to go; no matter what the obstacles seem to be. On the other hand, when He says stay, you will be able to stay – even in the face of great difficulty – because you will know that He will work everything out according to His perfect will for your life. This is faith. It is important for us to realize that faith is the very crux of our Christian experience. Hebrews 11:6a clearly says, "But without faith it is impossible to please Him…"

The New Testament quotes Abram's decision in Genesis 15 to believe and trust in God twice: in Romans 4:3 and Galatians 3:6. Abram's decision does not only have significance for Jewish people; it has significance for us Christians, who are Gentiles, as well. If you have made a decision to follow Jesus Christ, if you have placed your faith in Jesus and what He did for you on Calvary, then you are a child of Abram. You are an heir of the same promise that God gave to Abram and his descendants: "And if you are Christ's, then you are Abram's seed, and heirs according to the promise" (Galatians 3:29). Faith in Jesus Christ is the only criteria for Salvation, my friend. As you read this I ask you two questions: Are you living as a child of the promise? In whom are you placing your faith today?

Prayer
My Father God, thank You for Your Word that speaks to me. You are a great and awesome God. Thank You for my Salvation. I am so grateful for Your Son, Jesus Christ, my Saviour who died to give me Eternal Life. Thank You that through Abram I am a child of the promise. Amen.

Read Genesis 15:7–21

AND IT CAME TO PASS, WHEN THE SUN WENT DOWN AND IT WAS DARK,
THAT BEHOLD, THERE APPEARED A SMOKING OVEN AND A BURNING TORCH
THAT PASSED BETWEEN THOSE PIECES. ON THE SAME DAY THE LORD MADE A
COVENANT WITH ABRAM, SAYING: "TO YOUR DESCENDANTS I HAVE GIVEN
THIS LAND…"

Genesis 15:17–18a

Abram had questions for God. "Lord God, what will You give me, seeing I go childless, and the heir of my house is Eliezer of Damascus?" (Genesis 15:2). God answered Abram (Genesis 15:4b–7):

*"This one shall not be your heir, but one who will come from your own body
shall be your heir." Then He brought him outside and said, "Look now toward
heaven, and count the stars if you are able to number them." And He said
to him, "So shall your descendants be." And he believed in the Lord, and He
accounted it to him for righteousness. Then He said to him, "I am the Lord,
who brought you out of Ur of the Chaldeans, to give you this land to inherit it."*

Abram still wasn't satisfied so he asked God another question (verse 8): "Lord God, how shall I know that I will inherit it?" God then proceeded to cut a covenant with Abram. The thing about a covenant is that it was unbreakable. Once you made a covenant with someone you could not go back on your word to them. The punishment was death. God instructed Abram to take certain animals and cut them in half. They were placed opposite each other with a path between. The normal procedure would have been that the two people making the covenant would pass between the animals.

In this case that did not happen. Abram was only asked to lay them out. In our key verse only one half of the partnership passed between the halved animals; God's presence is indicated as doing so in the form of a smoking oven and a burning torch. Scripture says that this signifies the making of a covenant between God and Abram: "On the same day the Lord made a covenant with Abram". In His grace and mercy God knew that Abram was not able to keep this covenant. So God took on the responsibility of keeping His love covenant. It is a covenant based on faith. Ultimately Jesus Christ was the fulfilment of the covenant that God made with Abram – again it was all of God and nothing of us. Salvation is free, my friend; you cannot buy God's love. You can only accept it and love Him back, walking in faith and obedience with Him.

Prayer

My Father God, I come before You in the precious Name of Jesus my Lord and Saviour. Father, I thank You that You are a covenant-keeping God. You are faithful and You are true to Your Word and to Your character. Thank You for my Salvation. I love You, my Lord. Amen.

Read Genesis 15:1–6

> AND HE BELIEVED IN THE LORD, AND HE ACCOUNTED IT TO HIM FOR
> RIGHTEOUSNESS.
>
> Genesis 15:6

The Hebrew meaning of the word "believe" carries the idea of "the unqualified committal of oneself to another". So when Abram said that he believed in God, it wasn't an undefined belief. It was not a case of "Well, yes, I believe but…" It was an unqualified committal. The day that Abram believed was his day of Salvation. He was justified through his faith. There was nothing of works in it. He didn't do anything. We saw yesterday that after Abram made the commitment God followed it up by sealing it with a covenant between Himself and Abram. Did you notice that the Bible doesn't say that God and Abram made a covenant? No, it says that God made a covenant.

My friends, where do you stand regarding your relationship with Jesus Christ? Can you look back and pinpoint a day when you, like Abram, said: "I believe"? I have shared many times the story of my day of commitment in the little church in Greytown, South Africa. What has happened in the intervening years since the day of your commitment? Are you growing in your faith? Is Jesus becoming more and more to you? It is time for us to take stock of our commitment to Jesus, my friends. We will never accomplish great exploits for God if we have a mediocre commitment. A mediocre commitment equals a mediocre faith. Hebrews 11:6 tells us that without faith it is impossible to please God.

God is looking for men who will stand up for Him in these last days. He is looking for "mighty men" who will hold high Jesus' standards of truth and righteousness. None of us would be anything without God's grace. Isn't it precious that God showed us right back in Genesis 15 that He doesn't expect us to do it alone? He made it all possible through the sacrifice of Jesus Christ His Son. All we have to do is believe in the Hebrew sense – an unqualified commitment of oneself to God – and it will be reckoned to us as righteous. Not our righteousness, but the righteousness of Jesus.

Prayer
My Father, thank You for the reminder of that day when I committed my life to You. It was the best decision I have ever made. Lord, I want to walk true to that commitment each and every day of my life. I want to live out an unqualified commitment of myself to You. Amen.

Read Genesis 16:1–6

> SO SARAI SAID TO ABRAM, "SEE NOW, THE LORD HAS RESTRAINED ME FROM
> BEARING CHILDREN. PLEASE, GO IN TO MY MAID; PERHAPS I SHALL OBTAIN
> CHILDREN BY HER." AND ABRAM HEEDED THE VOICE OF SARAI.
>
> Genesis 16:2

When they left Ur Abram was seventy-five years old and Sarai was sixty-five. By the time we reach Genesis 16 they have been waiting eleven long years for the fulfilment of God's promise; God had promised Abram on several occasions that He would give him an heir. He had said that his heir would come from Abram's seed. It would not be someone who was adopted. As the years slipped by, despite the fact that Abram believed God and it was reckoned to him as righteousness, doubt crept in.

Before you judge Abram ask yourself whether this has ever happened to you. God has given you a promise or told you that He will do something. In the beginning you fervently believe the promise, but time ticks by and slowly you begin to lose heart. Life carries on, you make other plans, and the promise is tucked away somewhere. Maybe it is written at the back of your Bible. Occasionally you come across it, but you quickly turn the page. It is too painful to contemplate for too long. Maybe the time has come for you to wipe the dust off that promise. Bring it back before the Lord; repent of your unbelief; ask for His forgiveness and for Him to renew your faith.

We read in Numbers 23:19: "God is not a man, that He should lie, nor a son of man, that He should repent. Has He said, and will He not do? Or has He spoken, and will He not make it good?" If God makes a promise He will bring it to fruition. "For all the promises of God in Him are Yes, and in Him Amen, to the glory of God through us" (2 Corinthians 1:20). God is a gracious and forgiving God. Come before Him and allow Him to refresh you and restore you. God walked a walk with Abram and He walks a walk with us. Don't allow yourself to be cheated out of your inheritance because of unbelief. Choose to walk by faith and not by sight. It doesn't matter how long it takes – God will do what He promised.

Prayer

My Father, You are indeed a gracious, forgiving, and loving God. Forgive my unbelief, Lord. As I sit in Your presence I ask You to restore, refresh, and renew me. Lord, I want to walk by faith and not by sight. I want to trust You to fulfil Your promise to me. Thank You, Jesus. Amen.

Read Genesis 16:1–6

> THEN SARAI SAID TO ABRAM, "MY WRONG BE UPON YOU! I GAVE MY MAID
> INTO YOUR EMBRACE; AND WHEN SHE SAW THAT SHE HAD CONCEIVED, I
> BECAME DESPISED IN HER EYES. THE LORD JUDGE BETWEEN YOU AND ME."
>
> Genesis 16:5

Abram chose to listen to Sarai's voice instead of God's voice. When God's promise didn't materialize Abram probably began wondering what he should do to help God out. Clearly there was something that he should be doing. Don't we also feel like this sometimes? There is something we should be doing to solve our problem. We cannot just sit around waiting for a solution. Remember the maxim "God helps those who help themselves"? As men it is particularly difficult for us to stand back and wait. God created us to be the problem-solvers, to take responsibility – so the hardest thing is to wait.

After eleven years of waiting, both Abram and Sarai were despondent. You must remember that all the communication was between God and Abram. It was to Abram that God gave the instruction to go; to leave his country. It was with Abram that He spoke each time. It was with Abram that He made the covenant. It didn't mean that Sarai didn't benefit from it – but it was between God and Abram. So the responsibility for obeying God rested squarely on Abram's shoulders. When he chose to heed the voice of Sarai he was in direct violation of God's voice to him. No sooner had he done what Sarai suggested than the consequences began to manifest themselves. Disobedience to God's commands always brings consequences. Sometimes these can be dire.

Hagar became pregnant and this caused Sarai to become desperately unhappy. Abram washed his hands of the situation. Eventually it became impossible and Hagar the servant girl fled from her mistress. You would agree with me that this was not one of Abram's finest hours. What about your life – are you in a situation where you have disobeyed God and now you are sitting with the consequences of that disobedience? If this is so then I urge you to repent before the Lord, my friend. Don't let another day go by. He has promised you (in 1 John 1:9) that "If we confess our sins, He is faithful and just to forgive us our sin and to cleanse us from all unrighteousness."

Prayer

My Father, in this moment I bow humbly in Your presence. I ask You by Your Holy Spirit to search my heart. Lord, You know that I am so often guilty of making my own plans and finding my own solutions. Forgive me for this. Lord, from now on I want to wait upon You. I want to trust in You. Amen.

Read Genesis 16:6–15

> So she named the Lord who spoke to her, "You are El-roi"; for she said, "Have I really seen God and remained alive after seeing him?" Therefore the well was called Beer-lahai-roi; it lies between Kadesh and Bered.
>
> Genesis 16:13–14, NRSV

If you find yourself in a situation where you have been wronged then this reading is for you. There are times in our lives when something is done to us that we have no control over. Someone uses us and then treats us like the enemy. When human nature is involved there is always the opportunity for things to go awry. Hagar was used and then she was abused. She thought her only option was to run away from her problems. Is the flight syndrome your first course of action when you land in a difficult situation? You might feel that Hagar was justified in running away.

In her moment of need God met with her. He asked her where she came from and where she was going. When she told God He instructed her not to run away. God told her to go back and face her problems. He didn't send her back empty-handed though, did He? No, God assured her that He had seen her plight and that He was with her. Hagar chose to obey God and she named the place where God spoke to her "El-roi" – "You-Are-the-God-Who-Sees". Then she asked the question: "Have I also here seen Him who sees me?" Hagar no longer felt alone. She knew that there was someone who understood her plight and who cared about her.

Are you sitting by a spring of water feeling sorry for yourself? What you need is to meet with the "God-Who-Sees". Right now you need an interaction with your God – El-roi. You are not alone. He knows what has happened to you. He understands your hurt and confusion. Come to Him and allow Him to soothe and care for you. God has not deserted you. He does not despise you; He will never use and abuse you. He is the One in whom you can place your trust, no matter what happens. Don't allow the actions of other people to rob you of your blessing. Ask God what you should do next and then obey His instructions.

Prayer

My Father, I bow before You and ask You to touch my wounded heart and spirit. I have allowed myself to become cast down and filled with despair because of the things that have happened to me. Today I choose to look to You. You are my "God-Who-Sees". You know everything. I choose to follow You. Amen.

ABRAM RENAMED ABRAHAM

Read Genesis 16:15–16 and 17:1–14

AS FOR ME, BEHOLD, MY COVENANT IS WITH YOU, AND YOU SHALL BE
A FATHER OF MANY NATIONS. NO LONGER SHALL YOUR NAME BE CALLED
ABRAM, BUT YOUR NAME SHALL BE ABRAHAM; FOR I HAVE MADE YOU A
FATHER OF MANY NATIONS.

Genesis 17:4–5

Abram was eighty-six years old when Hagar bore him a son named Ishmael. Thirteen years later, when he was ninety-nine years old, God appeared to him again, as Almighty God, the All-Sufficient One. God says to Abram: "I am Almighty God; walk before Me and be blameless. And I will make My covenant between Me and you, and will multiply you exceedingly" (verses 1b–2). Abram responded by falling on his face before God. God then proceeded to talk to Abram as God the "Creator": God is the One who breathes the breath of life into all living beings. He is the Creator of Heaven and earth.

God the Creator decided the time was right to change Abram's name, which means "exalted father", to Abraham meaning, "father of a multitude". Do you see the significance of this act? God was breathing His Spirit into Abram; He was instilling His life-giving force into him. Besides being the father of Isaac, Abraham was also going to be the father of nations. This would be a "God thing" that only God the Creator could accomplish.

Abraham's journey was a journey of faith. We have observed God's call to him. We have traced his steps of obedience as he packed up and left his home. Abraham's journey had its ups and downs, but what comes through consistently is God's faithfulness to Abraham. God never gave up on Abraham. He believed in him, He forgave him, and He restored him each time. God patiently led Abraham toward the fulfilment of His purpose for his life. When you examine Abraham's walk you can see that it was definitely more of God than it was of Abraham. The same is true of us, isn't it? Take a moment to look back over your life; think of all the times that God has believed in you, forgiven you and restored you. Where would you be without His grace and His mercy, His faithfulness and His patience? Thank Him for breathing His Spirit into you. Thank Him for His commitment to you.

Prayer

Almighty God, Creator of the universe, I bow before You. Thank You for Your faithfulness and mercy toward me, a sinner. Lord, I would be nothing without You. I am so grateful to You as I bow in Your presence. Fill me anew today with Your Life-Giving Spirit, I pray. Make me, mould me, and use me. Amen.

Read Genesis 17:15–27

THEN ABRAHAM FELL ON HIS FACE AND LAUGHED, AND SAID IN HIS HEART, "SHALL A CHILD BE BORN TO A MAN WHO IS ONE HUNDRED YEARS OLD? AND SHALL SARAH, WHO IS NINETY YEARS OLD, BEAR A CHILD?"

Genesis 17:17

God reinforces His covenant with Abraham. He changes Abraham's name and He also changes Sarah's name – she was not excluded from the promise or the blessing. After all, without Sarah Isaac would not have been born. In chapter 15 we saw God making the covenant – Abraham was a silent bystander in the process. Now we see that God engages Abraham in the process. He has a part to play. Abraham has to take a further step of obedience.

God once again assured Abraham that he would have a child and that the child would be carried by Sarah. When God told him this, today's key verse says that "Abraham fell on his face and laughed". In his heart he found it hard to believe that God would come through in the way that He had promised. We see Abraham offering God another solution. He told God that he wished He would look favourably upon Ishmael. God was adamant though that His plan was still in place. I hope that as we have been experiencing Abraham's victories and struggles first hand it has given you some insight into your own life. Have you been able to identify those areas where you are struggling to believe God? As in Abraham's case, so often the evidence is heavily stacked against what God appears to be saying.

The important thing to realize is that, although Abraham doubted, in his heart he was still committed to obeying God. God is not scared of your questions. Make sure, though, that when you have questions you take them to Him. God told Abraham that he was to circumcise all the male members of his household. This was to be the sign of the covenant between God and Abraham. The circumcision was Abraham's "good faith" gesture, as it were. Abraham obeyed God and he circumcised all those in his household. He chose to walk by faith and not by sight. He chose obedience to God's commands above what he was feeling. What do you choose? Will it be faith and obedience or unbelief and disobedience?

Prayer

My Father, it is so easy to be caught up in the "logic" of doubt. If truth be told, though, it boils down to lack of faith. I know that I have to make a choice to believe You or to believe the evidence that I see before me. You are faithful and true; I choose to believe You. Lord, help me to act upon this belief. Amen.

Read Genesis 18:1–15

> "IS ANYTHING TOO HARD FOR THE LORD? AT THE APPOINTED TIME I WILL
> RETURN TO YOU, ACCORDING TO THE TIME OF LIFE, AND SARAH SHALL HAVE
> A SON."
>
> Genesis 18:14

Abraham recognized the Lord when He appeared to him. Over the years he had learned to recognize God's voice. Even though Abraham had his problems and his failures he never wavered in his commitment to doing what God told him to do. In Genesis 18:1 we read of how God appeared to Abraham "by the terebinth trees of Mamre, as he was sitting in the tent door in the heat of the day." Then three men appeared and Abraham immediately ran to meet them and bowed low; He had recognized the Lord.

The Bible tells us: "No one has seen God at any time. The only begotten Son, who is in the bosom of the Father, He has declared Him" (John 1:18). Despite the fact that no one had seen God, Abraham still recognized Him; he knew his God. Abraham fed the men and this time the Lord gave Abraham a specific date for the fulfilment of His promise. In Genesis 18:10, God says, "I will surely return to you at this time next year; and behold, Sarah your wife will have a son" (NASB). Sarah overheard the conversation and she laughed. It was inconceivable to her that what she had so longed for would actually happen.

The Lord heard her and He asked Abraham: "Is anything too hard for the Lord?" (verse 14). Today He is asking you the same question. What are you trusting Him for? Is it healing for yourself or a loved one; are you needing God to undertake on your farm or in your business; is your child not serving the Lord and you long to have them back in the fold; or is your marriage in trouble and you don't know what to do any more? Nothing is too difficult for the Lord. Trust Him, cling to His promises and choose to walk in obedience to His Word. He will come through for you and those whom you love. The key is obedient faith in a faithful God.

Prayer

My Lord and God, thank You for Your promises to me. You speak to me through Your Word, asking, "Is anything too hard for the Lord?" I answer You, "No, Lord, nothing is too hard for You!" I trust You. I believe in You. I choose to walk in obedient faith before You. I know you will undertake for me. Amen.

Read Genesis 21:1–7

> Now Abraham was one hundred years old when his son Isaac was born to him. And Sarah said, "God has made me laugh, and all who hear will laugh with me."
>
> Genesis 21:5–6

After twenty-five years God fulfilled His promise to Abraham. All those years ago God said to Abraham, "Get out of your country, from your family and from your father's house, to a land that I will show you. I will make you a great nation; I will bless you and make your name great; and you shall be a blessing. I will bless those who bless you, and I will curse him who curses you; and in you all the families of the earth shall be blessed" (Genesis 12:1–3). The Bible tells us that Abraham obeyed God: "So Abram departed as the Lord had spoken to him" (Genesis 12:4a). Throughout Abraham's life the overriding attitude of his heart was to obey God. Even when he didn't understand all that God was saying to him, Abraham chose to have faith in God.

This is what God asks of you and me, my friends. He does not expect us to be perfect. If we were we wouldn't need a Saviour, would we? He asks of us to place our trust in Him. He expects us to have faith in Him. Over and over I quote the Scripture to you that says, "without faith it is impossible to please [God]" (Hebrews 11:6a). We try many substitutes to replace simply having faith in God. He is not interested in any of your works. He does not care how smart you are. The fact that you are rich and you can replace the church's roof isn't of interest to Him. What God wants to know is this: Do you believe in Him? Is your faith in Him or in your own abilities?

Abraham's faith was in God. He had been on a journey with God for twenty-five years toward the fulfilment of the promise God made to him. If God has made you a promise, are you faithfully believing Him to fulfil that promise? We can only imagine the joy Abraham and Sarah felt. Sarah said, "God has made me laugh". She was expressing her absolute joy and happiness at God's faithfulness to her.

Prayer

My Lord, it is so easy to become discouraged and disheartened. I am so prone to looking toward my circumstances instead of looking toward You. Forgive me, I pray. Fill me afresh with Your Spirit. Help me to walk by faith and not by sight. Make me a man after Your own heart. Amen.

Read Genesis 22:1–5

> Now it came to pass after these things that God tested Abraham... .
>
> Genesis 22:1a

After promising Abraham that he would have a son; after telling him that through his son he would be the father of many nations; after making him wait twenty-five years for the promise to be fulfilled – it is inconceivable from a human perspective that God would then ask Abraham to kill that very son. Yet that is exactly what God did. Was God being perverse? Was He uncaring and unfeeling? My friends, was God playing games with Abraham? No, of course He wasn't. God is a loving God. He is a covenant-keeping God. He made a covenant with Abraham and He promised Abraham, "'Look now toward heaven, and count the stars if you are able to number them.' And He said to him, 'So shall your descendants be'" (Genesis 15:5b).

Abraham served a covenant-keeping God and so do you and I. The Bible tells us that He is the same yesterday, today, and forever. He does not change. Thinking about how God tested Abraham it reminds me of Job. Remember how God allowed Job to be tested too? Why did He allow Job to be tested? God allowed him to be tested so that Job's faith could be proved. Through his testing Job did not turn away from God. He continued to believe in God. Job said: "Though He slay me, yet will I trust Him" (Job 13:15a).

Abraham faced the biggest test of his life. The younger Abraham would have tried to find his own solution to his dilemma. Remember how he convinced Sarah to pretend to be his sister (not once, but twice) in order to avoid being killed. He took Sarah's maid and produced a son with her in order that he might have an heir. How about you, my friend, are you facing a test in your life at the moment? If you are then take a close look at how Job handled his time of testing. As we continue with our study of Abraham, take heart from the way that he handled his testing. Will you believe in your covenant-keeping God today?

Prayer

My loving, faithful Heavenly Father, thank You that You are my covenant-keeping God. You show Your love and mercy from generation to generation. Help me to believe in You in the same way that the mighty men of the Bible did. I too want to say, "Though He slay me, yet will I trust Him." Amen.

Read Genesis 22:6–10

> AND ABRAHAM SAID, "MY SON, GOD WILL PROVIDE FOR HIMSELF THE LAMB
> FOR A BURNT OFFERING." SO THE TWO OF THEM WENT TOGETHER.
>
> Genesis 22:8

As we've moved through this month, have you noticed the progression of Abraham's faith? It is doubtful that if God had fulfilled His promise to him earlier in his life that Abraham would have been able to trust God enough to be prepared to sacrifice Isaac. There must have been a million questions going around in Abraham's mind. I am sure you can think of many of them – they are the same ones that would be going through our minds, aren't they? Yet do we see Abraham asking questions? No, he simply obeys.

Isaac asks the question, "Look, the fire and the wood, but where is the lamb for a burnt offering?" (verse 7c). Abraham gives an answer based upon perfect trust in God: "My son, God will provide for Himself the lamb for a burnt offering" (verse 8a). My friends, this was a man who knew his God: a man who totally trusted his God. Abraham's faith in God was complete. When Isaac was eventually born there was no doubt in anyone's mind (least of all Abraham and Sarah's) that it was 100 per cent a God thing. Therefore, if God could give him a son when all hope of him having one due to his own virility was gone, then Abraham knew that God had a plan.

Abraham was willing to trust God no matter what the circumstances. He was willing to do the unthinkable because he knew, loved, and trusted his God. There are times in our lives that we are called to do difficult things. There are times when believing and trusting in God seems to be beyond human capability. If you are facing a time such as this, pause to consider Abraham. There cannot be a more difficult test of faith than what Abraham faced. Allow God's Spirit to speak to your spirit. My friend, no matter how tough the test you are facing, you have to make a choice: will you trust God, or are you trusting in yourself? "[W]ithout faith it is impossible to please [God]" (Hebrews 11:6a). Who do you choose today?

Prayer

My Loving Heavenly Father, I know that You love me with an everlasting love. Your love is constant, pure, and enduring. You know that I want to walk in Your ways. I want to be faithful to You. I want to choose to believe in You, trust in You, and obey You. Fill me with Your Spirit and strengthen me, I pray. Amen.

Read Genesis 22:11–19

> THEN THE ANGEL OF THE LORD CALLED TO ABRAHAM A SECOND TIME OUT
> OF HEAVEN, AND SAID: "BY MYSELF I HAVE SWORN, SAYS THE LORD, BECAUSE
> YOU HAVE DONE THIS THING, AND HAVE NOT WITHHELD YOUR SON, YOUR
> ONLY SON…"
>
> Genesis 22:15–16

Abraham had his arm raised ready to bring down the knife and thrust it right into the heart of his promised son. He was ready to kill his heir – his long-awaited, dearly loved son. Why? Because God told him to. He was willing to trust God above all. This was what God was looking for from Abraham – total and absolute obedience. We have often said that obedience and faith are interchangeable. The Word tells us: "Has the Lord as great delight in burnt offerings and sacrifices, as in obeying the voice of the Lord? Behold, to obey is better than sacrifice, And to heed than the fat of rams" (1 Samuel 15:22).

God stopped Abraham from killing Isaac. As Abraham looked up he saw a ram caught in the bushes. He took the ram, killed it, and sacrificed it to the Lord. Abraham called that place "The-Lord-Will-Provide" (Genesis 22:14). Abraham recognized that everything he had belonged to the Lord. The ram that was sacrificed is a beautiful picture of Jesus, the Son whom the Father loves, being sacrificed on our behalf. There was no ram in the thicket when Jesus hung upon the Cross of Calvary: God had to stand by and watch His Son suffer and die for the sins of this world.

My friend, Jesus suffered and died for your sins and for mine. Jesus is the fulfilment of the covenant that God made with Abraham. He is the promised Son. It is because of Jesus' death and sacrifice on Calvary that we, who are Gentiles, can benefit from the blessings God bestowed upon Abraham. Will you follow the example of your "father" Abraham? Take some time to meditate upon the life of Abraham. Allow God's Spirit to speak to you. Ask Him to show you the areas in your life where you need to open up and surrender to God. If you are still clinging to your own will, ask the Holy Spirit to help you to yield to God. Have faith in God; it is the only way that you can please Him.

Prayer

My Heavenly Father, I come to You in Jesus' Name. Thank You, Father, for sending Jesus as my Sacrificial Lamb. Thank You, Jesus, for Your obedience and submission to the will of Your Father; because of it I can come into the Father's presence today. I walk forward in faith believing in You. Amen.

Read Genesis 13

> AND LOT LIFTED HIS EYES AND SAW ALL THE PLAIN OF JORDAN, THAT IT WAS
> WELL WATERED EVERYWHERE (BEFORE THE LORD DESTROYED SODOM AND
> GOMORRAH) LIKE THE GARDEN OF THE LORD, LIKE THE LAND OF EGYPT
> AS YOU GO TOWARD ZOAR. THEN LOT CHOSE FOR HIMSELF ALL THE PLAIN
> OF JORDAN, AND LOT JOURNEYED EAST. AND THEY SEPARATED FROM EACH
> OTHER.
>
> Genesis 13:10–11

There was strife between Lot's servants and Abraham's servants. As a result they decided to go their separate ways. Abraham loved his nephew Lot and he allowed him to choose the land he wanted. Lot was greedy so he chose the Jordan, which was lush and green, because he thought it was the best land. We know from reading God's Word that this was not a good choice. Lot ended up in a very unhappy situation living in the midst of Sodom and Gomorrah.

In Genesis 14 Lot was taken captive in a war and Abraham had to go and rescue him. In chapter 18, when Abraham became aware that God was going to destroy Sodom and Gomorrah, he interceded on behalf of Lot. God spared Lot and gave him and his family the opportunity to escape from the city before He destroyed it. Lot's sons-in-law thought he was joking when he told them and urged them to leave. Lot lingered and eventually we are told in chapter 19 that the angels had to take the hands of Lot, his wife, and his daughters and lead them out of the city. Lot was not happy with being told to flee to the mountains. He asked to be allowed to go to the city of Zoar instead. Lot's wife was clearly unhappy about leaving Sodom and Gomorrah; she turned around to look back and God turned her into a pillar of salt. We leave Lot with his two daughters deceiving him into sleeping with them so that they could fall pregnant.

All in all, a sad tale isn't it? Lot made bad choices all the way through his life it would seem; and he suffered the consequences of them. He did not trust God. He did not have faith in God. My friend, if you find yourself in a similar position then I urge you to stop and to take stock of your life. You don't have to continue making bad choices. God is a God of mercy, but He is also a just God. Repent, come to Him, and He will forgive you.

Prayer

My Father, I thank You for Your grace, mercy, and forgiveness. I ask You to please forgive me that I so often fall into the trap of making bad decisions. I realize that most of the time this happens because I am not prepared to trust You and obey You. Forgive me, I pray. Help me to turn to You and walk in Your will and Your ways. Amen.

THE FAITH JOURNEY OF OBEDIENCE

The journey of obedience consists of moment-by-moment submission

1. Obey the voice of the Lord
2. Know, obey, love, and faith
3. Trust and obey, there is no other way…
4. Teach your children to obey God
5. Love equals obedience
6. You cannot serve two masters
7. If you love Me, obey Me
8. He who believes in Me
9. By grace, through faith
10. Upon whom do you rely?
11. The Helper has come
12. Seeking the Kingdom
13. Live as obedient children
14. Fruitful growth in faith
15. First mention of grace
16. Noah did as God commanded
17. God was grieved in His heart
18. Righteous in your generation
19. If God says it, He does it
20. God hasn't forgotten you
21. Noah built an altar
22. Promises and conditions
23. God's everlasting covenant
24. A more excellent sacrifice
25. Enoch pleased God
26. Keep My Word
27. Obedience brings peace
28. Perseverance + hope = faith
29. Nothing can separate us from God's love
30. Carry God's Word in your heart
31. Love the Lord your God

Read Deuteronomy 30:11–20

> THAT YOU MAY LOVE THE LORD YOUR GOD, THAT YOU MAY OBEY HIS VOICE,
> AND THAT YOU MAY CLING TO HIM, FOR HE IS YOUR LIFE AND THE LENGTH
> OF YOUR DAYS; AND THAT YOU MAY DWELL IN THE LAND WHICH THE LORD
> SWORE TO YOUR FATHERS, TO ABRAHAM, ISAAC, AND JACOB, TO GIVE THEM.
>
> Deuteronomy 30:20

"Obey" is one of the key words in the Old Testament. If you do a word search of the Old Testament then you will find that permutations of the phrase "obey the voice of the Lord" appear over and over again. God's people constantly chose to disobey Him. God sent prophet after prophet to His people to warn them and to exhort them to obey His voice. The Lord our God places a high premium upon obedience. We saw only a few days ago how the supreme test of Abraham's faith rested upon his willingness to obey God's command to offer up for sacrifice his only son, Isaac.

Throughout the Old Testament the disobedience of God's people stemmed from their unbelief. Time and again they chose to turn toward other gods. In situation after situation they chose to walk by sight and not by faith. Despite all the evidence that they had of God's faithfulness to them they still chose to go their own way. In our reading today, God is setting a choice before His people. The choice is life or death. Life comes as a result of obeying God's voice. Death comes as a result of disobeying His voice.

Verses 11–14 tell us:

> *For this commandment which I command you today is not too mysterious for you, nor is it far off. It is not in heaven, that you should say, "Who will ascend into heaven for us and bring it to us, that we may hear it and do it?" Nor is it beyond the sea, that you should say, "Who will go over the sea for us and bring it to us, that we may hear it and do it?" But the word is very near you, in your mouth and in your heart, that you may do it.*

God says His commands are not complicated – they are very simple. We have the same choice before us: obedience or disobedience. God has placed His Holy Spirit within us; the Spirit prompts us to walk in God's ways. Are you listening? If you are, then "do it" – obey!

Prayer

My Father God, Your Word is in my mouth and it is in my heart. I know what You require of me. Forgive my stubbornness; forgive my arrogance when so often I choose to walk my own way instead of following Your commands. I repent before You today. Cleanse me, fill me, and lead me, I pray. Amen.

KNOW, OBEY, LOVE, AND FAITH

Read Deuteronomy 11:13–32

> AND IT SHALL BE THAT IF YOU EARNESTLY OBEY MY COMMANDMENTS WHICH
> I COMMAND YOU TODAY, TO LOVE THE LORD YOUR GOD AND SERVE HIM
> WITH ALL YOUR HEART AND WITH ALL YOUR SOUL THEN I WILL GIVE YOU... .
> Deuteronomy 11:13–14a

The words "know", "obey", "love", and "faith" are interchangeable. You cannot love someone you do not know. It is hard to obey someone that you do not trust. Sadly, too many people in our world have trust issues. People have been let down so many times and it has left them with a very cynical view of life. We grow up with phrases such as: "Seeing is believing"; "God helps those who help themselves"; and "Each man for himself". I am sure you can add a few more to this list. None of them fit in with our reading and what God is saying to us in His Word.

Through our key verse God invites you to choose a path that is not paved with cynicism – He invites you to "earnestly obey My commandments which I command you today, to love the Lord your God and serve Him with all your heart and with all your soul". As a farmer I appreciate God's promises to bless the land and make it fruitful. If you are a businessman this promise applies just as much to you. God will bless your business; He will prosper your efforts. No one is excluded from this promise – whatever it is that you do, God is saying that He will bless you.

The criteria for receiving the blessing is obeying God's commands, loving God, and serving Him with all of your heart and soul. You will only be able to do this if you really know Him. I can guarantee you that the more you get to know God, your Father, the more you will love Him. I love Him more every day. Do you remember the words of the lovely hymn: "The longer I serve Him, the sweeter He grows, the more that I love Him, more love He bestows?" If you have a trust issue then you more than likely have a knowledge issue, which in turn leads to a love issue, which in the end will lead to an obedience issue. Come to Jesus; He will lead you into a deeper relationship with His Father.

Prayer

My Father God, I come to You in the Name of Jesus Christ, my Lord and Saviour. Father, I long to have a deeper love relationship with You. I realize that without a love relationship I will not be able to trust You and obey You as You want me to. Fill me afresh with Your Spirit of love and grace, I pray. Amen.

Read Psalm 5

> BUT LET ALL THOSE REJOICE WHO PUT THEIR TRUST IN YOU; LET THEM EVER
> SHOUT FOR JOY, BECAUSE YOU DEFEND THEM; LET THOSE ALSO WHO LOVE
> YOUR NAME BE JOYFUL IN YOU.
>
> Psalm 5:11

Another beautiful old hymn that reminds us of our theme for this month is "Trust and Obey":

> *Trust and obey, for there's no other way*
> *To be happy in Jesus, but to trust and obey….*
>
> *But we never can prove the delights of His love*
> *until all on the altar we lay; for the favour He shows,*
> *for the joy He bestows, are for them who will trust and obey.*

Outside of Jesus there is no way to find lasting happiness. He came to bring you abundant life. Jesus said: "I have come that they may have life, and that they may have it more abundantly" (John 10:10b). A life of obedience brings contentment and blessing. The first part of verse 10 says: "The thief does not come except to steal, and to kill, and to destroy." This is the enemy's purpose for your life. He will try to lure you away from God's purpose for your life. God's purpose is a path of obedient faith that leads to blessing and fulfilment; the enemy's plan is to lead you away so that he can rob you and take your blessing away from you.

We saw last month that even Abraham, the father of the faith, suffered the consequences of disobedience to God's commands to him. Deviating from God's plan brought Abraham nothing but heartache; it will be the same for us. Why would anyone settle for second best when they can live in the fullness of the very best? This is the question you need to ask yourself as you contemplate our discussion this month on the faith journey of obedience. This journey comprises moment-by-moment submission to God your Father. My friend, you'd better believe that time is short. We're living in the end times. Jesus is looking for mighty men who will take His Truth forward: men who will live lives of honour to the glory of His Name. Psalm 5 ends with this promise: "For You, O Lord, will bless the righteous; with favor You will surround him as with a shield" (verse 12).

Prayer

My Father, Your Word to me is one of love and exhortation. I place my trust in You. I want the outworking of this trust to be a life of obedience to You. I do not want the enemy to have the opportunity to rob and to steal from me. Thank You, Lord, that You promise to defend me as I walk in obedience. Amen.

Read Deuteronomy 6:1–9

> AND THESE WORDS WHICH I COMMAND YOU TODAY SHALL BE IN YOUR
> HEART. YOU SHALL TEACH THEM DILIGENTLY TO YOUR CHILDREN, AND SHALL
> TALK OF THEM WHEN YOU SIT IN YOUR HOUSE, WHEN YOU WALK BY THE WAY,
> WHEN YOU LIE DOWN, AND WHEN YOU RISE UP. YOU SHALL BIND THEM AS
> A SIGN ON YOUR HAND, AND THEY SHALL BE AS FRONTLETS BETWEEN YOUR
> EYES. YOU SHALL WRITE THEM ON THE DOORPOSTS OF YOUR HOUSE AND ON
> YOUR GATES.
>
> Deuteronomy 6:6–9

This instruction from God is preceded by another command: "Hear, O Israel: The Lord our God, the Lord is one! You shall love the Lord your God with all your heart, with all your soul, and with all your strength" (verses 4–5). This command is repeated countless times in different ways throughout the Old Testament. It is also quoted word for word in the Gospels of Matthew, Mark, and Luke. There is significance in it preceding God's instructions to us on how we are to educate our children regarding "The Faith".

You will never be able to teach and inspire your children to know, love, trust, and obey God with all of their hearts if you don't set an example for them to follow. You are their best example of what the Christian life should look like. We have a responsibility to teach our children to walk in obedience to God. However, these lessons are "best caught rather than taught". My friend, don't count your success by how much you accomplish in your career. Don't count it by how much money you accumulate. Count your success by the example that you are to your children of what it means to live a life of faith. A life committed to walking in obedience to Jesus your Saviour and God your Father.

It doesn't matter what the world thinks of you. What matters is what those closest to you think of you. When the front door closes do your wife and children experience what it means to live the Christian life through your example? This is your primary calling: to diligently teach your children what it means to love the Lord their God with all their heart, with all their soul, and with all their strength. If you are a parent who has – to the best of your ability – lived the Christian life, yet your children have still chosen to walk a different path, take heart. God is faithful; He will never leave you or forsake you. Continue to walk upright, continue to pray, and, above all, continue to trust God.

Prayer
My Father God, You are a loving, gracious Father to me. I am so grateful to be Your child. Help me to be a living example to my children of what it means to walk in obedience to You. I want to teach them through my actions and not only through my words how to love and obey You. Amen.

LOVE EQUALS OBEDIENCE

Read John 14:15–31

> Jesus answered and said to him, "If anyone loves Me, he will keep My word; and My Father will love him, and We will come to him and make Our home with him. He who does not love Me does not keep My words; and the word which you hear is not Mine but the Father's who sent Me."
>
> John 14:23–24

The verses we have just read basically tell us that if we say we love the Lord then we will obey His commandments. Not obeying is the equivalent of telling your wife that you love her but never doing anything for her. Then you wonder why she does not want to submit to you. I am sure you have heard the saying, "Love has feet". Whenever I have the privilege of performing a wedding service I remind the bridal couple that "love" is a verb – it is an action word.

It is not enough to only tell your family that you love them; you have to show them that you love them. You do this by the way in which you supply their needs. You provide for your family by putting bread on the table. You make sure that you arrive home at night in time for dinner so that you can spend time with your children before they go to bed. These are some of the ways of expressing love in action. Unfortunately some men think that saying the words "I love you" is enough. Sadly they do not back up their words with action. They are always either working or out with their friends.

The same can also be said for our relationship with Jesus. It is not enough for us to say the words, "I love You, Lord". God expects action from us. Verse 15 says, "If you love Me, keep My commandments" We have to walk our talk, my friends. God has given us everything that we need in order to walk obediently before Him. He has given us His Son, Jesus Christ; He has given us His Holy Spirit who dwells inside of us, empowering us to "walk our talk"; He has given us His Word to guide and direct us. We have all we need. What we have to do is make the decision to submit ourselves to God and "walk our talk" in every area of our lives. This is what a man of faith does – this is the path of obedience.

Prayer

My Father, You have spoken to me. Thank You for the reminder that "love" is an action word – it requires me to do something. I realize that the place to begin is my relationship with You. Once this is in order then the rest of my life will fall into place. I want to be a man of faith walking in obedience and love. Amen.

Read Matthew 12:22–30

> HE WHO IS NOT WITH ME IS AGAINST ME, AND HE WHO DOES NOT GATHER
> WITH ME SCATTERS ABROAD.
>
> Matthew 12:30

In today's verse Jesus made it very clear that you cannot serve two masters. Either you are for the Lord or you are against Him. Another way for the Lord to say this would be – "If you love Me then obey My commandments." Folks, you know by now that I am not about obeying the law. I am about grace – this is what I preach. I am about loving the Lord. Love is at the very centre of everything that Jesus stands for. It was love that drove Him to come down to this earth and die for you and me. The gospel is about love my friends.

However, if you say that you love the Lord then action has to follow your utterance. There is no way that you can say that you love the Lord and then continue to live exactly as you did before. People have to see a change in your life. You cannot say I've made a commitment to Christ and then continue committing adultery or stealing from your employers. You cannot continue wilfully sinning and say that you love God. In the same way that oil and water do not mix – nor do sin and obedience. You have to stop sinning and obey the Lord.

Too many Christians try and live with a foot in both camps. They want the benefits of Salvation, but they do not want to give up their favourite sin. You cannot flirt with the world my friends. Jesus is calling for a generation of men who are serious about serving Him. He is calling men to form a mighty army: men who will not be scared to stand up for righteousness; men who will not squirm, but who will proudly say: "I serve King Jesus." God wants men who will nail their colours to the mast, walking each day by faith and not by sight. Are you such a man? Is this how you are choosing to live your life?

Prayer

My Father, You are calling me to be a mighty man for You. I realize that I cannot have a foot in the world's camp and Your camp. It has to be one or the other. I cannot serve two masters. Lord, I desire to serve only one Master, and that is You. Help me to walk before You in integrity and love. Amen.

Read Titus 1

> THEY PROFESS TO KNOW GOD, BUT IN WORKS THEY DENY HIM, BEING
> ABOMINABLE, DISOBEDIENT, AND DISQUALIFIED FOR EVERY GOOD WORK.
>
> Titus 1:16

I have been telling you that God is not interested in your good works. Over and over we have read and quoted the text that says without faith it is impossible to please God. Ephesians 2:8 tells us: "For by grace you have been saved through faith, and that not of yourselves; it is the gift of God." Today's reading is a key one, telling us that there are those whose works deny God. My friend, God's Word doesn't contradict itself, so what is our text saying to us?

It is important not to confuse works done in order to try to earn your own Salvation with the actions of someone who is walking in obedient faith with God. Trying to make ourselves independent of God and doing things for our own glory is not what the Bible talks about. No, the Bible talks about the way we behave. We read the phrase over and over again in the Word of God – "If you love Me, keep My commandments" (for example, John 14:15). Sometimes people phrase it as – "If you love Me, obey My voice." What Titus is talking about in today's reading is obedience. If you truly know God then you will obey Him.

Obedience is the outworking of faith, and it is the outworking of love. We have read how Jesus said, "If you love Me then you will obey My commandments." I think this is the problem in the church today. There are a lot of people saying that they love God, but their actions don't support their words. *The Message*'s version of Titus 1:16 puts it like this: "They say they know God, but their actions speak louder than their words." By their lack of action they deny Him. I really believe we have reached the stage in the history of mankind where Christians have to stand up and be counted. You cannot straddle the fence any longer – you have to choose which camp you will live in. Will it be the world's camp or will it be Jesus' camp? Choose to live a faithful life of obedience, trusting God every day to lead you and guide you.

Prayer

My Father God, Your Word has spoken so clearly to me. I have to choose how I will live; which camp I will live in. I cannot remain sitting on the fence any longer. Lord, I want to serve You wholeheartedly. I want my words and my actions to line up with each other. I want to walk in obedient faith. Amen.

Read John 14:1–14

> MOST ASSUREDLY, I SAY TO YOU, HE WHO BELIEVES IN ME, THE WORKS THAT I
> DO HE WILL DO ALSO; AND GREATER WORKS THAN THESE HE WILL DO, BECAUSE
> I GO TO MY FATHER. AND WHATEVER YOU ASK IN MY NAME, THAT I WILL DO,
> THAT THE FATHER MAY BE GLORIFIED IN THE SON. IF YOU ASK ANYTHING IN MY
> NAME, I WILL DO IT.
>
> John 14:12–14

Jesus promised in John 14 that if we believe in Him we will do greater works than He did. He also promised that if we ask the Father anything in His Name He will give it to us. The belief that Jesus was speaking about here is not only Salvation belief – it goes beyond that. Verses 8–11 say:

> Philip said to Him, "Lord, show us the Father, and it is sufficient for us."
> Jesus said to him: "Have I been with you so long, and yet you have not known
> Me, Philip?… The words that I speak to you I do not speak on My own
> authority; but the Father who dwells in Me does the works. Believe Me that
> I am in the Father and the Father in Me, or else believe Me for the sake of the
> works themselves."

"Have I been with you so long, and yet you have not known Me…?" We therefore see two levels of knowing here. Philip and the other disciples knew Jesus. They believed in Him. Yet they did not fully trust Him, did they? They were always asking for more proof. Jesus said to Thomas: "Blessed are those who have not seen and yet have believed" (John 20:29b). I hope that when you read this one of our key Scriptures popped into your mind: "[W]ithout faith it is impossible to please [God]" (Hebrews 11:6a).

Again Jesus mentioned works: He says His Father does the works. By this He meant that the works that He did were done through His faith in His Father. Jesus trusted His Father and His Father did the works through Him. Jesus promised us that if we believe in Him the Father will do the same and greater works through us. If Jesus were standing before you right now He would ask you the same question that He asked Philip: "Have you not known Me?" Your actions will give Him the answer. Are you walking by faith, believing Him for both your needs and those of others, allowing Him to do His works through you?

Prayer

My God and Father, I come to You in the precious Name of Jesus, Your Son. Father, I want to have that deeper level of knowing. I want to believe – not superficially but with a deep assurance. Lord, I trust You to meet all my needs. Father, do Your works through me to the honour and glory of Your Name. Amen.

Read Ephesians 2:1–13

FOR BY GRACE YOU HAVE BEEN SAVED THROUGH FAITH, AND THAT NOT OF YOURSELVES; IT IS THE GIFT OF GOD, NOT OF WORKS, LEST ANYONE SHOULD BOAST. FOR WE ARE HIS WORKMANSHIP, CREATED IN CHRIST JESUS FOR GOOD WORKS, WHICH GOD PREPARED BEFOREHAND THAT WE SHOULD WALK IN THEM.

Ephesians 2:8–10

Your Salvation is the most precious, wonderful gift that you will ever receive, my friend. A gift is something you cannot earn – otherwise it wouldn't be a gift, would it? There is only one way to be saved, and that is through faith. Not faith in a religion, not faith in a dogma, not even faith in the Bible. No, we are saved through faith in Jesus Christ. No matter how rich, powerful, or influential you are you cannot buy your way into Heaven. No matter how driven and competitive you are you cannot earn your way into Heaven. It is an absolutely free gift that a loving Heavenly Father has bestowed upon you. He loves you, my friend. Are you revelling in His love as you read this? Are you praising Him for His amazing grace toward you? I hope so.

The reason Salvation is free is so that we cannot take the credit for it – hence "lest anyone should boast". God has a plan and a purpose for your life. We spent the whole of last month journeying with Abraham as he discovered God's purpose for his life. God doesn't love you any differently to the way that He loved Abraham. God has a plan and a purpose that He has especially designed for you. Our Scripture tells us that we are God's workmanship. We have been "created in Christ Jesus for good works". These works that Jesus was talking about are God's purpose for you.

God prepared them long before you were born. Our Scripture says God prepared them for you to walk in them. You will only be able to fulfil your purpose if you place your trust in God. You need to walk by faith and not by sight – trusting Him to reveal His plan to you step by step along the way. Don't settle for second best – live in the fullness of your Salvation. Walk by faith in the works that God prepared beforehand for you to accomplish. Don't settle for second best – Jesus died so that you can have the absolute best.

Prayer

My God and Father, thank You that You called me and saved me. I want to live in the fullness of Your Salvation. I want to walk the road of faith. I want to walk in the works that You have prepared for me to fulfil. These works are Your purpose for my life. Fill me and use me, I pray, in Jesus' Name. Amen.

Read 2 Chronicles 16

> AND AT THAT TIME HANANI THE SEER CAME TO ASA KING OF JUDAH, AND
> SAID TO HIM: "BECAUSE YOU HAVE RELIED ON THE KING OF SYRIA, AND HAVE
> NOT RELIED ON THE LORD YOUR GOD, THEREFORE THE ARMY OF THE KING OF
> SYRIA HAS ESCAPED FROM YOUR HAND."
>
> 2 Chronicles 16:7

Time after time in the Old Testament we read how God's people chose their own ways rather than His ways. They chose not to believe in Him. They chose to disobey God's commands to them. Each time there were dire consequences for His people and their land. King Asa, king of Judah, typifies this kind of behaviour. He chose to rely on man rather than on God. God is serious when He says to you that to obey is better than sacrifice. He means it when He says without faith it is impossible to please Him. When you face challenges upon whom do you choose to rely? Is your first inclination to sort it out yourself? Maybe you turn to other people and look to them for solutions to your problems.

In verse 8 God reminds King Asa through His servant Hanani: "Were the Ethiopians and the Lubim not a huge army with very many chariots and horsemen? Yet, because you relied on the Lord, He delivered them into your hand." When Asa was obedient to God and placed his faith in the Lord he was victorious. God goes on to say to him (verse 9): "For the eyes of the Lord run to and fro throughout the whole earth, to show Himself strong on behalf of those whose heart is loyal to Him" (verse 9a). God is looking for men who will be obedient to Him; men who will be loyal to Him no matter what. Loyalty, obedience, and faith are some of the important characteristics of a mighty man of God.

The world defines greatness through our accomplishments. God defines greatness through our loyalty to Him. The journey of faith is a moment-by-moment submission to God, your Father. Right up to his last breath King Asa chose not to rely upon God: "Asa became diseased in his feet, and his malady was severe; yet in his disease he did not seek the Lord, but the physicians" (verse 12b). How sad is that? Dire consequences indeed, wouldn't you say? Again I ask you: Upon whom do you rely, my friend?

Prayer

My Father God, I bow in Your presence and give You praise for Your goodness and Your mercy toward me. Forgive my unbelief. I want to be loyal to You above all. I desire to be a man who is known as Your obedient servant. Lord, You, and You alone, are my shield and my defender. Amen.

Read John 14:19–31

BUT THE HELPER, THE HOLY SPIRIT, WHOM THE FATHER WILL SEND IN MY
NAME, HE WILL TEACH YOU ALL THINGS, AND BRING TO YOUR REMEMBRANCE
ALL THINGS THAT I SAID TO YOU.

John 14:26

I find in my walk with the Lord that the more time I spend with Him the greater He manifests in my life. God reveals Himself to me in so many ways each day. One of the things that I have told you over and over again is that Christianity is not a quick fix. Christianity is a lifestyle. You either follow the Lord with all your heart or you do not follow Him at all. When I gave my life to the Lord on the 18 February 1979 something happened that changed my life forever.

What about you, my friend? You might reply that you have given your life to the Lord, but you are still working through issues. You cannot continually work through issues, sir. You need to surrender the things in your life that are not pleasing to God. I am not referring to outward things such as smoking, drinking, and swearing. All of those will stop in time. They must, because you don't need them and they are not good for you.

The issues that I am instead referring to are those things that outsiders don't always see. You may still be struggling with a bad temper, for instance. Maybe your problem is selfishness towards your family and your loved ones. It could be that you have other "gods" in your life – idols that continually trip you up. It is not good enough to say that you cannot stop these things – that you cannot help yourself. Jesus said: "He who has My commandments and keeps them, it is he who loves Me. And he who loves Me will be loved by My Father, and I will love him and manifest Myself to him" (John 14:21). Our key verse today tells you that God gave the Holy Spirit in order to help you. In obedience, surrender those things that are holding you back – then God will be able to move in your life. God is no respecter of persons. Walk forward in obedient faith and victory in Jesus through the power of His Spirit.

Prayer

My Father, forgive me for so often making excuses. Lord, I know that You have given me everything that I need to live a victorious Christian life. Help me to choose obedience; help me to choose submission to You above all else. I thank You for Your Holy Spirit whom You have sent to help me. Amen.

Read Matthew 6:24–34

> BUT SEEK FIRST THE KINGDOM OF GOD AND HIS RIGHTEOUSNESS, AND ALL
> THESE THINGS SHALL BE ADDED TO YOU.
>
> Matthew 6:33

Seeking the Kingdom of God means walking in obedient faith before the Lord each and every day of your life. It takes faith to obey God. Sometimes obedience to God can mean going against other people. This is why verse 24 says: "No one can serve two masters; for either he will hate the one and love the other, or else he will be loyal to the one and despise the other. You cannot serve God and mammon." What do you do when you face a situation at work where your boss tells you that you need to close a deal no matter what it takes – even if you have to do something underhanded and illegal? Do you choose to serve God or man? Do you choose the Kingdom of God or the kingdom of man?

These are difficult choices because losing your job means potential hardship for your family. Yet, in today's verse, Jesus said: "seek first the kingdom of God and His righteousness, and all these things shall be added to you." We often get it back to front, but Jesus was clear – first the Kingdom, then the blessing. This is where obedient faith comes in. You trust God that if you walk according to His commands He will undertake for you. God promised: "Now it shall come to pass, if you diligently obey the voice of the Lord your God, to observe carefully all His commandments which I command you today, that the Lord your God will set you high above all nations of the earth" (Deuteronomy 28:1).

We have established over and over again that God places a high premium on obedience. It is not what you do for Him that counts, but rather how you live before Him. Do not allow yourself to be swept up in the attitudes of the world. As a child of God you can rest secure in the knowledge that Your Father is in control of your life, the lives of your loved ones, and your circumstances. You can rest in His faithfulness and His goodness every day of your life.

Prayer

My Lord, You are calling me to walk a more dedicated walk with You. I am on a journey of discovery as I spend time in Your Word and in prayer. Lord, I want above all else to seek first Your Kingdom and Your righteousness. I realize that there is nothing of worth to be found anywhere else. Amen.

Read 1 Peter 1:13–25

> SINCE YOU HAVE PURIFIED YOUR SOULS IN OBEYING THE TRUTH THROUGH THE
> SPIRIT IN SINCERE LOVE OF THE BRETHREN, LOVE ONE ANOTHER FERVENTLY
> WITH A PURE HEART...
>
> 1 Peter 1:22

Every child of God is on a faith journey. We walk along this path in obedience to the Father. God calls us in the same way that He called Abraham and all of the other men of faith throughout history. We too have our own unique faith path. The only way to walk this path is to be committed and totally submitted to Jesus. He has gone before us – He has made the way for us to enter into the presence of the Father. When we take up our calling to walk as obedient children we please God.

As we read in verses 13–16:

> *Therefore gird up the loins of your mind, be sober, and rest your hope fully*
> *upon the grace that is to be brought to you at the revelation of Jesus Christ;*
> *as obedient children, not conforming yourselves to the former lusts, as in*
> *your ignorance; but as He who called you is holy, you also be holy in all your*
> *conduct, because it is written, "Be holy, for I am holy."*

An offshoot of this obedience is that we will love our brethren. We see that 1 John 4:20–21 puts it like this:

> *If someone says, "I love God," and hates his brother, he is a liar; for he who*
> *does not love his brother whom he has seen, how can he love God whom he has*
> *not seen? And this commandment we have from Him: that he who loves God*
> *must love his brother also.*

How are you doing when it comes to loving your brothers and sisters in the Lord? From the Scripture verses we have looked at it is obvious that if we love God we will love His children. He does not give us an option. God is very specific. It is so sad to all too often read of, or sometimes witness, the fights and rifts that occur between God's children. My friend, if you are involved in a dispute with a brother – stop immediately. Choose to live as an obedient child of God, go to him or her and make it right.

Prayer

Dear Father in Heaven, You have called me to live my life as Your obedient child. I know that often I fall short of this command. I allow myself to be caught up in conflicts that lead to pettiness, mistrust, and unloving behaviour towards my fellow Christians. Forgive me, I pray. Amen.

Read 2 Peter 1:1–11

> GRACE AND PEACE BE MULTIPLIED TO YOU IN THE KNOWLEDGE OF GOD AND
> OF JESUS OUR LORD, AS HIS DIVINE POWER HAS GIVEN TO US ALL THINGS
> THAT PERTAIN TO LIFE AND GODLINESS, THROUGH THE KNOWLEDGE OF HIM
> WHO CALLED US BY GLORY AND VIRTUE.
>
> 2 Peter 1:2–3

You cannot live a victorious Christian life outside of a knowledge of and a relationship with Jesus Christ. He is *the* way to the Father. There is no other way – despite what people may try to tell you. We have just read about all that we have in Jesus. Scripture uses words such as grace, peace, and divine power. It tells us that we have been given all things that pertain to life and godliness. This means that in Jesus you have everything that you need to be able to live an abundant, holy life. All of this is possible because of the knowledge we have of Jesus. This word – knowledge – does not mean an intellectual understanding or ability. What it means is an experiential knowledge. You know – because you have experienced it.

Our Scripture goes on to tell us how we should live in the light of this knowledge (verses 5–8):

> *But also for this very reason, giving all diligence, add to your faith virtue, to virtue knowledge, to knowledge self-control, to self-control perseverance, to perseverance godliness, to godliness brotherly kindness, and to brotherly kindness love. For if these things are yours and abound, you will be neither barren nor unfruitful in the knowledge of our Lord Jesus Christ.*

If we live a life of faithful obedience then we will be fruitful. Our lives will bear fruit. We will have a testimony that other people will be able to see. It is far more important for people to see your testimony by the way that you live, than what it is for them to hear you speak of it. "Actions speak louder than words" is a very apt saying when applied to a Christian's life. Like it or not, your life is a testimony every day. The only question is: what is your testimony saying? I hope it is pointing to a life of fruitful growth in faith and obedience. Peter concludes by telling us: "Therefore, brethren, be even more diligent to make your call and election sure, for if you do these things you will never stumble" (verse 10).

Prayer

My Lord and Saviour, thank You, Jesus, for all that You have given to me. I am so grateful that in You I have grace, peace, and divine power in abundance. Help me to live in the fullness of this so that I can have a life that testifies to fruitful growth in faith. Lord, I want to honour You and bring glory to Your Name. Amen.

Read Genesis 6:1–8

BUT NOAH FOUND GRACE IN THE EYES OF THE LORD.

Genesis 6:8

This is the first time that the word "grace" is mentioned in the Bible. "Noah found grace in the eyes of the Lord." In the midst of a corrupt and wicked generation Noah lived a life of obedient faith before God. Yesterday we said that whether we like it or not our lives are a testimony. The question is, what sort of a testimony are they? Well, certainly Noah's life was a testimony. We often think that it is too hard to live a righteous life in our society. There are so many temptations and things that can pull us away from walking in obedience with the Lord. It was no different in Noah's time, my friends.

Despite this Noah clearly made a choice. He did not run with the herd; instead he walked with the Lord. I want to encourage you if you are in a situation where it is difficult to serve God wholeheartedly. Maybe you are in an office environment where blasphemy and ungodly behaviour is the order of the day. It could be that you are at university and all your friends are running wild. Possibly you are a husband whose wife isn't serving the Lord, and you are walking a lonely road. Whatever your situation, it cannot be worse than the temptations and challenges that Noah faced.

It was so bad that the Word tells us: "And the Lord was sorry that He had made man on the earth, and He was grieved in His heart" (verse 6). Can you imagine what it must have been like trying to live a life of obedient faith at a time like that? Remember back at the beginning of February we said that Noah, who was Abraham's great grandfather several times removed, was a part of Abraham's godly heritage. You too have the opportunity to pass on a godly heritage – the decisions you make today that will determine the extent of the heritage you leave behind you. Will it be said of you: X found grace in the eyes of the Lord?

Prayer
My Father God, thank You for Your amazing grace. Your grace has not changed down through the ages. It is still as free and as abundant as it was when You extended it to Noah. You have called me to live a life of grace. A life that is sold out to You and Your purposes irrespective of what is happening around me. Amen.

NOAH DID AS GOD COMMANDED

Read Genesis 6:9–22

THUS NOAH DID; ACCORDING TO ALL THAT GOD COMMANDED HIM, SO HE DID.

Genesis 6:22

When God has a purpose for you to fulfil you can rest assured that He knows exactly what He wants you to do. He has it all worked out. God sees the bigger picture. Very often we can only see what is directly in front of us – and even then we tend to see what we want to see. God knew exactly what He wanted Noah to do. It was no accident that God chose Noah to build the ark. The Bible tells us that the people who were living on the earth at that time were wicked. They became so wicked that God eventually lost patience with them and He decided that He would destroy them along with the earth. However, God decided to save a remnant of the old world, and after the destruction everything was able to be begun anew.

As He looked down upon the earth He saw Noah. Yesterday we read: "But Noah found grace in the eyes of the Lord" (Genesis 6:8). In our reading today we see that "Noah walked with God" (verse 9c). Noah was a godly man, the only godly man of his time. He was a man of faith who chose to walk by faith and not by sight. So Noah was God's man for the job that needed to be done. God gave him exact instructions as to how he was to build the ark. God had the master plan. There had never been a flood before that time. So can you imagine how incredulous people were when Noah began telling them that the world was going to be flooded? No one believed him. The people ridiculed him and scoffed at him.

The antagonism from the people around him did not stop Noah from doing what God told him to do. He chose to believe God rather than listening to man: "Thus Noah did; according to all that God commanded him, so he did." This is the obedience of faith, my friends. This is what faith in action looks like. Remember the other day we said that faith is a doing word – it requires action.

Prayer

My Father God, You are a mighty and awesome God. You direct the affairs of this world with love and grace, but also with fairness and justice. Thank You for the example of a man of faith like Noah. Help me to be prepared to walk in obedient faith with You no matter what those around me think or say. Amen.

Read Genesis 6:3–7

AND THE LORD WAS SORRY THAT HE HAD MADE MAN ON THE EARTH, AND
HE WAS GRIEVED IN HIS HEART.

Genesis 6:6

In Genesis 1:26a we read: "Then God said, 'Let Us make man in Our image, according to Our likeness'" and then in verse 31: "Then God saw everything that He had made, and indeed it was very good. So the evening and the morning were the sixth day." It was only after God had created man that He felt His creation was "very good". When He had finished creating everything else He felt it was "good". Human beings were the crowning glory of God's creation. He made man in His image. God wanted to share His creation with mankind. Sadly, man did nothing but disappoint Him.

When we come to Genesis 6 we see that God had reached the end of His tether with mankind. Can you feel the tragedy of verse 6? "And the Lord was sorry that He had made man on the earth, and He was grieved in His heart." Imagine the immensity of God's pain and disappointment. His joy had turned to grief. He created man in His own image to have fellowship with Him. Man's wickedness had brought Him to the point where He could no longer allow things to continue the way they were going. Man was so sinful and had defiled the earth to such an extent that God saw no other outcome but to destroy His creation and begin over again.

God is a God of grace and mercy. He is long-suffering and kind. He is a covenant-keeping God. However, He is also the God of this universe. He is the Righteous Judge and He is a just God who demands punishment for sin. We so often only like to think of God in terms of His mercy and grace – and where would any of us be without it? We are all sinners who are saved by grace, aren't we? Never forget, though, that the grace and mercy you and I enjoy came at a tremendous price. God's holiness and righteousness had to be satisfied. There was only One who could satisfy Him – Jesus Christ, His Son. God gave everything in order to save His creation.

Prayer

My gracious Heavenly Father, I bow in Your presence and acknowledge You as my God, the Righteous Judge. Lord, I could never stand in Your presence. I am so grateful that I can come to You in the precious Name of Jesus Christ, Your Son. Thank You for my Salvation. Thank You that I am washed clean in the blood of Jesus. Amen.

Read Genesis 7:1–12

THEN THE LORD SAID TO NOAH, "COME INTO THE ARK, YOU AND ALL YOUR HOUSEHOLD, BECAUSE I HAVE SEEN THAT YOU ARE RIGHTEOUS BEFORE ME IN THIS GENERATION."

Genesis 7:1

Last month, when we were learning lessons together from Abraham's life, I mentioned to you that he came from a godly heritage. Noah was Abraham's great grandfather several times removed, but the heritage was still there. Noah was a man who walked his talk. He was a righteous man in his generation. He lived a righteous life in a time when it was not popular to do so. There were no doubt many temptations around him. If you look at the Bible's description of society in Noah's day they were rampantly evil. But despite all that was going on around him, Noah chose to walk uprightly with his God, and God honoured Noah's commitment to Him.

We live in wicked times. There is evil and mayhem all around us. People seem to be going from bad to worse. A lot of the time it is hard not to become despondent and discouraged when we see the crime that is running wild. We watch as people are caught up in all forms of sin and degradation. We can be forgiven for asking where and when will it all end. You might feel that given our society it is too difficult to stand up and be counted for God. At work you face so many temptations.

My friends, we do not live in more difficult times than Noah did. Our temptations are just different, but no worse. It comes down to choice, doesn't it? How do we choose to live? We can run with the crowd, going with the flow, or we can stand up and be a man who is righteous in his generation – a man whom God can use to fulfil His plans and purposes for this generation. What will your choice be today? We spoke last month about leaving a legacy. Noah left a legacy for Abraham to follow. You too have the opportunity to leave a legacy for those who will come after you. Will future generations of your family look back upon your life and be able to say, "He was a righteous man in his generation"?

Prayer

Father God, I so want to be known as a man who walked righteously before You. I want to leave a godly legacy for those who will come after me. Thank You that I am righteous because of what Jesus my Saviour has done for me. Help me to live in the fullness of my Salvation to the honour of Your Name. Amen.

IF GOD SAYS IT, HE DOES IT

Read Genesis 7:11–24

> IN THE SIX HUNDREDTH YEAR OF NOAH'S LIFE, IN THE SECOND MONTH, THE
> SEVENTEENTH DAY OF THE MONTH, ON THAT DAY ALL THE FOUNTAINS OF THE
> GREAT DEEP WERE BROKEN UP, AND THE WINDOWS OF HEAVEN WERE OPENED.
>
> Genesis 7:11

You can be assured that if God says He is going to do something He will do it. The Lord told Noah there would be a flood and "on that day all the fountains of the great deep were broken up, and the windows of heaven were opened." You can imagine how the scoffers felt as the first drops of rain turned into a steady drizzle, then the rain came down harder and harder, until eventually it was a non-stop downpour. I am sure their scoffing quickly turned to stark terror. As a child of God you can take comfort and courage from the fact that God is true and faithful to His Word.

The Bible tells us that God does not lie. "God is not a man, that He should lie, nor a son of man, that He should repent. Has He said, and will He not do? Or has He spoken, and will He not make it good?" (Numbers 23:19). So if God has made you a promise He will keep it. If He has told you something will happen, it will happen. This month we are on a faith journey of obedience. We have to choose whether we will walk by faith or by sight. The scoffers who watched Noah build the ark lived by sight. They believed what they could see and understand. Noah, on the other hand, lived by faith. He believed God when God said He was going to bring a flood. Noah didn't understand what a flood was – he had never seen one before. However, if God said it, then Noah believed it.

This is the choice we have to make each day in our lives. Will we believe everything we see around us or will we choose to believe God and His Word? It doesn't matter what your circumstances are: you can still choose to walk by faith. It is not faith if everything is going well and you know exactly what is going to happen next. Faith is clinging to the Lord and His word to you.

Prayer

My Father, help me, I pray, to remain faithful to You in the midst of a generation of people who so often are all too ready to turn away from You. You are faithful to me and to Your Word. I want to walk each day by faith and not by sight. Give me insight, give me courage, and fill me with Your Spirit. Amen.

GOD HASN'T FORGOTTEN YOU

Read Genesis 8:1–12

THEN GOD REMEMBERED NOAH, AND EVERY LIVING THING, AND ALL THE
ANIMALS THAT WERE WITH HIM IN THE ARK. AND GOD MADE A WIND TO PASS
OVER THE EARTH, AND THE WATERS SUBSIDED.

Genesis 8:1

Have you ever felt as if God has forgotten about you? It could be that you have been praying and trusting God for a long time for something. You believed that He gave you "a word" and you have been waiting for Him to make good on His promise to you. Each day the situation seems to become worse and you are reaching the place where you are becoming discouraged and ready to give up. Well, all I can say to you today, my dear friend, is, "Don't give up. Keep persevering."

James 5:11 says, "Indeed we count them blessed who endure. You have heard of the perseverance of Job and seen the end intended by the Lord – that the Lord is very compassionate and merciful." Peter encourages those of you who are suffering: "But may the God of all grace, who called us to His eternal glory by Christ Jesus, after you have suffered a while, perfect, establish, strengthen, and settle you" (1 Peter 5:10). If you are walking by faith and not by sight then you will remain steadfast no matter what is happening, or in some instances not happening, around you. Don't you love the end of verse 10 there – "and settle you"? Yes, my friend, even in the midst of the most severe trials you can be settled – safe and secure in the knowledge that God is in control.

Our key verse says: "Then God remembered Noah". After all those days locked up in the ark do you think Noah might have begun to wonder whether God had forgotten about him and his family? God had not forgotten about them – He was there with them every step of the way. The same is true for you. God has not forgotten you – He is right there with you. Don't lose heart; don't give up. Trust in your God. Cling to His Word. Spend time in prayer, praise, and worship. Look back through history and remember how God has come through for His children from generation to generation. He will do the same for you. He hasn't forgotten you!

Prayer

My Father, thank You for Your faithfulness that reaches down from generation to generation. Lord, You cannot lie – You are true to Your Word. Give me the courage to persevere and stand firm no matter what I see going on around me. I choose today to trust You. Thank You that You will never forget about me. Amen.

Read Genesis 8:13–22

> THEN NOAH BUILT AN ALTAR TO THE LORD, AND TOOK OF EVERY CLEAN
> ANIMAL AND OF EVERY CLEAN BIRD, AND OFFERED BURNT OFFERINGS ON THE
> ALTAR. AND THE LORD SMELLED A SOOTHING AROMA.
>
> Genesis 8:20–21a

Noah's journey of obedient faith continued as he patiently waited for the earth to dry out sufficiently for all of them to leave the ark. Eventually the day came when God said it was OK for them to step outside. What a different world awaited them to the one before the flood. Noah's first response was to offer a sacrifice to the Lord. Noah took of all the clean animals and clean birds. He built an altar and then sacrificed the animals and birds to the Lord: "And the Lord smelled a soothing aroma" (verse 21a).

Don't you find it amazing that God pre-planned for Noah to be able to offer the sacrifice to Him? "You shall take with you seven each of every clean animal, a male and his female… also seven each of birds of the air, male and female" (Genesis 7:2–3a). This meant that Noah's sacrifice would not hinder the re-population of the earth – there would still be a number of each type of animal and bird left. We serve a God who takes care of each and every detail in our lives. If God tells you to do something you don't have to stress about the details of how it will be accomplished. You simply have to faithfully obey Him, trusting Him to work it all out.

God accepted Noah's sacrifice: "And the Lord smelled a soothing aroma. Then the Lord said in His heart, 'I will never again curse the ground for man's sake, although the imagination of man's heart is evil from his youth; nor will I again destroy every living thing as I have done'" (Genesis 8:21). This meant that God had to find another way of dealing with the sin of mankind. He did not and could not change His character, which is of holiness and righteousness. So He chose to send His Son to die instead, so that mankind can live. Spend some time today bringing your own sacrifice of thanksgiving to the Lord. Bow before Him and thank Him for His faithfulness, His goodness and His mercy towards you.

Prayer

My Father God, I bow in Your presence. I come to You in the Name of Your Son and my Saviour, Jesus Christ. Jesus, thank You for sacrificing Yourself so that I can enter freely into the Father's presence. I praise You, my God and my Father, for Your everlasting love toward me. Amen.

Read Genesis 9:1–7

> So God blessed Noah and his sons, and said to them: "Be fruitful and multiply, and fill the earth."
>
> Genesis 9:1

As you read the verses in chapter 9 were you reminded of God's words to Adam and Eve in the Garden of Eden? "Then God blessed them, and God said to them, 'Be fruitful and multiply; fill the earth and subdue it'" (Genesis 1:28a). God had also said to Adam: "And the Lord God commanded the man, saying, 'Of every tree of the garden you may freely eat; but of the tree of the knowledge of good and evil you shall not eat, for in the day that you eat of it you shall surely die'" (Genesis 2:16–17). Adam failed the test of obedient faith. He didn't trust God when Eve ate of the apple. He followed her lead and lost the Garden of Eden.

After God wiped the earth clean He blessed Noah and his family. He gave them a promise with a condition: "But you shall not eat flesh with its life, that is, its blood… Whoever sheds man's blood, by man his blood shall be shed; for in the image of God He made man" (Genesis 9:4, 6). Throughout Scripture, if you look at God's promises they are usually accompanied by a condition. The condition is linked to obedience; it is linked to us complying with God's commands and His will – this takes faith. It means that you are willing to submit to God. We said at the beginning of the month that the journey of obedient faith consists of moment-by-moment submission to God.

So often we want the blessing without doing the time, so to speak. We crave the quick fix. When things don't work out as we want them to we look for our own solutions. This didn't work for Adam; it didn't work for Abraham either, if you remember. Every person throughout God's Word who sought their own solution rather than waiting upon, and having faith in God, ended up with a disaster on their hands. If you are facing a choice at the moment of finding your own solution or trusting God – what will your choice be?

Prayer

Dear Lord, I thank You for Your Word that speaks so clearly to me. You are a God of order and purpose. I know You love me, but I also know You expect obedience to Your ways and Your will. Help me not to fall into the trap of impatience – choosing my own solutions. Lord, I want to depend upon You. Amen.

Read Genesis 9:11–17

THE RAINBOW SHALL BE IN THE CLOUD, AND I WILL LOOK ON IT TO
REMEMBER THE EVERLASTING COVENANT BETWEEN GOD AND EVERY LIVING
CREATURE OF ALL FLESH THAT IS ON THE EARTH.

Genesis 9:16

"It shall be, when I bring a cloud over the earth, that the rainbow shall be seen in the cloud; and I will remember My covenant which is between Me and you and every living creature of all flesh; the waters shall never again become a flood to destroy all flesh" (Genesis 9:14–15). Hebrews 11:7 tells us: "By faith Noah, being divinely warned of things not yet seen, moved with godly fear, prepared an ark for the saving of his household, by which he condemned the world and became heir of the righteousness which is according to faith."

Never again would God destroy the whole earth through a flood. We said the other day that this meant that God had to find another way to satisfy His righteousness. Noah was an heir of this righteousness. You, my friend, if you are a follower of Jesus Christ, are an heir of this righteousness. What qualified Noah to be an heir? Faith qualified him. What qualifies you and me to be an heir of this righteousness? Yes, you've got it, faith qualifies us. Faith in Jesus Christ, the righteous Son of God. You serve a God who is faithful to His promises. Paul tells us in 2 Timothy 2:13: "If we are faithless, He remains faithful; He cannot deny Himself." God has never ever gone back on His word.

As the saying goes: "You can take God's promises to the bank". They will never default or bounce. What He looks for in return is for us to live lives of faithful obedience to Him. When you see a rainbow in the sky from now on, allow it to remind you of God's faithfulness, but also the responsibility of your faithfulness to Him. It is simple, my friend: if you love Him you will obey Him. If you obey Him, you will be walking in faith. If you are walking in faith then you will see His mighty hand stretched out, undertaking for you. Today, as never before, God is looking for men who will walk by faith – will you be such a man?

Prayer

My God and Father, Ruler of the universe, Creator of Heaven and earth. There is no one like You. Your greatness and majesty are beyond my feeble ability to describe. I can only bow before You in awe and wonder. Lord, I am so privileged to serve You. You are my covenant-keeping God. Amen.

Read Genesis 4:1–15

> BY FAITH ABEL OFFERED TO GOD A MORE EXCELLENT SACRIFICE THAN CAIN,
> THROUGH WHICH HE OBTAINED WITNESS THAT HE WAS RIGHTEOUS, GOD
> TESTIFYING OF HIS GIFTS; AND THROUGH IT HE BEING DEAD STILL SPEAKS.
>
> Hebrews 11:4

We have two men. Both brought sacrifices to God. He accepted Abel's sacrifice and rejected Cain's. This situation brings to mind God's words to the prophet Samuel when David was anointed king. Samuel's inclination was naturally to go with one of David's big strong brothers. Not God though – He was looking for something more; He was looking for something else entirely. He said to Samuel: "For the Lord does not see as man sees; for man looks at the outward appearance, but the Lord looks at the heart" (1 Samuel 16:7b). When God looked upon Cain and Abel – what He saw in Abel pleased Him, but what He saw in Cain didn't.

God has always been more interested in our obedience than in our sacrifices. The only sacrifice that counts with the Lord is one that comes from an obedient heart filled with faith and love. Why wouldn't we want to serve God with all our hearts? "Only fear the Lord, and serve Him in truth with all your heart; for consider what great things He has done for you" (1 Samuel 12:24). On the journey of faith there are no half measures. It is all or nothing. Cain did not want to take responsibility for his actions when God confronted him. He continued to act true to character. Cain didn't show any signs of repentance. Yet, despite this, when he complained to God that he would be killed, God showed him mercy (see Genesis 4:15).

Abel has the honour of being the first person mentioned in Hebrews' "Hall of Faith". Hebrews 11:4 says that he offered "a more excellent sacrifice than Cain". As you think about it today, how would you rate the quality of your sacrifice to God? Are you like Cain offering a mediocre sacrifice – a half-hearted commitment? Or are you like Abel – sold out to God giving Him only the best that you have to offer? When you "consider what great things He has done for you" how could you offer God anything less than excellence?

Prayer

My Father God, indeed I can agree with Samuel today when he said: "Only fear the Lord, and serve Him in truth with all your heart; for consider what great things He has done for you." Lord, You have done so much for me. I want to serve You with excellence in everything that I do for You. Amen.

Read Hebrews 11:1–6

> BY FAITH ENOCH WAS TAKEN AWAY SO THAT HE DID NOT SEE DEATH, "AND
> WAS NOT FOUND, BECAUSE GOD HAD TAKEN HIM"; FOR BEFORE HE WAS
> TAKEN HE HAD THIS TESTIMONY, THAT HE PLEASED GOD.
>
> Hebrews 11:5

In every generation there have been men who have walked with God. Men who have pleased Him. Men who wouldn't have wanted to have this epitaph on their tombstone: "His testimony is that he pleased God". We have been speaking for the past three months about walking by faith. What pleases God is a man who walks by faith. This is indeed the key to pleasing Him: "But without faith it is impossible to please Him, for he who comes to God must believe that He is, and that He is a rewarder of those who diligently seek Him" (verse 6).

Enoch didn't die. The Bible says: "And Enoch walked with God; and he was not, for God took him" (Genesis 5:24). Isn't that beautiful? I emphasize again: the journey of obedience consists of moment-by-moment submission. You do not suddenly wake up one day and find that you have the ability to live a faith-filled life. No, my friends, faith increases step by step; moment by moment; decision by decision; situation by situation. Remember last month when we looked at Abraham? We said that his faith journey began the moment he took the first step and left his home. Noah's faith journey began when he went out and fetched the wood to begin building the ark. Abel's began when he chose to give God of his best. What we know about Enoch is that he walked with God.

As this year progresses we will be looking at many other men of faith. Their stories like yours and mine are all different. However, one thing they all have in common is that they faced a decision as to whether it would be their way or God's way. None of them were perfect; they all made mistakes along the way. The common thread throughout, though, is that all of them had hearts that were for God. Each one of them desired above all else to walk in obedient faith with God. We all have the opportunity to walk the journey of faith with God. The only prerequisite is a heart that pleases Him.

Prayer

My Father in Heaven, You are merciful and kind. You love me more than I can ever understand. Lord, in Your graciousness You have invited me to walk the faith journey with You. Lord God, I want to faithfully walk with You each and every day so that You will be pleased with me. Amen.

Read John 14:19–24

> Judas (not Iscariot) said to Him, "Lord, how is it that You will manifest Yourself to us, and not to the world?" Jesus answered and said to him, "If anyone loves Me, he will keep My word; and My Father will love him, and We will come to him and make Our home with him."
>
> John 14:22–23

Jesus did not beat around the bush. He was absolutely 100 per cent clear about what He expects from those who claim to be His followers. If you love Him then you will keep His Word. What does it mean to keep His Word? It means that you will live your life in such a way that you will bring glory to God. When you are faced with decisions your first thoughts will be: "What does Jesus want me to do in this situation? What does His Word tell me to do?" God has not left us in the dark, my friends. He has given us His Word. In His Word He shares with us how we are to live the Christian life.

If you are a child of God your excuse can never be that you didn't know any better. In his epistle Peter tells us: "as His divine power has given to us all things that pertain to life and godliness, through the knowledge of Him who called us by glory and virtue" (2 Peter 1:3). We said the other day that God's promises come with conditions. The conditions are usually obedience. There is no way that you will be able to obey God if you do not trust Him. I remind you again of the old hymn "Trust and Obey" that goes, "Trust and obey, for there's no other way/To be happy in Jesus but to trust and obey".

In the light of all of this I want to ask you: are you walking in the ways of the Lord? I have to tell you that I grow tired of Christians telling me that Christianity is not working for them. They complain that God is not blessing their business or that God is not blessing their home, because they are still having problems in their family. I always reply, "Get back to basics. Ask yourself: am I living according to the Word of God?" God blesses obedience. He blesses those who walk in obedient faith, trusting Him and not themselves for the solutions to their problems.

Prayer

My Father, I come to You in Jesus' Name. Lord, as I stand in Your presence I ask You to search my heart. Show me any wicked, disobedient ways that are lurking within me. I know that You have called me to walk before You in love, faith, and obedience. Help me, Lord, to surrender to You. Amen.

Read John 14:25–31

PEACE I LEAVE WITH YOU, MY PEACE I GIVE TO YOU; NOT AS THE WORLD
GIVES DO I GIVE TO YOU. LET NOT YOUR HEART BE TROUBLED, NEITHER LET IT
BE AFRAID.

John 14:27

People go to great lengths to try and find peace. A lack of peace can drive a person insane. Many people live lives filled with fear because they do not have peace. Sadly, even some Christians lack peace in their lives. Every time we turn on the television, open a newspaper, or listen to the radio we are bombarded by news that has the potential to fill us with fear.

Our key Scripture today tells us that we do not have to live fear-filled lives. Jesus came to bring peace. In fact Jesus is Peace. Isaiah 9:6 says: "For unto us a Child is born, unto us a Son is given; and the government will be upon His shoulder. And His name will be called Wonderful, Counselor, Mighty God, Everlasting Father, *Prince of Peace*" (my italics). You see the problem is that people have it wrong. Peace is not a state of mind. It is not a place or an attitude – no, Peace is a Person – Jesus Christ.

Jesus came to reveal the Father to us. When He left to go back to Heaven He did not leave us without help. "These things I have spoken to you while being present with you. But the Helper, the Holy Spirit, whom the Father will send in My name, He will teach you all things, and bring to your remembrance all things that I said to you" (John 14:25–26). You never need to worry that you won't know what to do – you have the Holy Spirit living within you. He will bring to your remembrance everything that Jesus said. He will remind you of God's Word. If you live a life submitted to the Spirit He will lead you to walk in obedient faith. The Holy Spirit will help you to walk the journey of faith. His Spirit is powerful within each of us to help us to do God's will. The way to live a peaceful life is to live an obedient life, doing all that God your Father and Jesus your Saviour have commanded you to do in Their Word.

Prayer

My Father, I know that the path to peace is the path of faithful obedience to Your Word. Lord, thank You that You have filled me with Your Holy Spirit. Through Your Spirit I can live a life of power and fulfilment. I can live a life of peace and assurance of blessing. Keep me faithful, I pray. Amen.

Read Romans 8:12–25

> FOR WE WERE SAVED IN THIS HOPE, BUT HOPE THAT IS SEEN IS NOT HOPE; FOR
> WHY DOES ONE STILL HOPE FOR WHAT HE SEES? BUT IF WE HOPE FOR WHAT
> WE DO NOT SEE, WE EAGERLY WAIT FOR IT WITH PERSEVERANCE.
>
> Romans 8:24–25

"For as many as are led by the Spirit of God, these are sons of God" (verse 14). Being led by the Spirit of God means that you will do what the Spirit of God instructs you to do. Do you realize what it means to have the Holy Spirit of God living inside of you? It means that you have unlimited power. Not your own power, but God's power. This power is not for your own use. It is not for you to abuse or misuse. No, my friends, we are meant to live lives that are submitted to God. Then His Spirit can flow through us with power. God is looking for men of faith in this generation who will be willing to be used by Him to fulfil His purposes.

You are God's dearly loved child, as verses 15–17a illustrate:

> *For you did not receive the spirit of bondage again to fear, but you received the*
> *Spirit of adoption by whom we cry out, "Abba, Father." The Spirit Himself*
> *bears witness with our spirit that we are children of God, and if children, then*
> *heirs – heirs of God and joint heirs with Christ.*

Too many of God's children are living like step-children as opposed to living like heirs to the Kingdom of God. A hireling works for his wages and when five o'clock comes – or whenever he knocks off – he is out of there. He has no allegiance to the business. Doing his eight and a half hours or whatever he is contracted to do is all he is interested in. A son keeps working, because one day he is going to own the business.

We keep walking the path of patient perseverance. Our steps are bolstered by hope. It is possible to do this because we know that perseverance plus hope equals faith. God's Word tells us that without faith it is impossible to please Him. As His dearly loved children we know that He will keep His promises to us and one day we will see the fulfilment of all that we have hoped for.

Prayer

My Father, You have assured me that as Your dearly loved child I am an heir with Your Son, Jesus, to Your Kingdom. I am not a hireling, I am not a stepchild; I am a son. I walk the path of perseverance and hope, knowing that when my faith in You is strong I please You. Amen.

Read Romans 8:26–39

> FOR I AM PERSUADED THAT NEITHER DEATH NOR LIFE, NOR ANGELS NOR
> PRINCIPALITIES NOR POWERS, NOR THINGS PRESENT NOR THINGS TO COME,
> NOR HEIGHT NOR DEPTH, NOR ANY OTHER CREATED THING, SHALL BE ABLE TO
> SEPARATE US FROM THE LOVE OF GOD WHICH IS IN CHRIST JESUS OUR LORD.
>
> Romans 8:38–39

The verses that we have just read are some of the most beautiful in God's Word. I don't know what is going on in your life at the moment, my friend. It could be that you are going through some incredible hardship. I receive so many letters from Christians who are enduring trials and difficulties. Maybe you or one of your loved ones have been diagnosed with what the doctors are calling an incurable disease. There could be some of you who are facing what seem to be insurmountable difficulties in your marriage. Possibly your child is on drugs. If you are a businessman maybe you are facing bankruptcy. I know that there are many farmers who face daily hardships as they try to farm their land.

Whatever your situation – you do not have to be the victim of your circumstances. It is not a glib cliché when verse 28 tells you: "And we know that all things work together for good to those who love God, to those who are the called according to His purpose." If God's Word says it, then He means it. The question is: do you believe what His Word says? Verse 31 goes on to say: "What then shall we say to these things? If God is for us, who can be against us?" Whatever you feel is against you – know that God is for you. Have faith in Him; trust in Him. Walk the path of obedient faith.

"Yet in all these things we are more than conquerors through Him who loved us" (verse 37). Are you living like a conqueror or are you living as one who is defeated? Our key verse tells us that nothing can separate us from the love of God. If you are not feeling God's love right now it is not because He has changed towards you. He cannot – because His Word says that He will always love you. Reread Romans 8:26–39. Then spend some time in His presence and pray, asking God to reassure you once again of His love for you.

Prayer

My Father God, thank You for Your great love for me. I am so grateful that in the midst of my circumstances I can lift my eyes and look to You. You have promised me that nothing and no one can separate me from Your love. You also promise me that all things will work out according to Your will for my life. Amen.

Read Deuteronomy 11:18–21

> THEREFORE YOU SHALL LAY UP THESE WORDS OF MINE IN YOUR HEART AND
> IN YOUR SOUL, AND BIND THEM AS A SIGN ON YOUR HAND, AND THEY SHALL
> BE AS FRONTLETS BETWEEN YOUR EYES. YOU SHALL TEACH THEM TO YOUR
> CHILDREN, SPEAKING OF THEM WHEN YOU SIT IN YOUR HOUSE, WHEN YOU
> WALK BY THE WAY, WHEN YOU LIE DOWN, AND WHEN YOU RISE UP. AND YOU
> SHALL WRITE THEM ON THE DOORPOSTS OF YOUR HOUSE AND ON YOUR GATES,
> THAT YOUR DAYS AND THE DAYS OF YOUR CHILDREN MAY BE MULTIPLIED IN
> THE LAND OF WHICH THE LORD SWORE TO YOUR FATHERS TO GIVE THEM, LIKE
> THE DAYS OF THE HEAVENS ABOVE THE EARTH.
>
> Deuteronomy 11:18–21

Following Jesus is meant to be a lifestyle. It is something that permeates and takes over every single aspect of our lives. We are not meant to compartmentalize our walk with the Lord. You cannot live so that Monday to Saturday are for "other" activities and Sunday is for the Lord. Living this way is not a journey of faithful obedience to Jesus. If you try to live your Christian life with one foot in the world and one foot in the Kingdom, you will never be effective for the Lord. He demands either 100 per cent commitment or nothing.

He told us in His Word that we are either for Him or against Him. We have to choose. If you live a split life then you cannot be surprised when your family ends up in disarray. Your children need you to be the one who sets the example for them of what it means to walk by faith and not by sight. Where else are they going to learn it if they don't learn it from you, my friend?

I specifically placed the whole of our reading at the top of the page, because I want you to read it over again now. Then I want you to ask yourself some tough questions. Are you leading your children as the Lord has instructed you in these verses, or are you leaving it up to your wife to teach your children about the things of God? You need to take up your rightful place as the spiritual leader in your home and teach your children what it means to follow Jesus. Not only through your words, but far more importantly by the way that you live. I remind you again that faith is a doing word. It is not what you say that will remain with your children as they grow up, but rather how you have lived. Give them the godly legacy that we have spoken about earlier this month.

Prayer

My Father, You have been such an incredible Father to me. You are faithful, You are loving, and You are true. Help me, I pray, to be the same kind of father to my children. I want to teach them to love You, not only through what I say to them, but more importantly through the way that I live. Amen.

Read Deuteronomy 30:11–20

> THAT YOU MAY LOVE THE LORD YOUR GOD, THAT YOU MAY OBEY HIS VOICE,
> AND THAT YOU MAY CLING TO HIM, FOR HE IS YOUR LIFE AND THE LENGTH
> OF YOUR DAYS; AND THAT YOU MAY DWELL IN THE LAND WHICH THE LORD
> SWORE TO YOUR FATHERS, TO ABRAHAM, ISAAC, AND JACOB, TO GIVE THEM.
>
> Deuteronomy 30:20

I want to end with the same Scripture that we began the month with. I would like to invite you to take some time today to reflect back on the things we have discussed. There have been some vital truths that we have looked at. I sincerely pray that God's Holy Spirit has been speaking to you as you have read the Scriptures. At the end of the day, my friends, it is not my words that count, but God's Word. My sincere desire is to minister to you as the Holy Spirit leads me. I am committed to sharing the truth of God's Word as He reveals it to me. However, I am only too aware that it is only God's Spirit who can change your mind and your heart.

We have been looking at what it means to walk a faith journey of obedience. We said: "The journey of obedience consists of moment-by-moment submission." This submission is to God's will and His ways. What this world needs is men who walk in obedience to God's Word. When we see an army of men stand up and be counted for Jesus then we will see change take place in our land. What we see around us today is the result of people moving away from the Truth of God's Word. It is the result of people no longer loving the Lord their God with all of their hearts. When we turn the hearts of people towards God then their behaviour will follow suit.

Our Scripture today says that if we love God we will obey His voice. These two things go together. The Scripture goes on to say, "and that you may cling to Him". "Clinging" implies that there is closeness. When a person clings to someone you literally have to prise their arms loose. Are you clinging to God? If you cling to Him then there will be no room for doubt or sin to creep into your life. Your whole focus will be upon Him. Do you love Him in this way?

Prayer

My Father God, I want to cling to You. I want to have such a close relationship with You that nothing and no one will be able to prise me away from You. I love You, my Lord and God. I desire above all else to walk in moment-by-moment submission and obedience to You. Amen.

JOSEPH'S JOURNEY OF RESTORATION

Joseph's journey of restoration began with his heritage

1. Selling your birthright
2. Jacob receives the blessing
3. God blesses Jacob
4. Joseph, the much-loved son
5. Joseph, the dreamer
6. Envy destroys and distorts people
7. The consequences of sin
8. God's blessing upon Joseph
9. Faithfully flee temptation
10. Find grace in your time of need
11. God blesses Joseph in prison
12. Loving God under trials
13. Endure joyfully
14. Give God the glory
15. When people let you down
16. The faith to wait
17. God doesn't share His glory
18. Who is your Deliverer?
19. God will bring it to pass
20. A Spirit-filled man of faith
21. Faith is honoured
22. Fruitful in the midst of affliction
23. God is faithful to His Word
24. The remorse of wrongdoing
25. Joseph blesses his brothers
26. Joseph tests his brothers
27. The fulfilment of Joseph's purpose
28. Joseph provides for his family
29. Living a life of reconciliation
30. Joseph's journey of restoration

Read Genesis 25:19–34

AND JACOB GAVE ESAU BREAD AND STEW OF LENTILS; THEN HE ATE AND
DRANK, AROSE, AND WENT HIS WAY. THUS ESAU DESPISED HIS BIRTHRIGHT.

Genesis 25:34

Isaac's wife, Rebekah, had twins named Esau and Jacob. Esau was the eldest and therefore the heir to the blessing. The brothers grew up to become very different from each other. Esau was what I suppose you could call a hunter-gatherer, while Jacob worked in the fields. Esau was a rough diamond and Jacob was a smooth operator. As sometimes happens in families Isaac favoured Esau, while Rebekah favoured Jacob. As they grew up the differences between the siblings became increasingly apparent.

One day, when Esau returned home starving, he sold his birthright to Jacob for a plate of stew. Our key verse says that Esau "despised" his birthright. I guess in modern-day language you could say that he wanted instant gratification. We live in a society where people give away their souls for instant gratification. People steal or get into debt to afford the things they want. They take drugs and abuse alcohol in order to try and attain peace and harmony in their lives. These solutions always bring about stress and heartache.

Hebrews 12:12–17 has these words of warning for us:

> Therefore strengthen the hands which hang down, and the feeble knees, and make straight paths for your feet, so that what is lame may not be dislocated, but rather be healed. Pursue peace with all people, and holiness, without which no one will see the Lord: looking carefully lest anyone fall short of the grace of God; lest any root of bitterness springing up cause trouble, and by this many become defiled; lest there be any fornicator or profane person like Esau, who for one morsel of food sold his birthright. For you know that afterward, when he wanted to inherit the blessing, he was rejected, for he found no place for repentance, though he sought it diligently with tears.

If you find yourself in a place where you are tempted to sell your birthright in Jesus for something that will provide momentary gratification, consider today's story of Esau. Choose the path of faith, trusting God to provide what you need.

Prayer

My Father, thank You that Your Word speaks to me. It is a light to my path and a lamp to my feet. You instruct me and guide me. Today I have been warned regarding choosing instant gratification over faith in You. Lord, I want to walk the walk of faith, trusting You to provide for me. Amen.

Read Genesis 28:1–5

MAY GOD ALMIGHTY BLESS YOU, AND MAKE YOU FRUITFUL AND MULTIPLY
YOU, THAT YOU MAY BE AN ASSEMBLY OF PEOPLES; AND GIVE YOU THE
BLESSING OF ABRAHAM, TO YOU AND YOUR DESCENDANTS WITH YOU, THAT
YOU MAY INHERIT THE LAND IN WHICH YOU ARE A STRANGER, WHICH GOD
GAVE TO ABRAHAM.

Genesis 28:3–4

Isaac, the child of the promise, was old and he was about to die. It was time for him to pass on the blessing given to him by his father, Abraham, to his eldest son. Isaac did not know that Esau had sold his birthright to his brother. In Genesis 27 we read that Isaac sent Esau off to prepare his favourite meal. After the meal, Isaac was going to bestow the blessing upon his firstborn. While Esau was out hunting, Rebekah prepared the meal and had Jacob take it in to his father. Isaac was almost blind and he could not see which of his sons was before him. Esau was hairy and Jacob was smooth-skinned, so Rebekah had Jacob place animal skins on his forearms and neck.

Isaac didn't know any better and he passed the blessing that you read in our key verse on to Jacob. You will remember from our walk with Abraham that God had promised this blessing to Abraham and his descendants. Although Jacob was not without his faults we see that there was an inherent weakness and flaw within Esau that precluded him from receiving and being the bearer of the blessing. His lack of faith in God to provide his needs was indeed his downfall.

Throughout Jacob's life, even with his faults, there is a leaning towards God. Jacob had a desire for God's blessing upon his life. Later on Jacob fathered Joseph who became a mighty man of God. My friend, I urge you as you look at the story of Esau and Jacob, to examine your heart. Take stock of your life. What are the things that you are hankering after? Every day you are faced with the option of living in a way that will ensure God's blessing upon your life, or the choice to live in a way that will prevent God from being able to undertake in your life. Your choices don't only affect you and your life right now – they also have implications for the generations who will come after you.

Prayer

My Father God, You are a faithful God. You bless Your children from generation to generation. You were faithful to Your promise to Abraham. I am so grateful that through Jesus I am also a beneficiary of that promise. Help me to live a life of faith each day, bringing glory to Your Name. Amen.

Read Genesis 28:10–22

> AND BEHOLD, THE LORD STOOD ABOVE IT AND SAID: "I AM THE LORD GOD
> OF ABRAHAM YOUR FATHER AND THE GOD OF ISAAC; THE LAND ON WHICH
> YOU LIE I WILL GIVE TO YOU AND YOUR DESCENDANTS."
>
> Genesis 28:13

God continued speaking out His blessing upon Jacob:

> *Also your descendants shall be as the dust of the earth; you shall spread abroad
> to the west and the east, to the north and the south; and in you and in your
> seed all the families of the earth shall be blessed. Behold, I am with you and
> will keep you wherever you go, and will bring you back to this land; for I will
> not leave you until I have done what I have spoken to you.*
>
> Genesis 28:14–15

Isaac had passed the blessing on to Jacob, but it was not until God confirmed it that it was official.

Jacob had God's stamp of approval as the one who would be the carrier of the promise. In verses 20–22 Jacob makes a vow to God. He promises to serve God. I suppose you could say that was his moment of Salvation: the point at which he committed his life to God. Jacob set up a pillar or an altar and he worshipped God. Jacob called the name of the place where he met God Bethel – literally meaning "House of God". Calling the place by that name meant Jacob acknowledged God's presence there.

From that day on his walk with the Lord became real to Jacob. He became a man of faith on that day. Jacob married Rachel. "Then God remembered Rachel, and God listened to her and opened her womb. And she conceived and bore a son, and said, 'God has taken away my reproach.' So she called his name Joseph, and said, 'The Lord shall add to me another son'" (Genesis 30:22–24). Here we see Joseph making his appearance. God had a very specific plan and purpose for Joseph's life. I hope that as we spend this month learning faith lessons from his life that you will be blessed and encouraged in your faith walk with the Lord. When you see how God worked in the lives of His mighty men in the Bible are you not amazed and thankful that He is the same covenant-keeping God that He was then?

Prayer
My Father God, thank You once again today for Your incredible faithfulness down through the ages. I am so grateful that like Abraham, Isaac and Jacob I too am a child of the promise. Lord, help me to walk in humble obedience to You each day of my life. I want to please You in every area of my life. Amen.

Read Genesis 37:1–4

> Now Israel loved Joseph more than all his children, because he was the son of his old age. Also he made him a tunic of many colors.
>
> Genesis 37:3

From everything we read in the Bible about Joseph's older brothers it doesn't sound as if they were a very commendable bunch. They did not like Joseph. It wasn't simply a case of being irritated by, and therefore picking on, their younger brother. It went much deeper than that. They knew that their father not only favoured Joseph but that he loved him more than he loved the rest of them. One of the ways their father showed his love was by making Joseph a special coat of many colours.

One day the brothers were out watching their father's sheep. We don't know what it is that the brothers did wrong, but seventeen-year-old Joseph was with them at the time. He went back to his father and whatever it was that they did or didn't do, Joseph told his father about it. This clearly made the brothers very angry because no doubt they got into trouble with their father. We read in verse 4 that "they hated him and could not speak peaceably to him." At a young age Joseph showed signs of the man he was to become when he was grown up. He did the right thing even when those around him were doing wrong. He was a young man of principle.

It was at this young age of seventeen that Joseph began to trust and have faith in God. He didn't suddenly wake up one day and become obedient to God. It began when he was a young man out in the fields tending his father's herds. Whatever skulduggery his brothers were up to he would have no part in it. Joseph didn't become trustworthy the day he entered Potiphar's house – he was trustworthy already. Character is something that is built over time. Godly character comes from walking a steadfast walk of faith with the Lord. It comes from making the right choices each and every day. If you are a young man reading this how are you living your life? Are you standing true even when your friends aren't, or are you running with the crowd?

Prayer

My Father God, I thank You that I am Your much-loved son. I am so grateful that You do not have favourites. You love all Your children. Lord, I want to be known as an obedient child of Yours. I want to be faithful, true, and trustworthy. Help me to make the right choices each and every day. Amen.

Read Genesis 37:5–11

> "WHAT IS THIS DREAM THAT YOU HAVE DREAMED? SHALL YOUR MOTHER
> AND I AND YOUR BROTHERS INDEED COME TO BOW DOWN TO THE EARTH
> BEFORE YOU?" AND HIS BROTHERS ENVIED HIM, BUT HIS FATHER KEPT THE
> MATTER IN MIND.
>
> Genesis 37:10b–11

God has often spoken to His people in dreams down through the ages. Many, many times in the Bible we read of God coming to people in a dream with a specific message. In later years Joseph was given the ability to interpret dreams as well. The two dreams that we read about in our Scripture today were pictures of what would happen later on with regard to Joseph and his family. His brothers hated him even more as a result of these dreams. We are not talking about normal sibling rivalry here; their hatred of Joseph was deep-seated and evil.

It is interesting that although Jacob clearly didn't understand the full implications of the dream he realized that it was more than a young man's fantasies: "his father kept the matter in mind." Jacob had walked long enough with God and seen enough of His working in the lives of people to know that there was more to the dreams than met the eye. Jacob knew that God had a plan and a purpose for his son. One of the lessons that we learn from Joseph's life is that God does not bless you only for your own sake. As His children we are part of a much bigger picture. We are all part of God's ultimate plan of redemption for our world.

Joseph was Jacob's much-loved son. Ultimately Joseph became the instrument for his brothers' salvation and restoration. Jesus Christ is God's much-loved Son. God did not spare His Son, but sent Him to this world to effect the Salvation and restoration of mankind to Himself. Each day we, as God's children, have the opportunity to go out and live as ambassadors in our world proclaiming God's plan of Salvation and restoration. Do you realize that you are part of a much bigger plan than that which only affects your life? If so, are you faithful in daily living out that plan, sharing God's grace and goodness with those with whom you come into contact? Like Joseph, you too have a mission of restoration.

Prayer

My Father in Heaven, You sent Your precious Son to redeem me. As a result I have received Salvation and I have been restored in every area of my life. I am an ambassador for this Salvation and restoration. Help me to faithfully proclaim it to those You bring across my path. Amen.

ENVY DESTROYS AND DISTORTS PEOPLE

Read Genesis 37:12–24

THEN THEY SAID TO ONE ANOTHER, "LOOK, THIS DREAMER IS COMING! COME
THEREFORE, LET US NOW KILL HIM AND CAST HIM INTO SOME PIT; AND WE
SHALL SAY, "SOME WILD BEAST HAS DEVOURED HIM.' WE SHALL SEE WHAT
WILL BECOME OF HIS DREAMS!"

Genesis 37:19–20

Joseph's brothers were warped and blinded by envy. They were jealous of Joseph because they knew that their father loved him best. Even more than this they were envious of the kind of person that Joseph was. There was a big difference between Joseph and his brothers. Joseph didn't suddenly become a person of integrity when he landed up in Potiphar's home in Egypt. His integrity was developing all through his childhood. He didn't suddenly become a man of faith when faced with his first challenge. No indeed, Joseph's faith grew as he did.

His brothers could not identify and understand the difference between them and Joseph so they envied him, and they plotted against him. Isn't it so often true of human nature that we destroy what we do not understand? Envy is a dangerous emotion, my friend. Proverbs 14:30 warns us: "A sound heart is life to the body, but envy is rottenness to the bones." Envy will literally eat away at you until you are nothing but an empty shell if you allow it to. The devil uses it to sow discontent in our lives. If we allow him to he will always have us looking at what other people have and comparing it to what we have.

"For where envy and self-seeking exist, confusion and every evil thing are there" (James 3:16). Envy ruins relationships; it breaks up marriages and can destroy families. "Let us not become conceited, provoking one another, envying one another" (Galatians 5:26). Envy and deceit broke up Jacob's family. From the moment his sons decided to sell their brother Joseph into slavery all their lives were dominated by the ramifications of that one decision. Are there people whom you envy? Have you ever considered that envy is caused by a lack of faith? If I believe that God is my Provider, then I will be content with whatever He has given me. I will rest in His love and His provision. I will leave you with my wife Jill's favourite verse: "Now godliness with contentment is great gain" (1 Timothy 6:6).

Prayer

My Father in Heaven, thank You that I am Your much-loved son. You do not play favourites. You love all Your children equally. Therefore, I do not need to envy anyone. I have everything that I need in Jesus Christ, my Saviour. I am so grateful to You. You abundantly supply all of my needs. Amen.

Read Genesis 37:25–36

So Judah said to his brothers, "What profit is there if we kill our brother and conceal his blood? Come and let us sell him to the Ishmaelites, and let not our hand be upon him, for he is our brother and our flesh." And his brothers listened.

Genesis 37:26–27

Reuben seemed to be the only one of Joseph's brothers who had a conscience. He couldn't go through with killing Joseph and so he convinced his brothers to throw him into a pit instead. His plan was to sneak back to the pit and save Joseph. However, while he was gone the traders came by and Judah convinced his brothers to sell Joseph to them. Joseph's brothers betrayed him for twenty shekels of silver. When Reuben returned the deed was done. Then they had to cover up their first sin by deceiving their father into believing that a wild animal had killed and eaten Joseph. From that day on the brothers lived a lie.

Sin has consequences. One lie leads to another lie. Deception breeds deception. This is why sin leads to guilt, depression, and for some people even suicide. It is not worth it, my friend. So many of God's children are living lives of defeat because they have allowed sin to take root in their hearts. Jesus gave some very direct admonition regarding sin (Matthew 5:29–30):

If your right eye causes you to sin, pluck it out and cast it from you; for it is more profitable for you that one of your members perish, than for your whole body to be cast into hell. And if your right hand causes you to sin, cut it off and cast it from you; for it is more profitable for you that one of your members perish, than for your whole body to be cast into hell.

If you find yourself caught in a web of sin, stand still for a moment – remember who you are. You are a child of God. Jesus came to this earth to die for your sins. You can stop. Turn back to Him. We are promised in God's Word: "If we confess our sins, He is faithful and just to forgive us our sins and to cleanse us from all unrighteousness" (1 John 1:9). Often when Jesus healed or delivered someone He told them to go and sin no more.

Prayer
My Father, I come to You with a humble heart and spirit. I ask You to cleanse me and forgive me. I know that choosing to turn from You and walk in my own ways is not living a life of faith. I turn back to You – I choose to live for You; I choose to trust You and to love You above all else. Amen.

Read Genesis 39:1–8

So it was, from the time that he had made him overseer of his house and all that he had, that the Lord blessed the Egyptian's house for Joseph's sake; and the blessing of the Lord was on all that he had in the house and in the field.

Genesis 39:5

God didn't stop Joseph's brothers from selling him into slavery. Why? Because He had a bigger plan and purpose for Joseph's life. Joseph was a man of faith. He chose to obey and to walk with God no matter what. This was one of the main things that riled his brothers and caused them to envy him so much. Instead of learning from Joseph they chose rather to hate him. Potiphar quickly realized that he had struck gold in Joseph. God blessed Potiphar because of Joseph; he prospered as a result of having Joseph in his house.

Soon Potiphar entrusted the running of his household to Joseph. This was such an unusual thing to do. Only God's favour upon Joseph could cause this to happen. God's blessing upon Joseph was not only for his benefit, it was also to fulfil the larger purposes of God. I am sure that when Joseph was travelling to Egypt he must have wondered what would become of him. I am sure that by faith he held fast to the dreams God had given him. In the same way that God had blessed his great-grandfather Abraham, God's blessing was upon Joseph.

Joseph found himself in a strange land all alone without his family. His response wasn't to bemoan his fate. No, instead he set about faithfully serving God and his master. He walked the walk of faith day after day. I don't know what situation you find yourself in right now. I want to ask you a question though. Is your boss (if you have one) being blessed as a result of having you work for him or her? Can they trust you with all that they have, knowing that you will be a good steward? This is what God expects from us. This is the path of faith. We are blessed in order to be a blessing. Joseph was a true witness to the greatness of God in Potiphar's house. You too have the opportunity to be a witness in your place of employment. Remember faith is a doing word – what are you doing?

Prayer

My Lord and Saviour, thank You for Your amazing blessing upon my life. I want to walk in faith before You. I want to be a good steward of all that You entrust to me. Keep me humble, keep me faithful, and keep me committed to You. Lord, I want to be used by You to bless other people. Amen.

Read Genesis 39:6–10

> THERE IS NO ONE GREATER IN THIS HOUSE THAN I, NOR HAS HE KEPT BACK
> ANYTHING FROM ME BUT YOU, BECAUSE YOU ARE HIS WIFE. HOW THEN CAN I
> DO THIS GREAT WICKEDNESS, AND SIN AGAINST GOD?
>
> Genesis 39:9

Joseph enjoyed great success in Potiphar's house. He was in charge of everything. The Bible tells us that Potiphar didn't even know how much money or goods he had – he completely trusted Joseph to oversee it all and to keep check on his behalf. Joseph took his duties seriously. He was committed to his master. He was a hard worker and an example to all those who worked with him. The devil doesn't like it when God's children are successful, does he? No, he doesn't. He wasn't pleased with Joseph. He decided that he would try and trip Joseph up. He used Potiphar's wife to try and lure Joseph into temptation.

Joseph consistently denied the attempts of Potiphar's wife to seduce him. It is not easy for a young man to resist temptation, is it? It takes moral integrity and it takes faith. It takes a firm belief in the God you serve as well as knowledge of who you are in Him. Paul exhorted Timothy: "Flee also youthful lusts; but pursue righteousness, faith, love, peace with those who call on the Lord out of a pure heart" (2 Timothy 2:22). One of the lessons to learn from this Scripture is that you will become like those you hang around with. Choose to be with people who will build you up in the Lord, not break you down.

On the other hand, if you find yourself in a situation like Joseph where you have nowhere to run, you can take comfort in this promise from God. "No temptation has overtaken you except such as is common to man; but God is faithful, who will not allow you to be tempted beyond what you are able, but with the temptation will also make the way of escape, that you may be able to bear it" (1 Corinthians 10:13). The pathway of faith is one of obedience to God's Word. By faith Joseph resisted Potiphar's wife at the expense of his own freedom. Even though obedience to God's principles landed him in a prison cell, Joseph was victorious in his faith.

Prayer

My God and Father, You have called me to walk a path of faithful obedience to You. I choose to walk by faith and not by sight. No matter what the cost I want to be true to You and Your calling upon my life. I realize that nothing is worth disappointing You and walking contrary to Your principles. Amen.

Read Hebrews 4:11–16

LET US THEREFORE COME BOLDLY TO THE THRONE OF GRACE, THAT WE MAY
OBTAIN MERCY AND FIND GRACE TO HELP IN TIME OF NEED.

Hebrews 4:16

"Seeing then that we have a great High Priest who has passed through the heavens, Jesus the Son of God, let us hold fast our confession. For we do not have a High Priest who cannot sympathize with our weaknesses, but was in all points tempted as we are, yet without sin" (verses 14–15). There is nothing that you can go through that Jesus hasn't already endured and gained the victory over. He has gone before us; He has led the way. He is a sure and present help in times of trouble.

Jesus was falsely accused by the religious leaders of His day. They trumped up charges against Him, so that they could eventually nail Him to a cross to die. Was this a random act? No, of course it wasn't – God was in control. He had a plan and a purpose. When Joseph was unfairly accused of committing adultery with Potiphar's wife, was the outcome random? Of course not – God was in control. He had a plan and a purpose for Joseph's life that stretched far beyond the outcome of that incident. Joseph found grace to help him in his time of need. He held fast to his confession and God blessed him, even in a jail cell.

You may have heard me tell many stories of missionaries who left everything to serve God in faraway places. I have shared with you the hardships that they often endured. Some of them were falsely accused and even put to death for their faith. Each and every one of them knew what it meant to boldly approach the throne of grace. They all found grace to help them in their time of need. Some of them even found the courage to die for that which they believed. No matter what you are going through today, approach the throne of grace. Don't try and do it alone. You have a High Priest who understands your weaknesses and who will give you the strength that you need to stand firm in your faith so that you do not slip or fall.

Prayer

My Father, I come to You in the Name of Jesus. I boldly approach Your throne of grace in this time of need. You have promised me in Your Word that You will not turn me away. Jesus, I look to You for help and support right now. Strengthen me, encourage me, and empower me to keep the faith. Amen.

Read Genesis 39:10–23

> BUT THE LORD WAS WITH JOSEPH AND SHOWED HIM MERCY, AND HE GAVE
> HIM FAVOR IN THE SIGHT OF THE KEEPER OF THE PRISON. AND THE KEEPER OF
> THE PRISON COMMITTED TO JOSEPH'S HAND ALL THE PRISONERS WHO WERE IN
> THE PRISON; WHATEVER THEY DID THERE, IT WAS HIS DOING.
>
> Genesis 39:21–22

Joseph found himself in prison because he refused to give in to temptation. Looking at it from a human perspective it would seem most unfair. Surely he should have been rewarded for doing the right thing, not punished. Once again God takes bad circumstances and He uses Joseph in that situation. Can you see a pattern developing here? God is moving Joseph step by step toward his ultimate destiny. Each of the situations in Joseph's life is a stepping stone towards the end goal.

God blessed Joseph in the prison and he was put in total control of the jail and all the prisoners. "The keeper of the prison did not look into anything that was under Joseph's authority, because the Lord was with him; and whatever he did, the Lord made it prosper" (verse 23). A man of faith and principle can be trusted no matter where he finds himself. It is not the circumstances that make the man; it is the Spirit of God living inside of the man. It is the state of the man's heart and his commitment to God.

So often we have it all back to front, don't we? We strive after success, which we equate with wealth, popularity, possessions, and prestige, only to find that we have placed our ladder against the wrong wall. Joseph understood that God was in control of his life; not his brothers; not the traders who bought him. Certainly not Potiphar or his wife. He was committed to living right and living by faith no matter where he found himself. It was because of this attitude that he was qualified to fulfil God's plan and purpose both for his life as well as that of Israel. Are you able to see God's hand in your circumstances? As you look at your circumstances, commit to serving God faithfully in the midst of the situation. Choose to be a man who walks by faith and not by sight. Like Joseph you can glorify God irrespective of what is happening around you. This is the path to true success and fulfilment.

Prayer

My Father in Heaven, I realize that all too often I allow myself to be at the mercy of my circumstances. This means that outside factors control my emotions and actions. I want to change this and in the future I want to be controlled by Your Spirit who dwells within me. Amen.

Read James 1:12–16

> BLESSED IS THE MAN WHO ENDURES TEMPTATION; FOR WHEN HE HAS BEEN
> APPROVED, HE WILL RECEIVE THE CROWN OF LIFE WHICH THE LORD HAS
> PROMISED TO THOSE WHO LOVE HIM.
>
> James 1:12

It seems when you look at Joseph's life he endured one trial after another. Who could have blamed him if when he landed in prison he decided that living right was no longer a viable option? After all, the only thing it got him was a prison sentence. He could easily have decided to go into business for himself in prison – to cheat on the jailer and line his own pockets. This was not an option for Joseph, though, was it? Instead he chose to continue to serve God. His faith was firmly placed in his God – his God is the same yesterday, today, and forever; He is the God of Abraham, Isaac, and Jacob. Joseph loved God more than he loved his freedom or his own comfort.

The question before each of us is whom do we love more: God, or ourselves and our own desires? God is looking for men who will stand up and be counted. Mighty men who will rally to His call, living lives that bring glory to His Name and the Name of His Son, Jesus Christ. "But each one is tempted when he is drawn away by his own desires and enticed. Then, when desire has conceived, it gives birth to sin; and sin, when it is full-grown, brings forth death" (verses 14–15).

My friend, how do you handle the temptations that come your way? So often people play the blame game: it was the devil who made me do it, or so-and-so is responsible. We don't take responsibility for our own actions. If you want to be a man of integrity who will stand up under temptations and trials you need to make good decisions. Like Joseph, you need to be prepared to live right and obey God no matter what the provocation to do otherwise. Don't sell yourself short. You have an inheritance waiting for you: "Blessed is the man who endures temptation; for when he has been approved, he will receive the crown of life which the Lord has promised to those who love Him."

Prayer

My Father God, today I confess my sinfulness before You. Forgive me for so often blaming other people or circumstances for my lack of obedience. Cleanse me and fill me anew with Your Spirit so that I can walk in obedience to You and Your Word. Amen.

Read Hebrews 12:1–17

> LOOKING UNTO JESUS, THE AUTHOR AND FINISHER OF OUR FAITH, WHO FOR THE JOY THAT WAS SET BEFORE HIM ENDURED THE CROSS, DESPISING THE SHAME, AND HAS SAT DOWN AT THE RIGHT HAND OF THE THRONE OF GOD.
>
> Hebrews 12:2

We do not read anywhere that Joseph was depressed or angry about his situation. He went from being his father's much loved son, with a privileged place in the family, to being in a prison cell. From the time that he obeyed his father's request to go and visit his brothers who were tending the herds in the fields, his life had seemingly spiralled out of control. The Bible doesn't say a great deal about Joseph's character prior to his being sold into slavery. However, I think that we can safely assume that he was a young man of integrity and faith. As we said the other day, Joseph's character was developed by making one good decision after another.

Joseph had the option to become bitter and twisted about his situation. Instead he chose to do what our reading instructs us to do. He chose to look at the bigger picture. He chose joy over being disgruntled. He held on to the dreams that God had given him back home. Joseph knew that God had a plan. It is not easy when you are in the midst of the battle to always see the wood for the trees. This is why we need to keep our eyes firmly fixed upon Jesus our Saviour and Lord. "[L]ooking unto Jesus, the author and finisher of our faith, who for the joy that was set before Him endured the cross, despising the shame, and has sat down at the right hand of the throne of God. For Jesus there was a bigger picture.

For men and women down through the ages who have served God at great personal cost, there has always been a bigger picture. Our problem is that so often our vision is limited. This is where faith comes in. "For now we see in a mirror, dimly, but then face to face. Now I know in part, but then I shall know just as I also am known. And now abide faith, hope, love, these three; but the greatest of these is love" (1 Corinthians 13:12–13).

Prayer

My Father in Heaven, thank You for Your Son. Jesus, thank You for Your example. You suffered joyfully because You knew there was a bigger picture. Even though I can only see dimly now, help me to trust You above all. I want to walk the faith walk. I want to endure joyfully for Your Name's sake. Amen.

Read Genesis 40:1–8

> So Joseph said to them, "Do not interpretations belong to God? Tell them to me, please."
>
> Genesis 40:8b

Joseph recognized that everything he had had come from God. Any abilities that he might have had, God had given them to him. Therefore he could not take credit for anything. The Pharaoh's butler and baker landed up in jail with Joseph. They both had dreams that left them disturbed. When Joseph came in to them in the morning he was concerned when he saw that they were looking sad. We learn something new about Joseph as we observe his attitude to the baker and butler: Joseph was compassionate. He was not so self-involved that he could not recognize other people's difficulties. Joseph took time to find out what their problems were.

When they told him they had both had dreams he immediately pointed them to God as the source of wisdom and knowledge. He did not take the credit for himself. He did not try to show them how smart he was because he could interpret their dreams. This is humble faith, isn't it? It was another step along the journey that God was taking Joseph on. If Joseph hadn't chosen to obey God that day his story might have had a different outcome.

If you find yourself in a difficult situation take a moment to stop and contemplate Joseph's attitudes and reactions. We have seen that he obeyed God no matter what, even at the expense of his own freedom. He served God faithfully wherever he found himself. He blessed those around him by doing the best job that he could for them. He did not become bitter and twisted about his circumstances. Instead he used his circumstances to serve God and those around him. He had compassion for other people despite himself also being in difficult circumstances. He gave the glory to God and made sure that the baker and the butler understood that it was God who would be the One who would give the interpretation of their dreams. These are the actions of a man of faith. How do you choose to walk – by faith, or by sight? Give God the glory today!

Prayer

My God in Heaven, You deserve all the honour, glory, and praise that I am able to give You. You are a great and an awesome God. There is none like You. I bow before You. Lord, I submit my circumstances to You right now and ask You to use me to Your glory despite what I am going through. Amen.

Read Genesis 40:9–23

> BUT REMEMBER ME WHEN IT IS WELL WITH YOU, AND PLEASE SHOW KINDNESS
> TO ME; MAKE MENTION OF ME TO PHARAOH, AND GET ME OUT OF THIS
> HOUSE.
>
> Genesis 40:14

Joseph interpreted the butler's dream, which had a good outcome. The baker's dream, on the other hand, did not have a good outcome for him. It happened for both of them exactly as Joseph had said it would. When he interpreted the butler's dream he asked him to remember him when he got out of prison. Three days after the dream the butler was released from prison and he promptly forgot about Joseph. He went on with his life as if the incident with Joseph had never taken place.

Have you ever found yourself in a situation where you helped someone else only to have them promptly forget about you? Maybe you were in trouble yourself and that person never bothered to come and see if they could help you. It is very easy to become resentful and bitter when this happens. If we entertain these emotions they can quickly move from unforgiveness to hatred. In the case of Joseph, he was disappointed, but we don't see any evidence of bitterness.

The important thing to remember here is that God had a plan and a purpose for Joseph's life. The time had not yet come for that plan to move to the next stage. So Joseph needed to remain in prison until God was ready for him to move forward to the next phase. The same is true for us. Perhaps you find yourself in a similar situation to Joseph and you are wondering why someone has let you down. You were so sure that they would come through for you – after all, look at everything that you did for them. Consider the fact that maybe God is not yet ready to move you to the next stage in His plan and purpose for you. Stay where you are. Submit to Him; faithfully and joyfully continue to serve Him where you find yourself. When the time is right, and He is ready to move, nothing will be able to stop Him.

Prayer

My Father, I thank You that I am dependent upon no one else save You. You and You alone can I trust. Lord, I am so grateful that You are never late with Your answers to my needs. Help me to patiently wait for You. Your timing is perfect and I submit to Your will for my life. Amen.

Read Genesis 41:1–8

> THEN IT CAME TO PASS, AT THE END OF TWO FULL YEARS, THAT PHARAOH
> HAD A DREAM...
>
> Genesis 41:1a

Joseph was not alone. Every person in whose life God has moved mightily has had to endure a waiting period. Each man down through history who has been used by God to accomplish great things has had to learn to wait upon the Lord. Abraham had to wait twenty-five years for the promise God made him to be fulfilled. Noah had to wait in the ark after it stopped raining until God was ready to let him and his family out – by the time he came out it had been just over a year since he entered the ark. Job had to wait patiently as he endured his trials over several months. Paul spent three years in the wilderness being taught by the Lord. There are many, many others that we could name.

In our reading today we learn that Joseph spent another two years in the prison. It would appear that throughout the two-year period he continued to walk by faith with the Lord. Joseph conscientiously fulfilled his duties running the prison, and he was faithful in all that was entrusted to him. After two years we once again see God's hand move to unfold the next phase in the plan. God had not forgotten about Joseph. He knew exactly where Joseph was; He knew exactly what was happening in his life every moment of every day. Behind the scenes God was busy working His plan and purpose.

The same is true for you, my friend. If you find yourself in what seems to be a holding pattern at the moment, please don't despair. Hang in there. Trust God and continue to faithfully walk with Him. At exactly the right moment He will intervene in your circumstances and show you the next step along your faith path. Remember we have said before: God is never too early and He is never a second too late – He is always perfectly on time, every time. Jeremiah 29:11 assures us that He has a plan: "For I know the thoughts that I think toward you, says the Lord, thoughts of peace and not of evil, to give you a future and a hope." Do you have the faith to wait?

Prayer

My Father, I realize that so often I become impatient and I want to take matters into my own hands. Lord, You have spoken to me again through Your Word and the example not only of Joseph, but of so many men of faith. Lord, I also want to be a man of faith. I want to wait faithfully for You. Amen.

Read Genesis 41:9–16

"BUT I HAVE HEARD IT SAID OF YOU THAT YOU CAN UNDERSTAND A DREAM, TO INTERPRET IT." SO JOSEPH ANSWERED PHARAOH, SAYING, "IT IS NOT IN ME; GOD WILL GIVE PHARAOH AN ANSWER OF PEACE."

Genesis 41:15b–16

I want us to spend two days on this portion of Scripture because there are two valuable lessons to be learned here. Joseph had come to understand a key factor in being used by God. This fact is that God does not share His glory with anyone. How many men have fallen because of pride and vanity? Sadly, way too many. The Bible is littered with the corpses of men who tried to claim God's glory. It is no different in modern-day history. It is an all too common occurrence to read or hear of another man of God who has been discredited, who has failed God, and those he led. Most often the rot sets in when a person begins to take the glory that should be God's alone.

Joseph had learned this early on in his life. He knew that the favour he gained in both Potiphar's as well as the jailer's household was not due to his own abilities. He was a man with a destiny. I am sure that on many occasions, when circumstances became tough, he thought back to the two dreams that God had given him as a youth. He kept his faith strong. He believed that God was in control of his life. Joseph chose to walk by faith and not by sight. He did not define himself by his circumstances, but rather he defined himself by who he knew himself to be in God.

I am constantly aware that it is God who not only deserves, but demands the glory. My friends, the closer one draws to Jesus, the more you become aware of your ever-increasing need. "… but with God all things are possible" (Matthew 19:26b). The inverse is also true; without God nothing is possible. Joseph wanted Pharaoh to be very clear about who was going to be giving the interpretation to his dream. If you have been taking God's glory go before Him and repent. Ask His forgiveness and purpose in your heart to walk humbly before Him from now onwards. God doesn't share His glory!

Prayer

My Father God in Heaven, You are a mighty and an awesome God. There is none like You on earth or in the heavens. I come before You on bended knee. I pay homage to Your Great Name. Help me to walk before You in humility, always giving the honour and glory to You in every situation. Amen.

Read Genesis 41:9–16

> "BUT I HAVE HEARD IT SAID OF YOU THAT YOU CAN UNDERSTAND A DREAM,
> TO INTERPRET IT." SO JOSEPH ANSWERED PHARAOH, SAYING, "IT IS NOT IN
> ME; GOD WILL GIVE PHARAOH AN ANSWER OF PEACE."
>
> Genesis 41:15b–16

Another sign of Joseph's integrity was that when he appeared before Pharaoh he didn't see Pharaoh as his deliverer. Think back on Joseph's experiences since the day his brothers threw him in the pit. Who could blame him if he grabbed his first real opportunity at freedom with both hands? It was Joseph's chance to shine and make a good impression upon Pharaoh. He had sat for two long years after Pharaoh's butler was released, waiting for the butler to honour his promise to him. It was only when it suited the butler's purposes that he remembered Joseph. He saw it as a way to gain favour with his master.

Joseph was brought before Pharaoh. You would expect him to be prepared to go along with anything, and do whatever he was commanded to do – no questions asked – and no comments made. One certainly wouldn't expect to hear him putting Pharaoh in his place by telling him, "It is not in me; God will give Pharaoh an answer of peace." Pharaoh was not a God-fearing man. Joseph didn't know what his reaction would be to this statement. Joseph stated it clearly – he was not unsure about his faith – he was not ashamed or reserved about the fact that he trusted in God. If Pharaoh wanted help he needed to know from Whom the help was coming.

The other important lesson for you and me to learn from this is that it was not Pharaoh who was Joseph's deliverer – it was God. Joseph understood that all too clearly. He knew that it was God who would save him, not Pharaoh. Knowing that meant he could be faithful to God no matter what happened. He didn't have to compromise on his faith because he trusted God. Joseph could boldly proclaim to Pharaoh that it was God who would give the understanding about what his dreams meant. My friend, do you believe that God is your deliverer? If so, be faithful to Him first and foremost. He is your security. He is the One who will undertake for you.

Prayer
My Father God, I am so grateful to You for all Your goodness to me. I know that I can trust and rely upon You to undertake for me according to Your will and good purposes for my life. I do not trust in anyone or anything else – only You. Lord, I pray that You will help me to walk faithfully with You. Amen.

Read Genesis 41:16–32

AND THE DREAM WAS REPEATED TO PHARAOH TWICE BECAUSE THE THING IS ESTABLISHED BY GOD, AND GOD WILL SHORTLY BRING IT TO PASS.

Genesis 41:32

So far we have learned the following about Joseph's faith walk with God. Joseph was a young man of integrity: he told his father when his brothers got up to mischief while tending to the herds. He was conscientious: he faithfully fulfilled his assignments. He was honest and upright in all his dealings: he didn't succumb to Potiphar's wife. He was trusted by his masters: their households prospered because of his diligence. Joseph was generous: he helped his fellow inmates out when they had dreams that they didn't understand. Joseph was a young man of remarkable faith: he trusted God implicitly. He knew beyond a shadow of a doubt that God was in charge of his life.

Joseph gave God the glory due to His Name: he didn't hesitate to tell Pharaoh that it was God who would give the understanding regarding his dreams. Yesterday we learned that Joseph knew not only in Whom he believed, but he also knew Who his Deliverer was. Today we learn another faith lesson through Joseph: if God wills something it will come to pass: "because the thing is established by God, and God will shortly bring it to pass." In other words, if God says it you can believe it. It doesn't matter how much evidence there is to the contrary. You can take God's promises to the bank, my friend.

If we take a look at 2 Corinthians 1:20 we see that Paul puts it this way: "For all the promises of God in Him are Yes, and in Him Amen, to the glory of God through us." What do you need to believe God for right now? Hold fast to the promise He has given to you. If God has made you a promise, are you faithfully believing Him to fulfil it? He is true to His Word. Don't allow yourself to be caught in a web of doubt and fear. Trust God and He will bring it to pass at exactly the right time. Joseph was a witness to Pharaoh. He spoke boldly about God. We too need to speak out boldly proclaiming God's goodness and faithfulness each day.

Prayer

My God in Heaven, thank You once again for reminding me that You are a faithful God. Your faithfulness is indeed new every morning. You are the same yesterday, today, and forever more. I can trust in You no matter what. I can take Your promises to me to the bank. Amen.

Read Genesis 41:33–41

AND PHARAOH SAID TO HIS SERVANTS, "CAN WE FIND SUCH A ONE AS THIS, A MAN IN WHOM IS THE SPIRIT OF GOD?"

Genesis 41:38

Pharaoh recognized something in Joseph. Remember, Pharaoh was not a man of faith. He did not believe in the God of Abraham, Isaac, and Jacob. He had no religious training or understanding. Yet, he was able to discern that there was something unusual about Joseph. He could see that Joseph was of a different calibre to his other aides. Indeed, what made Joseph stand out was his heart for God. It was that characteristic that made even non-believers stop and take note.

You cannot fake a heart that is for God, my friend. Sooner or later something will give. Have you heard the saying "grace under pressure"? It is when the chips are down and the rubber hits the road that the real you comes out. When you are under pressure, what spills from your heart, my friend? Is it the love, light, and goodness of the Holy Spirit, or is it the darkness of the devil? You cannot serve two masters: either you serve the King of the universe or you serve the king of this world – which will it be? Pharaoh didn't choose Joseph to be over all of his kingdom because Joseph was clever. He didn't choose him because he was capable. He didn't even choose him because he was honest and trustworthy. No, Pharaoh chose Joseph because "Can we find such a one as this, a man in whom is the Spirit of God?"

God can use anyone – He is not limited by our limitations. What He needs is someone who is open and filled with His Spirit. He looks for people who are prepared to be controlled by His Spirit; people who will be open to being filled with power and grace. Now is the time to turn to God. Now is the time to be filled with His Spirit. God is looking for men of this generation to stand up and be counted for Him. He is looking for men who can be used by Him to bring Salvation to our nation and to Africa. Are you such a man, my friend?

Prayer

My God and Father, I am so thirsty for the infilling of Your Holy Spirit. Cleanse me, fill me, and use me, I pray. I want to walk rejoicing in You. I want to remain close to You at all times – listening to Your voice. I want to walk in bold assurance of Your love and grace towards me. Amen.

Read Genesis 41:42–49

THEN PHARAOH TOOK HIS SIGNET RING OFF HIS HAND AND PUT IT ON JOSEPH'S HAND; AND HE CLOTHED HIM IN GARMENTS OF FINE LINEN AND PUT A GOLD CHAIN AROUND HIS NECK. AND HE HAD HIM RIDE IN THE SECOND CHARIOT WHICH HE HAD; AND THEY CRIED OUT BEFORE HIM, "BOW THE KNEE!" SO HE SET HIM OVER ALL THE LAND OF EGYPT.

Genesis 41:42–43

The years of faithfulness paid off. God gave Joseph the interpretation of Pharaoh's dreams. In the dreams God warned of the coming famine and gave Pharaoh the opportunity to prepare well in advance. Once again we see God's favour resting upon Joseph. Pharaoh chose to believe the interpretation of his dreams. He immediately realized that he needed someone very special to be in charge of the preparation for the coming famine. Who better than Joseph? Do you see how Joseph's faithfulness paid off? All those years he chose to do the right thing, stretching right back to his boyhood. Integrity is a path that needs to be walked, step by step, day by day. Living by faith and not by sight is a lifestyle that needs to be lived decision by decision.

Joseph didn't blow hot and cold as we so often do. His devotion to God, and to doing what pleased God, did not waiver throughout his time of captivity. In circumstances that one could have understood him faltering in, Joseph stood firm. No matter what came his way he didn't falter. This is the kind of faith that God is looking for in us. Joseph was a man on a mission. He didn't know or understand what that mission was – but all through the years he clung to the dreams God had given him as a young man. He knew that when the time was right God would make it clear to him.

God honours faith, my friends. You only have to look at Hebrews 11 to see this. There we see God's "Hall of Faith" – He salutes all the biblical heroes of the faith. Joseph is there among them. Pharaoh honoured Joseph with worldly goods and symbols of prestige. These were all well and good, and befitted his new status. Pharaoh even gave Joseph a new name (Genesis 41:45) – Zaphnath-Paaneah – meaning "the man to whom mysteries are revealed". However, no honour was as important to Joseph as God's stamp of approval upon his life. Are you living so that God can honour your faith?

Prayer

My Father God, thank You for the example of Joseph's life. All these centuries later I can still be inspired by him and his faithfulness to You. Help me, I pray, to walk the path of integrity and of faith day by day. Lord, I want nothing more than to receive Your stamp of approval upon my life. Amen.

FRUITFUL IN THE MIDST OF AFFLICTION

Read Genesis 41:46–57

> JOSEPH CALLED THE NAME OF THE FIRSTBORN MANASSEH: "FOR GOD HAS
> MADE ME FORGET ALL MY TOIL AND ALL MY FATHER'S HOUSE." AND THE
> NAME OF THE SECOND HE CALLED EPHRAIM: "FOR GOD HAS CAUSED ME TO
> BE FRUITFUL IN THE LAND OF MY AFFLICTION."
>
> Genesis 41:51–52

I want to stop right here and ask you something: Where do you find yourself right now? Are you in a good place in your life, or are you hanging on by the skin of your teeth? I am sure that each one of you reading this devotional have known "skin of your teeth" times. Sometimes illness is the cause, either our own or that of a loved one. It might be as a result of some unspeakable tragedy. Maybe you lost your business or your farm due to the downturn in the economy and you don't know where to turn next. Your heart may have been broken because of a betrayal by someone you loved and trusted.

All these, and many other scenarios that occur in our lives, can potentially trip us up as we walk the path of faith. It is not what happens to you that defines you, but rather how you react to it. This was true of Joseph; he had so many unfair things happen to him throughout his young life. Who could have blamed him if he had decided to give up? However, this was never an option for Joseph. He walked a straight line of faith. Joseph was only thirty years old when Pharaoh made him ruler over Egypt; he was still a young man. As Paul exhorted to Timothy, "Let no one despise your youth, but be an example to the believers in word, in conduct, in love, in spirit, in faith, in purity" (1 Timothy 4:12). Joseph certainly lived up to this instruction, didn't he?

When God blessed Joseph with two sons he named them for the experiences that he had been through. The first, Manasseh, was named in remembrance of what Joseph had been through as a result of his brothers' actions. The second, Ephraim, in response to the fact that God had made Joseph to be fruitful despite what he had been through. My friend, have you remained fruitful through the good and the bad times? This is what walking by faith is about.

Prayer

My God in Heaven, I bow in Your presence. Lord, I am so weary of the trials and tribulations that I am experiencing right now. I feel beaten and battered. I come to You for strength and courage. I ask You to lift my feeble head. Help me to remain fruitful through it all, no matter what, so that Your Name will be honoured. Amen.

Read Genesis 42:1–20

> AND JOSEPH'S BROTHERS CAME AND BOWED DOWN BEFORE HIM WITH THEIR
> FACES TO THE EARTH... SO JOSEPH RECOGNIZED HIS BROTHERS, BUT THEY DID
> NOT RECOGNIZE HIM. THEN JOSEPH REMEMBERED THE DREAMS WHICH HE
> HAD DREAMED ABOUT THEM...
>
> Genesis 42:6b, 8–9a

I have said it many times before and no doubt will say it many times in the future: if God says He will do something, you can believe that He will do it. Don't let the enemy rob you of your birthright in Jesus. There are so many blessings that are ours because of what Jesus accomplished on Calvary. One of them is: "For all the promises of God in Him [Jesus] are Yes, and in Him [Jesus] Amen, to the glory of God through us" (2 Corinthians 1:20). When God makes you a promise or gives you a word, hang on to it for dear life. Don't allow anyone or anything to make you believe that He will not honour His Word.

Joseph never forgot the dreams that he had as a young boy. He held them safely in his heart. Eventually the day came when he saw the reality of the dreams in front of his very eyes. Can you imagine what it must have been like for Joseph when he saw ten of his brothers (all except Benjamin) kneel in front of him? One can only guess at the emotions that he must have experienced.

At long last the pieces had begun to fall into place. God had prepared Joseph throughout his life for that moment. There was a much bigger plan in God's heart than Joseph could ever have imagined. God's plan went all the way back to Joseph's great grandfather Abraham. God had promised to bless Abraham and his descendants. Part of God's plan to keep that promise required Joseph being in Egypt, in charge of the food, during the time of the famine. Jacob sent his sons to Egypt to buy food. Who had God put in place to provide for Jacob and his family? None other than Jacob's much-loved son, Joseph. Isn't God amazing, my friends? Why do we ever doubt Him? He has your life in His hands. He has the lives of your loved ones in His hands. You can trust Him to do what is best.

Prayer

Dear Lord, You are an amazing and wonderful Father. There is none like You. You are faithful from generation to generation. You bless Your children. I am so grateful that I am Your child. A child of the Promise. My trust is in You, Lord; my hope is in You – in no one and nothing besides You. Amen.

Read Genesis 42:18–24

AND REUBEN ANSWERED THEM, SAYING, "DID I NOT SPEAK TO YOU, SAYING, "DO NOT SIN AGAINST THE BOY'; AND YOU WOULD NOT LISTEN? THEREFORE BEHOLD, HIS BLOOD IS NOW REQUIRED OF US."

Genesis 42:22

All those years ago Joseph's brothers had sought to harm him. Although Joseph's life had not always been easy, he had known success and satisfaction. He had lived with a definite sense of God's presence and blessing upon his life. On the other hand, what his brothers had done to Joseph had haunted them all of their lives. When Joseph told them to bring Benjamin to him, how did they react? "Then they said to one another, 'We are truly guilty concerning our brother, for we saw the anguish of his soul when he pleaded with us, and we would not hear; therefore this distress has come upon us'" (verse 21).

Everything that happened in their lives was coloured by that one action. They had to live all those years with their father's grief over the loss of Joseph. Their jealousy must have quickly turned to remorse when they realized what a terrible, irreversible thing they had done. Now they find themselves in a foreign country at the mercy of the Egyptian ruler and they are terrified. They feel that it is payback time.

My friends, it is no different for us. When we choose to sin it has consequences in our lives. Sometimes, as a number of you will know, the consequences reach down through the years. Where would any of us be without the grace of the Lord Jesus Christ? None of us could stand apart from, and outside of, God's gracious mercy towards us. Jesus died so that you and I can know forgiveness and restoration. God is in the restoration business. He used Joseph to bring restoration to his father's house. God uses His Son, Jesus, to bring restoration into your life and mine. If you, like Joseph's brothers, are walking around with a heavy burden of guilt today – it is time to lay down the load. Come to Jesus, kneel at the foot of His cross, and repent before Him. Turn from your sin and allow Him to soothe, cleanse, forgive, and heal your broken heart. Don't go another day without experiencing His restoration and love.

Prayer

My Father, I come to You in the Name above all names – Jesus Christ, my Saviour and Lord. Father, forgive me for the sin that I committed. Lord, You know how it has haunted me all of these years, robbing me of my joy. Cleanse me, forgive me, heal me, and restore me to Yourself, I pray. Amen.

Read Genesis 42:25–38 and 43:1–14

> THEN JOSEPH GAVE A COMMAND TO FILL THEIR SACKS WITH GRAIN, TO
> RESTORE EVERY MAN'S MONEY TO HIS SACK, AND TO GIVE THEM PROVISIONS
> FOR THE JOURNEY. THUS HE DID FOR THEM.
>
> Genesis 42:25

Amazingly, Joseph blessed his brothers! The normal human reaction would have been to have taken the opportunity to get even. He didn't do this because he was not filled with a need for revenge. Why was that? It was because he knew that God was in control of his life. Joseph was a man of faith. He had been on a journey of faith with God for many years. He believed that God had a plan and a purpose for his life. Joseph believed that he wasn't the victim of his brothers' crime – rather he believed that he was the subject of God's purposes and plans. That made all the difference to the way Joseph viewed life. How do you view your life?

The brothers, on the other hand, were filled with terror when they realized that their money had somehow found its way back into their saddlebags. "… My money has been restored, and there it is, in my sack!" Then their hearts failed them and they were afraid, saying to one another, "What is this that God has done to us?" (verse 28). It seems as if they constantly expected doom and disaster – they were unable to simply accept a blessing. There is no doubt, though, that the brothers had changed over the years. The young men who sold Joseph into slavery would have been quick to take advantage of the windfall. They would have more than likely hidden it and not told their father about what had happened.

As soon as they arrived home they shared what had happened with their father. It is interesting to note their protectiveness towards Benjamin, their youngest brother. Judah said to his father: "I myself will be surety for him; from my hand you shall require him. If I do not bring him back to you and set him before you, then let me bear the blame forever" (Genesis 43:9). So they returned to Egypt with Benjamin. They took double the amount of money: half to pay for the new grain, and the other to return what had been placed in their saddlebags.

Prayer

My Father God, I realize as I come before You that I am not at the mercy of other people's actions. I am instead the subject of Your plans and purposes. Therefore I can walk by faith and not by sight. I can treat others with compassion and grace because of Your love for me. Amen.

Read Genesis 44:1 – 45:2

> NOW THEREFORE, PLEASE LET YOUR SERVANT REMAIN INSTEAD OF THE LAD AS
> A SLAVE TO MY LORD, AND LET THE LAD GO UP WITH HIS BROTHERS. FOR HOW
> SHALL I GO UP TO MY FATHER IF THE LAD IS NOT WITH ME, LEST PERHAPS I SEE
> THE EVIL THAT WOULD COME UPON MY FATHER?
>
> Genesis 44:33–34

Joseph tested his brothers a second time. He again returned their money, and had his silver cup placed in Benjamin's saddlebag. The brothers hadn't travelled far when Joseph sent a servant after them. When the cup was found in Benjamin's bag they were taken back to appear before Joseph. Imagine their dread. Joseph decreed that Benjamin should remain behind as his slave. Judah then stepped forward, and in our key verses we read that he offered to take Benjamin's place as Joseph's slave.

What a turnaround! Remember when Joseph was sold into slavery? Judah had said to his brothers, "'What profit is there if we kill our brother and conceal his blood? Come and let us sell him to the Ishmaelites, and let not our hand be upon him, for he is our brother and our flesh.' And his brothers listened" (Genesis 37:26–27). When Judah realized that they could make money out of Joseph, he convinced his brothers to sell him into slavery rather than killing him. Yet, here he was years later offering himself as a slave to save his youngest brother. Clearly something had brought about a change in Judah's life. Over the years he'd had plenty of opportunity to regret his actions. He must have often wished that he'd had the courage to stand up to his brothers and stop what had happened to Joseph. The text tells us that when Joseph realized the extent of Judah's love for Benjamin he was overcome with emotion.

The Bible speaks about the fruits of repentance. It tells us that when our hearts change then so will our actions. What God does through His Spirit on the inside of us, will find its way to the outside. My friends, what do your actions tell people about your walk with the Lord? Can your family, your neighbours, your friends, and your colleagues see the evidence of your walk of faith with God? Do they see a man who walks humbly before his God? Does your family witness a husband and a father who walks by faith and not by sight?

Prayer

My Father, daily I have to choose whether to walk by faith or by sight. I realize, Lord, that my choices are witnessed by those around me. Forgive me for so often taking the path of least resistance. Help me to walk a consistent walk of faith with You each and every day of my life. Amen.

Read Genesis 45

> THEN HE SAID: "I AM JOSEPH YOUR BROTHER, WHOM YOU SOLD INTO EGYPT. BUT NOW, DO NOT THEREFORE BE GRIEVED OR ANGRY WITH YOURSELVES BECAUSE YOU SOLD ME HERE; FOR GOD SENT ME BEFORE YOU TO PRESERVE LIFE."

Genesis 45:4b–5

I don't think we will ever be able to fully appreciate the emotion of that moment when Joseph revealed himself to his brothers. They must have experienced so many different feelings. Relief that he was alive; abject fear that he was alive. The thought that their father would find out about what they had kept hidden all those years. The shame, remorse, and hopefully deep, genuine repentance. They no doubt also keenly remembered the dreams that Joseph had when he was a young man and their reaction to them. It was those dreams that had been the final straw and that had caused them to no longer be able to contain their hatred for Joseph.

However, the brothers' emotions were not the key factor at that moment. The key was the eventual unveiling of Joseph's purpose. At that moment all of the years of hardship and suffering made sense to Joseph. He realized with absolute clarity why he had been sold into slavery. Joseph's purpose was one of restoration; to preserve life. He had been sent ahead to provide for his father's household. As we said the other day: God used Joseph to help Him keep His promise to Abraham. At last, after all the years of separation, Joseph would be reunited with his father.

My friend, I hope that you have been inspired and challenged as a result of our walk with Joseph. What has God been saying to you through the Scriptures we have read? Has He been speaking to you about a specific area of your life? As we look at Joseph's life and his commitment to walking with God through thick and thin there are so many lessons we can learn from him. We are approaching the end of the month, but I want to encourage you to take some time over the next couple of days to be alone with God. Allow the Holy Spirit to examine your heart. Let God speak to you and show you how He wants you to apply these lessons from the life of Joseph to your life.

Prayer

My Father God, You have been speaking to me on so many levels this month. I know that I need to take some time to be alone with You, so that I can listen carefully to Your Spirit speaking to me. Lord, help me to listen, obey, and walk forward in faith and renewed commitment to You. Amen.

Read Genesis 46:26–34 and 47:1–12

> AND JOSEPH SITUATED HIS FATHER AND HIS BROTHERS, AND GAVE THEM A
> POSSESSION IN THE LAND OF EGYPT, IN THE BEST OF THE LAND, IN THE LAND
> OF RAMESES, AS PHARAOH HAD COMMANDED. THEN JOSEPH PROVIDED HIS
> FATHER, HIS BROTHERS, AND ALL HIS FATHER'S HOUSEHOLD WITH BREAD,
> ACCORDING TO THE NUMBER IN THEIR FAMILIES.
>
> Genesis 47:11–12

God used Joseph to restore the fortunes of his father and his brothers. They received the best that the land of Egypt had to offer. Not because they deserved it, but because of the high regard in which the Pharaoh held Joseph. He denied Joseph nothing. Joseph used Pharaoh's good favour to bless his family. If you read the rest of chapter 47 you will see that Joseph continued to serve the Pharaoh well. He wisely dispensed the grain that he had stored up. In the process he made the Pharaoh even wealthier than he'd been before. Joseph remained faithful and diligent. I am sure that as his brothers watched him they must have been in awe of the type of man that their brother was.

Joseph's power was absolute, yet he did not abuse it. He recognized that all he was and all he had belonged to God. He was what he was because of God's favour upon his life. His job was to walk in obedience and faith with God, fulfilling God's purposes. There is no greater satisfaction in life than knowing that you are where God wants you to be, doing what God wants you to do. So many people try to run away from God's plans for them. You cannot do this, my friend; there is not enough room in this world for you to outrun God. The place of satisfaction and fulfilment is the path of obedience and submission.

There is also no safer place on earth than the place where God wants you to be. I always say that I fear no man. No man can take my life. God is in control of my every breath. When the day comes that I take my last one, the next thing that I will know is Heaven. Until then I will live all-out, 100 per cent for Jesus. By His grace I will walk the path of faith that He has laid out for me, fulfilling His purposes for my life and the lives of those He wants to bless through me.

Prayer

My Father, thank You for the joy of serving You. I praise Your Holy Name. I am so grateful that You have called me, saved me, and commissioned me to serve You. Keep me faithful, keep me humble, keep me loving You. Lord, thank You that I am a man with a mission and a purpose. Amen.

Read 2 Corinthians 5:12–21

> NOW ALL THINGS ARE OF GOD, WHO HAS RECONCILED US TO HIMSELF
> THROUGH JESUS CHRIST, AND HAS GIVEN US THE MINISTRY OF
> RECONCILIATION, THAT IS, THAT GOD WAS IN CHRIST RECONCILING THE
> WORLD TO HIMSELF, NOT IMPUTING THEIR TRESPASSES TO THEM, AND HAS
> COMMITTED TO US THE WORD OF RECONCILIATION.
>
> 2 Corinthians 5:18–19

Joseph lived a life of reconciliation. After revealing himself to his brothers he said: "I am Joseph your brother, whom you sold into Egypt. But now, do not therefore be grieved or angry with yourselves because you sold me here; for God sent me before you to preserve life" (Genesis 45:4b–5). He could have sought retribution, but Joseph realized that God had called him to walk a different path. He realized that his purpose was to restore his brothers. Joseph's actions meant that his brothers were freed of their guilt over what they'd done to him. They were also freed of their lifelong deception of their father. For the first time in many years their burden was lifted.

We find ourselves in the same position as Joseph's brothers. We are guilty sinners who need a Saviour. We need someone who will offer us restoration. Jesus came to this world to restore us to the Father. The Bible tells us Jesus said, "I am the way, the truth, and the life. No one comes to the Father except through Me" (John 14:6). Our key verse reads "God, who has reconciled us to Himself through Jesus Christ". God's plan and purpose to see humankind reconciled to Himself was through His Son, Jesus Christ.

Once we have received God's gift of restoration and reconciliation it is our duty to share it with other people. As you look around you each day, you are faced with people who are guilty and lost – the same as you were. What are you doing to offer them the same gift that you received? Our key verse also tells us that God has given us the ministry of reconciliation. He has committed to us the word of reconciliation. The life of faith is a life of reconciliation. We are to trust God to use us to further His purposes and plans for this world. God was, in Christ, reconciling the world to Himself. You have a part to play in His plan – how are you doing when it comes to fulfilling your role?

Prayer

My Father God, I come before You with gratitude and thanksgiving in my heart for Your great love, mercy, and grace towards me. Thank You that I have received Your wonderful gift of reconciliation through Jesus Christ, my Saviour. Help me to live a life of reconciliation, drawing others to You. Amen.

Read Genesis 50:1–22

> JOSEPH SAID TO THEM, "DO NOT BE AFRAID, FOR AM I IN THE PLACE OF
> GOD? BUT AS FOR YOU, YOU MEANT EVIL AGAINST ME; BUT GOD MEANT IT
> FOR GOOD, IN ORDER TO BRING IT ABOUT AS IT IS THIS DAY, TO SAVE MANY
> PEOPLE ALIVE. NOW THEREFORE, DO NOT BE AFRAID; I WILL PROVIDE FOR YOU
> AND YOUR LITTLE ONES." AND HE COMFORTED THEM AND SPOKE KINDLY TO
> THEM.
>
> Genesis 50:19–21

What a man of God! Joseph's brothers didn't understand grace, did they? Genesis 47:28 tells us that Jacob lived in Egypt for seventeen years. All that time the brothers believed that Joseph was only being good to them because of their father. When Jacob died they were deeply fearful for their lives, and the lives of their families. They came before Joseph ready to plead with him to be merciful towards them. Joseph's response was amazing, wasn't it? It was so different to what we often witness happening between people. I don't know about you, but I have known of family feuds that have stretched from generation to generation – over things far less dire than what happened between Joseph and his brothers.

What made the difference in Joseph's situation? How was he able to so wholeheartedly forgive his brothers? Not only did he forgive them, but he restored them and cared for them. "'… do not be afraid; I will provide for you and your little ones.' And he comforted them and spoke kindly to them." Joseph was able to do this because he knew that God was in control of his life. God had taken what was meant for evil and used it for good. "… you meant evil against me; but God meant it for good, in order to bring it about as it is this day, to save many people alive." There you have the purpose of Joseph's life in a nutshell.

The question before you and me as we come to the end of this month's journey with Joseph is: What about us? Is there someone you have a feud with – someone who has harmed you and you are unable to forgive, no matter how hard you have tried? I have news for you today: there is no such thing in a Christian's life as being unable to forgive. God has given us Joseph as an example of faith. Will you choose to live a life of faith trusting God? Will you choose to live a life of forgiveness and restoration today?

Prayer

My Father God, You have taught me so many lessons over this past month. Above all You have shown me that my life and my times are in Your hands. You and You alone are in control of my life. Help me to extend forgiveness, restoration, and kindness to those who have wronged me. Amen.

MOSES' JOURNEY OF DELIVERANCE

Moses' journey of faith began at the burning bush

1. God's people in bondage
2. God protects Moses
3. God acknowledges His people
4. Moses' burning bush experience
5. How God speaks to us
6. God of the everyday
7. Moses, the reluctant messenger
8. The Lord prepares the way
9. Darkness before the dawn
10. I am the Lord
11. Preparations to leave
12. The Passover Lamb
13. God's abiding faithfulness
14. See the salvation of the Lord
15. The parting of the Red Sea
16. Don't become discouraged
17. Help in times of suffering
18. The Lord is my strength and song
19. Bitter waters become sweet
20. Bread from Heaven
21. The-Lord-Is-My-Banner
22. Obedience to God's Laws
23. God's Word – our lamp and light
24. Showing your love
25. The presence of the Lord
26. God's Holiness
27. God defends Moses
28. God loses patience
29. Moses' faith journey
30. Moses' death
31. Enjoy the journey

Read Exodus 1:1–14

> AND JOSEPH DIED, ALL HIS BROTHERS, AND ALL THAT GENERATION. BUT
> THE CHILDREN OF ISRAEL WERE FRUITFUL AND INCREASED ABUNDANTLY,
> MULTIPLIED AND GREW EXCEEDINGLY MIGHTY; AND THE LAND WAS FILLED
> WITH THEM. NOW THERE AROSE A NEW KING OVER EGYPT, WHO DID NOT
> KNOW JOSEPH.
>
> Exodus 1:6–8

A new Pharaoh came into power who had not known Joseph and all that he had done for Egypt. Fear entered his heart when he realized that the Israelites were under the protection of their God. One of the ways that people deal with fear is to destroy what they do not know or understand. "And he said to his people, 'Look, the people of the children of Israel are more and mightier than we; come, let us deal shrewdly with them, lest they multiply, and it happen, in the event of war, that they also join our enemies and fight against us, and so go up out of the land'" (verses 9–10).

Fear caused the Pharaoh to act harshly against God's people. The land that had provided them with protection was suddenly enslaving them. Even though the Israelites were in bondage and experienced great hardship under their Egyptian taskmasters, God was still with them. "But the more they afflicted them, the more they multiplied and grew. And they were in dread of the children of Israel" (verse 12). Remember what God had promised Abraham back in Genesis 13:16, "And I will make your descendants as the dust of the earth; so that if a man could number the dust of the earth, then your descendants also could be numbered."

God looked after and provided for Abraham throughout his life. He blessed him and fulfilled His promise to him. He did the same for Isaac. Then when famine threatened to wipe out Jacob and his family, God provided for them with a plan that He had set in motion many years before. Now once again Abraham's descendants were being threatened. The God of Abraham, Isaac, and Jacob would not allow His people to be brought to nothing. God never goes back on His Word. God had a plan: He would deliver His people. My friend, He remains the same today as He was yesterday. He hasn't gone back on His Word before and He will not go back on His Word now. You can trust Him because He remains faithful.

Prayer

My Father, thank You for a new month with new opportunities to walk with You and to learn from Your Word. Lord, I look forward to journeying with Moses and taking courage from his walk of faith with You. You have been faithful to Your people down through the ages, and You are faithful to me, too. Amen.

Read Exodus 1:15–22 and 2:1–10

> BUT WHEN SHE COULD NO LONGER HIDE HIM, SHE TOOK AN ARK OF
> BULRUSHES FOR HIM, DAUBED IT WITH ASPHALT AND PITCH, PUT THE CHILD IN
> IT, AND LAID IT IN THE REEDS BY THE RIVER'S BANK.
>
> Exodus 2:3

We've seen before how God preserved life through an ark. Here we see that Moses' mother made an ark and placed him in it. He floated around until Pharaoh's daughter came down to the river and found him. God had a plan, not only to save Moses' life, but to deliver His people. Abraham, Noah, and Joseph's lives were about so much more than only themselves and the same was true for Moses. God chose him out of all the Hebrew boys born at that time to carry out His plan of deliverance for the children of Israel.

No matter how the Pharaoh tried to destroy God's people, he couldn't. He wasn't in charge; God was in charge. It is the same with our world. The enemy, Satan, may try as he will to bring down God's Kingdom, but he will never succeed. The ultimate deliverance and victory took place on Calvary. When Jesus cried, "It is finished!" Satan was defeated. Then when Jesus arose from the grave, finally overcoming the sting of death, the victory was sealed. My friends, you and I can walk confidently because we serve a risen Saviour. We have been delivered once and for all as a result of Calvary. Throughout the Old Testament we see God's people moving in and out of captivity. Each time God delivered them; then through disobedience they would land up enslaved once again.

We have freedom. Jesus said, "Therefore if the Son makes you free, you shall be free indeed" (John 8:36). Why is it, then, that so many of God's children are living lives enslaved to sin? It is time for us to believe in what Jesus did for us. It is time for us to start walking by faith and not by sight. It is time to take God's Word to us seriously when it says: "But without faith it is impossible to please Him, for he who comes to God must believe that He is, and that He is a rewarder of those who diligently seek Him" (Hebrews 11:6).

Prayer

My Father God, I do not want to be like the children of Israel constantly falling into slavery through disobedience. Help me to trust and obey You. Lord, Your faithfulness is new every morning. You remain the same. Help me to walk by faith and not by sight. I want to please You. Amen.

Read Exodus 2:11–25

Now it happened in the process of time that the king of Egypt died. Then the children of Israel groaned because of the bondage, and they cried out; and their cry came up to God because of the bondage. So God heard their groaning, and God remembered His covenant with Abraham, with Isaac, and with Jacob. And God looked upon the children of Israel, and God acknowledged them.

Exodus 2:23–25

Moses was adopted by Pharaoh's daughter and he grew up in the palace. It is safe to say, though, that he never forgot his roots. He was very aware of his people's suffering. So much so that one day he killed an Egyptian taskmaster who was ill-treating one of the Israelites. As a result of this action Pharaoh sought to kill Moses when he heard about it. So Moses fled from Egypt. He went to the land of Midian and there he married the priest of Midian's daughter, Zipporah. He was content to tend his father-in-law's sheep. Moses literally hid in the desert. He was an introverted man and did not in any way seek the limelight.

On the other hand, the plight of the children of Israel grew worse. They called out to God and He heard them. Our key verses say that "God remembered His covenant with Abraham, with Isaac, and with Jacob. And God looked upon the children of Israel, and God acknowledged them." The time was drawing near when the next phase of God's plan was about to be put into action. Noah had played his part, then Abraham, followed by Joseph, so the next in line was Moses. It was his turn to step on to centre stage.

God often uses the people that we would never dream of using to accomplish His purposes. Moses was such a person. "Then Moses said to the Lord, 'O my Lord, I am not eloquent, neither before nor since You have spoken to Your servant; but I am slow of speech and slow of tongue'" (Exodus 4:10). "But God has chosen the foolish things of the world to put to shame the wise, and God has chosen the weak things of the world to put to shame the things which are mighty" (1 Corinthians 1:27). It is never an excuse to tell God you cannot do something. If He has called you, then He will equip you. God was going to save His people and Moses was His man to do it.

Prayer

My Father, You have loved Your people down through the ages. You have always remained faithful. Lord, You have chosen to use ordinary men to accomplish Your purposes. You do not look for superheroes, You look for obedient servants. Men who will choose to walk by faith and not by sight. Amen.

Read Exodus 3

> THEN HE SAID, "DO NOT DRAW NEAR THIS PLACE. TAKE YOUR SANDALS OFF
> YOUR FEET, FOR THE PLACE WHERE YOU STAND IS HOLY GROUND." MOREOVER
> HE SAID, "I AM THE GOD OF YOUR FATHER – THE GOD OF ABRAHAM, THE
> GOD OF ISAAC, AND THE GOD OF JACOB." AND MOSES HID HIS FACE, FOR HE
> WAS AFRAID TO LOOK UPON GOD.
>
> Exodus 3:5–6

The day no doubt started off like any other for Moses. He didn't realize that by the end of it his life would never be the same again. It was the day that he would meet God for the first time. He definitely knew who God was. His mother would have made sure of that. However, it didn't matter how much Moses knew about God: what was important was that God knew about Moses. God had His hand upon Moses way back when he was bobbing around in the little ark that his mother had built to protect him. It was no accident that Pharaoh's daughter found him and took him in. It was not a coincidence that she allowed Moses' mother to rear him.

Moses landing up in the wilderness looking after sheep was no accident either. The time he spent in seclusion was his preparation period. At exactly the right moment in time the God of Abraham, the God of Isaac, and the God of Jacob appeared to Moses. Can you imagine Moses' surprise when the bush suddenly burst into flames? Moses immediately knew that something unusual was happening. God spoke to Moses and told him what He wanted him to do. Moses wanted none of it. He was a "wanted man" in Egypt. Even though the previous Pharaoh had died, he did not want to take a chance on returning.

God began revealing to Moses what He planned to do for His children. He told Moses that he would be the one to lead them out of captivity into freedom. He was the one whom God had chosen to deliver His people. Moses didn't immediately obey God. There proceeded a long discussion. God was patient with Moses and took him through the plan step by step – answering all of his concerns and doubts. God is gracious and merciful. If He has been speaking to you and you have doubts and concerns about what God is saying, you can take them to Him. He loves you and He will lead you step by step, as He did Moses.

Prayer

My Father God, I am so grateful that I can come to You with whatever is worrying me. Lord, I want to walk in faith and obedience to You. I want to be used by You. Thank You that I can bring my concerns to You. Please help me to work through these issues so that I can wholeheartedly walk forward with You. Amen.

Read Exodus 3:1–6

> AND THE ANGEL OF THE LORD APPEARED TO HIM IN A FLAME OF FIRE FROM THE MIDST OF A BUSH. SO HE LOOKED, AND BEHOLD, THE BUSH WAS BURNING WITH FIRE, BUT THE BUSH WAS NOT CONSUMED.
>
> Exodus 3:2

Why is it that we think that if we didn't have a huge experience with God we are somehow second-rate Christians? Maybe it is because some Christians, I don't say all, exaggerate their experiences with God. You know the ones who are always saying, "God spoke to me." I want to tell you something, my friend. God has never spoken audibly to me. I don't want to cross swords with anyone out there, but God has spoken audibly to very few people. He is so big and so huge and amazing; He is omnipresent and omnipotent. If He had to speak audibly to you, you would die. God told Moses not to approach the burning bush. He told him to remove his shoes because he was on holy ground.

Later on, God hid Moses in the cleft of the rock and shielded him with His own hand when He passed him by. Moses only saw the back of God. God protected Moses. This is why I am sceptical when someone tells me they had a conversation face to face with Jesus. I don't want to call them a liar, because I wasn't there. Nevertheless, I want to caution you to carefully weigh up any "word" relayed to you as a result of "a direct conversation" with God.

The Lord speaks to all of His children every day, in all kinds of ways. He speaks to us through His Word. He speaks to us through the prompting of His Spirit. He speaks to us in our workplace. He speaks to us through circumstances. He also speaks to us through other Christians. There are times when God dramatically manifests Himself to a person. When He does so it is not a sign of the person's superiority. Think of Moses' case – he was a lowly shepherd. God chooses how He communicates with us. Our job is to obey Him when He speaks. To act upon what He says by faith. So don't put store by how God speaks; rather examine your reaction to what He says to you.

Prayer

My Father God, thank You that You speak to me each and every day. I realize that so often I am not listening because my mind is full of other things. Help me to slow down, stand still, and listen for Your voice. Help me to be open to hear, and then to believe and obey You. Amen.

Read Exodus 3:1–6

> NOW MOSES WAS TENDING THE FLOCK OF JETHRO HIS FATHER-IN-LAW, THE
> PRIEST OF MIDIAN. AND HE LED THE FLOCK TO THE BACK OF THE DESERT,
> AND CAME TO HOREB, THE MOUNTAIN OF GOD.
>
> Exodus 3:1

Moses wasn't doing anything particularly spiritual when God spoke to him. Moses wasn't up the mountain on a forty-day fast praying. He hadn't gone on a pilgrimage. He was working. He was looking after Jethro's sheep. God met him as he went about his everyday business. This is exciting; it means that God will talk to the boilermaker as he works in the factory. He will talk to the farmer as he drives his tractor. God will speak to the executive as he runs his company. The sportsman can hear God speak to him as he practises on the field. The student can hear from the Lord as he studies. Jesus will meet you in your place of work, because that is where He met Moses.

God didn't meet Moses in Pharaoh's palace. He met Moses at the back end of the world in the desert. The other lesson you can learn from Moses' encounter with the Lord is that God will not forget about you. Moses was happy to be in the back of the desert – he wanted to be inconspicuous. However, God had His eye on Moses right from the time he was hidden in the reeds. God knew exactly where to find Moses when the time was right.

In the same way that God had His hand upon Noah, Abraham, and Joseph, so He also had His hand upon Moses. With each of them, when the moment was right He revealed His purpose for their lives. It was Moses' turn to play his part in God's plan for the redemption of His people. So don't wait for some huge experience before you begin to serve God – simply go about your daily business. Be open and available; God will speak to you in the everyday moments of your life. He is the God of the everyday. We often miss out on the blessing because we are sitting around waiting. He is with you wherever you are. Walking a faith walk is about choosing each day to walk by faith and not by sight.

Prayer

My God of the everyday, thank You for Your Word to me. I realize that I spend a lot of time sitting around waiting. By doing this I know that I am missing out on so much of the adventure of serving You. Help me to get on with my life and be open to You as You speak to me. Amen.

Read Exodus 4:1–12

> THEN MOSES SAID TO THE LORD, "O MY LORD, I AM NOT ELOQUENT,
> NEITHER BEFORE NOR SINCE YOU HAVE SPOKEN TO YOUR SERVANT; BUT I
> AM SLOW OF SPEECH AND SLOW OF TONGUE." SO THE LORD SAID TO HIM,
> "WHO HAS MADE MAN'S MOUTH? OR WHO MAKES THE MUTE, THE DEAF, THE
> SEEING, OR THE BLIND? HAVE NOT I, THE LORD? NOW THEREFORE, GO, AND
> I WILL BE WITH YOUR MOUTH AND TEACH YOU WHAT YOU SHALL SAY."
>
> Exodus 4:10–12

As we said yesterday, Moses was very happy in the back end of the desert. He had no desire whatsoever to move to centre stage. He did not want to be the person whom God sent to deliver the children of Israel. You will remember that his attempts to intervene on their behalf when he was a young man had ended badly for him. He had found peace and contentment and he wasn't keen to give that up. However, God had other plans for Moses and saying no wasn't an option; even if saying yes was a process.

In order to quell Moses' fears God performed two miracles through him (verses 2–7). Then God told him that if the Israelites still wouldn't believe that God had sent him he was to take water from the river. When Moses poured the water on the ground it would turn to blood (verse 9). Even after all that, Moses was still not keen. He begged God to send someone else. My friends, in some ways we can take courage from Moses. It is amazing to think that God would have been prepared to entrust the monumental task of saving His people to an introverted man such as Moses. Our human thinking would expect God to look for a charismatic personality who was larger than life: someone with leadership skills who could rally the people.

But no, God wanted a man who above all would be obedient to Him. A man who would walk in humility before Him. A man who would know that it was God who was in charge. God wanted someone who would be dependent upon Him. He wanted a man with a servant's heart; a patient man. Have you looked around at the "big names" in Christianity and thought to yourself that God will never use someone like you? Well, if you have then Moses is your example, isn't he? My friend, God is not interested in your abilities. He is interested in your willingness – never forget this. He is looking for men of deep faith who will walk in obedience with Him.

Prayer
My Father God, thank You for Your Word. Thank You for the encouragement of Moses' calling. I am inspired to walk in humility, obedience, faithfulness, and availability with You each and every day. I am Yours, Lord, to do with as You choose. All I want is to serve You faithfully. Amen.

Read Exodus 4:13–31

AND AARON SPOKE ALL THE WORDS WHICH THE LORD HAD SPOKEN TO
MOSES. THEN HE DID THE SIGNS IN THE SIGHT OF THE PEOPLE. SO THE
PEOPLE BELIEVED; AND WHEN THEY HEARD THAT THE LORD HAD VISITED THE
CHILDREN OF ISRAEL AND THAT HE HAD LOOKED ON THEIR AFFLICTION, THEN
THEY BOWED THEIR HEADS AND WORSHIPED.

Exodus 4:30–31

God allowed Aaron, Moses' brother, to speak on his behalf. Jethro, Moses' father-in-law, permitted him to return to his people. God had warned them that Pharaoh would not be prepared to listen to God's decree to free His people. On the other hand, after meeting with the priests of Israel, and sharing God's words with them, as well as the signs He had told them to perform, the children of Israel believed Moses and Aaron. The stage was now set. God had put His master plan in motion. There was no going back – no stopping Him. He had His man of faith through whom He would deliver His people. The journey of faith that had begun for Moses in the tiny ark among the reeds was about to take a new path.

Moses didn't even realize that all the years he'd spent in the desert God was preparing him for the next phase in his life. Remember that God did the same with Joseph; all the things that Joseph went through prepared him for his destiny, for his purpose. My friends, it is no different with you and me. God is constantly preparing us. He is teaching us lessons through the things we experience. He is leading us each day along the path of our purpose and destiny.

He has a plan and a purpose for each of His children. Paul tells us in Ephesians 2:10: "For we are His workmanship, created in Christ Jesus for good works, which God prepared beforehand that we should walk in them." We have been saved for a purpose. God has had His hand upon you from the time you were in your mother's womb. Psalm 139:16 says: "Your eyes saw my substance, being yet unformed. And in Your book they all were written, the days fashioned for me, when as yet there were none of them." This is how special and precious you are to God, your Father. Are you living as a child of the promise? Are you living in the fullness of your destiny and purpose with God?

Prayer
My Father God in Heaven, You are a great and a mighty God. There is none like You. I bow before You in praise and worship. I honour You and I lift my voice in grateful thanksgiving. Lord, I want to live in the fullness of my purpose and destiny. I submit to You and Your will for my life. Amen.

Read Exodus 5

> So Moses returned to the Lord and said, "Lord, why have You brought trouble on this people? Why is it You have sent me? For since I came to Pharaoh to speak in Your name, he has done evil to this people; neither have You delivered Your people at all."
>
> Exodus 5:22–23

As God had predicted, Pharaoh was not in the least bit interested in allowing the children of Israel to leave Egypt. Why would he? After all, if he let them go he would lose all his cheap labour. He had no knowledge or fear of God. "And Pharaoh said, 'Who is the Lord, that I should obey His voice to let Israel go? I do not know the Lord, nor will I let Israel go'" (verse 2). Pharaoh believed that he was the highest authority; there was no one of whom he needed to be afraid. His reaction was to double the suffering of the children of Israel. He gave the order to make their lives even more miserable than they had been before.

It is understandable, in a way, that Moses would have been confused by this turn of events. After all, God was supposed to have sent him to free His people – to lift their burden. It seemed that once again he had only made things worse. The children of Israel immediately blamed Moses and Aaron for their added suffering. They had clearly moved far from their God; in doing so they had forgotten that they served the God of Abraham, Isaac, and Jacob – the God who had promised that He would bless the descendants of Abraham. They had turned from God and placed their trust in the things that they could see and touch. They felt more comfortable in Egypt, in captivity, than they did at the prospect of walking in freedom with God.

Isn't this so often our story? When things become hard we are quick to turn away from God. We clutch on to the familiar. We complain and moan instead of clinging to God. In times of suffering and hardship it is often darkest before the moment of release and provision arrives. Faith is not faith when all is sunshine and roses, my friend. True faith valiantly, and often stubbornly, clings on when everything looks as black as night. Truly, the darkest hour often comes before the dawn.

Prayer

My Father, thank You for the encouragement of Your Word to me. Help me to cling on to You no matter what happens. Give me the courage and the strength to remain standing through thick and thin. Don't let me slip away or lose my way in the dark. I know that You are right there with me. Amen.

Read Exodus 6:1–9

> AND I APPEARED UNTO ABRAHAM, UNTO ISAAC, AND UNTO JACOB, BY THE
> NAME OF GOD ALMIGHTY, BUT BY MY NAME JEHOVAH WAS I NOT KNOWN TO
> THEM.
>
> Exodus 6:3, KJV

God reveals Himself to Moses by a new name: Jehovah. He appeared by several different names to Abraham, including El Shaddai, which revealed God as the Covenant Maker (Genesis 17:1). "Jehovah" reveals Him as the covenant-keeping God. Jehovah, according to the *Zondervan Bible Dictionary*, means: "eternal, to be, to exist, always is and unchangeable". The name Jehovah is unique to God alone. Moses' amazing faith journey took on a new dimension when God revealed Himself as Jehovah to him. God reminded Moses of his history. He drew Moses' attention to what He had done for Abraham, for Isaac, and for Jacob. God told Moses that he, Moses, was to play a part in God making good on His promise to his forefathers.

God had not been absent or inattentive to what the Israelites had been going through. He had been there all along. The time was right for Him to intervene and Moses was God's choice to deliver His people from bondage. This was not only a journey of faith for the Israelites; it was also an intensely personal journey of faith for Moses. He had to choose to trust God. Moses had to be prepared to step up to the plate and accept the responsibility that God was entrusting to him. And God didn't leave Moses without help: He gave him his brother, Aaron, to assist him.

However, Moses' primary Source was God. This is why God revealed Himself to Moses as Jehovah. God wanted Moses to experience Him as the covenant-keeping God. It was important for Moses to know that God would be with him every step of the way. Moses could rely upon the Eternal God, the God who "always is; the unchangeable God". My friend, you can rely upon this same God. If you have accepted Jesus, then the Lord Jehovah is your covenant-keeping God too. He is there with you no matter what you are going through. He invites you to continue walking with Him by faith, trusting Him to undertake for you. He didn't let Moses down and He won't let you down either.

Prayer
My Father God, in the midst of all that is going on around me I am so grateful that I can stop and take time to bow in Your presence right now. Lord, thank You that You are my Jehovah God. You are my covenant-keeping God. You have always been and will always be; there is no end to You. Amen.

"SPEAK NOW IN THE HEARING OF THE PEOPLE, AND LET EVERY MAN ASK FROM HIS NEIGHBOR AND EVERY WOMAN FROM HER NEIGHBOR, ARTICLES OF SILVER AND ARTICLES OF GOLD." AND THE LORD GAVE THE PEOPLE FAVOR IN THE SIGHT OF THE EGYPTIANS.

Exodus 11:2–3a

Between chapters 7 and 11 God sent nine plagues upon the Egyptians. Each time Pharaoh hardened his heart. He was stubborn and he refused to allow the children of Israel to leave Egypt. Nothing seemed able to move him. No matter what Moses and Aaron said or did, Pharaoh remained steadfast. The time had approached for the final plague – this would be the one that would cause Pharaoh to relent and allow the Israelites to leave. God told Moses that the time was imminent and He told Moses to prepare.

The children of Israel had been slaves in the land of Egypt for over 400 years. Despite, over the centuries, contributing through their labour toward making the Egyptians wealthy, the Israelites did not own many material possessions that they could take with them. God had a plan for His people to leave with some of the wealth that they had helped accumulate. Our key verse says that He gave the people favour with the Egyptians. They were instructed by Moses to ask for items of silver and gold – things that they could carry with them when they left. God granted them favour and the Egyptians gave generously to them. Later these items would be used to build Solomon's Jerusalem Temple that housed the Ark of the Covenant.

God had planned ahead. He had provided for His people before there was even a need. God was showing them that they could trust Him to be their Provider. He has not changed. He does the same for us, doesn't He? If you look back I am sure that, like me, you can see God's hand of preparation in many areas of your life. He knows what we will need long before we do, and He will never leave us wanting, my friends. All we have to do is walk in obedient faith with Him day by day. If we are prepared to concentrate on our relationship with Him, then He will do the rest for us. "But seek first the kingdom of God and His righteousness, and all these things shall be added to you" (Matthew 6:33).

Prayer
My Father, thank You that You are in control of every aspect of my life. There is nothing that escapes Your attention. You know the end from the beginning and I have nothing to fear as long as I walk in faithful obedience with You. Lord, I want to be a man of faith who believes Your Word. Amen.

Read Exodus 12:21–28

> Then Moses called for all the elders of Israel and said to them,
> "Pick out and take lambs for yourselves according to your families,
> and kill the Passover lamb."
>
> Exodus 12:21

God tested Abraham by telling him to sacrifice Isaac, his only son, on the altar. When God saw that Abraham was willing to obey Him, He provided a ram in the thicket to take the place of Isaac upon the altar. God revealed Himself to Abraham as "Jehovahjireh" – "The Lord our Provider" (Genesis 22:14, KJV). Now we read of another instance where a sacrifice was required. This time it was to save the firstborn of each Israelite family. God would pass over the land of Egypt and put to death all the firstborn of the Egyptians.

The children of Israel would be spared through the shedding of the blood of a lamb. Exodus 12:5 tells us: "Your lamb shall be without blemish, a male of the first year." As per God's instructions Moses tells them: "For the Lord will pass through to strike the Egyptians; and when He sees the blood on the lintel and on the two doorposts, the Lord will pass over the door and not allow the destroyer to come into your houses to strike you" (verse 23). Once again a sacrifice would save the firstborn – those who would carry forward the promise that God made to Abraham. Jehovah, their covenant-keeping God, would provide the way of escape for them. He would keep His covenant with their forefather, Abraham.

The Passover instituted in Egypt was a forerunner of the Passover at which Jesus, the "spotless Lamb of God" (1 Peter 1:19, NLT) would put an end to the need for blood sacrifices. He would once and for all pay the price to satisfy God's need for a pure, sin-free sacrifice. Jesus' sacrifice would pay the debt of sin. His sacrifice would make it possible for us to be reconciled to God. Jesus' death on Calvary and His shed blood would wash away the sin of the world. Jesus made it possible for us to walk and live by faith. Our Salvation is by faith; and our Christian walk is by faith. We are permanently covered and protected by the shed blood of Jesus Christ.

Prayer
My God and Father, thank You for the once-and-for-all sacrifice of Jesus Christ Your Son and my Saviour. Lord, I stand in Your presence today because of what Jesus did for me on Calvary. I am redeemed and restored because of Jesus' sacrifice. Thank You, Jesus, that You and You alone could save me. Amen.

GOD'S ABIDING FAITHFULNESS

Read Exodus 12:29–32, 40–41 and 13:17–22

AND MOSES TOOK THE BONES OF JOSEPH WITH HIM…

Exodus 13:19a

For 400 years the children of Israel had been slaves in Egypt, just as the Lord had told Abraham they would be: "Then He said to Abram: 'Know certainly that your descendants will be strangers in a land that is not theirs, and will serve them, and they will afflict them four hundred years. And also the nation whom they serve I will judge; afterward they shall come out with great possessions'" (Genesis 15:13–14; see also Exodus 11:2–3a). How many times have we said that God is never too early and He is never too late? Exactly as He had promised Abraham, so He delivered His children from the hands of their oppressors.

God also didn't forget about Joseph. In Genesis 50:24–26 we read: "And Joseph said to his brethren, 'I am dying; but God will surely visit you, and bring you out of this land to the land of which He swore to Abraham, to Isaac, and to Jacob.' Then Joseph took an oath from the children of Israel, saying, 'God will surely visit you, and you shall carry up my bones from here.' So Joseph died, being one hundred and ten years old; and they embalmed him, and he was put in a coffin in Egypt." Joseph's desire was to leave Egypt with the Israelites when the time came. Hundreds of years later, when the time was right, Joseph's bones moved with his people. God never forgets, my friends. He is the God of time. We fret and worry about things happening "on time"; we agonize over the fact that if something doesn't happen "right now" it will be "too late".

Whatever it is that you are waiting for God to do in your life, I hope that you have taken comfort and courage from our reading today. I pray that you will understand in your spirit that God is in control. He will do what He has promised, but it will be in His timing, which is always perfect. The question is – will you trust Him, or will you try and make your own plans?

Prayer
My Father God, Your faithfulness stretches from generation to generation. You are not inhibited by time. I know that as I abide in You and trust in You, You will keep me in perfect peace and that You will provide for me. I know that You and You alone are my help and my refuge. Amen.

Read Exodus 14:1–14

AND MOSES SAID TO THE PEOPLE, "DO NOT BE AFRAID. STAND STILL, AND
SEE THE SALVATION OF THE LORD, WHICH HE WILL ACCOMPLISH FOR YOU
TODAY. FOR THE EGYPTIANS WHOM YOU SEE TODAY, YOU SHALL SEE AGAIN
NO MORE FOREVER. THE LORD WILL FIGHT FOR YOU, AND YOU SHALL HOLD
YOUR PEACE."

Exodus 14:13–14

Moses gave the children of Israel some good advice that will also work for us when
we face a "Red Sea" situation in our lives. The first thing he said to them was: "Do not
be afraid." Why? Because they had the Lord Jehovah on their side. He is a covenant-
keeping God. They had just witnessed Him honouring the covenant He'd made
generations previously with Abraham. My friends, He is the same covenant-keeping
God now as He was back then. You do not need to be afraid today, no matter what the
threat is that you are facing.

The next thing that Moses told them was that they should "stand still". Our
first inclination when danger lurks is to either take flight or attack. Moses told the
Israelites: "Stand still, stand firm, stand strong". It is only when we stand still that
we can hear God speak to us. We are often so busy "doing" that we do not hear God
speaking to us, telling us what to do next. So, stand still – wait for, and listen to, God.
Moses told them that if they were not afraid and if they stood still then they would
"see the salvation of the Lord". There was no doubt in Moses' mind that God would
show up. Moses believed that God would do what He said He would do. He didn't
know exactly what it was that God would do, but he knew that if God had promised
to deliver His people then He would do it.

Moses went on to tell them – "The Lord will fight for you." If you are facing a battle
today, then you can know that God is on your side. He will fight the battle for you;
don't try and do it on your own. The last instruction Moses gave was: "and you shall
hold your peace." When God is fighting your battle for you, you can hold your peace,
and you can remain in perfect peace, because He is your Peace. God honours faith, He
honours trust, and He honours His Word.

Prayer

*My covenant-keeping God, I come before You right now. I am not afraid, because I trust You.
I stand still in Your presence and I wait to see what You will accomplish for me. I trust You,
Lord, to fight on my behalf. I stand before You in perfect peace knowing that I am Your child.
Amen.*

Read Exodus 14:15–31

> THUS ISRAEL SAW THE GREAT WORK WHICH THE LORD HAD DONE IN EGYPT;
> SO THE PEOPLE FEARED THE LORD, AND BELIEVED THE LORD AND HIS
> SERVANT MOSES.
>
> Exodus 14:31

Moses' walk of faith with the Lord was a progressive one in much the same way as yours and mine is. If you remember, Abraham too had a progressive walk of faith. We saw Abraham's faith in God growing over the years; until the day came when he was able to trust God with the one thing that he loved more than life itself – his son of the promise. The Moses who stood at the burning bush was not the same Moses who stood on the banks of the Red Sea. His faith had grown as he had witnessed God come through for His people. Moses' faith would grow even more over the coming years, but that day he believed God when God told him to reach out his rod across the sea.

Moses did what God told him to and the sea parted. The next step was the Israelites being prepared to walk on to the pathway that had been cleared through the sea. They had to take the first step. Once they did, the rest, as they say, is history. It was indeed a great and awesome miracle that the Lord did that day. It is no different for us, my friends. At times we face challenges and difficulties in our lives that seem every bit as daunting as the Red Sea. We stand on the banks and our enemies seem to be gaining ground behind us. There is nowhere to go; there appears to be no escape.

Like the children of Israel you have to make a choice. Will you trust yourself, or will you trust God? What will it be? So often we exhaust every avenue before we turn to God for help. This is not faith, and without faith it is impossible to please God. If you are standing on the banks of a "Red Sea" situation right now – what choice are you going to make? If you are prepared to take the first step of faith, God will do the rest. There really is no other option. With God all things are possible.

Prayer

My Father God, You are the covenant-keeping God who parted the Red Sea for the children of Israel. I know that You will undertake for me in the same way that You did for them. Help me to take the first step of faith into the sea. Lord, I thank You that I can trust You. Amen.

16 May   DON'T BECOME DISCOURAGED

Read Psalm 136

To Him who divided the Red Sea in two, for His mercy endures forever; and made Israel pass through the midst of it, for His mercy endures forever; but overthrew Pharaoh and his army in the Red Sea, for His mercy endures forever.

Psalm 136:13–15

Can you imagine the Israelites standing on the shore of the Red Sea, the ocean stretching in front of them and their enemies gaining ground behind them? They looked back and saw the most powerful army in the world pursuing them. There was nowhere to go; they had no artillery or weapons. They were not an army; after all they had been in captivity for over 400 years. All they were was a vast crowd of people: men, women, children, and elderly people.

Moses stood alone at the Red Sea, but he was not discouraged. He wasn't sure what God would do, but he knew that He had a plan. That is what happens when you step out on to the water; it's what happens when you intend great things for God and when you expect great things from God. All of a sudden the battlefield is level and you realize, "Lord, if You don't do this I am finished." Moses knew God would come through. It is amazing how clearly God speaks to someone who is desperate. You cannot say that you are trusting God when you have a few million in the bank, and you're not doing anything to stretch your faith.

The children of Israel had nowhere to turn to, but to God. Moses knew that God alone was their Refuge and their Deliverer. It is the same in your life and mine, my friend. We have no help other than God, our Father. The truth is that you don't need anyone else to help you. Sadly, like the Israelites, we all too often look everywhere but to God for help. Yet the psalm we read tells us that "His mercy endures forever." He undertakes for His children today, just as He did in Moses' day. So don't be discouraged; don't be downhearted. "[Look] unto Jesus, the author and finisher of our faith" (Hebrews 12:2a). It doesn't matter how great the army approaching you appears to be, you are part of a much larger army – you belong to the Army of the Kingdom of God.

Prayer

My Father God, You and You alone are my Help, my Refuge, and my Deliverer. There is no one besides You. I want and need no one other than You. Lord, I stand at the edge of my "Red Sea" today. I look to You; I call out to You. Lord, answer me and undertake for me, I pray. Amen.

Read 1 Peter 5:5–11

> BUT MAY THE GOD OF ALL GRACE, WHO CALLED US TO HIS ETERNAL GLORY
> BY CHRIST JESUS, AFTER YOU HAVE SUFFERED A WHILE, PERFECT, ESTABLISH,
> STRENGTHEN, AND SETTLE YOU.
>
> 1 Peter 5:10

Yes, there are times of suffering. Times we have to step out and walk on water. It is then we call out: "God, help me!" He hears us and reaches out to us. Moses might not have become discouraged, but he certainly suffered that day standing by the Red Sea. He had all the people clamouring around him. They did not believe as he did; they had not been at the burning bush. They wanted someone to blame and Moses was right at hand.

Moses must have cried, "God, help me!" When he did, what do you think happened? Yes, we read about it a couple of days ago. God told him to stretch out his arm. He told Moses to stretch his rod out over the sea. The very same rod that God used to perform the miracles before Pharaoh in Exodus 7. Immediately the ocean began parting – two high walls of water on either side. Can you imagine what it must have been like? Then God placed a cloud in front of the Egyptian army so that they couldn't see where the Israelites were. The cloud remained in place until the last Israelite had walked over to the other side.

If you don't believe this account, my friend, then I feel very sorry for you. Do you know that there is more evidence to support the Bible than any of the other philosophies that people follow? Isn't it strange that people never seem to feel the need to check and test the truth of anybody else's philosophy, but they are always trying to punch holes in the Bible? I want to tell you the Word of God has stood the test of time. After the Israelites passed through, the cloud lifted. The most powerful army thundered into the Red Sea after the Israelites. When they were halfway across the Lord told Moses to stretch out his arm again; as he did so that mighty ocean closed up and swallowed the Egyptian army. If you are suffering, know that in a while He will "perfect, establish, strengthen, and settle" you.

Prayer

My Father in Heaven, today I reach out to You. I am at the end of my tether. Lord, it feels as if this suffering has gone on forever. I stand at the edge of my "Red Sea" with the enemy fast approaching. "Lord, help me!" Save me, deliver me, and restore me, I pray. Amen.

THE LORD IS MY STRENGTH AND SONG

Read Exodus 15:1–21

I WILL SING TO THE LORD, FOR HE HAS TRIUMPHED GLORIOUSLY! THE HORSE
AND ITS RIDER HE HAS THROWN INTO THE SEA! THE LORD IS MY STRENGTH
AND SONG, AND HE HAS BECOME MY SALVATION; HE IS MY GOD, AND I WILL
PRAISE HIM; MY FATHER'S GOD, AND I WILL EXALT HIM.

Exodus 15:1b–2

Imagine the celebration and euphoria that the children of Israel must have experienced when the last person stepped on to the bank on the other side of the Red Sea. They witnessed a spectacular miracle first-hand. God undertook for them in a very visible way. It was official; they were out of Egypt and on their way to the Promised Land.

Moses led the people in a beautiful song of praise to Jehovah, their covenant-keeping God. Miriam, Moses' sister, who had stood guard over him as he bobbed around in the reeds when he was a baby, was part of the crowd. "Then Miriam the prophetess, the sister of Aaron, took the timbrel in her hand; and all the women went out after her with timbrels and with dances" (verse 20). Imagine her excitement at how God was using her baby brother! When last did you sing a song of praise and thanksgiving to God, your Father? David understood the importance of praising God: "And now my head shall be lifted up above my enemies all around me; therefore I will offer sacrifices of joy in His tabernacle; I will sing, yes, I will sing praises to the Lord" (Psalm 27:6).

It is all too easy to allow the burdens of life to weigh us down so that we forget to praise God. The enemy knows that praise is a powerful weapon in the hands of God's children. If you have fallen into a rut, then it is time for you to resume praising God. He loves it when His children spend time praising Him. If you need help then turn to the psalms, and use them to inspire you, as you verbalize your praise to God. There are times in our lives when we have to praise God by faith. When things are not going well, and we are in the midst of trials, this is the time that praising God is crucial. In Psalm 59:17 David says the following: "To You, O my Strength, I will sing praises; for God is my defense, my God of mercy."

Prayer

My Father God, my covenant-keeping God, I come before You with songs of praise and thanksgiving. Lord, You have always been there for me. You have never let me down. You are a faithful God. Your mercies are new to me every morning. Day after day You love and care for me. Amen.

Read Exodus 15:22–27

> AND THE PEOPLE COMPLAINED AGAINST MOSES, SAYING, "WHAT SHALL WE DRINK?"
>
> Exodus 15:24

We move from the euphoria of the Red Sea crossing to three days later when the Israelites are grumbling because they are thirsty. They came to Marah and the water was bitter so they could not drink. It took them no time at all to forget what God had done for them. You would think that their first thought would be: "If God could part the Red Sea for us to walk across on dry land, then He can provide suitable drinking water for us. Let's pray to Him and ask Him to meet our need." But no; this was not their first reaction – their first instinct was to moan and complain to Moses.

We are quick to judge them, aren't we? Yet we have to face the fact that we often react exactly the same when things don't go our way. It is all very well to be full of faith when the road is smooth and there are no challenges. However, this is not what it means to live and walk by faith. Faith is only faith once it has been tried and tested. We all have times when the bitter waters of Marah flow through our lives. It is what we choose to do in those times that speaks volumes about our faith, or lack of it. Moses knew who his Source of help and Provision was – he called out to God. "So he cried out to the Lord, and the Lord showed him a tree. When he cast it into the waters, the waters were made sweet" (verse 25a).

It doesn't matter how bitter a situation is: the Lord can make it sweet. It is not always the change in circumstances that makes the difference, but rather the presence of the Lord in those circumstances. Jesus died and hung upon the Cross of Calvary so that the bitter places in our lives can be made sweet through His sacrifice for us. He has reconciled us to the Father of Light where we can always find hope and healing, no matter what we are going through.

Prayer

My Father in Heaven, I thank You for Your great love for me. Thank You for Jesus' death on Calvary that turned my bitter situation into a sweet one – filled with hope and peace. Now, no matter what happens in my life, I know that I am Your child and You will be with me each and every day. Amen.

Read Exodus 16

> THEN THE WHOLE CONGREGATION OF THE CHILDREN OF ISRAEL COMPLAINED
> AGAINST MOSES AND AARON IN THE WILDERNESS. AND THE CHILDREN OF
> ISRAEL SAID TO THEM, "OH, THAT WE HAD DIED BY THE HAND OF THE LORD
> IN THE LAND OF EGYPT, WHEN WE SAT BY THE POTS OF MEAT AND WHEN
> WE ATE BREAD TO THE FULL! FOR YOU HAVE BROUGHT US OUT INTO THIS
> WILDERNESS TO KILL THIS WHOLE ASSEMBLY WITH HUNGER."
>
> Exodus 16:2–3

Moses had an unenviable task leading the children of Israel. All they did was moan and complain. As soon as anything went wrong they immediately looked backward toward Egypt and lamented that Moses had led them out of captivity. Sin has that effect upon people, doesn't it? So often people will choose to rather live in their sin, than to accept the freedom and redemption that God offers them through Jesus Christ. Sadly, too many Christians would rather live in sin than repent and turn from it. Jesus offers forgiveness – but forgiveness comes as a result of repentance and a turning away from sin.

The Israelites were hungry and they wanted food. Moses again turned to God. With each test he faced, Moses' faith grew stronger and stronger. God again came through and He gave the people manna in the morning and quail in the evening. Exodus tells us that for forty years the people ate the manna that God provided. They had to gather only enough for the needs of that day. Anything left over would go bad overnight. There is a lesson there for us, isn't there? God will provide what you need when you need it. When Jesus taught His disciples to pray the Lord's Prayer, what does it say? "Give us this day our daily bread" (Matthew 6:11).

Like the children of Israel we so often want to hoard. Faith trusts that God will provide as we need it. Unbelief prompts us to make our own plans. We look to our own resources and abilities. But, as we have read, "without faith it is impossible to please Him, for he who comes to God must believe that He is, and that He is a rewarder of those who diligently seek Him" (Hebrews 11:6). When the chips are down in your life what is your first reaction: seeking God or finding your own solution? Jesus is the Bread of Life – feed off Him. In Him you have everything that you need to live a victorious Christian life. He will never leave you nor forsake you, no matter what happens.

Prayer
My Lord and God, thank You for Jesus who is the Bread of Life. Jesus promised that if I eat of Him I will never again go hungry. Lord, thank You that You are faithful to Your Word. I know that no matter what happens I can trust You and Your Word to me. Help me to live for You each day. Amen.

Read Exodus 17

> AND MOSES BUILT AN ALTAR AND CALLED ITS NAME, THE-LORD-IS-MY-BANNER.
>
> Exodus 17:15

Are you facing a battle in your life right now? Does it feel as if you have a war on your hands? My friends, the Word of God warns us: "Be sober, be vigilant; because your adversary the devil walks about like a roaring lion, seeking whom he may devour" (1 Peter 5:8). We have an enemy far more deadly than any earthly army. We have an enemy of the soul – Satan. He seeks to prevent us from serving God faithfully. Have you ever experienced that just when you feel led to do something big for God everything begins to go wrong in your life? This is the enemy, my friend – he does not want you to do great things for God.

The Israelites faced the Amalekite army. The man who stepped forward to lead the Israelites into battle was none other than Joshua. This is the first time that we encounter him. Joshua, the man of faith. Joshua, the obedient one. Again take note: Joshua became a mighty man of valour over time. Joshua had lived a lifetime of faith before Moses sent him and Caleb off to scout out the Promised Land. Faith builds over time, my friends; it is like a muscle – you have to exercise it, for it to grow strong.

Joshua led the Israelites into battle and Moses stood on the hill holding up his arms. When he became weary Aaron and Hur held up his arms for him. As long as his arms were lifted the Israelites were the stronger side. God gave them the victory and Moses built an altar to the Lord. He named it "The-Lord-Is-My-Banner". God is your Banner. He is my Banner. We have nothing to fear from the war that the enemy tries to wage against us, as long as we are covered and protected by God-Our-Banner. God does not send us out into the fray without protection. In the same way that He protected and cared for the children of Israel, He protects and cares for us.

Prayer

My Father God, thank You that You are my Banner. You are there for me night and day. I have nothing to fear from anyone or anything as long as I walk covered and protected by You – my Banner. Lord, help me to walk forward boldly. Help me to fight valiantly. Amen.

Read Exodus 20

> NOW ALL THE PEOPLE WITNESSED THE THUNDERINGS, THE LIGHTNING
> FLASHES, THE SOUND OF THE TRUMPET, AND THE MOUNTAIN SMOKING; AND
> WHEN THE PEOPLE SAW IT, THEY TREMBLED AND STOOD AFAR OFF. THEN THEY
> SAID TO MOSES, "YOU SPEAK WITH US, AND WE WILL HEAR; BUT LET NOT
> GOD SPEAK WITH US, LEST WE DIE."
>
> Exodus 20:18–19

Jesus said: "If you love Me, keep My commandments" (John 14:15). Our God is a Holy and Righteous God. I don't care what office you hold, it does not give you a licence to sin. Jesus says you must be the husband of one wife. He says we have to obey the Law. Nowhere in the Bible does Jesus condone homosexuality. I don't hate homosexuals, believe me, I don't. I love them, but I cannot condone their lifestyle because the Lord says it is not right. When you sleep with a woman who is not your wife and she becomes pregnant, abortion is not the solution. There are consequences to sin. The child must be brought up in the fear of the Lord.

God hates divorce. If you are reading this and you are divorced – don't do it again. Repent and ask God to forgive you and move on. If you are contemplating divorce I want you to pray about it. God doesn't like it. You made a promise, didn't you? You made a covenant with God on the day you were married. You said until death do us part. Well that stands, sir.

Maybe you feel I am coming on too strong. Well I'm sorry, I am only telling you what the Word says. Why? Because I want the Lord to set you free today. I sense that many of you reading this are like a bird in a cage. The Lord says that if you obey His Law He will open the gate and you can fly free. You can't do things your way and ask God to bless you. It doesn't work like that. God has put His Law in place for our own good. I am a sinner; this is why I am telling you to do it God's way. I don't want you to walk the road I walked. I caused a lot of pain and suffering to myself and those around me because I was determined to do things my way. Don't do it your way – do it God's way.

Prayer
My Father in Heaven, You have once again reminded me of how seriously You take Your Laws. You put them in place to protect me and to keep me walking the faith road with You. Lord, help me to faithfully live in the centre of Your love and protection. Amen.

Read Psalm 119:97–112

> YOUR WORD IS A LAMP TO MY FEET
> AND A LIGHT TO MY PATH.

Psalm 119:105

God's commandments are there for our good, not His. He is God. He doesn't have to obey commandments. He made them. For the same reason He instructs you to be the husband of one wife, He says you must discipline your children. He knows what happens if you don't – you make a rod for your own back. If your children are unruly it isn't their fault, sir, it is yours: because you didn't discipline them when they were babies. I know a man who is born again, Spirit-filled and baptized. He believes it is wrong to discipline a child with a rod. I told him that he can just as well take the Bible and throw it away. My Bible tells me that if you chastise a child, he'll grow up and thank you for it. My Bible tells me that a good hiding will not harm a child; in fact one day it might save their life.

We cannot change God's Laws. We have to obey them so that we can live a fulfilled life. Jesus said: "The thief does not come except to steal, and to kill, and to destroy. I have come that they may have life, and that they may have it more abundantly" (John 10:10). Why? Young man, this is why you don't play the field as those in the world do. It leads to debauchery, sickness, and death. Keep yourself pure until your wedding day. Why? Because the Bible says so.

The Bible also says that a man who sleeps around with an unmarried woman is a fornicator. God also hates adultery and warns us against it. I remind you of these truths, because obeying the truth sets us free. Picture a huge boil on your arm. You keep putting a poultice on it, covering it up. No matter what you do it doesn't heal. It is time to remove the poultice, take up a nice sharp scalpel and lance the boil, so that all the muck can be cleaned out. Repent before the Lord today – then you will know healing and freedom.

Prayer

My God and Father, truly Your Word is a lamp to my feet and a light to my path. Your Word brings healing and freedom. This is the road of faith. I choose to walk by faith and not by sight. I choose to live the abundant life that Jesus died to give me. Keep me faithful, I pray. Amen.

Read Deuteronomy 6:1–9

> HEAR, O ISRAEL: THE LORD OUR GOD, THE LORD IS ONE! YOU SHALL LOVE THE LORD YOUR GOD WITH ALL YOUR HEART, WITH ALL YOUR SOUL, AND WITH ALL YOUR STRENGTH.
>
> Deuteronomy 6:4–5

If you love somebody you won't intentionally hurt them. My wife, Jill, is so very special to me; we've been married for over forty years now. I can honestly say that I love her more today than on the day we were married. I don't like to do things that hurt or dishonour her. I know the things that she likes: one of them is that she likes to know where I am when I am away from home.

As you may know, I travel frequently and I am often away from home. So what do I do? I use my cell phone to keep in touch. When I travel from my farm into Durban to catch my plane, I call her from the airport before I board. When I arrive in Johannesburg, I let her know that the plane has touched down. If I am flying out of the country I speak to her again before the plane takes off. When I arrive at my destination I phone her every single day that I am away. You are quite right if you are thinking that it must cost me a fortune – it does – an absolute fortune. So much so that every time I return home I have to sell another ox to pay for the phone calls. Now I have no oxen left, but I still have my wife.

What about you, my friend? What's the point of having a lot of oxen and no wife? The same is true of our relationship with God. Show Him you love Him. Do things that make Him happy. Spend time speaking to Jesus. When was the last time you had a good chat with Him? Your love for Him will stop you from sinning. This is an absolute truth, because if you really love someone you won't hurt them. Think about that. How do you learn to love someone? You spend time with them. "Love the Lord your God with all your heart, with all your soul, and with all your strength." Obey God's commandments and serve Him.

Prayer

My Father God, thank You for Your wonderful love toward me. You have loved me from the beginning of time. Every day You show Your love for me in so many different ways. Help me to love You in return. Help me to show You through my actions that I love You with all of my heart, soul, and mind. Amen.

Read Exodus 33

> THEN HE SAID TO HIM, "IF YOUR PRESENCE DOES NOT GO WITH US, DO NOT
> BRING US UP FROM HERE. FOR HOW THEN WILL IT BE KNOWN THAT YOUR
> PEOPLE AND I HAVE FOUND GRACE IN YOUR SIGHT, EXCEPT YOU GO WITH US?
> SO WE SHALL BE SEPARATE, YOUR PEOPLE AND I, FROM ALL THE PEOPLE WHO
> ARE UPON THE FACE OF THE EARTH."
>
> Exodus 33:15–16

Over and over the children of Israel disappointed God. He had heard their cries and delivered them out of captivity in Egypt. Yet they constantly looked backward wishing that they could return to their shame and imprisonment. We read that Moses went up the mountain to meet with God. When he took too long to come down the people pressured Aaron into allowing them to build a golden calf for them to worship. God was furious with them and He punished the Israelites (Exodus 32). Our reading today follows on from this incident.

God is still angry. Moses took his tent and went out, far from where the people were, to meet with God. Moses realized that without God's presence and mercy upon them the Israelites wouldn't last a day. God was literally their lifeline. He was the cloud who protected them by day and the pillar of fire who guided them by night (Exodus 13:21). On behalf of the people Moses begged God not to depart from them. Moses fully realized that they didn't deserve God's forgiveness for their sin. He asked God to have mercy upon them.

"So the Lord said to Moses, 'I will also do this thing that you have spoken; for you have found grace in My sight, and I know you by name'" (Exodus 33:17). Have you ever wondered where you would be without the grace of God, my friend? Like the Israelites, we wouldn't last a day without God's grace and mercy upon our lives. Isn't it so sad that all too often, like the Israelites, we take His grace and mercy for granted? If you find yourself in a position where you have been treating God's grace with disdain, re-evaluate your life right now. Turn back to God and repent before it is too late. God is a gracious, merciful, and loving God; but He is also the Righteous Judge. He is Holy and He demands that His people be holy too. Come before Him today and ask His forgiveness. Don't move forward without His presence in your life.

Prayer

My Father, in the same way that You spoke to Moses Your servant, You are speaking to me today. You require of me that I should live a life that brings glory and honour to Your Holy Name. Lord, there is none like You. You have called me out to be a child of the King. Help me to live up to that name. Amen.

Read Exodus 33:17–23 and 34:1–11a

> AND THE LORD PASSED BEFORE HIM AND PROCLAIMED, "THE LORD, THE
> LORD GOD, MERCIFUL AND GRACIOUS, LONGSUFFERING, AND ABOUNDING
> IN GOODNESS AND TRUTH, KEEPING MERCY FOR THOUSANDS, FORGIVING
> INIQUITY AND TRANSGRESSION AND SIN, BY NO MEANS CLEARING THE GUILTY,
> VISITING THE INIQUITY OF THE FATHERS UPON THE CHILDREN AND THE
> CHILDREN'S CHILDREN TO THE THIRD AND THE FOURTH GENERATION."
>
> Exodus 34:6–7

Lack of obedience equates to lack of faith. Moses trusted God and because he trusted God he did what God told him to do. It must have been endlessly frustrating for Moses to observe the children of Israel's continuing lack of faith. Every time they were faced with a challenge they chose to complain instead of trusting God. This happened time and time again. They didn't seem capable of learning or changing. When Moses came down the mountain to find the children of Israel worshipping the golden image he was so angry that he smashed the tablets on the ground. Eventually, after Moses asked God to show him His glory, God renewed His covenant with the Israelites (Exodus 34:10):

> Then He said, "I will make all My goodness pass before you, and I will proclaim the name of the Lord before you. I will be gracious to whom I will be gracious, and I will have compassion on whom I will have compassion." But He said, "You cannot see My face; for no man shall see Me, and live." And the Lord said, "Here is a place by Me, and you shall stand on the rock. So it shall be, while My glory passes by, that I will put you in the cleft of the rock, and will cover you with My hand while I pass by. Then I will take away My hand, and you shall see My back; but My face shall not be seen."
>
> Exodus 33:19–23

No man can see God and live to tell the tale. God is Holy. His glory is beyond anything that we can imagine. We would be struck dead by it. God protected Moses as He passed before him. God is merciful, He is gracious, He is long-suffering and abounding in goodness; but He is a Holy, Righteous Judge. Do not play around with His mercy and grace, my friend. Be serious about your faith walk with Him. God demands and deserves our full allegiance and love. Walking by faith and not by sight means living all-out for God.

Prayer

My Holy Father in Heaven, I bow in awe and wonder before Your throne. You are a Holy and a Righteous God. You deserve all of my love, all of my obedience, all of me – 100 per cent. There is no place for a half-hearted commitment to You. I want to walk as a man of faith before You. Amen.

Read Numbers 12

> Not so with My servant Moses;
> He is faithful in all My house.
> I speak with him face to face,
> Even plainly, and not in dark sayings;
> And he sees the form of the Lord.

Numbers 12:7–8a

Moses had a special relationship with God. He saved Moses when he was a baby, helped him escape after killing the Egyptian, and appeared to him in a burning bush. All through the time it took for Pharaoh to allow the Israelites to leave, Moses' relationship with God grew stronger. Once they were out of Egypt and on their journey towards the Promised Lands Moses grew ever closer to God. This closeness was driven by Moses' dependence upon God. At every turn the people complained and moaned. It must have taken a lot of patience to deal with them.

There is no doubt, though, that Moses had a great love for his people. I am sure he learned this love at his mother's knee. Moses' destiny was to lead God's people on a journey of deliverance out of slavery and bondage. God loved Moses too. We see the evidence of this love all along his journey. We have a great example of it in our reading today. An altercation developed between Moses and his siblings, Aaron and Miriam. God took Moses' side in no uncertain terms. Read again our key verse – isn't this amazing? God says He speaks face to face with Moses. He speaks plainly to him. God even goes so far as to say that Moses saw His form.

As a result of the disagreement Miriam ends up with leprosy. Moses immediately beseeches God to heal her. Moses is gracious and forgiving. He does not hold grudges. My friend, when you walk close to God there is no time or place for pettiness in your life. When you are in a faith relationship with God your focus is upon Him, and not on the things that would try to bring you down. There is so much in our world that would try and distract us from serving God wholeheartedly. A man who chooses to walk by faith and not by sight will not be sidetracked by these things. You have a higher purpose. You have a destiny to fulfil in the same way that Moses had.

Prayer

My Father God, I come to You on bended knee. I bow my head in Your presence. I thank You that I, like Moses, have a destiny to fulfil. Help me not to become sidetracked by pettiness or disagreements. These things are only sent to lead me astray. Keep me focused and keep me faithful. Amen.

Read Numbers 32:1–13

> SO THE LORD'S ANGER WAS AROUSED AGAINST ISRAEL, AND HE MADE THEM WANDER IN THE WILDERNESS FORTY YEARS, UNTIL ALL THE GENERATION THAT HAD DONE EVIL IN THE SIGHT OF THE LORD WAS GONE.
>
> Numbers 32:13

Eventually the day came that God ran out of patience with the children of Israel. He had brought them out of Egypt. He delivered them and promised them that He would lead them to Canaan. They chose not to trust Him. Their faith was in what they could see – not in God. They chose to walk by sight and not by faith. Through it all God remained faithful. He protected them; He cared for them; He fed them and sheltered them. None of it satisfied them. After they chose not to cross the Jordan river a second time, God had had enough. So He decreed that they would wander around in the desert for forty years – until the last of those who had come out of Egypt had died.

Their behaviour is a lot like ours sometimes. We know what God expects from us, what He wants us to do, but we choose to walk our own path, instead of walking His way. You see many of us land up in the predicaments we do because we don't want to obey the Word of the Lord. Every time in my life that I have got myself into trouble, it has been because I was disobedient to what the Word of God says.

My friend, if you find yourself in this position then I urge you to turn to God's Word – confess your sins. The Bible tells us: "If we confess our sins, He is faithful and just to forgive us our sins and to cleanse us from all unrighteousness" (1 John 1:9). This is all you have to do. I don't know how many people, me included, walk around carrying burdens: sins we have committed in the past that we are so sorry about, and if we could relive our lives we would never do them again. The good news is that God does forgive us. So we can lay down our burdens right now. Learn from the mistakes of the Israelites and obey God; walk in His ways and He will give you abundant life.

Prayer

My Father, You are merciful, kind, long-suffering, faithful, and true. You love Your people with an everlasting love. Yet You are also the Righteous Judge. Lord, I stand in Your presence asking for Your forgiveness today. Forgive me, cleanse me, fill me, and use me, I pray. In Jesus' Name. Amen.

Read Hebrews 11:23–29

> By faith he forsook Egypt, not fearing the wrath of the king; for he endured as seeing Him who is invisible.
>
> Hebrews 11:27

Moses was a great man of faith. Yet, I don't believe Moses had the same amount of faith when he called the people out of Egypt as he had at the end of the forty years in the desert. No, just like you and me, Moses was on a faith journey. The more he exercised his faith, the stronger it grew. The more he opened himself up to receive from God, the greater his capacity to believe became. It is no different for us. If you want more faith then begin to exercise the faith you have. Believe God; trust Him to do what He says He is going to do. Get to know His Word and His promises: believe them; stand upon them.

When Moses observed God feeding 2.5 million people every day in the desert his faith grew. I have been to the Negev desert. Believe me, there is nothing there; not even a blade of grass to be seen – nothing, except rocks and sand. Yet, God faithfully fed those 2.5 million people for forty years. That's a miracle! Moses witnessed miracle upon miracle performed by God. Each time his faith was strengthened. Have you ever wondered why God's miracles had that effect upon Moses, yet the Israelites who experienced those same miracles did not believe? It comes down to choice, my friends. Either you are going to be open to God and His ways or you are going to close yourself off.

Moses was on a journey of deliverance. His journey required a huge amount of faith. I want to tell you, if Moses needed faith in his days, we need ten times more faith today simply to survive. The God who parted the Red Sea is the same God that you serve today. The God who brought water forth from a rock and who, for four decades, fed millions of people in a desert is your God. He is the same yesterday, today, and forever. Will you trust Him and walk the faith walk with Him?

Prayer

My Father, You are indeed the same yesterday, today, and forever. You will never change. You are as powerful today as You were in Moses' day. Help me to trust You and to believe in You. Help me to exercise my faith muscles each day so that I can grow in faith. Amen.

Read Numbers 20:1–13

THEN THE LORD SPOKE TO MOSES AND AARON, "BECAUSE YOU DID NOT BELIEVE ME, TO HALLOW ME IN THE EYES OF THE CHILDREN OF ISRAEL, THEREFORE YOU SHALL NOT BRING THIS ASSEMBLY INTO THE LAND WHICH I HAVE GIVEN THEM."

Numbers 20:12

God instructed Moses: "Take the rod... Speak to the rock before their eyes, and it will yield its water" (verse 8a). Moses was so frustrated with the children of Israel that he didn't obey God: "Then Moses lifted his hand and struck the rock twice with his rod" (verse 11a). God is no respecter of persons, my friends. He loved Moses so much, but Moses dishonoured God before the Israelites. That could not go unpunished.

You might think this was harsh after everything that Moses went through – all the years of faithful service. Isn't it sad that so near the end he fell short? It is a sober reminder to us that it is not how we start that counts, but how we finish. We need to keep pressing on to the ultimate goal – to the end of our faith journey. Paul understood this when he said: "Not that I have already attained, or am already perfected; but I press on, that I may lay hold of that for which Christ Jesus has also laid hold of me" (Philippians 3:12).

God didn't abandon Moses though, did He? We see the final scene of Moses' life play out:

> Then Moses went up from the plains of Moab to Mount Nebo, to the top of Pisgah, which is across from Jericho... Then the Lord said to him, "This is the land of which I swore to give Abraham, Isaac, and Jacob, saying, 'I will give it to your descendants.' I have caused you to see it with your eyes, but you shall not cross over there." So Moses the servant of the Lord died there in the land of Moab, according to the word of the Lord. And He buried him in a valley in the land of Moab, opposite Beth Peor; but no one knows his grave to this day... But since then there has not arisen in Israel a prophet like Moses, whom the Lord knew face to face....

Deuteronomy 34:1a, 4–6, 10 (my emphasis)

Did you notice God buried Moses, His beloved servant, Himself? God never abandoned Moses – He was with him to the very end.

Prayer

My God and Father, Your faithfulness and mercy amaze me over and over again. In the same way that You were Moses' covenant-keeping God right up to the end, so You are mine too. I thank You that I can depend upon You. Help me to keep faithful and obedient to You and Your Word. Amen.

Read Numbers 6:24–26

THE LORD BLESS YOU AND KEEP YOU; THE LORD MAKE HIS FACE SHINE UPON YOU, AND BE GRACIOUS TO YOU; THE LORD LIFT UP HIS COUNTENANCE UPON YOU, AND GIVE YOU PEACE.

Numbers 6:24–26

Moses led the children of Israel on a journey of deliverance. You and I are also on a journey. Our journey is a learning experience. I want you to realize that it's not about the destination; it's about the actual journey that you are on at this moment in time. You need to live an abundant life; you need to live life to the full. Some people live for the future, always thinking about tomorrow; or, worse, people live in the past, always looking backward. Put the past behind you. Some of us are so busy with the details of our lives that we forget to enjoy the here and now. Our ambition drives us, until one day we accomplish what we set out to do, only to find that we are still empty.

This happened to me many years ago when I packed up my family and left Zambia to come to South Africa. I believed that if I could purchase a farm in South Africa, and make a success of it, I would be happy. But I realized with time that the only thing that brings lasting satisfaction is knowing God. He alone is the Source of fulfilment. The Israelites had to learn this in the desert. It took them forty years and the sad news is that all of the Israelites who left Egypt perished in the desert. Do you know why? Yes, because they did not have faith in the Living God.

There were only two men out of 2.5 million people who crossed into the Promised Land. Have you ever thought about that? One was Joshua, and the other one was Caleb. They alone believed and obeyed God. Even Moses, Aaron, and Miriam didn't enter because they doubted. I want to urge you today to walk by faith. Each day you need to make a new choice to walk by faith. Yesterday's faith doesn't work today. Yes, you do build on each day's faith, like building blocks, one upon the other – but each day you have to choose anew to believe God.

Prayer

My Father, the way of faith is the way of blessing. Thank You for the wonderful blessing that Moses spoke out upon the children of Israel. Today, I claim this blessing for myself. The Lord bless me and keep me; the Lord make His face shine upon me, and be gracious to me; the Lord lift up His countenance upon me, and give me peace. Amen.

JUNE

JOSHUA, SAMUEL, AND JOB'S JOURNEYS

Their journeys began with commitment to God

1. The courage to wage war
2. On the mountain with God
3. Faithful in the little things
4. The persistence of faith
5. An example of what faith isn't
6. Don't run with the crowd
7. Punishment and reward
8. Joshua – God's man
9. God is with Joshua
10. Be strong and courageous
11. Samuel's godly heritage
12. The blessing of obedience
13. Obedient Samuel
14. Samuel heard from God
15. God was with Samuel
16. Israel demands a king
17. Obey the voice of the Lord
18. Samuel mourns Saul
19. Samuel anoints David
20. Samuel dies
21. Job, a blameless man
22. Job's reaction to tragedy
23. Keep on going, no matter what
24. Job's reaction to affliction
25. Job's grief
26. Though He slay me…
27. The Lord delivers the righteous
28. My Redeemer lives
29. Now my eye sees You
30. Finishing stronger

Read Exodus 17:8–16

> AND MOSES SAID TO JOSHUA, "CHOOSE US SOME MEN AND GO OUT, FIGHT
> WITH AMALEK. TOMORROW I WILL STAND ON THE TOP OF THE HILL WITH THE
> ROD OF GOD IN MY HAND." SO JOSHUA DID AS MOSES SAID TO HIM, AND
> FOUGHT WITH AMALEK.
>
> Exodus 17:9–10a

In our discussions concerning Moses' faith journey last month we saw how God miraculously undertook for the children of Israel when the Egyptian army pursued them. In Exodus chapter 17 they once again faced a foe who came to wage war against them. It was the first time they had faced attack since the Egyptians. As usual Moses turned to God to find out how he should handle the situation. Moses chose someone he could trust to lead the troops. When we read of Joshua for the first time it is apparent that he was a special young man. Our key verse tells us: "So Joshua did as Moses said to him." We don't see any of the questioning, arguing, moaning, or complaining that is so typical of the majority of the Israelites. Joshua simply obeyed. He obeyed Moses, yes, but ultimately he was obeying God, wasn't he?

We see Joshua exhibiting some of the courage that characterized his entire life. A life of faith is a life of courage, my friend. Faith definitely takes courage, because so often the act of stepping out and walking by faith means going against popular opinion, logic, and so-called wisdom. A man of faith knows that the only wisdom that ultimately counts is God's wisdom, shared through His Spirit and His Word with those who will listen. Hearing from God is our lifeline. Believe me, you cannot afford to listen to anyone else. Joshua understood this. He knew that it was God who would give him victory.

God is looking for modern-day men like Joshua. Men who have the courage of their convictions. He wants men who will stand up and be counted for Him. God is the same God of power who helped Joshua gain victory over the Amalekites. As we have mentioned before, Moses built an altar and called the name of the place "The-Lord-Is-My-Banner" (verse 15). God is our Banner. He stands firmly behind every man of courage who steps out in faith in His Name. As we spend time learning faith lessons from Joshua's life, ask God to show you the areas where you need to grow in courage and obedience to Him.

Prayer

Dear Lord, I thank You for the testimony of a man of courage like Joshua. I want to be known as a man of courage too. A man who obeys You no matter what. I ask You to fill me with Your Spirit, Lord. Help me to step out and be available to You. Amen.

ON THE MOUNTAIN WITH GOD

Read Exodus 24:1–12

THEN THE LORD SAID TO MOSES, "COME UP TO ME ON THE MOUNTAIN
AND BE THERE; AND I WILL GIVE YOU TABLETS OF STONE, AND THE LAW AND
COMMANDMENTS WHICH I HAVE WRITTEN, THAT YOU MAY TEACH THEM."

Exodus 24:12

Growing in God and being used by Him means spending time with Him. I have often shared with you how I love to go up into the mountains and spend time with God. The title of one of my previous devotional books was *Time on the Mountain*. I want to share with you some of the words I wrote for the preface of that book, as they are so relevant to what we are talking about today.

Time spent with God is the most critical responsibility of any believer. It will determine the depth of your relationship with God. If we look at Titus 1:16 the Bible says: "They say they love God, but by their actions they deny Him." It is no use telling somebody you love them but you never ever spend time with them. The same applies to God. I read a beautiful story many years ago where the writer said, "first the mountain and then the ministry". We cannot hope to help others if we are not spending regular time with God. So we need to go up the mountain first to hear from God. We must follow Jesus' example. Only then can we go down into the valley and meet the needs that are waiting there.

Often we use the excuse that we are too busy to spend a prolonged period of time with God. The bottom line is we can never spend enough time with God. So the busier we get the earlier we should get up in the morning. That is what Martin Luther did: the more he was used by God to help others, the earlier he would rise in the morning to have his quiet time. I often share with people how I love to go up into the Drakensberg Mountains to spend time with God. Nothing can take the place of that "alone time" with Him. It is in those alone times that God speaks and it is then that He imparts His power. Remember, my friend: "first the mountain and then the ministry".

Prayer
My Father in Heaven, You speak so clearly to me. I know that the only way to grow in You, the only way to be powerfully used by You, is to spend time in Your presence. Lord, forgive me that so often I want to take short cuts. I love You and want to spend time with You. Amen.

Read Exodus 24:12–18

So Moses arose with his assistant Joshua, and Moses went up to the mountain of God.

Exodus 24:13

We saw that when Moses sent Joshua out to war he did not shrink from the task that Moses set before him. He didn't ask questions or make excuses. He was a man who obeyed God. He was a man of faith who trusted God to undertake for him. He was a loyal person who supported his leader, Moses. It was these qualities that led to him becoming Moses's trusted assistant. God had a plan and a purpose for Joshua's life. Day by day, Joshua learned to depend upon God one situation at a time. With each challenge that presented itself he chose to turn to God and believe in Him. Joshua's faith grew because he was faithful in the small things, my friend. His obedience and faithfulness led to God being able to entrust him with bigger and bigger assignments.

How is it in your life? Are you faithful in the small things? Are you careful to obey God when no one else is looking? In Matthew 25 Jesus told the parable of the talents. The master said the same thing to two of his servants: "His lord said to him, "Well done, good and faithful servant; you were faithful over a few things, I will make you ruler over many things. Enter into the joy of your lord'" (verse 21).

However, it was a different kettle of fish altogether when it came to the servant who wasn't faithful. Then the master had no mercy (read verses 24–28). Jesus further said: "For to everyone who has, more will be given, and he will have abundance; but from him who does not have, even what he has will be taken away" (verse 29). Jesus was not being unfair or unkind when He told this parable. No, He was telling us how important faithfulness is. Ultimately Joshua's faithfulness led to him being entrusted with one of the most important assignments in the history of the world. God has a plan and a purpose for your life – but it requires you living a life of faithfulness and obedience. God honours faithfulness.

Prayer

My Father God, I know that You have a plan and a purpose for my life. I pray that You will help me to be faithful in the day to day things. My faith will grow as I walk with You. I want to be a man who is obedient to You, Lord, in every area of my life. Amen.

Read Exodus 33:7–11

So the Lord spoke to Moses face to face, as a man speaks to his friend. And he would return to the camp, but his servant Joshua the son of Nun, a young man, did not depart from the tabernacle.

Exodus 33:11

The Word tells us: "So Moses went into the midst of the cloud and went up into the mountain. And Moses was on the mountain forty days and forty nights" (Exodus 24:18). For forty days Joshua waited while God spoke to Moses. He didn't waver; he patiently waited as God gave Moses the Ten Commandments. Can you imagine the dedication that it took to sit up on that mountain? I am sure that Joshua didn't really understand all that was happening, but he knew that God wanted him there and that was enough for him. God finished giving Moses the Law and they made their way down the mountain.

It was Joshua who alerted Moses to the fact that there was something wrong in the camp as they came down the mountain (Exodus 32:17). As they approached they saw the golden calf that the Israelites had made to worship. Joshua was not a part of the false worship of Israel. Instead he was sitting in God's presence waiting on the Lord. In our reading today we see that once again Joshua was where the presence of God was. He accompanied Moses out of the camp to meet with God. There they pitched the tent and called it the Tabernacle of Meeting. "So the Lord spoke to Moses face to face, as a man speaks to his friend." Can you imagine what it must have been like to witness that? Joshua did.

Joshua did not depart from the Tabernacle – he faithfully remained in the presence of the Lord. Nothing was more important to him than being in God's presence. Do you long for the presence of the Lord in this way? Is it your greatest joy to sit with God? My dear friends, I am sure that if we had this kind of relationship with God so many of the things that hold us back from living by faith and not by sight would simply evaporate in the power of His presence. He wants the same relationship with you that He had with Joshua.

Prayer

My Father God, forgive me that so often I am all too eager to move on and go about my business. Lord, help me to become more interested in Your business than my own. Help me to learn from Joshua's life what it means to be persistently faithful to You. Amen.

Read Numbers 13:21–33

BUT THE MEN WHO HAD GONE UP WITH HIM SAID, "WE ARE NOT ABLE TO GO UP AGAINST THE PEOPLE, FOR THEY ARE STRONGER THAN WE."

Numbers 13:31

Here we have a classic example of what faith isn't. After everything God had done for them; after all the miracles that they had witnessed – the children of Israel still didn't trust God to undertake for them. He had delivered them out of Egypt in order to take them to the Promised Land. They stand on the doorstep, as it were, and they refuse to step over the threshold because of fear. Can you relate to this, my friends? Maybe you have stood at the brink of blessing, but unbelief has prevented you from taking the first step out of the boat.

Remember that Hebrews 11:6 tells us: "But without faith it is impossible to please Him, for he who comes to God must believe that He is, and that He is a rewarder of those who diligently seek Him." We always focus on the first part of the verse, but take a look at the second phrase: "for he who comes to God must believe that He is". If you have trouble believing God it is because you have never seen God for who He really is. Last month we saw that He revealed Himself to Moses as Jehovah – the covenant-keeping God. God is always faithful, my friend. The question is: are you? Don't allow fear to keep you from experiencing God's blessing in your life.

Out of the twelve men who went on the fact-finding mission, it was only Caleb and Joshua who came back with a positive report. Caleb said: "Let us go up at once and take possession, for we are well able to overcome it" (verse 30b). They saw with the eyes of faith instead of the eyes of doubt. The other men would have none of it and they convinced the people with their negative report. We need to be careful what we say. So often we can be tempted to speak our negative thoughts to others, which can erode their faith, causing them to mistrust and disbelieve God. Take a lesson from Caleb and Joshua – speak hope and faith into situations.

Prayer

Dear Father, this is a sober reminder of the consequences of negativity and lack of faith. Lord, after You have done so much for me and shown me in so many ways that You love me, please forgive me for those times when I doubt You. Lord, I want to walk forward in faith. Amen.

Read Numbers 13:21–33

THERE WE SAW THE GIANTS (THE DESCENDANTS OF ANAK CAME FROM THE GIANTS); AND WE WERE LIKE GRASSHOPPERS IN OUR OWN SIGHT, AND SO WE WERE IN THEIR SIGHT.

Numbers 13:33

What I love about Joshua is his faithfulness to Moses, but obviously also to God. Moses climbed up Mount Sinai to receive instructions from God as to how to lead the children of Israel. The Israelites grew tired of waiting for Moses to come down the mountain so they persuaded Aaron to make a golden calf for them to worship. They committed idolatry. As I said a few days ago, Joshua had no part of this pagan worship. He was where his master was; he was where the presence of God was. Joshua was a great man of faith.

Moses sent twelve spies into Canaan to scout the land. The twelve returned; ten came back with negative reports and only two gave positive reports. It was only Joshua and Caleb who saw the opportunities instead of the problems. Joshua would look at a mountain and see it as a molehill; whereas the other ten spies only saw the mountain. The Bible tells us very clearly that because of this the giants saw these men as grasshoppers, and so they became as grasshoppers. The Word says, "There we saw the giants (the descendants of Anak came from the giants); and we were like grasshoppers in our own sight, and so we were in their sight."

The ten spies doubted. Why? Because they looked at the enemy, they looked at the situation and they looked at themselves. Caleb and Joshua had faith, not in the situation or themselves – no, they had faith in God. This is the difference between a mighty man of God and an ordinary man. The challenge is the same, but the perspective is vastly different. What I really appreciate about Joshua is his steadfastness and his faithfulness to God. He did not run with the crowd. I have often spoken about how it takes a live fish to swim against the current, and a dead fish to flow with the current. It is very easy to go with the crowd. Joshua however, was not a man who was influenced in any way by the crowd.

Prayer

My Father in Heaven, I thank You that You have called me to walk by faith. It is not a blind faith that You ask for, but rather a considered faith – a faith where I choose, despite what is happening around me, to look to You and place my trust in You. I will not run with the crowd. Amen.

Read Numbers 14:1–30

> EXCEPT FOR CALEB THE SON OF JEPHUNNEH AND JOSHUA THE SON OF NUN,
> YOU SHALL BY NO MEANS ENTER THE LAND WHICH I SWORE I WOULD MAKE
> YOU DWELL IN.
>
> Numbers 14:30

Wasn't this a tragic outcome to what was supposed to be a victory for God's people? They chose to believe a lie rather than the truth. They chose to walk by sight and not by faith. They chose to accept the bad report rather than the good report. Where did it get them? Absolutely nowhere – it brought down God's punishment upon them. God had had enough; His patience had run out and He brought down judgment upon Israel. Joshua and Caleb were horrified at the reaction of their fellow Israelites; they pleaded with them to trust God rather than man, but to no avail.

> *But Joshua the son of Nun and Caleb the son of Jephunneh, who were among those who had spied out the land, tore their clothes; and they spoke to all the congregation of the children of Israel, saying: "The land we passed through to spy out is an exceedingly good land. If the Lord delights in us, then He will bring us into this land and give it to us, "a land which flows with milk and honey.' Only do not rebel against the Lord, nor fear the people of the land, for they are our bread; their protection has departed from them, and the Lord is with us. Do not fear them."*
>
> Numbers 14:6–9

This is a sobering passage of Scripture that we are dealing with today, my friends. We serve a God of love and grace; but He is also God Almighty, and He demands obedience from His children. For Joshua and Caleb it was a simple matter: if God said it, then He would do it. The size of the enemy didn't matter – it was only God's Word that was important to them. So God punished the rest of the Israelites, but He rewarded Joshua and Caleb for their faith. "But without faith it is impossible to please Him, for he who comes to God must believe that He is, and that He is a rewarder of those who diligently seek Him" (Hebrews 11:6). In whom are you placing your trust?

Prayer
My Father God, You are God Almighty. I bow before You and acknowledge You as Holy and Righteous. Lord, You demand obedience from Your children. Help me, Lord, I pray, to walk in faith with You. I choose to trust You above my circumstances and people. Amen.

Read Deuteronomy 31:1–23

> THEN HE INAUGURATED JOSHUA THE SON OF NUN, AND SAID, "BE STRONG
> AND OF GOOD COURAGE; FOR YOU SHALL BRING THE CHILDREN OF ISRAEL
> INTO THE LAND OF WHICH I SWORE TO THEM, AND I WILL BE WITH YOU."
>
> Deuteronomy 31:23

Joshua was God's man – His chosen one to take the children of Israel across the River Jordan into the Promised Land. God appointed Joshua to do it. Joshua was eighty years old when he led the Israelites into the land of milk and honey. He had served his apprenticeship. He had served Moses for forty years in the desert. He was fully equipped and qualified. This is such an important point to remember. Joshua was not inexperienced. If we want to be used by God we need to be humble enough to carry a man of God's suitcase as it were, to serve him in order to receive the anointing.

Joshua was a very bold and brave man. He'd paid his dues in the desert, so when he met with the enemy in the land of Canaan they didn't frighten him at all. The reason he wasn't frightened was because he had seen the miracles God had performed through Moses over the years: miracles like parting the Red Sea so that the children of Israel could walk through and feeding an entire nation for forty years with manna from Heaven every single day, ensuring that the animals and children didn't perish in the desert. Joshua was a man who grew in faith and stature as he observed with his physical as well as his spiritual eyes the faithfulness of his God. Therefore nothing could deter him.

People who desire to operate in faith need to start small and then allow God to grow them into men who can perform great miracles for Him. Joshua was a man on a journey. He did not allow the enormity of the journey to frighten him because his faith and his courage were in God. He knew that the same God who had walked with Moses all the years would lead and guide him as well. When he spent all that time at the Tent of Meeting with Moses while he waited on God, Joshua too learned to wait on God. So Joshua knew that he wasn't alone on his journey.

Prayer
My Father God, thank You for the lessons I am learning from the life of Your servant Joshua. He truly was a man of faith, a man of substance, a mighty man for You. Lord, help me too to be faithful to You, humble, obedient, and patient, as You work out Your purposes in my life. Amen.

Read Joshua 6

> So the Lord was with Joshua, and his fame spread throughout all the country.
>
> Joshua 6:27

This must surely be one of the most exciting stories in Scripture. Can you picture it? What an amazing sight! The armed men, then the seven priests holding the seven rams' horns, followed by the Ark of the Lord bringing up the rear of the procession. This is not your average battle plan, is it? Can you imagine an army general coming up with a plan such as this? No, I am sure they would laugh off an idea like this; they would think it would be sure to fail.

It reminds me of this Scripture: "Some trust in chariots, and some in horses; But we will remember the name of the Lord our God" (Psalm 20:7). The way of the world is to trust in our own plans and strategies. The spiritual way is to trust in God and God alone. He is the One who can deliver us from our enemy. He is the One who can make a way when there seems to be no way. For Joshua it meant trusting God's way, not his own. He had to be willing to put aside his own ideas and do what God was telling him to do. Joshua learned to trust God over many years. He chose on many occasions to walk by faith and not by sight. These choices meant that when the time came he was able to lead the children of Israel in God's ways.

God was with Joshua. What about you, my friend? Are you at a place in your life where you have a wall of Jericho that needs to come down? If so, how are you tackling your problem? Are you stressing yourself out trying to come up with a man-made solution, or are you waiting on God, listening to His voice and expecting Him to give you the solution? Our plans will come to nought – His plans will always succeed, bringing glory to His Name. God was with Joshua and He will be with you too. Walk in His ways, obey His commands, and place your faith in Him.

Prayer

My Father God, thank You for the wonderful encouragement of the story about the walls of Jericho coming down. I know that the walls in my life are no challenge at all for You. Help me to wait on You, to be attentive, and to obey Your commands to me. Amen.

Read Joshua 1

HAVE I NOT COMMANDED YOU? BE STRONG AND OF GOOD COURAGE; DO
NOT BE AFRAID, NOR BE DISMAYED, FOR THE LORD YOUR GOD IS WITH YOU
WHEREVER YOU GO.

Joshua 1:9

God spoke these words directly to Joshua. Moses was dead and God had entrusted
Joshua with the job of leading the children of Israel into the Promised Land. We read a
few days ago how Joshua had been many years in training for this assignment, having
faithfully served both God and Moses. We also noted how, when everyone else was off
doing their own thing, Joshua remained at the Tent of Meeting. He didn't want to miss
anything that God might do or say. Joshua was not only a man of faith, he was also a
faithful man. He was just the person that God needed to take His people through the
final steps of entering their Promised Land.

Joshua was up for the task, not because of his own strength – he was a very strong
man: physically, morally, and emotionally – but it was his spiritual strength that made
him the ideal person for the job. As we said yesterday, this strength was built up over
many years from the time when he was a young man serving Moses: "Joshua the son
of Nun, Moses' assistant, one of his choice men" (Numbers 11:28a). Joshua made his
choices and he stuck with them. He told the people, "choose for yourselves this day
whom you will serve... But as for me and my house, we will serve the Lord" (Joshua
24:15).

Each of us face challenges in our lives that seem impossible when viewed in our
own strength. My friend, if you are walking by faith, living in God's Word and in His
will, then you can know that you are not alone. In the same way that God was with
Joshua, He is with you and me. If you have chosen to serve Him then He is for you,
and if He is for you, who can be against you? I want you to repeat our key Scripture
out loud inserting your own name. "Have I not commanded you, X? Be strong and of
good courage; do not be afraid, nor be dismayed, for the Lord your God is with you
wherever you go." This is God's Word to you.

Prayer

*My Father, as I repeat Your Word to me I am filled with faith, courage, and strength. In You I
can do anything. I choose to serve You and You alone. I choose to walk by faith and not by sight.
I choose to praise You, to worship You, and to honour Your Holy Name. Amen.*

Read 1 Samuel 1

> "FOR THIS CHILD I PRAYED, AND THE LORD HAS GRANTED ME MY PETITION
> WHICH I ASKED OF HIM. THEREFORE I ALSO HAVE LENT HIM TO THE LORD;
> AS LONG AS HE LIVES HE SHALL BE LENT TO THE LORD." SO THEY WORSHIPED
> THE LORD THERE.
>
> 1 Samuel 1:27–28

When Samuel was born he was a much-wanted and much-loved baby. His mother Hannah had waited many years to conceive. She had at one point become quite desperate. She took her distress to the Lord. "And she was in bitterness of soul, and prayed to the Lord and wept in anguish" (verse 10). Hannah promised God that if He gave her a male child: "I will give him to the Lord all the days of his life, and no razor shall come upon his head" (verse 11b). Eli the priest watched her praying and he mistook her sadness for drunkenness. When he realized what her problem was, he had compassion for her. He said, "Go in peace, and the God of Israel grant your petition which you have asked of Him" (verse 17).

In due course Hannah fell pregnant and had a baby boy. She named him Samuel. True to her word, once she had weaned him, she took Samuel to the temple and presented him to Eli, the High Priest. Who would have blamed Hannah if after Samuel was born she simply couldn't bear to part with him? After all, she had waited so long, surely God would understand. To Hannah a promise was a promise. She fulfilled her vow to God. In doing this Hannah secured a godly heritage for her son. Her actions set the course for his life.

Samuel was probably the godliest of all the prophets in the Bible. He never ever fell into disgrace. He was faithful to his God right to the very end of his life. When we look through God's Word we see that many of the leaders such as Moses, Noah, and Solomon (more of him later) started well, but they didn't finish strong. Not Samuel, though. From the day that his mother took him to the temple – when he was little more than a toddler – until the day he died, Samuel never disappointed or forsook the Lord. Hannah set the example for Samuel. She presented him to Eli with these inspiring words: "… as long as he lives he shall be lent to the Lord" (verse 28).

Prayer

My Father God, You are a covenant-keeping God. You are faithful from generation to generation. You love Your people, and You show Your loving kindness to Your children. Thank You, Lord, that I am Your child. I want to walk in faith with You. Amen.

Read 1 Samuel 2:1–21

> AND THE LORD VISITED HANNAH, SO THAT SHE CONCEIVED AND BORE THREE
> SONS AND TWO DAUGHTERS. MEANWHILE THE CHILD SAMUEL GREW BEFORE
> THE LORD.
>
> 1 Samuel 2:21

God blesses obedience, my friends. We can never out-give God. When Hannah took Samuel to the temple it seemed as if she was giving up everything. However, in reality what she was doing was opening the way for God to bless her beyond measure. Not only did she have the joy of seeing her firstborn grow up to serve God, but she knew the joy of motherhood five more times. God blessed her abundantly. So often we hold back from obeying God because we cannot see the end from the beginning. We look at the situation in front of us and it seems impossible. So what do we do? We make our own way; we find our own solution. The result of doing this is usually disastrous.

As I have said before, every mistake I have made, every mess I have landed myself in throughout my life, has been because I did it my way instead of God's way. Hannah continued to exert a godly influence over Samuel. Our reading tells us that every year when Hannah and her husband, Elkanah, went up to the feast she took Samuel a little robe that she made for him. Hannah continued to care for and love Samuel.

How proud she must have been year after year to see him grow. Hannah must have felt so blessed when she saw how God was using Samuel. She is an example to us. Her choices tell us that we shouldn't hesitate to choose obedience over our own wishes and desires. Obedience takes faith. Faith is based upon hope. Hebrews 11:1 says: "Now faith is the substance of things hoped for, the evidence of things not seen." Everything of significance that has ever been achieved for God down through the ages has been done through faith. "But without faith it is impossible to please Him, for he who comes to God must believe that He is, and that He is a rewarder of those who diligently seek Him" (Hebrews 11:6). Is there something that you need to bring before the Lord and offer to Him today?

Prayer

Lord, help me to lay my all at the altar of sacrifice. I realize that I can never out-give You, my Father. Thank You that You love me and that You have called me to serve You. Lord, I want to give you my life 100 per cent. There is nothing that I want to hold back from You. Amen.

Read 1 Samuel 3:1–7

(NOW SAMUEL DID NOT YET KNOW THE LORD, NOR WAS THE WORD OF THE
LORD YET REVEALED TO HIM.)

1 Samuel 3:7

We have already said that Samuel came from a godly heritage. His father and mother were people of faith. They were obedient to God; they worshipped Him and they loved Him. Samuel grew up in the temple. He worked there with Eli the High Priest and became his right-hand man. As he grew Samuel learned to obey Eli. Our Scripture tells us that he "did not yet know the Lord". God had not, up to that point in time, spoken directly to Samuel. He had knowledge of God. He spent his days serving God in His temple. But Samuel didn't know God personally. He had not yet communicated with God; nor had God communicated with him.

Obedience was a theme that would run throughout Samuel's life. One of the lessons for us to learn from his life is that obedience is a day-by-day walk with God. We can see that he obeyed God in the small things. This lifestyle of obedience led to his being able to be used in a mighty way by God throughout his life. When it comes to our lives, we so often are looking for the big assignments. We want the grand gestures. Yet, what God wants most from us is a daily walk of obedience. He wants us to be faithful in the small things. "He who is faithful in what is least is faithful also in much" (Luke 16:10a).

God is not as interested in what we do for Him as He is in how we live for Him. He places a high premium upon obedience. If you look at all of the great men of faith throughout history, obedience was a key component of their walk with the Lord. We cannot say that we love God if we are not obedient to Him. The Bible tells us: "You shall love the Lord your God with all your heart, with all your soul, and with all your strength" (Deuteronomy 6:5). If you love God in this way then obedience will be the outworking of your love.

Prayer

My Father in Heaven, You are a great and an awesome God. You have shown Your love from generation to generation. Down through the ages You have called men to serve and love You. Lord, I want to be known above all as a man who obeys and loves You. Amen.

Read 1 Samuel 3:8–21

> NOW THE LORD CAME AND STOOD AND CALLED AS AT OTHER TIMES,
> "SAMUEL! SAMUEL!" AND SAMUEL ANSWERED, "SPEAK, FOR YOUR SERVANT
> HEARS."
>
> 1 Samuel 3:10

In the Hebrew language the word for "listen" and the word for "obey" is the same. So as far as the Israelites were concerned, if you listened then you were obedient, and if you obeyed it meant that you had listened. We often say to children: "Listen to me!" What we mean when we say this is, "I want you to obey me and do what I am telling you to do." So there is only one word for both listen and obey. Samuel was a prime example of what it means to live in "listening-obedience" to God.

How did his life of obedience begin? It began by his listening to God. We read about Samuel's first encounter with hearing the voice of God. Not only did Samuel have to be willing to hear what God said to him; but he also had to be willing to share it. We see the listening and the obedience working hand in hand here. Samuel was a young boy and it must have been a great temptation for him not to tell Eli what God has said. It was not an easy word. It was a word of judgment upon Eli's family. Samuel showed tremendous courage. I wonder if he had shrunk from obeying God's voice in this instance if God would have been able to use him so mightily throughout the rest of his life.

From a young age Samuel learned and chose to walk with God. He chose to listen to the voice of the Lord and to obey what God said to him irrespective of what it was. He was faithful to the end, and what impresses me most about Samuel was his faithfulness to God rather than to men. He was totally committed to the Lord. Throughout his life Samuel never wavered in his commitment to God's Word and God's Truth. There were times in Samuel's life where obeying God was painful and meant that he suffered as a result of it. This never stopped him, though – he listened, heard, and obeyed, no matter what the cost.

Prayer

My Father God, I bow in Your presence and praise Your Holy Name. You are a great God. There is none like You. You speak to me in so many different ways. Help me to listen to You. When I am listening, help me to hear and then to obey Your commands, no matter what. Amen.

Read 1 Samuel 7

> SO THE PHILISTINES WERE SUBDUED, AND THEY DID NOT COME ANYMORE
> INTO THE TERRITORY OF ISRAEL. AND THE HAND OF THE LORD WAS AGAINST
> THE PHILISTINES ALL THE DAYS OF SAMUEL.
>
> 1 Samuel 7:13

Exactly as God said He would, He dealt with Eli's family. The nation of Israel went through troubled times; they wandered away from following God. They found themselves at war with the Philistines. When they were facing defeat they took the Ark of the Lord thinking it would help them to win. Instead they were defeated, and as part of the spoils of war the Philistines took the Ark of the Lord. This displeased God greatly, and He sent a plague upon the Philistine men (1 Samuel 5). In chapter 6 we read that they returned the Ark and it remained in Kirjath Jearim for twenty years. The people then approached Samuel, requesting him to intercede before the Lord for them. Samuel gathered them together at Mizpah and he prayed for them.

When the Philistines heard that the children of Israel had gathered together they went up against them. The Israelites were fearful of the Philistines, but God undertook and He caused confusion among them. This meant that the children of Israel were able to destroy the Philistines. All of this happened because the Lord intervened and undertook for them. He did this not because they deserved it, but because Samuel asked Him to. The Israelites were so far from God that they didn't see that their strength lay in Him and Him alone. He was the One who helped them to overcome their enemies, not their military prowess. God did it because Samuel, His faithful servant, beseeched Him to do so.

Our verse tells us that the Philistines were subdued and that they did not bother Israel again for as long as Samuel lived. God blessed Israel because of Samuel's obedience to Him. Samuel was God's prophet to Israel. He travelled throughout the land judging the people. Samuel continued to live a life of obedience and faith irrespective of what the people were doing around him. Samuel was not influenced by the behaviour of other people. He stayed true and strong. As a result God blessed his life and made him a blessing to others.

Prayer

My Father God, thank You that You are my Help, my Strength, and my Fortress. I have no other help but You. Lord, I come before You today and I ask You to help me to defeat the enemies who have come up against me. I know that I can only do this in Your strength. Amen.

Read 1 Samuel 12:1–24

> IF YOU FEAR THE LORD AND SERVE HIM AND OBEY HIS VOICE, AND DO NOT
> REBEL AGAINST THE COMMANDMENT OF THE LORD, THEN BOTH YOU AND THE
> KING WHO REIGNS OVER YOU WILL CONTINUE FOLLOWING THE LORD YOUR
> GOD.
>
> 1 Samuel 12:14

For many years Samuel was the voice of the Lord to the people of Israel. God would speak to Samuel, and then Samuel would speak to the people. He ruled wisely and fairly; he was faithful to God, listened to Him and obeyed all that the Lord told him. Sadly, though, Samuel's sons (like Eli's) did not follow in their father's footsteps. They did not walk in the ways of the Lord. The people came to Samuel in chapter 8 and they demanded a king to rule over them. Samuel was unhappy about this, and as usual he took the matter to God. God told him that He would grant the people's request.

Between chapters 8 and 12 we see the process of Saul being chosen as king of Israel. Our reading today speaks of his coronation. Whenever God chooses a man for a job He gives him what he needs to fulfil the assignment. "Then the Spirit of the Lord will come upon you, and you will prophesy with them and be turned into another man. So it was, when he had turned his back to go from Samuel, that God gave him another heart" (1 Samuel 10:6, 9a).

Once again, in the matter of choosing a king, Samuel obeyed God down to the last syllable of what He said to him. "And now here is the king, walking before you; and I am old and grayheaded, and look, my sons are with you. I have walked before you from my childhood to this day" (1 Samuel 12:2). Even though the children of Israel didn't get it, Samuel understood that all they needed was God. They didn't need an earthly king when they had the Heavenly King. Instead of trusting God they wanted to find their own solutions to their problems. It is the same with us sometimes: we think that we can do a better job than God. Men particularly feel that they have to be the ones coming up with the answers. My friends, God has the answer and He is the Answer to whatever your need is.

Prayer
My Father God, I realize that so often I fall into the trap of trying to sort things out for myself. I look for earthly solutions and use human logic. You have reminded me today that You are the Answer to my every need, to my every challenge, and to every situation in my life. Amen.

Read 1 Samuel 15:1–23

> So Samuel said: "Has the Lord as great delight in burnt offerings and sacrifices, as in obeying the voice of the Lord? Behold, to obey is better than sacrifice, and to heed than the fat of rams."
>
> 1 Samuel 15:22

Obedience has always been of paramount importance to God. Despite everything that God had given to Saul, he was not an obedient man. In chapter 13 we see that he is pressurized by the people and he makes the sacrifice himself instead of waiting for Samuel. When Samuel arrives he tells Saul: "But now your kingdom shall not continue. The Lord has sought for Himself a man after His own heart, and the Lord has commanded him to be commander over His people, because you have not kept what the Lord commanded you" (1 Samuel 13:14).

In chapter 15 we see that Saul again disobeys the commands of God. His excuse to Samuel: "I have sinned, for I have transgressed the commandment of the Lord and your words, because I feared the people and obeyed their voice" (verse 24). As a result of his disobedience Saul is rejected as king. Samuel was not intimidated by any man, not even the king of Israel – Saul. He obeyed God to the letter when God told him to anoint the next king of Israel after Saul had lost his anointing.

We are confronted with choices every day of our lives. The choice is to do things God's way or our own way. God's Word is very clear about how He wants us to live. My friends, like Samuel we have to choose obedience or disobedience. Whatever the situation you are facing in your life right now, ask yourself the following questions. Are you listening to God? If you are and He speaks to you – are you hearing Him? Once you have heard Him, the choice is obedience or disobedience. Very often obedience comes with a price attached to it. There are times when because you obey God's voice you will not be very popular with some people. That is OK as long as you are following His will: living your life with love and integrity. You can trust God to take care of the other details. Our job is to listen, to hear, and to obey.

Prayer

My Father, You are so clear in Your Word that obedience is key to my experiencing and enjoying Your blessing upon my life. Lord, I want to walk in obedience to You above everything. Help me to drown out all other voices other than Yours speaking to me. Amen.

Read 1 Samuel 15:24 – 16:5

> AND SAMUEL WENT NO MORE TO SEE SAUL UNTIL THE DAY OF HIS DEATH.
> NEVERTHELESS SAMUEL MOURNED FOR SAUL, AND THE LORD REGRETTED
> THAT HE HAD MADE SAUL KING OVER ISRAEL.
>
> 1 Samuel 15:35

Despite the fact that Samuel was against the people's desire for an earthly king, he had obviously grown fond of King Saul. It was clearly a great source of sorrow to him that Saul had not shaped up to be the king that God had called him to be. Even though God had given Saul a change of heart and placed His Spirit upon him, Saul still had to choose to walk with God. Each day he had to choose whether he would obey God or not. We see from Saul's life that he chose disobedience. He was more concerned with what man thought than with what God did. Saul never learned what Samuel had learned at a very young age: obedience is better than sacrifice.

So we see a very human side to Samuel as he mourns Saul. He no doubt mourned the waste of so much potential for good. The Word tells us that Saul was an impressive man. Throughout the story of Samuel's life the theme repeats itself that God does not look on the outward appearance. God looks upon and judges what He finds in a person's heart. So often we see that men who are serving God have big personalities and presence. They are charismatic leaders and people flock to them. This is great and it is an amazing thing to see God's hand upon someone's life as they serve Him and He uses them. However, sadly we all too often see high-profile men of God falling and bringing disgrace upon the Name of the Lord.

Each one of us has to be mindful of how we walk before the Lord. We are to serve Him and live lives based upon truth as well as integrity. We might not have an earthly kingdom to lose, but we do have a Heavenly one. We need to remember God's Word and His dealings with His people down through the ages. No matter what the temptation is that faces us, we must choose to walk in obedience before Him. Fear God and not man.

Prayer

My Father, Your Word is Truth and Your Word is Light. It is a lamp to my feet as I follow You and live for You. Jesus, You are the Way, the Truth, and the Life. In You I have everything that I need to live a life of obedience. I want nothing more than to honour You. Amen.

Read 1 Samuel 16:4–13

AND THE LORD SAID, "ARISE, ANOINT HIM; FOR THIS IS THE ONE!"

1 Samuel 16:12b

The Lord commanded Samuel to go to the house of Jesse. He told him that He had chosen a king from among Jesse's eight sons. It seemed obvious and logical from a human perspective that the new king would be Jesse's eldest son. It might have been easy for Samuel to be persuaded to think that he was the right choice. Samuel looked at all seven young men who stood before him. Then he did what he had been doing his whole life: he waited for the Lord to talk to him. When the Lord started talking he listened carefully. Then he obeyed the Lord.

The Lord told him that none of the seven were to be the new king. Samuel asked Jesse if he had any other sons. Up until that moment all of them had forgotten about David, who was out in the fields tending the sheep. Jesse sent for David. The moment he walked into the room the Lord said, "Arise, anoint him; for this is the one!" Samuel immediately anointed him with oil and proclaimed that he would be the next king of Israel. David was a young boy, and no doubt Samuel was reminded of how young he himself was when he began serving the Lord.

Again we see the matter of the heart coming up. When Samuel looks at Eliab and believes him to be God's chosen king, God says to Samuel, "Do not look at his appearance or at his physical stature, because I have refused him. For the Lord does not see as man sees; for man looks at the outward appearance, but the Lord looks at the heart" (verse 7). God isn't really interested in how clever or educated you are. He doesn't care about when you were born or what class you are from, whether you are rich or poor. God really isn't concerned about what your profession is. What concerns Him is whether you have a heart that is for Him. He wants to know whether you will obey Him above everyone and everything else. God wants to know that He has your absolute allegiance – does He?

Prayer

My Father God, I come before You in the precious Name of Jesus, my Saviour and Lord. Father, You have called me to be Your child. You have given me a new life and a new heart. Lord, help me to keep my heart pure and committed to You, no matter what the temptation. Amen.

Read 1 Samuel 28:1–20

> NOW SAMUEL HAD DIED, AND ALL ISRAEL HAD LAMENTED FOR HIM AND
> BURIED HIM IN RAMAH, IN HIS OWN CITY.
>
> 1 Samuel 28:3a

It can truly be said of Samuel that he was a man after God's own heart. He loved God above all else. His whole life was dedicated to serving God. From the time that his mother, Hannah, took him to the temple as a toddler to his dying breath, Samuel walked with God. He carried out God's commands. Samuel did exactly what God told him to do – no more and no less. He judged among the people fairly and with integrity. He took nothing from any man. Samuel knew that God and God alone was his Source.

He was a man who walked by faith and not by sight. He learned to discern God's voice that very first night when God called to him as a young boy, and he answered, "Speak, for Your servant hears" (1 Samuel 3:10b). Samuel was not only a man of faith, but he was also an extremely faithful man. As we said before, in the Hebrew language the word for listen and obey is the same word. He learned to hear God's voice as a young boy; he also learned to listen to what God had to say to him. Then, even more importantly than hearing and listening, he obeyed. When he uttered the words to Saul, "to obey is better than sacrifice", he was testifying to the norm by which he had lived his life.

Samuel was not a respecter of persons. King or common man: he shared God's Word with them. He was not impressed in any way by rank or by station. He only submitted himself to God. He did not shrink back from the hard messages. He faithfully said what God told him to say. That is why God was able to so powerfully use Samuel. As you have spent the past few days looking at Samuel's life, what has God been saying to you through His Spirit? I hope that you have been inspired by this great man of faith. My friends, how has God challenged you, and what are you going to do about it?

Prayer

My God and Father, thank You for the life of Samuel. Thank You that You have spoken to me through Your Word as I have been reading and thinking upon this great man of faith. Help me to live for You alone. Help me to hear, listen, and obey, no matter what. Amen.

Read Job 1:1–12

> THERE WAS A MAN IN THE LAND OF UZ, WHOSE NAME WAS JOB; AND THAT
> MAN WAS BLAMELESS AND UPRIGHT, AND ONE WHO FEARED GOD AND
> SHUNNED EVIL.
>
> Job 1:1

Anyone can praise and worship God when things are going well in their lives. However, the crunch comes when things do not go well. This is why I love Job so much. He is one of my heroes of the faith. Even though we are going to spend ten days examining the life of Job together, we will not be able to look at every aspect of his life. If you have a chance, set aside some time and read through the book of Job. I hope that you will be encouraged and inspired in your faith as you study his life.

God's opinion of Job was that he was blameless, upright, and God fearing. He was a good man. One day the devil came before God, and he told God that it was easy for Job to praise Him. After all, he was a rich farmer, with a beautiful wife and children. The devil taunted God, saying that if He took everything away from Job he would no longer praise and serve God. So God gave Satan permission to touch Job's life. And the Lord said to Satan, "Behold, all that he has is in your power; only do not lay a hand on his person" (verse 12a). It is important to note two things here. First, Satan couldn't touch Job's life without God's permission. Second, God was in complete control of how far Satan could go. He told Satan what he could and couldn't do.

My friends, it is God and not Satan who is in control of your life. If you are His child then He is your Father and He directs your life according to His will for you. You can trust God to care for you, no matter what comes your way. If you faithfully choose to walk by faith and not by sight, He will lead you every step of the way. Romans 8:28 tells us: "And we know that all things work together for good to those who love God, to those who are the called according to His purpose."

Prayer

My Father in Heaven, I bow before You and I worship You. Lord, I don't want to be one of those people who only serve and praise You when everything is going well in their lives. I know that no matter what happens You are in control of my life. Nothing can touch me outside of Your will. Amen.

Read Job 1:13–22

> THEN JOB AROSE, TORE HIS ROBE, AND SHAVED HIS HEAD; AND HE FELL TO
> THE GROUND AND WORSHIPED. AND HE SAID: "NAKED I CAME FROM MY
> MOTHER'S WOMB, AND NAKED SHALL I RETURN THERE. THE LORD GAVE, AND
> THE LORD HAS TAKEN AWAY; BLESSED BE THE NAME OF THE LORD."
>
> Job 1:20–21

I tell you, my friends, Satan went for it. He took Job's farm, all his animals, and his crops. They were wiped out – just like that! As if that wasn't bad enough he killed all of Job's children as well. They were having a party and the Bible tells us that a strong wind came up and blew the house over, killing all of them. Not only was Job penniless, but he also lost his family. The loss of material things, although uncomfortable, is nothing compared to your whole family being wiped out in one clean sweep. Satan clearly believed that that was what it would take to cause Job to turn against God. Can you imagine yourself in Job's position – how would you react?

As one lot of bad news after the other was delivered to Job he must have been devastated and heartbroken. It is clear that he loved his children. We read in verses 4 and 5:

> And his sons would go and feast in their houses, each on his appointed day,
> and would send and invite their three sisters to eat and drink with them. So
> it was, when the days of feasting had run their course, that Job would send
> and sanctify them, and he would rise early in the morning and offer burnt
> offerings according to the number of them all. For Job said, "It may be that my
> sons have sinned and cursed God in their hearts." Thus Job did regularly.

Job was a caring, godly father who was concerned for the spiritual well-being of his children. Satan must have been dancing with glee at the thought of how Job would reject and curse God. Instead, what was Job's reaction?

> Then Job arose, tore his robe, and shaved his head; and he fell to the ground and
> worshiped. And he said: "Naked I came from my mother's womb, and naked
> shall I return there. The Lord gave, and the Lord has taken away; blessed be the
> name of the Lord." In all this Job did not sin nor charge God with wrong.
>
> Job 1:20–22

Prayer

My Father God, I am so in awe of the great faith that Your servant Job had in You. Lord, I want to have a faith like that. I want to be able to love You, serve You, worship You, and praise You, irrespective of what life brings my way. Lord, give me strength; give me courage, I pray. Amen.

Read Romans 5:1–21

AND NOT ONLY THAT, BUT WE ALSO GLORY IN TRIBULATIONS, KNOWING THAT TRIBULATION PRODUCES PERSEVERANCE; AND PERSEVERANCE, CHARACTER; AND CHARACTER, HOPE. NOW HOPE DOES NOT DISAPPOINT, BECAUSE THE LOVE OF GOD HAS BEEN POURED OUT IN OUR HEARTS BY THE HOLY SPIRIT WHO WAS GIVEN TO US.

Romans 5:3–5

The Lord is in full control, my dear friend. You know the world really sits up and takes notice of Christians when the going becomes tough. They watch to see whether the Christians will persevere. I want each of us to take a moment to ask ourselves what kind of witness we are to the world. What do your unsaved family and colleagues see when they look at your life? Do they see a fair-weather Christian, or one who sticks through thick and thin? Are you praising God irrespective of your circumstances?

Some time back I visited Australia. At that time Western Australia – in fact the whole of Australia – was going through the worst drought of the millennium. In the outback, some people had come by a copy of my book, *Faith Like Potatoes*. One of the pastors had read the book and he wrote inviting me to come over and help them. He shared with me that he was a "city slicker", and because of that, when he told the young farmers there was a better way, they looked at him in disbelief. They didn't believe that he knew or understood what they were going through. The situation had reached a crisis point. Tragic stories were reported. Up to five farmers a week were committing suicide. They were so desperate they didn't know where to turn.

So we went to Australia to share with them, to encourage them, and to pray with them. The good news is that it began to rain and they had the best rains they had had in over a decade. It had nothing to do with me, Angus Buchan; it had everything to do with Jesus Christ. When people repent and bow the knee, acknowledging Jesus Christ as Saviour, He comes through for them. "[I]f My people who are called by My name will humble themselves, and pray and seek My face, and turn from their wicked ways, then I will hear from heaven, and will forgive their sin and heal their land" (2 Chronicles 7:14).

Prayer

My God, thank You for Your Word that encourages me. I know that You are in the midst of every circumstance of my life. Help me to humble myself before You, and to call upon Your Holy Name. Help me to keep going, no matter what happens. Amen.

Read Job 2:1–10

> But he said to her, "You speak as one of the foolish women speaks. Shall we indeed accept good from God, and shall we not accept adversity?" In all this Job did not sin with his lips.
>
> Job 2:10

There was no letting up for Job. He lost his material goods, he lost his family, and still the devil was not satisfied. In our reading we see that he once again appeared before God, telling Him that it was all very well for Job not to turn his back on God, but if God allowed him to afflict Job personally then He would see a different outcome. God again gives Satan permission to touch Job, and again sets limits on what he can and cannot do. "And the Lord said to Satan, 'Behold, he is in your hand, but spare his life'" (verse 6). So Satan proceeded to afflict Job with painful boils from the top of his head to the soles of his feet. Can you imagine anything worse?

Job's wife, who is heartbroken no doubt over the loss of her children, encourages Job to curse God. We read Job's response to her urging: "Shall we indeed accept good from God, and shall we not accept adversity?" (verse 10). The Scripture goes on to say: "In all this Job did not sin with his lips." This is faith, my friends, is it not? Faith is not faith if it hasn't been tested. It has been said that Job is possibly the oldest book in the Bible. I feel that of all the men of faith Job is probably the greatest. As you know, faith is my subject. I have studied the men of the Bible and I feel that Job is very likely the man who had the most faith.

My friends, I don't know what you are dealing with in your life. It could be sickness – your own or that of a loved one – or maybe you've recently been bereaved. You may be going through the pain of a marriage break-up. You might be facing financial disaster and you don't know which way to turn. Take your need to Jesus. Give it to Him. Choose to trust Him, and allow Him to work out your situation according to His good and perfect will for you.

Prayer

My Father God in Heaven, You are in control of this world and all who live in it. You have every circumstance and situation under control. There is nothing that can touch my life that You cannot deal with and help me to deal with. I choose right now to trust and believe in You. Amen.

Read Job 2:11–13 and 3:20–26

"FOR THE THING I GREATLY FEARED HAS COME UPON ME, AND WHAT I DREADED HAS HAPPENED TO ME. I AM NOT AT EASE, NOR AM I QUIET; I HAVE NO REST, FOR TROUBLE COMES."

Job 3:25–26

The fact that Job's faith in God did not waver does not mean that he did not suffer greatly as a result of what happened to him. I think it is important for us to spend some time looking at Job's pain. It would be wrong to give the impression that having faith means that we don't experience pain or that it is wrong to express our feelings of grief and pain. If you have time then read the whole of chapter 3. There you will learn of Job's intense feelings of pain and grief. Three of Job's friends came to see him when they heard what had befallen him. They were no doubt shocked to witness the level of Job's pain.

And when they raised their eyes from afar, and did not recognize him, they lifted their voices and wept; and each one tore his robe and sprinkled dust on his head toward heaven. So they sat down with him on the ground seven days and seven nights, and no one spoke a word to him, for they saw that his grief was very great.

Job 2:12–13

They were at a loss as to know how to comfort him. If you have ever experienced great tragedy then you will know what Job was going through. It is OK to express your grief and pain. God does not expect you to bottle it up inside yourself. He doesn't expect you to pretend that nothing has happened. That is not faith.

Faith is when you go through indescribable agony, but you choose to turn to God with your feelings and not from Him. Faith is when you come and lay your pain down at the foot of the cross. It is when you allow the Holy Spirit to comfort, calm, and soothe you. It is when slowly but surely you allow the Holy Spirit to apply the balm of Gilead to the raw and wounded areas of your life. Faith is when each day you make the decision to follow Jesus. To trust Him and to submit to Him.

Prayer
My Loving Father in Heaven, I thank You that I don't have to pretend with You. I can share my pain with You. I can grieve, I can lament and I can cry out to You. You hear me, You enfold me in Your arms and You love me. Lord, I choose to open myself up to Your healing work in my life. Amen.

Read Job 13:1–19

Though He slay me, yet will I trust Him. Even so, I will defend my own ways before Him.

Job 13:15

Job's three friends Eliphaz, Bildad, and Zophar supposedly came to be with him during his time of trouble to encourage him. However, this was not the case. They spent their time with Job plying him with human wisdom. Among other things their judgment of the situation was: Job must have sinned and therefore he was being chastened by God. They accused Job of folly and wickedness. They urged him to repent and assured him that the wicked are punished by God. We know from what we have read that none of this was true of Job.

What did God Himself say about Job? He said to Satan, "Have you considered My servant Job, that there is none like him on the earth, a blameless and upright man, one who fears God and shuns evil?" (Job 1:8). So if God proclaimed Job blameless, what right did his friends have to say otherwise? The problem with human wisdom is that it always has to try and find a "logical" reason for things. God's ways are not our ways: it is as simple as that. So trying to figure things out from a human perspective won't get us anywhere.

This is what faith is about – it is about trusting God, even when we cannot see the end from the beginning. Even when things are murky and dark, we need to cling to the promise Jesus has made to us: "For He Himself has said, 'I will never leave you nor forsake you'" (Hebrews 13:5b). "God is not a man, that He should lie, nor a son of man, that He should repent. Has He said, and will He not do? Or has He spoken, and will He not make it good?" (Numbers 23:19). Job understood this, irrespective of what his friends had to say to him. This is why he could say: "Though He slay me, yet will I trust Him." You are safer in the hands of the Living God than anywhere else on earth! Like Job, make the choice to trust Him today.

Prayer
My Father God, I bow before You. I realize that in the midst of suffering You are always there. You said You will never leave and You never do. Help me to cling to You. Help me not to be distracted by the voices and noise around me. I want to keep my eyes fixed upon You and only You. Amen.

Read Psalm 34

> MANY ARE THE AFFLICTIONS OF THE RIGHTEOUS, BUT THE LORD DELIVERS
> HIM OUT OF THEM ALL.
>
> Psalm 34:19

I hope that you are encouraged by this wonderful psalm of faith. If there was ever a man who understood suffering, it was Job. I have said it to you many times, but I'll say it again, this idea that people have, that when you come to Jesus all your problems will be over, is not true. It is a lie from the devil to discourage people. The truth is: come to Jesus and He will walk with you through the fire and through your trials (read Isaiah 43).

Are there trials in your life that are starting to sink you? Maybe you, like Job, are saying, "Lord, why are You contending with me? Lord, why are You fighting me? Lord, why are You punishing me?" This is what Job said: "I will say to God, 'Do not condemn me; show me why You contend with me'" (Job 10:2). My dear friend, it's not God who's fighting with you. I'll tell you who's fighting with you: it's probably yourself. We are so often our own worst enemy, aren't we? Face the enemy of your soul head on – not in your own strength, but in God's strength.

The Lord says we have to put on the armour of God every day when we wake up. We do this in our house. Every morning, when we wake up, the first thing I do is turn over and tell my wife, Jill, "I love you." Then I start putting on the armour of God, on the two of us, our children, and our grandchildren. Did you put the armour of God on this morning? If you're going through a trial, it means you're in a war. If you go to war, you need the armour of God. The helmet of Salvation, the breastplate of Righteousness, the belt of Truth, the shoes of the Gospel of Peace, the shield of Faith, the sword of the Spirit, the Word of God, covered by the blood of the Lamb. You go out with the joy of the Lord, which is your strength.

Prayer

Lord God, Ruler of the universe, You are my Lord and my Master. I worship at Your throne. I give You praise. I give You glory for Your infinite goodness and mercy. Thank You that You never leave me nor forsake me. You are always there. I know that, no matter the trial, I am Your beloved child. Amen.

Read Job 19

> FOR I KNOW THAT MY REDEEMER LIVES, AND HE SHALL STAND AT LAST ON
> THE EARTH.

> Job 19:25

In spite of all his suffering; despite losing all of his family, his farm, and his animals, Job never lost his faith. For I know that my Redeemer lives! Even when the people around him tried to bring him down – his wife and his friends were no help to him at all. His faith was all he had left after everything had been taken away, but it was more than enough, wasn't it? Job knew his God, and because he knew his God, he could withstand the trial. The time to learn to know your God is before the trials strike. So many Christians neglect their walk with God, and then they wonder why it is that their faith cannot sustain them in the difficult times. You prepare beforehand, my friends. Yesterday we spoke about putting on the armour of God. When a soldier goes into battle he suits up beforehand – not once the enemy begins attacking him. By then it's too late.

We need to understand that the trials we are going through are to prepare us for the life that is yet to come. We have to understand that we are involved in a war. Job was in a war – it was a war for his soul. We are in a war. Job understood that he was not alone in the battle. Neither are we: the battle is not ours, it is the Lord's. Our part is to stand.

And when those fiery trials come we need to know the Word of God. Don't begin trying to get to know the Lord after the trials have come. Spend time now fortifying yourself. Make the Word part of who you are – let it penetrate your spirit man. Grow closer to Jesus every day by having good quiet times. Spend time praying. Then, when the trials come, you'll be able to stand. Like Job you will not be moved. You will be able to cry out in the midst of your pain: "For I know that my Redeemer lives, and He shall stand at last on the earth."

Prayer
My Father God, my Redeemer and Deliverer. I call out to You and I stand upon the promises in Your Word today. Lord, You have given me Your strength and Your righteousness. I take hold of Your Holy Name and I proclaim that I am Your child. I am Your servant and I know that You are alive! Amen.

Read Job 42:1–6

> I HAVE HEARD OF YOU BY THE HEARING OF THE EAR, BUT NOW MY EYE SEES
> YOU. THEREFORE I ABHOR MYSELF, AND REPENT IN DUST AND ASHES.
>
> Job 42:5–6

Nothing can prepare you for an encounter with the Living God. Job was a righteous man. God Himself declared him blameless. Yet in all his days of worshipping God before his trials began, Job had never really encountered Him. Through the many days (and we don't know exactly how many they were) he began to encounter God. We are spared none of the details as we watch Job work through his suffering and pain. He is honest about his feelings. One of the big lessons we can learn from Job is that, no matter how much he was hurting, he took his hurt to God. He poured his heart out before God.

We have already seen that the people in Job's life weren't much help to him. They brought him down, rather than building him up. God saw all of this and He didn't let it pass without comment, as we will see when we conclude our time with Job. Not only was he a man of faith and integrity, but Job was also a man who knew how to persevere. So when everything was said and done, God and Job had a conversation. You can read the full script of it in chapters 38–41. After everything that Job had been through, God revealed Himself to Job in a new and different way. God revealed His omnipotence to Job.

Job came to experience God in a whole new way. Job said, "I know that You can do everything, and that no purpose of Yours can be withheld from You" (verse 2). Then Job repented before God and he uttered these beautiful words: "I have heard of You by the hearing of the ear, but now my eye sees You. Therefore I abhor myself, and repent in dust and ashes." My friend, if you are in the midst of a trial, ask God to give you a new revelation of Himself. Ask Him to open your eyes so that you will not just hear of Him, but that You will see Him for who He is – God Almighty!

Prayer

My Father, God Almighty, I bow humbly in Your holy presence. You have filled me once again with awe and wonder as I have read Your Word. Lord, I want to experience You in the way that Job did. I want to know You, not only with my mind, but also with my heart. Amen.

Read Job 42

Now the Lord blessed the latter days of Job more than his beginning; for he had fourteen thousand sheep, six thousand camels, one thousand yoke of oxen, and one thousand female donkeys. He also had seven sons and three daughters.

Job 42:12–13

In verses 7–8 of our reading we see how God dealt with Job's three friends. He did not let them get away with the way they had behaved. What is interesting, and I wonder if you noticed it as you read the Scripture? "And the Lord restored Job's losses when he prayed for his friends" (verse 10a). We have spoken many times about the need to forgive those who try to cause us harm. Here we see clearly in God's Word that He restored Job after he prayed for his friends. If there are people who have been insensitive to your pain, who have maybe hurt you by what they have said or done, or in some instances not done – forgive them. Let it go, my friend: it is not worth missing out on God's blessing.

Job was a man whom we can honestly hold in great esteem. He was a man who took his tribulation, his testing, his pain, his suffering, and gave it back to God. And in the end God blessed him very richly. So much so that the Bible says that Job received back everything he lost seven times over. After these events Job lived 140 years and saw his children and his grandchildren for four generations. He died a very old man. The Word tells us, "So Job died, old and full of days" (verse 17).

"And the Lord restored Job's losses…" (verse 10). The word used for "losses" here is "captivity". The enemy, Satan, took captive Job's family by killing them; he took captive Job's farm and all he owned. It was temporary and God returned to him what had been taken captive (and we know the Lord restored it sevenfold). My friend, if Satan has taken something captive from you, don't despair. Remain faithful, walk righteously, and keep believing. God is faithful; He will come through for you. James tells us: "Indeed we count them blessed who endure. You have heard of the perseverance of Job and seen the end intended by the Lord – that the Lord is very compassionate and merciful" (James 5:11).

Prayer

My Father God, I thank You for the past days and the lessons You have taught me from the life of Your servant Job. Lord, You are a faithful God. You keep Your promises to Your children. You are in complete control of my life. I commit everything I am to You. Lord, I trust You to do Your will in my life. Amen.

JULY

DAVID'S JOURNEY OF FRIENDSHIP WITH GOD

David's journey began with his spending time with God

1. David, a man with a destiny
2. David, anointed king
3. Jesus, the Anointed One
4. The Lord is with him
5. Wait on the Lord
6. The mind of Christ
7. Waiting renews strength
8. Lord, show me Your ways
9. Be available and ready
10. Resting and waiting
11. The consequences of not waiting
12. Unanswered prayers
13. While you are waiting
14. Dealing with detractors
15. Absolute faith in God
16. The right armour for battle
17. David slays Goliath
18. Remaining faithful
19. The tragic end of King Saul
20. God's covenant with David
21. Surely He shall deliver me
22. Dealing with a rebellious child
23. David's treachery
24. God confronts David
25. The consequences of David's sin
26. David repents before the Lord
27. David counts the people
28. Remember the name of the Lord
29. To whose voice do you listen?
30. Now the Lord loved him
31. My soul waits for God

Read Ruth 4:13–22

> ALSO THE NEIGHBOR WOMEN GAVE HIM A NAME, SAYING, "THERE IS A SON BORN TO NAOMI." AND THEY CALLED HIS NAME OBED. HE IS THE FATHER OF JESSE, THE FATHER OF DAVID.
>
> Ruth 4:17

The first time the Bible mentions David is in the book of Ruth – a beautiful love story of redemption. Ruth married Boaz and they had a baby named Obed, who had a son named Jesse. When he grew up he in turn had a son named David, who ultimately became the king of Israel. The faithfulness of God is a golden thread that runs throughout Scripture. In Matthew 1 we read that Jesus Christ, our Saviour, was descended from the line of David.

Long before Samuel showed up at Jesse's door to anoint the new king of Israel, God had His hand upon David. In fact, long before David was born, it was in God's heart that David would fulfil a special part in His plan of redemption. David was a man with a destiny, there is no doubt about that. As a young boy, while he tended his father's sheep in the fields, David developed a special relationship with God. The life of a shepherd is a solitary one and David spent many hours alone with the sheep. It was during his time as a shepherd that he learned to know and trust God.

When in danger God came to his aid; with His help, David slayed both a bear and a lion: "The Lord, who delivered me from the paw of the lion and from the paw of the bear, He will deliver me from the hand of this Philistine" (1 Samuel 17:37a). David feared nothing and no one because he knew that God was on his side. You too are a man with a destiny, my friend – do you realize this? Are you living each day in a vital, faith relationship with God? I don't know what the "lions" and the "bears" are that you are facing in your life right now. What I do know is that the same God who undertook for David will undertake for you. Spend time with Him; get to know Him like David did – then you will see His power manifested in your life in a new and fresh way.

Prayer

My Father, we are at the beginning of the second half of this year. It is amazing where the time has gone. I thank You that I am a man with a destiny. Forgive me that I don't always live in the truth of this. Help me, I pray, to get to know You better and stay close to You. Amen.

Read 1 Samuel 16:1–13

> SO HE SENT AND BROUGHT HIM IN. NOW HE WAS RUDDY, WITH BRIGHT EYES,
> AND GOOD-LOOKING. AND THE LORD SAID, "ARISE, ANOINT HIM; FOR THIS
> IS THE ONE!" THEN SAMUEL TOOK THE HORN OF OIL AND ANOINTED HIM
> IN THE MIDST OF HIS BROTHERS; AND THE SPIRIT OF THE LORD CAME UPON
> DAVID FROM THAT DAY FORWARD. SO SAMUEL AROSE AND WENT TO RAMAH.
>
> 1 Samuel 16:12–13

The story of David's anointing is a perfect illustration of the Scripture that says: "But God has chosen the foolish things of the world to put to shame the wise, and God has chosen the weak things of the world to put to shame the things which are mighty" (1 Corinthians 1:27). Samuel arrived at Jesse's home expecting to anoint one of his strong, strapping sons. In Samuel's mind they fit the description of what a king should look like. In his defence, Jesse didn't think to have David called in when Samuel said he wanted to see all of his sons.

The moment was approaching when David would step centre stage as he walked into his destiny. Samuel, a man who listened to God, heeded the instruction not to settle for anything less than God's perfect will in the situation. What about you, my friend, do you hold out for God's perfect will in your circumstances, or are you happy to settle for second best? God has so much more for us than we can ever imagine: "Now to Him who is able to do exceedingly abundantly above all that we ask or think, according to the power that works in us" (Ephesians 3:20).

Have you ever felt that God might have overlooked you or forgotten about you? You don't need to worry that this will ever happen. David was stuck away in a field, far from anyone. His own father didn't even think to call him in to meet the prophet. Yet God didn't forget about David. He knew exactly where David was and, when the moment was right, He had him brought in. God will never ever forget you or abandon you, my friend. You can wait for His perfect time. You can rely upon God to know when the best moment is to move forward. We so often want to jump the gun – to disastrous effect. As I have said, every time I have messed up in my life, it is because I didn't wait on God – I chose to go with my timing instead of His.

Prayer

My Father in Heaven, as I bow in Your presence today, I give You praise and honour. You are a great and awesome God. There is none like You, my Lord. Thank You that You are in perfect control of my life. I need have no anxiety; You will make all things clear in Your time. Amen.

JESUS, THE ANOINTED ONE

Read Luke 4:16–22

THE SPIRIT OF THE LORD IS UPON ME, BECAUSE HE HAS ANOINTED ME
TO PREACH THE GOSPEL TO THE POOR; HE HAS SENT ME TO HEAL THE
BROKENHEARTED, TO PROCLAIM LIBERTY TO THE CAPTIVES AND RECOVERY
OF SIGHT TO THE BLIND, TO SET AT LIBERTY THOSE WHO ARE OPPRESSED; TO
PROCLAIM THE ACCEPTABLE YEAR OF THE LORD.

Luke 4:18–19

Down through the ages God has been anointing men and women to fulfil His purposes. Yesterday we read of David's anointing that took place in his father's home, in front of his family. "Then Samuel took the horn of oil and anointed him in the midst of his brothers; and the Spirit of the Lord came upon David from that day forward" (1 Samuel 16:13a). Today we read about the ultimate anointing – of Jesus Christ, our Saviour. There never was before, and never has been since, One greater than He. Yet, God chose to humble Himself and come to this earth as a defenceless baby to save you and me.

My friends, if Jesus, who is God, needed the Spirit of the Lord to be upon Him in order to minister to people, then how much more do we need Him? Time and time again we read of God manifesting Himself to people whom He chose to use in some way or another. To list only a few of them: Abraham, Noah, Joseph, Moses, Joshua, Samuel, David, Isaiah, Jeremiah, and Daniel – and these are only the Old Testament men. We can rest assured that if God calls us, then He also equips us. Has God been speaking to you? Is He calling you to fulfil a purpose and a plan that He has for you? If so, what has been your reaction to His call upon your life?

There is no greater thrill or joy than to be used by God to touch the lives of people. I never cease to be amazed and humbled as I watch God at work when we've held our Mighty Men Conferences. To see so many men come together to seek God is an awesome thing to behold. It takes faith to accept your calling and God's anointing upon your life, my friends. Accepting His Father's anointing upon Him led Jesus to the Cross of Calvary, didn't it? Sometimes the road of anointing is a hard and lonely road – but, oh, so worthwhile and fulfilling, isn't it?

Prayer

My Father God, I come before You the God of all that there was, is, and will be. You are a great, awesome, and majestic God. I worship You, my Lord. I offer my life as a living sacrifice to You. Use me, dear Lord, as You see fit. In Jesus' Name. Amen.

Read 1 Samuel 16:14–23

> THEN ONE OF THE SERVANTS ANSWERED AND SAID, "LOOK, I HAVE SEEN A
> SON OF JESSE THE BETHLEHEMITE, WHO IS SKILLFUL IN PLAYING, A MIGHTY
> MAN OF VALOR, A MAN OF WAR, PRUDENT IN SPEECH, AND A HANDSOME
> PERSON; AND THE LORD IS WITH HIM."
>
> 1 Samuel 16:18

How sad it was that Saul, who had known God's blessing upon his life, no longer enjoyed that blessing. Saul, who had known what it was to "have the Lord with him", no longer had that closeness: "But the Spirit of the Lord departed from Saul" (verse 14a). Chilling words indeed! This is David's introduction to Saul, the king of Israel – a man demented by "a distressing spirit" (verse 14b), sent upon him by the Lord. Saul landed in this position because of his lack of faith and his disobedience to God's instructions.

In chapter 15 the Lord gave Saul an instruction and he did not carry it out. "Now the word of the Lord came to Samuel, saying, 'I greatly regret that I have set up Saul as king, for he has turned back from following Me, and has not performed My commandments'" (1 Samuel 15:10–11a). God sent Samuel to Saul to inform him that the Lord had rejected him as the king of Israel. We serve a God of mercy and grace, my friends. He is long-suffering and forgiving, but He is also a Holy God and calls for obedience from His children. So often we want to skirt around the issue of obedience – but, as we have said before, an obedience issue is a faith issue.

"So Samuel said: 'Has the Lord as great delight in burnt offerings and sacrifices, as in obeying the voice of the Lord? Behold, to obey is better than sacrifice, and to heed than the fat of rams'" (1 Samuel 15:22). David was a young man who walked with God; he obeyed God, and he trusted God. Saul's servants, in today's verse, described David as "a mighty man of valour". How would those who know you describe you to a stranger? Would they say: "X is a mighty man of valour. He is a man who walks by faith and not by sight. He is a man who obeys and honours his God above all else. The Lord is with him"? God is looking for the same attributes in men today as He has since the beginning of time.

Prayer

My Father, I am so conscious of You speaking to me right now. I realize that You want to cut through all the hype and the noise – You want to get down to basics. The basics of character, obedience, and faith. Lord, I want it to be known that You are with me. Amen.

Read Isaiah 64

FOR SINCE THE BEGINNING OF THE WORLD MEN HAVE NOT HEARD NOR PERCEIVED BY THE EAR, NOR HAS THE EYE SEEN ANY GOD BESIDES YOU, WHO ACTS FOR THE ONE WHO WAITS FOR HIM.

Isaiah 64:4

Over the next few days I want to look at what it means to wait upon God. There was a period of waiting between the time that Samuel anointed David to be king, and when he actually became king. He had to wait until the time was right. Most of us are not very good at waiting. I think this is why the fast-food chains do so well; everything is "hurry up" now. We live so much of our lives on the run. As a result of our "hurry, I want things now" mentality, we have a hard time waiting upon God.

We are so busy with our lives that we often don't make the time for those closest to us. How often do you sit down with your family around the table for a meal? In so many homes the dining room table has become an ornament. There are several mentions in the New Testament of Jesus sitting down and eating with His disciples. The most important sacrament in the Christian faith is Holy Communion, or Breaking Bread, as some people refer to it. This took place at the dinner table the night before the Lord was betrayed. Makes you think, doesn't it?

How can you spend time hearing from God when you don't wait for Him to speak? How can you impart Christian values to your family if you never sit down together? You can't tell them about Jesus rushing off to school or to sports. Life is becoming so hectic even the Lord is slowly but surely being pushed out of the picture. Let's have a look at the New Testament view: "Eye has not seen, nor ear heard, nor have entered into the heart of man the things which God has prepared for those who love Him" (1 Corinthians 2:9). If you love someone you make the time to spend with them. You cannot say you love your wife and then never spend time with her. The same is true of God – if you love Him you will spend time with Him.

Prayer

Heavenly Father, I pray that the words of my mouth and the meditations of my heart will be acceptable to You, my Lord and my Refuge. Help me to put aside all the cares and busyness of this world. Lord, I want to sit in Your presence and wait upon You. In Jesus' Name. Amen.

Read 1 Corinthians 2:6–16

> FOR "WHO HAS KNOWN THE MIND OF THE LORD THAT HE MAY INSTRUCT
> HIM?" BUT WE HAVE THE MIND OF CHRIST.
>
> 1 Corinthians 2:16

Many of us are missing God's blessing because we do not take the time to sit down and hear what the Master is saying to us. Instead we are doing our own thing, and we are suffering as a result. "Now we have received, not the spirit of the world, but the Spirit who is from God, that we might know the things that have been freely given to us by God" (verse 12). The only way that you will come to know the mind of Christ is if you spend time learning from God's Spirit. These things are not understood in the normal human way.

Gently, and with love, I want to tell you that I am tired of people coming up to me and asking: "Why did God allow this to happen to me?" "Why is God taking my business away from me?" "Why did God break up my relationship?" Let's stop right there, folks. Half the time we make our own plans and then we ask God to bless them. God says: "I don't want you to do so-and-so. I don't want you to leave South Africa and go to Australia." Or on the other hand He might say: "I want you to leave South Africa and go to Australia." How do you find out what you should do? Not by thumb-sucking (guessing), that's for sure. No, sir, you find out by waiting on God.

With some people it is almost like spiritual fortune telling. They take their finger and point to a verse in the Bible and say, "Thus says the Lord". That is not waiting on God. What happens if your finger falls on that Scripture that says "and [Judas] went and hanged himself" (Matthew 27:5)? Are you going to hang yourself? Of course not. You need to read your Bible systematically; you need to pray regularly, and then God will start to show you what to do. "But God has revealed them to us through His Spirit" (1 Corinthians 2:10a). What has God revealed? "The things which God has prepared for those who love Him" (verse 9b).

Prayer

My Father God, I come before You and bow in Your presence. Lord, forgive me for the frantic way that I live my life. Forgive my questioning and my doubt. Right now I choose to sit at Your feet and wait upon You. I am attentive and listening to what You want to say to me. Amen.

Read Isaiah 40:25–31

> BUT THOSE WHO WAIT ON THE LORD SHALL RENEW THEIR STRENGTH; THEY
> SHALL MOUNT UP WITH WINGS LIKE EAGLES, THEY SHALL RUN AND NOT BE
> WEARY, THEY SHALL WALK AND NOT FAINT.
>
> Isaiah 40:31

Folks, I find as I am maturing in the faith that I am spending less time talking and more time waiting. You have to be very careful when, having listened and heard from God, you then say: "Thus says the Lord", because people are listening. You need to be sure you have heard God correctly, and the only way to be certain is to spend time with God.

We have just read the beautiful Scripture from Isaiah that I am sure you all know by heart. Have you ever seen an eagle? An eagle doesn't flap around like a crow sitting on a power line. An eagle locks its wings and catches the thermal current, soaring ever higher in the sky. This is what God wants for you. Too many Christians flap around like crows on the power lines instead of soaring like the eagles. You were created to soar, not to flap, my friend. There may be those reading this devotional who suffer from depression. Anxiety, fear, and stress dog their lives. The Lord says: "Wait on Me and I will reassure you. I will show you a way. My peace will come upon you and you will start to sleep well and think correctly."

If you wait on the Lord you will renew your strength; you will mount up with wings like an eagle; you will run and not be weary; you will walk and not faint. When you run an ultra-marathon, you have to wait, you have to walk, you have to eat, and you have to drink – no matter how strong you are. You will never finish an ultra-marathon running at the pace of a 100-metre sprint. The Christian life is a marathon; it is not a sprint. We need to be prepared to wait on God so that we can hear from Him. So today, right now, choose to be an eagle rather than a crow. Stop the frantic movement and slow right down. Sit at the Master's feet and hear what He has to say to you.

Prayer
My Father God, You speak so clearly, and yet so often I cannot hear You – because of all the noise and commotion I have allowed into my life. Help me to clear it all out, to stop, sit down, and not move until I am able to hear Your voice speaking to me. Amen.

Read Psalm 25

> SHOW ME YOUR WAYS, O LORD; TEACH ME YOUR PATHS. LEAD ME IN YOUR
> TRUTH AND TEACH ME, FOR YOU ARE THE GOD OF MY SALVATION; ON YOU I
> WAIT ALL THE DAY.
>
> Psalm 25:4–5

David learned to wait on God when he was tending his father's sheep in the fields. As he sat there he would hear from God; he would write his psalms to the Lord and compose his music. Is it any wonder that he was able to soothe Saul's troubled spirit? When we spend time with the Lord He stills the storm within us. He is our Peace and our Wisdom.

What is the qualification for hearing from God? Quite simply, one thing: that we love Him. I have said it many times before, but it bears repeating: if you love somebody then you will be prepared to spend time with them. There is a very sad Scripture that reads, "They profess to know God, but in works they deny Him, being abominable, disobedient, and disqualified for every good work" (Titus 1:16). You cannot tell God you love Him yet never take the time to wait on Him. Stop your busyness and begin spending time in the presence of God. Do you think that maybe if King Saul had spent more time in God's presence listening, he might not have disobeyed God? The outcome of this was his being rejected as king.

You cannot earn your way to Heaven. "For by grace you have been saved through faith, and that not of yourselves; it is the gift of God, not of works, lest anyone should boast" (Ephesians 2:8–9). Yet, so much of our often frantic busyness for God is nothing other than works. It takes faith to wait – then it takes faith to act on God's Word to you. I looked at the meaning of the word "wait" in the *Oxford English Dictionary*; this is what is says: "To remain inactive in expectation of something". Isn't that beautiful? To remain inactive. Hey, guys, come on! How hard is it to do this? Remain inactive and in expectation. What are you expecting from God right now? If your answer is nothing, then that is exactly what you will receive: nothing. Don't settle for less than God's best for you, my friend.

Prayer

My Father in Heaven, You are a loving Father to me. So often I block Your voice because of my own busyness. I realize that even when I am busy for You it doesn't count if it comes from a place of works. Help me to stop and wait expectantly on You. Amen.

Read Psalm 27

> WAIT ON THE LORD; BE OF GOOD COURAGE, AND HE SHALL STRENGTHEN
> YOUR HEART; WAIT, I SAY, ON THE LORD!
>
> Psalm 27:14

Another meaning of the word "wait" is to delay temporarily. Now I am the worst culprit when it comes to this. My wife Jill, on the other hand, is the one who waits upon God. She always says to me, "Angus, sit down for a minute." To delay temporarily. The final meaning of "wait" that I want us to explore is: to be available or in readiness. Are you available for God to speak to you right now? Are you ready for God to give you a new game plan for your life? You say yes – well then you had better be prepared to wait, because He wants to speak to you.

There was a time several years ago that I was very much in demand as a preacher. It was a great honour and very affirming, but if you don't check your heart, it can very quickly become an ego trip. If it is not of God it doesn't work. Around that time Jill and I went to a beautiful game reserve in the northern part of Zululand. After a couple of days, the Holy Spirit impressed upon me that I had forsaken my first love. "Nevertheless I have this against you, that you have left your first love. Remember therefore from where you have fallen; repent and do the first works, or else I will come to you quickly and remove your lampstand from its place – unless you repent" (Revelation 2:4–5).

A lampstand represents light. The Holy Spirit is Light. God said to me, "If you don't repent and stop running around like a mad thing, I am pulling out." For me that would be the greatest nightmare of all time because I know my natural limitations. I could not imagine standing on a platform speaking to thousands of people and suddenly realizing that God is not there. So I said, "Lord, I am going to listen to You." You see, I could hear Him because I was waiting on Him. There were no distractions, just Jill and me alone in the bush – listening to God.

Prayer

My Father God, I know that the worst nightmare of my life would be to realize that You have pulled out, and left me to my own devices. Lord, I need You. I want to be filled and empowered by Your Spirit. I need You to strengthen my heart. Lord, I wait upon You. Amen.

Read Psalm 37

REST IN THE LORD, AND WAIT PATIENTLY FOR HIM.

Psalm 37:7a

With great shame I have to say it took me a couple of days to quieten down when we were at the game reserve. I believe I am not alone; there are many men who will identify with me regarding the difficulty of stopping, and being quiet. We become so busy that it is very difficult to switch off. We make the excuse that we have responsibilities. There are people depending upon us. Our responsibility is to provide for our family and our employees and so on. All this does is it takes away our peace and makes it difficult to hear God speak to us.

As I said, after a few days I had settled down, and the Holy Spirit was able to start talking to me. He said, "Angus, I want you to close down. I want you to cancel all your appointments for the next year." I replied, "Lord, I am fully booked for the next year." He came back, "All of them." I was booked to speak in Newfoundland, India, up in Africa, all over the place. "But Lord, what will they say?" I felt the Lord reply, "They won't say anything because I am telling you to do it." Well, reluctantly, and I am telling you, it was reluctantly, folks, I did what He told me to do. Praise God that I did. I do listen to the Lord sometimes. I hope you are listening to Him right now.

I picked up the phone when I returned home and I cancelled every single appointment. Amazingly, not one of those men were angry with me, and some of them had been waiting for two years for those appointments. I simply told them, "I cannot come. The Lord says that I have got to draw aside and wait on Him." "Commit your way to the Lord, trust also in Him, and He shall bring it to pass. He shall bring forth your righteousness as the light, and your justice as the noonday" (verses 5–6). When we wait on the Lord we will be able to trust Him.

Prayer

My Father God, You are so true and faithful. You remain the same throughout the generations. I bow before You. Lord, I wait patiently upon You. I am ready to hear and obey Your Word to me today. Speak, Lord; I am Your servant. Amen.

Read 1 Samuel 13:1–15

> AND SAMUEL SAID TO SAUL, "YOU HAVE DONE FOOLISHLY. YOU HAVE NOT
> KEPT THE COMMANDMENT OF THE LORD YOUR GOD, WHICH HE COMMANDED
> YOU… BUT NOW YOUR KINGDOM SHALL NOT CONTINUE. THE LORD HAS
> SOUGHT FOR HIMSELF A MAN AFTER HIS OWN HEART…"
>
> 1 Samuel 13:13a and 14a

Wait on the Lord. Folks, what would have happened, if back then when God spoke to me, I had said no to Him; if I had refused to change my plans, and continued with the trips and speaking engagements I had lined up? There would possibly have been a measure of success, but it would not have been what God wanted. Now, as I look back, I realize that was a turning point. God continues to do amazing things. Why? Quite simply because I waited on Him.

You have just read a sad story about what happens when a man doesn't wait on God. It certainly cost King Saul dearly. It cost him his kingship. He was the first king of Israel. Saul stopped listening to God. He started to bend the word of the Lord to suit himself. His ego became too big. He believed that he could disobey God and get away with it. What did God say to him? "Your kingdom will not continue, I am going to find a man after My own heart." God looks upon the heart, my friend. We saw this when He chose David to succeed Saul. God told Samuel not to look on the outward appearance, but to look at the heart of the man. Don't become caught up in the trivia of life – seek the essence that is God's will for your life.

Saul did not get away with his sin and neither will we. You might think that you can have an affair with that woman; it will be a one-off thing; nobody will find out about it. My friend, the Bible says: "take note, you have sinned against the Lord; and be sure your sin will find you out" (Numbers 32:23). Possibly you might believe that you don't have to pay your taxes – you are clever and you have found a way to cover it up. God knows. Straight away God won't want to speak to you any more because He is a Holy God. Do you understand? God is looking for men after His own heart.

Prayer

My God and Father, I pray that You will forgive me for thinking that there are things that I can get away with. Lord, all that happens is that I am losing out on my relationship with You. I want to be a man after Your heart. I want to hear from You. Amen.

Read 1 Samuel 15:10–35

> ... HAS THE LORD AS GREAT DELIGHT IN BURNT OFFERINGS AND SACRIFICES, AS IN OBEYING THE VOICE OF THE LORD? BEHOLD, TO OBEY IS BETTER THAN SACRIFICE, AND TO HEED THAN THE FAT OF RAMS.
>
> 1 Samuel 15:22

Some people say: "Oh, Angus, God never answers my prayers." He won't receive your prayers if you go and do it your way. Repent this morning, return to God, and live right. Pay your debts. Be faithful to your wife. Love your children. Treat your employees honourably. Then watch what happens. All of a sudden your life will change.

Unfortunately, Saul didn't do this, did he? He went and offered up a sacrifice to God before the prophet Samuel arrived because he saw that his soldiers were becoming tired and leaving (1 Samuel 13). Ahead of them was a massive army. *'n Boer maak 'n plan* (a farmer makes a plan). Isn't that right? I've been farming for nearly forty years, and not one of my plans have ever worked out. Let's do it God's way and then wait to see how differently things turn out. Saul took matters into his own hands, and offered up a sacrifice, instead of trusting God. Samuel came over the hill; he looked at Saul and asked, "What have you done?" Saul replied, "Well, I have offered up a sacrifice to God because you were late." Samuel said, "I told you I was coming."

As a result Samuel sadly continued: "As of this moment, you have lost your anointing. You have lost your gifting. You have lost your calling. You have lost your mantle. You have lost your authority. As of this moment you are no longer king of Israel." And that is exactly what happened. Why? Because Saul didn't wait. You know, the tragedy if you continue reading the story is that eventually King Saul committed suicide, and his blessed son Jonathan also died on the battlefield. I want to tell you, it is never too late to start waiting on God. You say, "Angus, I have made such a hash of my life. Is it too late for me?" It's never too late for those who are prepared to wait on the Lord. I don't care if you are sixteen or sixty-six. God has a plan for you.

Prayer

My Father in Heaven, You are a gracious, but righteous God. Thank You for Your Word that has come through to me so strongly. Lord, I want to be a man who waits upon You. I want to be a man who listens to You, who walks with You by faith and not by sight. Amen.

Read 1 Samuel 17:1–15

BUT DAVID OCCASIONALLY WENT AND RETURNED FROM SAUL TO FEED HIS FATHER'S SHEEP AT BETHLEHEM.

1 Samuel 17:15

The day that David was called in from the fields, where he was tending his father's sheep, signalled a major change in the direction of his life. Shortly after that we see him being summoned to soothe Saul's troubled spirit. Yet, the important lesson for us to learn is that there was still a waiting period for David. He continued to perform his duty as shepherd to his father's sheep. He did not immediately rush off and claim the throne. There was a plan and a process. God was working out the details of how it would all fall into place. There were important lessons still for David to learn.

My friend, you need to understand that sometimes living by faith means waiting. You have to spend time waiting on God in His presence. When He gives you a Word for your situation or a promise of what He will bring to pass, sometimes it happens immediately, but there are times when there is a waiting period. This waiting period requires faith. You have to believe that you did hear from God. It takes faith to then hold on to that Word. We live in an instant society, and we want everything to happen yesterday. God doesn't always work like that. He knows the end from the beginning of every situation.

How many times have we said that He is never too early and He is never ever late? Walking by faith and not by sight sometimes means waiting. Abraham had to wait. Noah had to wait. Moses had to wait. Throughout history men of faith have had to wait for God's timing. What do you do while you are waiting? You continue to draw closer to God. You continue doing what you have always done (like David). You walk in the Spirit, listening to His voice. You move when God tells you to move. You stand still when He tells you to stand still. As He has done for His children throughout history, when the time is right, He will bring His promises to fruition in your life.

Prayer

My Father, waiting is always the hardest. I realize, though, that the waiting is not a period of inactivity. It is a time to build my relationship with You; to draw closer to You; to learn to know You even better; and to prepare myself for what lies ahead. Keep me faithful. Amen.

Read 1 Samuel 17:16–29

Now Eliab his oldest brother heard when he spoke to the men; and Eliab's anger was aroused against David, and he said, "Why did you come down here? And with whom have you left those few sheep in the wilderness? I know your pride and the insolence of your heart, for you have come down to see the battle."   1 Samuel 17:28

When you are intent on following God's plan for your life, walking by faith and not by sight, you will always encounter detractors. Those who try to convince you that you are crazy to believe what God is telling you. In our reading we encounter David's oldest brother, Eliab. Being the oldest, he no doubt believed that he should have been the one chosen to be king. But, as I have said before, God is not concerned with outward appearance:

So it was, when they came, that he [Samuel] looked at Eliab and said, "Surely the Lord's anointed is before Him!" But the Lord said to Samuel, "Do not look at his appearance or at his physical stature, because I have refused him. For the Lord does not see as man sees; for man looks at the outward appearance, but the Lord looks at the heart."
     1 Samuel 16:6–7

This must have been a bitter pill for Eliab to swallow. Isn't it interesting that Eliab's retort to David is "I know your pride and the insolence of your heart"? He accuses David of the very thing of which he himself is guilty. Yet, God looked at both of their hearts, and decreed that David had the purer heart. The lesson here is that we are to run our own race. Check your own heart – make sure that you are walking in integrity and honesty before God.

Paul put it this way:

I'm not saying that I have this all together, that I have it made. But I am well on my way, reaching out for Christ, who has so wondrously reached out for me. Friends, don't get me wrong: By no means do I count myself an expert in all of this, but I've got my eye on the goal, where God is beckoning us onward – to Jesus. I'm off and running, and I'm not turning back. So let's keep focused on that goal, those of us who want everything God has for us.
     Philippians 3:12–15, *The Message*

If you are encountering detractors you are in good company – to mention only one, remember Noah and those who ridiculed him for building the ark?

Prayer
My Father, it is You who has called me. You have spoken to me. Help me to keep my eyes focused upon You and the goal You have set before me. Strengthen me, empower me, and equip me to remain faithful, no matter what the opposition is that I may encounter. Amen.

Read 1 Samuel 17:31–37

> MOREOVER DAVID SAID, "THE LORD, WHO DELIVERED ME FROM THE PAW OF
> THE LION AND FROM THE PAW OF THE BEAR, HE WILL DELIVER ME FROM THE
> HAND OF THIS PHILISTINE."
>
> 1 Samuel 17:37a

Matthew 19:26 says: "Jesus… said to them, 'With men this is impossible, but with God all things are possible.'" As I have emphasized, Hebrews 11:6 says, "But without faith it is impossible to please Him, for he who comes to God must believe that He is, and that He is a rewarder of those who diligently seek Him". These words were uttered by Jesus and written by the author of Hebrews long after David lived, but they perfectly sum up his faith. One young boy, with no battle experience. The Israeli army, skilled at war. The opposing Philistine army, a giant as their mascot. Sadly, Saul had lost his faith; he had lost his ability to lead his men. He was no longer the man he had been before the Spirit of God departed from his life.

This is a sobering reminder, my friend. We are nothing without the Spirit of God within us and upon us. David, on the other hand, came with none of this baggage. For him it was a simple matter. If God had done it before, He could do it again. To him the giant didn't seem any different or scarier than the bear and the lion had. You can imagine how frightening it had been for a young boy to be all alone in the field and there before him is a wild animal. He had no spears or special weapons. All he had was his faith in God. All he needed was faith in God. This is why he could later write: "Some trust in chariots, and some in horses; but we will remember the name of the Lord our God" (Psalm 20:7).

One man and God is an army, my friend. I don't know what the threat is that you might be facing in your life right now. It could be the scary giant of a terminal illness, it could be bankruptcy, or maybe the break-up of your marriage, or perhaps one of your children has got themselves into serious trouble. There are many giants out there – but remember: "with God all things are possible."

Prayer

My Father God, I long to have the profound, yet uncomplicated faith that David had. Lord, I realize that it came from a deep relationship with You. He knew his God. I know that this only comes from spending time with You. Waiting upon You, and walking faithfully with You. Amen.

Read Ephesians 6:10–18

> FINALLY, MY BRETHREN, BE STRONG IN THE LORD AND IN THE POWER OF
> HIS MIGHT. PUT ON THE WHOLE ARMOR OF GOD, THAT YOU MAY BE ABLE TO
> STAND AGAINST THE WILES OF THE DEVIL.
>
> Ephesians 6:10–11

No soldier in his right mind goes into battle without wearing his full battle gear. He takes all the precautions that he can, making sure that he has every advantage over his enemy. In the story of David and Goliath we read that this was exactly what Saul tried to do for David. "So Saul clothed David with his armor, and he put a bronze helmet on his head; he also clothed him with a coat of mail" (1 Samuel 17:38). You could say David was armed to the teeth.

What Saul didn't realize was that he wasn't dealing with a "normal" situation. What did David do? "David fastened his sword to his armor and tried to walk, for he had not tested them. And David said to Saul, 'I cannot walk with these, for I have not tested them.' So David took them off" (1 Samuel 17:39). Crazy, right? No: obedient. David knew that his strength didn't lie in Saul's armour. His strength lay in the armour of God – which cannot be seen with the naked eye.

It is no different for you and me, my friend. If you are facing a giant in your life you don't need human wisdom, strength, or weapons. You need the right armour: God's armour. Paul also understood this principle and he wrote about it in Ephesians. David knew that if he was going to be successful he needed God's armour; if you are going to overcome your enemy – the enemy of your soul, the devil – you too need to clothe yourself for battle. God has given us everything that we need to be victorious. If a soldier, fighting a war, wouldn't dream of going into battle unequipped, why do Christians so often think they can fight spiritual battles in their own strength? Battles in the spiritual realm can only be fought with spiritual weapons. Don't go out unprepared; listen to the apostle Paul's advice: "Therefore take up the whole armor of God, that you may be able to withstand in the evil day, and having done all, to stand" (Ephesians 6:13).

Prayer

My Father in Heaven, You reign supreme over the Heavens and the Earth. I am Your child and You have not left me defenceless. Help me to gird up and put on Your full armour. I do not go out into the battle unprepared. I have everything that I need for victory. Amen.

Read 1 Samuel 17:40–58

> THEN DAVID SAID TO THE PHILISTINE, "YOU COME TO ME WITH A SWORD, WITH A SPEAR, AND WITH A JAVELIN. BUT I COME TO YOU IN THE NAME OF THE LORD OF HOSTS, THE GOD OF THE ARMIES OF ISRAEL, WHOM YOU HAVE DEFIED."
>
> 1 Samuel 17:45

This was all the protection that David needed: the Name of the Lord of hosts. "I come to you in the name of the Lord of hosts". Although Goliath may have been the superior soldier, with better armour and more deadly weapons, David was not fighting alone. He came in the Name of the Lord of hosts – the Commander, not only of the army of Israel, but of all of Heaven as well. The Lord of hosts only had to speak a word to guide David's pebble to Goliath's forehead, causing him to drop to the earth before David.

All created agencies and forces are under the leadership and dominion of the Lord of hosts. My friends, the same Lord of hosts who gave David victory is my God and He is your God. He is the same yesterday, today, and forever. David knew his God, and because he did know Him he was able to take down a giant. It took faith, yes, but the faith came from knowing, and knowing came from being with God. There are no short cuts to a powerful Christian life. It is one day at a time. One step of obedience at a time. One act of faith at a time. God is with us for the long haul.

So, no matter what the giant or giants are in your life right now, you do not need to fear them. You do not need elaborate weapons or armour to fight them. What you need is to hear from the Lord of hosts. You need to wait upon Him, receive His orders, and then faithfully carry them out. Victory will be yours. Often God's instructions will go against human logic. This is because He does not operate as man operates. "But the natural man does not receive the things of the Spirit of God, for they are foolishness to him; nor can he know them, because they are spiritually discerned" (1 Corinthians 2:14). So you have to choose whom you will follow and obey – God or man? David chose that which is spiritually discerned – what will you choose?

Prayer

My Father in Heaven, You are the Lord of hosts, the Ruler over all that is in Heaven and all that is on the Earth. I am Your child and You will bring the forces of Your great power to bear upon the giants in my life, just as You did for David. Father, help me to walk in faith. Amen.

Read 1 Samuel 24

> THEN HE SAID TO DAVID: "YOU ARE MORE RIGHTEOUS THAN I; FOR YOU
> HAVE REWARDED ME WITH GOOD, WHEREAS I HAVE REWARDED YOU WITH
> EVIL."
>
> 1 Samuel 24:17

David faced an uphill battle with King Saul. The further Saul drifted from God, the more he grew to hate David. Not long after killing Goliath, while David played to soothe Saul's troubled spirit, he tried twice to pin David to the wall with his spear. There is nothing more devastating and frightening than the Spirit of God withdrawing from someone's life. If you want to fear something, my friends, this is what you should fear. Saul's life went from bad to worse. David, on the other hand, grew stronger and stronger.

People watched and they saw how David handled situations. He was a natural born leader. People gravitate towards natural leaders. "And David behaved wisely in all his ways, and the Lord was with him. Therefore, when Saul saw that he behaved very wisely, he was afraid of him. But all Israel and Judah loved David, because he went out and came in before them" (1 Samuel 18:14–16). In our reading today we see David being handed a golden opportunity to rid himself of King Saul once and for all. "Then the men of David said to him, 'This is the day of which the Lord said to you, "Behold, I will deliver your enemy into your hand, that you may do to him as it seems good to you"'" (1 Samuel 24:4a). David's response was: "The Lord forbid that I should do this thing to my master, the Lord's anointed, to stretch out my hand against him, seeing he is the anointed of the Lord" (verse 6).

David stood over Saul as he slept, but instead of killing him as his men wanted him to, he cut off a piece of Saul's robe. David knew that it was God who would protect him. He understood that it was God who had anointed him king and therefore it was God who would put him on the throne when the time was right. His job was to remain faithful until then. The same is true for us – we are to remain faithful to God's call upon our lives.

Prayer
My Father in Heaven, You are in control of this universe. You control the lives of each and every person. I am so grateful that I can rest in Your will for my life. I do not need to scheme and make plans – all I have to do is faithfully serve and follow You. Amen.

Read 1 Chronicles 10

> SO SAUL DIED FOR HIS UNFAITHFULNESS WHICH HE HAD COMMITTED AGAINST THE LORD, BECAUSE HE DID NOT KEEP THE WORD OF THE LORD, AND ALSO BECAUSE HE CONSULTED A MEDIUM FOR GUIDANCE. BUT HE DID NOT INQUIRE OF THE LORD; THEREFORE HE KILLED HIM, AND TURNED THE KINGDOM OVER TO DAVID THE SON OF JESSE.
>
> 1 Chronicles 10:13–14

The thing that ultimately killed Saul was his unfaithfulness to the Lord. It really was a tragedy to see someone who was at one time a mighty man of God fall and have his life end so badly. This year our focus is upon walking by faith and not by sight. There are so many situations and circumstances that come our way that can cause us to wander off course. Yet, God is clear about what He wants from us. He is looking for men who will trust Him; men who will obey Him above all else.

So many people profess to love God, but they are not prepared to obey Him. You cannot have one without the other; it just doesn't work like that. Saul learned this to his detriment. When he chose to disobey God and to lie to Him, it was the beginning of the end for him. Sadly, the day Saul died so did his whole family. His three sons perished in the same battle. When David heard of Saul's death he didn't celebrate over his enemy's demise as one would expect. "How the mighty have fallen, and the weapons of war perished!" (2 Samuel 1:27). David knew only too well that it was God and God alone who gave victory.

The day would come when David too would experience the awful consequences of disobedience to God's laws. God is serious about us obeying His Word, my friends. Never mistake God's grace as licence to sin. The annals of history are littered with the corpses of those who have floundered upon the rocks of sin. God offers forgiveness to those who repent. King Saul never truly repented before God, and thus he sealed his fate. If you find yourself in a position where you have violated God's laws, now is the time for you to repent of your sin. Don't tempt God. Instead come before Him, repent, ask His forgiveness, then go and sin no more. Repentance means that you turn from the sin and don't do it again.

Prayer

My Father God, I come before You on bended knee. I realize that there is nowhere else for me to go but to You. Lord, I confess before You. I ask You to forgive me. I am sorry for what I have done, Lord. I ask You to cleanse me, fill me with Your Spirit, and renew me. Amen.

Read 2 Samuel 7:8–22

"For You, Lord God, know Your servant. For Your word's sake, and according to Your own heart, You have done all these great things, to make Your servant know them. Therefore You are great, O Lord God."

2 Samuel 7:20b–22a

In the same way that God made a covenant with Abraham, Isaac, Jacob, Noah, and Moses, so He also made one with David. God promises David that no matter what happens He will not punish David's house as He had Saul's: "But My mercy shall not depart from him, as I took it from Saul, whom I removed from before you. And your house and your kingdom shall be established forever before you. Your throne shall be established forever" (verses 15–16). When we spent time journeying with Moses a couple of months ago we saw God revealed for the first time as the covenant-keeping God (Jehovah).

Before that, we had seen Him revealed by many other names. Abraham experienced God as Creator, God Almighty, and Provider, to name but a few. David had already come to know God as the Lord of hosts – when He undertook for him in battle. In verses 15 and 16 God reveals Himself as merciful. This is important given the circumstances that will play out in David's life in later years. David had a unique journey with God. The Lord speaks about this as He details the covenant He is making with David. "Thus says the Lord of hosts: 'I took you from the sheepfold, from following the sheep, to be ruler over My people, over Israel'" (verse 8b).

God doesn't choose people based upon their standing in society, or upon their education. He takes the simple things of this world and uses them to confound the wise. I am a farmer; nothing more and nothing less. God has chosen to use me to spread His gospel. I am constantly awed and humbled by this. My friends, your background never needs to stand in the way of God using you. Education is a good thing, don't get me wrong, but it cannot on its own prepare you for serving the Master. What will make it possible for God to use you mightily is spending time with Him, learning to know Him and His Word. David received most of his training in the fields looking after the sheep.

Prayer

My Father, I praise You today that You are a covenant-keeping God. You never change. You show Your mercy from one generation to another. Your love and goodness know no end. Keep me faithful, so that You can use me in Your service. Amen.

Read Psalm 91

> HE WHO DWELLS IN THE SECRET PLACE OF THE MOST HIGH SHALL ABIDE
> UNDER THE SHADOW OF THE ALMIGHTY. I WILL SAY OF THE LORD, "HE IS MY
> REFUGE AND MY FORTRESS; MY GOD, IN HIM I WILL TRUST."
>
> Psalm 91:1–2

From a young age, starting when he encountered the bear and the lion, David knew what it was to face danger. It didn't stop when he entered King Saul's court. As we know, Saul tried on numerous occasions to harm and even kill David. Even after Saul's death danger didn't go away – David was a warrior and he faced many enemies who wanted him dead. As you read the psalms, many of them are written by David as he entreated God to deal with his enemies. David's relationship with God continued to be a close one; he expressed his love and trust in the Lord very beautifully through the many psalms that he wrote.

David took all of his emotions to the Lord. Whatever he was feeling, he shared it with God. We see David ranting about the unfairness of life, because it seemed as if it was more beneficial to be wicked than righteous (Psalm 73). We read of him beseeching God to heal him (Psalms 6 and 30). He asks God to forgive his sins (Psalm 38 and 41). David comes to God and repents after his sin of adultery and murder (Psalm 51). No matter what he was going through, David knew that the only Person to turn to was God.

So often we make the mistake of turning everywhere else before we turn to God. Don't get me wrong, I believe in doctors, my friends. I am not saying don't go to the doctor. What I am saying is go to God as well. He is the ultimate Healer. We go to psychologists and spend thousands – but we don't go to the Prince of Peace. We look to man to provide for us instead of going to Jehovah Jireh – our Provider. People go on quests to find truth and enlightenment, when it is Jesus who is the Light: He is "the way, the truth, and the life" (John 14:6). David understood that God was everything that he needed. Do you understand this truth, and do you live in the fullness of it?

Prayer

Lord Most High, because I love You, therefore You will deliver me; You will set me on high, because I know Your Name. When I call upon You, You answer me; You are with me in trouble; You deliver me and honour me. You satisfy me with long life, and show me Your Salvation. Amen.

Read Psalm 3

I LAY DOWN AND SLEPT; I AWOKE, FOR THE LORD SUSTAINED ME. I WILL
NOT BE AFRAID OF TEN THOUSANDS OF PEOPLE WHO HAVE SET THEMSELVES
AGAINST ME ALL AROUND.

Psalm 3:5–6

If you read through 2 Samuel then you will find that Absalom, one of David's sons, ended up being one of his father's worst enemies. He did not fear God as his father David did. He was ambitious and crafty, determined to get what he wanted, no matter whom he hurt in the process. He did everything that he could think of to undermine his father. He cunningly turned many of the Israelite men against David. The psalm we have just read was written by David while he was under attack from Absalom and his supporters. One of the mainstays of David's life, as we have already noted, is that no matter what he faced he always turned towards God for help.

Here again we see David reaching out to God, realizing that God was his only help. As a father, it is heartbreaking to even try and imagine what it must have been like for David to have a son like Absalom. Yet, all through Absalom's treachery David didn't waver in his love for him. If anything, David was too lenient with him, and maybe that is where the problem came in. As fathers we have a duty to train our children in the things of the Lord. We do this through love and grace, but with a firm hand. It is not for nothing that the Bible cautions us: "He who spares his rod hates his son, but he who loves him disciplines him promptly" (Proverbs 13:24).

The other important lesson to learn from the relationship between David and Absalom is the importance of perseverance and forgiveness. David never gave up on Absalom. He continued to care about him and love him. If you have a child who has chosen, despite your best efforts, to walk an ungodly path, take a lesson from David. Continue to pray for them; keep loving them and make sure they understand that the day they repent and turn back to God your door is open to them. Sometimes we become mixed up. We must hate the sin and love the sinner.

Prayer
My Father God, You know that I come to You with a heavy heart when I think about those that I love who have chosen not to serve You. Lord, help me to keep faithful to You no matter what. Give me Your love, grace, and mercy so that I can share them with my loved ones. Amen.

Read 2 Samuel 11:1–27

BUT THE THING THAT DAVID HAD DONE DISPLEASED THE LORD.

2 Samuel 11:27b

If ever there was a case in point for the saying: "It's not how you start, but how you finish that counts", David's life is one. The young man trusted God so implicitly that he could take on an entire army, with nothing more than a slingshot and a few stones. The same boy fought bears and lions with the sure knowledge that his God was protecting him. The mighty warrior, whom God had blessed over and over again with victory. This man, whom people referred to as the greatest king that Israel had ever known (besides Jesus Christ), was taken down by his lack of discipline and his desire for what did not belong to him.

Sin breeds sin, doesn't it, my friends? Once David had committed adultery with Bathsheba the die was cast. She became pregnant; David tried to cover his sin by calling Uriah, her husband, home from battle. Due to a deep-seated loyalty and respect Uriah refused to be with his wife. So David had to come up with another plan. His plan was to place Uriah in the front line of battle, so that he would be killed. David added murder to his list of sins. Isn't it so true, my friends, that once we begin sinning, it is a downward spiral and we don't seem able to put on the breaks.

These are truly terrible words: "But the thing that David had done displeased the Lord." We said before that one of the scariest things is having the Spirit of the Lord withdraw from your life. I urge you today that if you find yourself in a place where you have embarked on a road of sin: Stop! Don't go any further – turn around, come back to God, and repent. He has promised that He will always forgive you; but you have to stop what you are doing and repent. This is the only way. Don't walk the road of rebellion against God that will surely end in death and destruction. Instead choose life, love, and forgiveness.

Prayer

My Father in Heaven, I bow before You. You are a Holy and Awesome God. There is none like You, not on earth or in Heaven. Lord, Your grace, mercy, and forgiveness reach to the ends of the earth. Today, I turn to You and I ask You to forgive me, cleanse me, heal me, and restore me. Amen.

Read 2 Samuel 12:1–9

THEN NATHAN SAID TO DAVID, "YOU ARE THE MAN!"

2 Samuel 12:7a

God sent the prophet Nathan to confront David about his sin. Nathan told David a story, and by the time he came to the end David was terribly angry with the man in the story. He decreed that the man should die.

> Then Nathan said to David, "You are the man! Thus says the Lord God of Israel: 'I anointed you king over Israel, and I delivered you from the hand of Saul. I gave you your master's house and your master's wives into your keeping, and gave you the house of Israel and Judah. And if that had been too little, I also would have given you much more! Why have you despised the commandment of the Lord, to do evil in His sight?'"

2 Samuel 12:7–9a

What a terrible day for David. There are valuable lessons for us to learn from this period of David's life. So often we only want to focus upon the good and the positive. However, we are all human; we all fail, we sin, and we all make mistakes. Every one of the mighty men of faith in the Bible experienced times in their lives where they sinned and failed. Each one of them had their weaknesses. Jesus came to save sinners, my friend. His grace does not give us licence to sin – be very sure of that. Paul says:

> What shall we say then? Shall we continue in sin that grace may abound? Certainly not! … knowing this, that our old man was crucified with Him, that the body of sin might be done away with, that we should no longer be slaves of sin. Therefore do not let sin reign in your mortal body, that you should obey it in its lusts.

Romans 6:1–2a, 6 and 12

Jesus Christ came to this earth to save us from our sin. He came to give us eternal life. As Christians we must become more and more like Jesus each day. When we do sin we must be quick to repent and turn from our sin. Repentance means that you do not commit that sin again.

Prayer

My Father in Heaven, thank You for Your grace and mercy that is new every morning. You are faithful even when I am faithless. Forgive me that so often I wander away from You. So often I disappoint You by sinning. I repent before You today; I turn from my sin. Amen.

Read 2 Samuel 12:10–23

> AND NATHAN SAID TO DAVID, "THE LORD ALSO HAS PUT AWAY YOUR SIN;
> YOU SHALL NOT DIE. HOWEVER, BECAUSE BY THIS DEED YOU HAVE GIVEN
> GREAT OCCASION TO THE ENEMIES OF THE LORD TO BLASPHEME, THE CHILD
> ALSO WHO IS BORN TO YOU SHALL SURELY DIE."
>
> 2 Samuel 12:13b–14

David paid a terrible price for his sin because the first child that was born to him and Bathsheba died. From then onward you never again read of David doing any mighty works for God. You never hear of him killing another "Goliath". I don't doubt that he was saved, and I am sure he is in Heaven, because he repented.

Furthermore, he is still mentioned in the "Hall of Faith" in Hebrews 11:32–34:

> *And what more shall I say? For the time would fail me to tell of Gideon and
> Barak and Samson and Jephthah, also of David and Samuel and the prophets:
> who through faith subdued kingdoms, worked righteousness, obtained
> promises, stopped the mouths of lions, quenched the violence of fire, escaped
> the edge of the sword, out of weakness were made strong, became valiant in
> battle, turned to flight the armies of the aliens.*

But there were consequence to David's sin, and there are consequences to our sin. Remember that. David's family was in disarray. We read of all kinds of intrigue and dissention among them. Absalom, of whom we read a few days ago, is a prime example of this. David, the mighty man of God, risked everything for a few moments of pleasure. Sin has a way of escalating. Once he had committed the one sin he had to find a way to cover it up, and then he committed another one. So the web of sin will ensnare us if we are not careful. We need to be on the alert and awake to the wiles of the enemy. Peter warns us about this: "Be sober, be vigilant; because your adversary the devil walks about like a roaring lion, seeking whom he may devour" (1 Peter 5:8). Don't play with fire because you will get burned, my friends. Paul tells Timothy: "Flee also youthful lusts; but pursue righteousness, faith, love, peace with those who call on the Lord out of a pure heart" (2 Timothy 2:22). This Scripture applies whether you are sixteen, twenty-six, or sixty-six – flee lust and seek a pure heart.

Prayer

My Father God, You are serious about calling those who love You and serve You to walk in holiness before You. Lord, I realize that it takes a decision of the will to walk by faith and not by sight. It takes a decision of the will to choose a pure heart and to turn away from lust. Amen.

Read Psalm 51

AGAINST YOU, YOU ONLY, HAVE I SINNED, AND DONE THIS EVIL IN YOUR SIGHT...

Psalm 51:4a

David went to God with his sin. Throughout his life we see that David turned to God in the good times and the bad times. He knew that life was not worth living if he was separated from God. One thing David never forgot was that everything he had and was came about as a result of what God had done for him. So in what must have been the worst moment of his life he ran to his God. David had been through many battles in his life; he had known what it was to be hunted down and have enemies who had tried to kill him. Through all of those experiences, no matter how tough they were, he always had the moral high ground.

Now for the first time in his life he faced his own inadequacies. He had failed the God whom he had loved and served since he was a young boy. He faced a choice once again: turn to God or turn away from God. David trusted God's mercy more than he trusted any human being. We have the beautiful psalm that David wrote to God expressing his repentance. David acknowledged his sin, he didn't try and make excuses or blame anyone else; he took responsibility: "For I acknowledge my transgressions, and my sin is always before me" (verse 3).

My friend, if you find yourself in a similar place to the one in which David found himself, you too have a choice. Are you going to turn towards God or away from Him? Are you going to take responsibility or try to blame someone else? Repentance is owning up and taking responsibility, then turning away and not doing it again. God is merciful, He is gracious, and He is faithful. He will not cast anyone who has a sincerely repentant heart away from Him. "For You do not desire sacrifice, or else I would give it; You do not delight in burnt offering. The sacrifices of God are a broken spirit, a broken and a contrite heart – these, O God, You will not despise" (verses 16–17).

Prayer

My Father God, I bow in Your presence and I ask that You "Create in me a clean heart, O God, and renew a steadfast spirit within me. Do not cast me away from Your presence, and do not take Your Holy Spirit from me" (verses 10–11). Amen.

Read 2 Samuel 24:1–9

> SO THE KING SAID TO JOAB THE COMMANDER OF THE ARMY WHO WAS WITH
> HIM, "NOW GO THROUGHOUT ALL THE TRIBES OF ISRAEL, FROM DAN TO
> BEERSHEBA, AND COUNT THE PEOPLE, THAT I MAY KNOW THE NUMBER OF THE
> PEOPLE."
>
> 2 Samuel 24:2

David decided after he had conquered the enemy through the power of God that he wanted to see how strong he was. So he sent Joab, his commander, to go and count how many able men there were in the kingdom. Why did he do this? I'll tell you why he did it: because he was beginning to place his trust in his army instead of in God. That made God very angry.

My dear friend, in whom are you trusting right now? If your trust is in anyone or anything other than God you are going to come up short. Maybe you are trusting in your finances, or in your farm; it could be that your trust is in your business – if it is, I say it again: you are going to come up short. Are you trusting in your spouse? If you are then that is unfair of you. You're putting tremendous pressure on her. You cannot do that, my friend. You have to trust God, and God alone. "So we may boldly say: 'The Lord is my helper; I will not fear. What can man do to me?'" (Hebrews 13:6). This is what God wants from us: to trust Him alone.

God is looking for a man: maybe it is you sitting quietly reading this. "For the eyes of the Lord run to and fro throughout the whole earth, to show Himself strong on behalf of those whose heart is loyal to Him" (2 Chronicles 16:9a). He wants you to trust Him. Then He will work great exploits through you. "… but the people who know their God shall be strong, and carry out great exploits" (Daniel 11:32b). All his life David had known what it was to do great exploits for God. He had seen God working on his behalf. Then he sinned and even though God forgave him it seemed as if he lost his edge. Don't let that happen to you, my friend. Choose well, stay strong, stay sharp, and finish well. After all, it is not how we start, but how we finish that counts.

Prayer

My Father God, thank You that Your hand is upon my life. Help me to walk moment by moment in the power of Your Spirit. Lord, I realize that when left to my own devices it is so easy for me to wander off the path. Keep me faithful, keep me strong, and keep me close. Amen.

Read Psalm 20

SOME TRUST IN CHARIOTS, AND SOME IN HORSES; BUT WE WILL REMEMBER THE NAME OF THE LORD OUR GOD.

Psalm 20:7

As a boy, when David faced the bear and the lion, he didn't consider their size and weigh up whether he could take them or not. His only thought was to trust God to help him, and he took them out. When he went up against Goliath, he did not rely upon Saul's army. David did not look at the number of soldiers on each side and calculate what his chances were. No, he totally relied upon God. God gave him the victory and after that David went from strength to strength. David was a mighty man. When he went out to battle his mighty men went with him. They did not need to be mighty in number, only in faith. I want to challenge you that it is not about numbers; it is about faith in Christ.

"Some trust in chariots, and some in horses; but we will remember the name of the Lord our God." Today we don't have chariots pulled by horses, but we have a myriad of things we can substitute in their place. We need to constantly remember that God is in control of our destiny. Not man, not circumstances, not politics, not the economy, and not even our health; God alone is in control.

Folks, He is a jealous God: "for you shall worship no other god, for the Lord, whose name is Jealous, is a jealous God" (Exodus 34:14). God's jealousy is not the bad kind. It is borne out of love for us. He gave His only begotten Son, who died on a cross, so that you and I can have eternal life. He has a right to be jealous over us. He has a right to be angry when we start to prostitute ourselves with other gods. I am not only referring to physical idols. The idols in our lives can take on many forms; to name but a few: money, security, education, our appearance. An idol is anything that takes our focus off of Jesus and causes us to place our trust in something or someone else.

Prayer

My Lord and God, I bow humbly in Your presence. Lord, search my heart, I pray. Show me where I am placing my focus. Forgive me and help me, I pray, to look to You and only You for everything of which I have need. Lord, I realize that without You I am nothing. Amen.

Read 1 Chronicles 21:1–30

> AND JOAB ANSWERED, "MAY THE LORD MAKE HIS PEOPLE A HUNDRED
> TIMES MORE THAN THEY ARE. BUT, MY LORD THE KING, ARE THEY NOT ALL
> MY LORD'S SERVANTS? WHY THEN DOES MY LORD REQUIRE THIS THING? WHY
> SHOULD HE BE A CAUSE OF GUILT IN ISRAEL?"
>
> 1 Chronicles 21:3

Even David's trusted general Joab was scared. He begged David not to take the census. He knew it was going to upset the Lord. Joab did as David asked, but he did not count the men of God. He didn't count the Levites, only the soldiers – even though David told him to count everybody. Who inspired David to take a census? That's right, Satan did. The devil himself. I am telling you now as I sit here, there are many in this world of ours at the moment who are being inspired by the devil. The devil is telling you that our nations have gone to the dogs. It is the devil who says to you that there is no hope for this world.

The devil himself is telling you to trust only yourself. He is telling you that you cannot trust anyone else, not even God. He says don't trust your children; they will let you down when the going gets tough. No, they won't. I have handed my farms over to my children with the title deeds, the cheque book, and the debts. Why? Because my trust is in God, who is in my children. Exactly.

There are always consequences to your actions. I repeat: there are always consequences to your actions. Of course, if you repent God forgives you every time. He is a merciful God. He is a forgiving God. The consequences remain, though. Young man, if you are sleeping with that girl, you know you're not supposed to, because she is not your wife. If you make her pregnant, and then realize you don't really love her, it is too late because you have an obligation to her and the baby. The baby in that girl's womb is yours. As long as that child lives, every time you see the child you will remember what you did. God will forgive you if you repent. As I have said before, repentance means don't do it again. God's forgiveness does not take away the consequences, however – they remain forever.

Prayer

My Father God, I come before You and I realize that You are speaking to me right now. Forgive me that I allow the devil to speak negatively to me about certain things. I realize that he cannot do it if I don't allow him to. Help me to only listen to Your voice. Amen.

Read 2 Samuel 12:15–25

THEN DAVID COMFORTED BATHSHEBA HIS WIFE, AND WENT IN TO HER AND LAY WITH HER. SO SHE BORE A SON, AND HE CALLED HIS NAME SOLOMON. NOW THE LORD LOVED HIM, AND HE SENT WORD BY THE HAND OF NATHAN THE PROPHET: SO HE CALLED HIS NAME JEDIDIAH, BECAUSE OF THE LORD.

2 Samuel 12:24–25

David never again knew the full glory of God's blessing after he sinned. He knew forgiveness, but not the former greatness that he had known. However, God did not abandon David or his seed. As we know, Jesus was directly descended from David's line. He was of the house of David. Our reading today talks of the birth of Solomon. It tells us: "Now the Lord loved him". God acknowledged Solomon's birth and sent "word" with the prophet Nathan. This shows the mercy of God. It shows Him as the covenant-keeping God.

We see in 2 Samuel 7:12–16 how God's covenant with David spoke of Solomon and the part he would play in the perpetuation of the house of David, as well as Jesus being the ultimate fulfilment of the covenant:

When your days are fulfilled and you rest with your fathers, I will set up your seed after you, who will come from your body, and I will establish his kingdom. He shall build a house for My name, and I will establish the throne of his kingdom forever. I will be his Father, and he shall be My son. If he commits iniquity, I will chasten him with the rod of men and with the blows of the sons of men. But My mercy shall not depart from him, as I took it from Saul, whom I removed from before you. And your house and your kingdom shall be established forever before you. Your throne shall be established forever.

Where would any of us be without God's grace, mercy, and faithfulness in our lives? Paul writing to Timothy says: "If we are faithless, He remains faithful; He cannot deny Himself" (2 Timothy 2:13). We know from Scripture that Solomon grew up to be a wise and godly man. He chose to serve God and He used him. I don't know what is going on in your life and where you find yourself right now. I want to say to you, turn toward God and not away from Him. He will lead you, and He will guide you in His paths of righteousness.

Prayer

My Father, thank You for Your great love for mankind. You have shown Your love from the beginning of time. I am so encouraged as I read of Your faithfulness and goodness. Lord, I turn to You today. I ask You to take my hand and lead me in Your paths of righteousness. Amen.

Read Psalm 62

> TRULY MY SOUL SILENTLY WAITS FOR GOD; FROM HIM COMES MY SALVATION.
> HE ONLY IS MY ROCK AND MY SALVATION; HE IS MY DEFENSE; I SHALL NOT BE
> GREATLY MOVED.
>
> Psalm 62:1–2

Looking back over this past month and the lessons we have learned from David's life, as well as his walk with God, I hope that you have been encouraged. There have been so many truths that God has imparted to us through His Word. David was a man who loved God with all his heart. Even when he sinned he didn't turn away from God; he turned to Him. He was a man who showed great faith in God. There have been few men who have shown greater faith than David – think of his days as a shepherd, and the time of his battle with Goliath.

God chose him to be king of Israel and God doesn't make mistakes. When God chose David it was because of his heart. His was on a journey of friendship with God; a journey of trust and love. God never turned His back on David, even though David had to accept that there would be consequences for his actions. In the midst of the consequences God was there. God did not break the covenant that He made with David and He redeemed David's sin by making Solomon, the child of David and Bathsheba, part of the fulfilment of that covenant.

What does this say to you and to me? We've already established that God's grace and mercy doesn't give us licence to sin. No, indeed! It gives us motivation to love God with all of our heart, soul, and mind. We are encouraged today to trust God for every aspect of our lives; to depend upon Him and Him alone for all of our needs.

> *My soul, wait silently for God alone, for my expectation is from Him. He only is my rock and my salvation; He is my defense; I shall not be moved. In God is my salvation and my glory; the rock of my strength, and my refuge, is in God. Trust in Him at all times, you people; pour out your heart before Him; God is a refuge for us.*
>
> Psalm 62:5–8

Choose to wait upon the Lord, and choose to walk by faith and not by sight.

Prayer
My Father God, I thank You for the example of David's journey of friendship with You. I thank You that I have learned so many lessons from his life. Help me now to walk forward with You in trust and obedience, waiting upon You and relying only on You. Amen.

ELIJAH AND ELISHA'S JOURNEY OF PURPOSE

Their journey of faith began when they heeded the call to serve

1. Elijah's God
2. God provides for Elijah
3. What do you choose?
4. To blame or not to blame?
5. Questioning God
6. Elijah, a man of God
7. At the crossroads
8. Where do you stand?
9. Whom do you fear?
10. Toward whom is your heart turned?
11. Increase our faith
12. The Lord is with you
13. Walking the narrow way
14. Be prepared for a fight
15. Greater is He that is in you
16. Zealous for the Lord
17. Elijah was not alone
18. From Elijah to Elisha
19. Elisha's persistence
20. The Father longs to give
21. God's Elijahs and Elishas
22. God uses what we have
23. What can I do for you?
24. I shall not want
25. Sharing Jesus – the Light
26. Accept, obey, and believe
27. Take hold of your miracle
28. Open your eyes to the miracles
29. God restores what was lost
30. God honours His Word
31. Power even in death

Read 1 Kings 17:1–7

> AND ELIJAH THE TISHBITE, OF THE INHABITANTS OF GILEAD, SAID TO AHAB,
> "AS THE LORD GOD OF ISRAEL LIVES, BEFORE WHOM I STAND, THERE SHALL
> NOT BE DEW NOR RAIN THESE YEARS, EXCEPT AT MY WORD."
>
> 1 Kings 17:1

Elijah was a man with a purpose. The first time we read about him he is delivering a message from God to wicked King Ahab. Elijah the Tishbite is one of my biblical heroes. You know that King Ahab was a terrible tyrant – one of Israel's worst ever kings. He dominated Israel through violence, oppression, and fear. However, there was one man for whom King Ahab had tremendous respect, and that was Elijah the Tishbite. Elijah was known as the hairy man who wore a leather belt (2 Kings 1:8). He was the predecessor of John the Baptist, because the same spirit that was in Elijah was in John the Baptist.

I want to tell you a little bit about Elijah. What happened to him also occurs today. When a man of God with a backbone stands up and calls sin by its name, some people don't like it. Elijah was just such a man. You can be sure that if you stand up for Jesus Christ, my dear friend, you may be hated, you may be despised, or you may be loved. But one thing people won't be is indifferent to you. Elijah was a "black or white" kind of man – there were no grey areas for him. He was a man who gave all or nothing. He was either in or he was out. We need more men like Elijah today.

D. L. Moody (1837–99) was one of the greatest evangelists who ever lived. He spoke to over 100 million people during his life. There was no television or radio at that time. Once he travelled from America to Britain to preach on what he thought would be a short campaign, but in fact it lasted for three years. Whole trainloads of people followed him from station to station. Soon revival broke out. D. L. Moody used to say, "If man has nothing bad to say about you, you can rest assured that the Lord Jesus has nothing good to say about you." Elijah wasn't popular with King Ahab because he pointed out his sin to him.

Prayer
My Father God, it is such a privilege to begin another month examining the life of yet one more of Your mighty men of faith. Lord, I pray that You will teach me lessons from the life of Elijah. I want to have the same spirit that he did. I too want to serve You wholeheartedly. Amen.

GOD PROVIDES FOR ELIJAH

Read 1 Kings 17:8–16

THE BIN OF FLOUR WAS NOT USED UP, NOR DID THE JAR OF OIL RUN DRY, ACCORDING TO THE WORD OF THE LORD WHICH HE SPOKE BY ELIJAH.

1 Kings 17:16

As we have moved through this year looking at some of the key men of faith in the Bible, have you noticed how each one walked their own road of obedience to God? Each one of them had their own journey of faith; each of them had their own test of obedience. Faith and obedience; obedience and faith – interchangeable with each other. Elijah's journey was a path of obedience to God. It cost him because it made him unpopular with the king. We saw in our reading yesterday that God told Elijah to leave and go eastward. He found himself by the Brook Cherith, where God looked after him until the brook dried up.

Then he went to Zarephath. Have you noticed that each time the Bible says: "Then the word of the Lord came to him, saying…" (verses 2 and 8), Elijah waited upon God? He heard from Him and then he obeyed Him. God had prepared the way and when Elijah arrived in Zarephath he went to a widow who looked after him; in turn God looked after the widow. For the length of the drought she never ran out of flour and oil with which to feed her family. She obeyed God and God blessed her.

So often we complicate our lives with our human logic. We expect to see the end from the beginning of a situation. Faith doesn't work like this, does it? Faith is taking one right step after another. Faith is obeying, even when it is hard to do so. Faith is knowing that God will come through for you – not a moment too soon and not a moment too late. Are you facing a drought in your life at the moment? Does it feel as if nothing is going right? If so, then you need to come before the Lord and seek His face. Allow His Spirit to minister to you. Check your walk with Him. If everything is as it should be then simply hang in there. Know for certain that He will never leave you, nor forsake you. Continue to faithfully walk through the drought with Him.

Prayer

My Father in Heaven, in the midst of turmoil You are always there. You are my Rock and my Fortress. You are a very Present Help in times of trouble. Lord, I cling to You. I hold fast to Your love and Your faithfulness. Keep me steady, keep me faithful, and keep me true. In Jesus' Name. Amen.

Read 1 Kings 17:14–24

> FOR THUS SAYS THE LORD GOD OF ISRAEL: "THE BIN OF FLOUR SHALL NOT
> BE USED UP, NOR SHALL THE JAR OF OIL RUN DRY, UNTIL THE DAY THE LORD
> SENDS RAIN ON THE EARTH."
>
> 1 Kings 17:14

Elijah told King Ahab that it wouldn't rain for three-and-a-half years, and there wasn't any rain. This meant that there was very little food and water available. Elijah went and stayed at a widow's house. When he arrived she had just enough flour and oil to make one more cake for her son and herself; then they were going to lie down and die. The prophet came and he tested her. He told her that he was hungry. He asked her to give him some bread to eat and water to drink. She told him she only had enough for one last meal for her and her son. The choice she faced was to be obedient to the man of God or not. She made the cake and she gave it to him. When she looked in her flour bin there was enough flour to make a cake for her and her son to eat. This went on each day of the drought. There was enough flour to feed them; because of her faithfulness God honoured her, and she never went hungry.

We experienced a similar miracle on our farm during one of our men's conferences. We had 7,400 men for a whole weekend. However, we only had enough food for 5,000 men. I want you to remember God always honours faith. If you forget everything else, remember this. I want to tell you folks that God multiplied the food so that we collected thirty-six baskets of leftovers from the three meals. Divided by three that is twelve baskets per meal. Exactly what Jesus' disciples collected after He had fed 5,000 men with two fishes and five barley loaves.

God is faithful; He will never let you down. Trust Him no matter what the situation. If He has told you to do something then obey Him; He will do what He has said He will do. The widow's part in the story was to choose to obey – to do what Elijah asked of her. God's part was multiplying the flour and the oil.

Prayer
My Father, You speak to me so clearly through Your Word. Lord, the bottom line is that You want me to choose to obey You above all else. When I do as You want me to then You undertake. Lord, miracles are as much for today as they were for Bible times. Lord, I am looking to You for a miracle. Amen.

Read 1 Kings 17:17–24

NOW IT HAPPENED AFTER THESE THINGS THAT THE SON OF THE WOMAN WHO
OWNED THE HOUSE BECAME SICK. AND HIS SICKNESS WAS SO SERIOUS THAT
THERE WAS NO BREATH LEFT IN HIM.

1 Kings 17:17

We understand miracles here at Shalom Ministries. We also know that after a miracle the devil sometimes tries to test us. The powers of darkness come against us. The enemy will try to drag us down when we are on a spiritual high. It is tempting to cry out, "Lord, what is happening? You have just done this amazing thing and now things seem to be getting worse!" Can you relate to this? Well, maybe you can. Certainly, in the case of the widow's son dying, Elijah could. This was the widow's reaction when her son became ill and died. She immediately blamed Elijah for the disaster that had befallen her. She asked him, "Have you brought death to my house?" Has this ever happened to you? You led somebody to Christ, or rather you were instrumental in their conversion. Everything went well until suddenly difficulties arose. The new Christian turned around and blamed you. They may have suggested that they were better off in their old life.

The widow questioned God's goodness despite the fact that He had been providing for her all through the terrible drought. Elijah, on the other hand, immediately turned to God and not away from Him. This is the test, my friends. How does your faith hold up in times of crisis? What is your first reaction: to blame God and sometimes other Christians, or to turn towards Him? He is your Strong Tower. He is your Ever-Present Help in times of trouble. Learn to call upon His Name rather than to rant and rave about your misfortunes. He was faithful to Elijah; He will be faithful to you as well, but you have to call upon Him and believe that He will answer you.

Shalom Ministries are committed to pulling people out of hellish situations and restoring them to Christ. This can be a messy business sometimes, in the same way the widow's situation was for Elijah. We have to take it on the chin. Jesus says, "When people say all manner of evil about you for My Name's sake, jump for joy" (Matthew 5:11b–12a, my paraphrase).

Prayer

My Father, I realize that the business of saving people for Your Kingdom is a messy business. Yet there is nothing that I would rather be doing than working in Your vineyard, bringing in the harvest. Keep me faithful. Help me to have courage and to take it on the chin when necessary. Amen.

Read 1 Kings 17:17–24

SO SHE SAID TO ELIJAH, "WHAT HAVE I TO DO WITH YOU, O MAN OF GOD? HAVE YOU COME TO ME TO BRING MY SIN TO REMEMBRANCE, AND TO KILL MY SON?"

1 Kings 17:18

There have been times, during periods of drought in the area where I live, when people have come to me asking, "Where is the rain?" I in turn have asked them, "Do you think I am the Rainmaker?" They have answered, "Yes," and I reply, "No, I am not; I am the son of the Rainmaker." I have to admit that I love saying this. If you believe in Him, then, my friend, you too are the son of the Rainmaker. From the beginning of time people have looked for something or someone they can physically see, to either blame or to worship.

Remember how the Israelites behaved towards Moses? He was their hero when he led them out of Egypt; the Red Sea parted allowing them to march through, and Pharaoh's soldiers were drowned. It didn't take long before they began feeling hungry and thirsty. Then they moaned and complained to Moses, "Why didn't you leave us in Egypt? At least there we had onions and leeks to eat. There we could be buried properly." So, folks, beware of this. Why do people lay blame? They see you as representing the Lord. So when things don't go well they come to you for answers.

You also see this when someone becomes ill. So often the first thing people ask is, "Where is this God of yours? He is supposed to be a God of love." Or if there is a bad accident they ask, "How can your God allow this to happen?" Often it is people who have given their lives to the Lord who ask these questions. When they do, you have to be strong, patient, and loving because frequently they are new Christians, and they are still learning. My friends, the lesson to learn from this is that we have to walk by faith and not by sight. We have to share God's truth with other people. We must not question God; He is in control of every aspect of our lives. Trusting Him is a choice each individual must make.

Prayer

My Father God, forgive me, I pray, for those times that I have been tempted to doubt You. Lord, I know that You and You alone are my Rock, and my Fortress. I shelter under Your wings. I nestle in Your loving arms. There is no other Help but You. Lord, undertake for me, I pray. Amen.

Read 1 Kings 17:17–24

> THEN THE WOMAN SAID TO ELIJAH, "NOW BY THIS I KNOW THAT YOU ARE
> A MAN OF GOD, AND THAT THE WORD OF THE LORD IN YOUR MOUTH IS THE
> TRUTH."
>
> 1 Kings 17:24

There are many men who claim to be men of God. However, the question I want us to explore today is: What does it really mean to "be a man of God"? A man of God walks his talk. Too many people who claim to be followers of Jesus, who proclaim themselves to be men of God, do not take care to ensure that their walk and their talk match up. God looks on the heart, my friends; we have said this many times. He knows the condition of each man's heart. He is more concerned with your inner life than He is with your outer life. It is what goes on in a man's mind and heart that defines his actions.

A man of God is not scared to speak the truth of God's Word. Now we don't run around trying to make enemies when we preach the truth. The Bible will condemn you, but it will also set you free. You don't have to try and be controversial. All you have to do is preach the truth, and you will be controversial. Why? Because Jesus was controversial. We need Elijahs more today than we've ever needed them since the foundation of the world. Men who are ready to put their faith on the line. Men who will act upon their convictions. Men who will not be afraid to stand up and proclaim God's Truth.

A man of God ministers first and foremost to his own family. Your loved ones need to know who you are before the world does. Are you the same person on a Sunday morning in church that you are when you arrive home from church, and the front door closes? It is no good us running around trying to save the world when those in our own homes are lost. Your first responsibility is to share Jesus with your children. Be an example to them of what God the Father is like. Allow them to experience love, grace, forgiveness, and discipline. A loving father leads and guides his family in the ways of God.

Prayer

My Father God, You are a Loving Father to me. You have shown me Your ways, Lord. You lead me in paths of righteousness, for Your Name's sake. Help me to be Your man. I want my walk to match up with my talk. I want to lead my family to You and I want to be a witness to others. Amen.

Read 1 Kings 18:1–16

> NOW AS OBADIAH WAS ON HIS WAY, SUDDENLY ELIJAH MET HIM; AND HE
> RECOGNIZED HIM, AND FELL ON HIS FACE, AND SAID, "IS THAT YOU, MY LORD
> ELIJAH?" AND HE ANSWERED HIM, "IT IS I. GO, TELL YOUR MASTER, "ELIJAH
> IS HERE.'"
>
> 1 Kings 18:7–8

Ahab's servant Obadiah was a godly man. He loved the Lord. When Elijah appeared before him he found himself standing at a crossroads. Would he have the faith to do what Elijah asked him to do or would he run scared? It was a difficult choice because Ahab would as soon kill him as look at him. Obadiah was scared that Elijah would disappear again, and leave him to face the music. However, he chose to do as Elijah asked and he informed Ahab that Elijah wanted to meet with him. Do you face a crossroads in your life right now? There are two options before you: one is a godly option; the other will lead you away from the Lord.

Have you ever seen a railway siding where the railway lines cross over each other leading off into the siding? When the train comes along the regular lines it has to change tracks in order to pull into the siding. A decision has to be made to continue on or cross over into the siding. This is what the choices that we sometimes have to make are like. Do we carry on as usual, or do we choose to cross over to follow the path God has for us? Are you at a crossroads right now? Are there choices you have to make?

I don't know what is happening in your life. I don't know what choices you are facing. But I want you to take courage from Elijah. He knew exactly who he was, he knew where he was going, and he knew where his destiny lay. Time and again people come to me. They say things like: "Angus, I don't know what to do."; "Angus, I don't have any direction in my life, can you please pray for me?" Folks, all you have to do is ask God and He'll tell you. It's been said, "The world stands aside for the man who knows where he's going." Be like Obadiah and Elijah: choose the path you're going to walk and then follow through.

Prayer

My Father, thank You that in the midst of all the chaos and uncertainty You are always the same. You are calling me to choose to follow You. To walk in Your ways and according to Your will for my life. You are inviting me to be a man of courage and of principle who always chooses the right way. Amen.

Read Revelation 3

BEHOLD, I STAND AT THE DOOR AND KNOCK. IF ANYONE HEARS MY VOICE AND OPENS THE DOOR, I WILL COME IN TO HIM AND DINE WITH HIM, AND HE WITH ME.

Revelation 3:20

In our reading yesterday Elijah was about to meet with King Ahab. Ahab didn't know it but he was about to face a choice. The land had gone through a terrible drought. You would have thought that this would have caused him to come before the Lord in repentance, but no, he stubbornly refused to humble himself before God. What about you today? Where are you standing? Are you a Christian in name only? Are you one of those fair-weather Christians? It depends on how things are going. If things are going well, then: "Praise God, Hallelujah!" But if things are going tough, then: "God where are you? Why have you rejected me?"

Folks, this is not what it means to serve God! Elijah served God unconditionally, and when he called out to God, God heard his prayers and He answered him. And that's what He wants you to do: to say, "God, I'm standing at a crossroads." Now folks, as I have said, there are railway lines: one to the left and one to the right. I have to "get in" or "get out", as they say. It has to be one or the other because God cannot tolerate a lukewarm Christian. "So then, because you are lukewarm, and neither cold nor hot, I will vomit you out of My mouth" (verse 16).

Are you going to be red hot like Elijah was? I'll tell you something: when Elijah walked into a place everyone knew what he stood for. We need more people like Elijah in our generation. He fearlessly carried out God's commands. He did not run hot and cold. He stood firm and listened to the voice of the Lord. Are there voices around you clamouring so loudly that the voice of the Lord is being drowned out? He stands at the door and He knocks. Will you let Him in? Will you choose today to serve Him above all others? For Elijah there was no other choice. He loved God wholeheartedly and He didn't care who knew about it. What is your choice?

Prayer

My God and Father, as I bow in Your presence, I hear Your voice calling out to me. I hear You knocking. I choose to open the door to You, Lord, and never close it again. I choose to stand tall for You. I want to serve You with all of my heart and strength for as long as I live. Amen.

Read 1 Kings 18:9–24

> Then it happened, when Ahab saw Elijah, that Ahab said to him, "Is that you, O troubler of Israel?" And he answered, "I have not troubled Israel, but you and your father's house have, in that you have forsaken the commandments of the Lord and have followed the Baals."
>
> 1 Kings 18:17–18

After three-and-a-half years of drought Ahab's heart was still hardened towards God. He had not come to the place of realizing that his wickedness was the cause of Israel's suffering. It was easier for him to blame the man of God, Elijah. Once again we see Elijah's fearlessness. He chose to obey God rather than man. He was the only prophet of the Lord left. This did not fill him with fear, because he knew that God was on his side.

Sin is a terrible thing and it blinds us to the realities that are staring us in the face. So many people have chosen to walk the broad road that leads to destruction instead of the narrow road that leads to eternal life. We live in desperate times, my friends. They are desperate because we are in a war for souls of people. The enemy continually tries to blind them, but we have the message of the Good News of Jesus Christ that can shine the light into their darkness. We need to be people like Elijah. We need to be fearlessly spreading the message of the gospel to those around us.

Too often we are cowered by the comments and ridicule of the world. We are scared of what people will think of us. We do not want to be known as fanatics. My friends, this is not how a man of faith behaves. A man who chooses to walk by faith and not by sight trusts his God to lead him. He chooses obedience to God and His Word above the world. This is how Elijah lived. He was single-minded and focused completely upon what God was calling him to do. Everyone else feared King Ahab. We saw that even Obadiah, who was a godly man, feared him. He was convinced that when he went back and told Ahab that Elijah wanted to meet with him, he would be put to death. In the end, even though he was scared, Obadiah obeyed God. Where do you stand today: do you choose to obey man or God?

Prayer

My Father, I am so grateful for the example of men like Elijah. You are looking for modern-day Elijahs who will fearlessly proclaim Your Word. Lord, I want to be such a man. Fill me with Your Holy Spirit, I pray. Give me the power and strength to walk in Your ways and obey You. Amen.

Read 1 Kings 18:21–40

AND ELIJAH CAME TO ALL THE PEOPLE, AND SAID, "HOW LONG WILL YOU FALTER BETWEEN TWO OPINIONS? IF THE LORD IS GOD, FOLLOW HIM; BUT IF BAAL, FOLLOW HIM." BUT THE PEOPLE ANSWERED HIM NOT A WORD.

1 Kings 18:21

I have visited the very same mountain that Elijah stood on, folks: Mount Carmel. He said, "Right, now is the time of truth: let's see who God is. You serve Baal (a false god). I serve the God of Israel. Let's see whose god is the greatest. You make your sacrifice and I will make mine. Then let's see what happens." You have read the story. What a scene it must have been! On the one side the 450 prophets of Baal, erecting an altar to him. Elijah, one lone man, on the other side, building an altar to his God.

Once the altars were built the sacrifices were laid on them. Then Elijah told them to pour water over the wood on his altar, to make it good and wet. He did this so that they could not later claim that he had cheated in any way. The scene was set: all of Israel were watching, along with King Ahab and his entourage. You see, my friends, faith means to believe unconditionally. Elijah was a man of faith; he didn't only see things from a natural perspective. He knew he was going to see fire come down from Heaven. Why? Because God had told him what to do. He obeyed God and he trusted in God. Have we not said so many times that obedience and faith go hand in hand?

You read about the antics of the prophets of Baal. No matter how much they performed nothing happened. Yet all that Elijah had to do was call upon the Name of the Lord. "Lord God of Abraham, Isaac, and Israel, let it be known this day that You are God in Israel and I am Your servant, and that I have done all these things at Your word. Hear me, O Lord, hear me, that this people may know that You are the Lord God, and that You have turned their hearts back to You again" (verses 36b–37). I ask you, my friend, what about your heart: is it turned toward God or away from Him?

Prayer

My Father in Heaven, I realize again as I read Your Word that You demand wholehearted commitment from me. I cannot falter between two opinions. I have to be 100 per cent committed to You and Your purposes for my life. Lord, I choose to serve You, the Living God. Amen.

Read Luke 17:1–10

AND THE APOSTLES SAID TO THE LORD, "INCREASE OUR FAITH." SO THE
LORD SAID, "IF YOU HAVE FAITH AS A MUSTARD SEED, YOU CAN SAY TO THIS
MULBERRY TREE, "BE PULLED UP BY THE ROOTS AND BE PLANTED IN THE SEA,'
AND IT WOULD OBEY YOU."

Luke 17:5–6

I want to share the story of evangelist Duncan Campbell with you. He was a modern-day man of faith. This story I am sharing with you took place on the Isle of Lewis in the Scottish Hebrides in 1950. Christians in that area had been praying for revival for many years. Duncan Campbell was at a prayer meeting in a bothy (a small stone cottage found in Scotland). He found the meeting to be hard going, and asked a blacksmith who had already witnessed God's hand in bringing people to faith, to pray.

The godly young man, who had the spirit of Elijah, stood up and began praying. It was nearly two in the morning. "God, do You know that Your honour is at stake?" he said. "You promised to pour water on the thirsty and floods on the dry ground and, God, You are not doing it!" Campbell recounts that once the young man had finished speaking the walls of the cottage started rattling. Stone walls, folks, began vibrating. They ran out into the street; the whole village fell on their knees in repentance before God. Revival had come to the Hebrides.

Duncan Campbell had embarked on a ten-day campaign and he ended up staying for two years. Folks, people came from all over the world. The pubs and dance halls closed down. Farmers had prayer meetings in the middle of their fields. Elijah told the prophets of Baal to stand back; then he called to the God of gods, and fire came down. Fire came straight down from Heaven and consumed the sacrifice; consumed the wet wood, the meat, even the stones until there was only a black hole left. I want to ask you, where is the God of Elijah today? That's what Elisha, the prophet who came after Elijah asked: "For the eyes of the Lord run to and fro throughout the whole earth, to show Himself strong on behalf of those whose heart is loyal to Him" (2 Chronicles 16:9a).

Prayer

My Lord, God of Elijah, You are the same God who brought fire down from Heaven. In Your Word You say that if I have faith like a mustard seed I can uproot the mulberry tree and plant it in the sea. Lord, like the disciples, I ask You to increase my faith. Give me the spirit of Elijah, I pray. Amen.

Read Psalm 23

> HE MAKES ME TO LIE DOWN IN GREEN PASTURES; HE LEADS ME BESIDE
> THE STILL WATERS. HE RESTORES MY SOUL; HE LEADS ME IN THE PATHS OF
> RIGHTEOUSNESS FOR HIS NAME'S SAKE.
>
> Psalm 23:2–3

We forget that the tongue is very powerful. What you say is what you get: "I am not feeling well"; "I will never get over this flu"; "I will never get a job" – and you won't. You have to begin walking in the Spirit. We have to start believing that God will do His best for us. We are going to look at what can happen in our lives after a miracle takes place. We will also look at what happened to Elijah. It has a lot of relevance for your life and mine. I have shared with you before that I do not subscribe to the theology that states: "Come to Jesus and all your problems will be over." This is definitely not the whole truth. It is a half-truth, and a half-truth is a lie.

There is nowhere in the Bible where Jesus says: "Come to Me and all your troubles will be over." He does, however, say, "Come to Me, all you who labor and are heavy laden, and I will give you rest. Take My yoke upon you and learn from Me, for I am gentle and lowly in heart, and you will find rest for your souls. For My yoke is easy and My burden is light" (Matthew 11:28–30). This does not mean that you will have no more trouble.

Your burden may be heavy, but the Lord walks with you. He takes the burden and sees you through the fire safely to the other side. I'd rather be in a little rowing boat with Jesus Christ, rowing around the southern-most tip of South Africa, with waves about twenty metres high, than to be without Him on a lake with water as smooth as glass. Why? Because to be with Jesus is to be at peace. Being without Him is being in hell. As you know, I am a simple man, a farmer, and I want to simplify Heaven and hell. Heaven is being with God and hell is being without Him. I think that pretty much sums it up. Don't you agree?

Prayer

Dear Lord, I thank You that You are with me no matter what happens in my life. You didn't promise that everything would be smooth sailing; but you did promise that You will lead me beside still waters even in the midst of the storm. Thank You that Your yoke is easy and Your burden is light. Amen.

Read Matthew 7:13–29

> ENTER BY THE NARROW GATE; FOR WIDE IS THE GATE AND BROAD IS THE
> WAY THAT LEADS TO DESTRUCTION, AND THERE ARE MANY WHO GO IN BY IT.
> BECAUSE NARROW IS THE GATE AND DIFFICULT IS THE WAY WHICH LEADS TO
> LIFE, AND THERE ARE FEW WHO FIND IT.
>
> Matthew 7:13–14

Very often when a person gives their life to Christ they say: "I am going to walk the Christian road, I am going to walk the Calvary Way, and I am going to serve the Lord"; "I am going to stop drinking and doing drugs"; "I am going to quit smoking"; or "I am not going to watch pornography any more." Then all of a sudden all hell breaks loose. Have you ever noticed this? The next day, whatever the problem is, it seems to be worse than ever before. Of course! The devil doesn't want to let go of you. Nevertheless, I want to tell you, you have to break with whatever it is, because you are on the wrong road.

In our reading we saw that there are two roads. The narrow road is difficult; few find it, but it leads to Heaven and eternal life. The broad road is wide; many people walk on it, but it leads to hell. You have to choose the narrow road, my friend, the so-called "hard way". Although, truth be told, it is not a hard way at all. Think of it as preparation for a race. You have to get up two hours earlier than you normally do in the morning. It is freezing cold outside. You begin to run, but your limbs are stiff and sore; your muscles are still aching from last week. You press through the barrier. Then all of a sudden one morning you wake up and you feel stronger. You feel fit because you have lost that extra fat and you have built muscle. Your energy levels soar and you have a breakthrough. But getting to that point is painful and takes perseverance.

The same analogy can be applied to walking the Christian road. The Christian walk is not for wimps. I don't know where that mindset ever came from. As a young man I too thought that the guys who went to church were wimps. In reality it is quite the opposite! It takes a great deal of courage to walk the narrow way.

Prayer

My Father in Heaven, You have called me to walk the narrow way. You have called me to prepare for the race and to run it with courage and perseverance. Like Elijah, Your servant of old, You call me to faithfully serve You no matter what the temptations and difficulties that I may face. Amen.

Read Isaiah 54:1–17

> "NO WEAPON FORMED AGAINST YOU SHALL PROSPER, AND EVERY TONGUE
> WHICH RISES AGAINST YOU IN JUDGMENT YOU SHALL CONDEMN. THIS IS THE
> HERITAGE OF THE SERVANTS OF THE LORD, AND THEIR RIGHTEOUSNESS IS
> FROM ME," SAYS THE LORD.
>
> Isaiah 54:17

I have occasionally told the tale of Gypsy Smith, the great British evangelist, who preached from the back of his painted wagon. Remember that he said a dead fish flows with the current, but it takes a live fish to swim against it. When your friends want you to watch a blue movie with them, it takes courage to say, "I don't do that." If they offer you drugs and you say, "I don't do that," it takes courage. I tell you, God will honour you for it. Often when we take a stand for God it seems as if the enemy intensifies his efforts in our lives. It has often happened to me.

Isn't the Scripture that we read from Isaiah 54 beautiful? I have another one for you: "When the enemy comes in like a flood, the Spirit of the Lord will lift up a standard against him" (Isaiah 59:19b). Friends, when you sign on the bottom line and you say: "As from today I am a child of God, and I am walking with the Lord", you can expect a fight. You are entering a war. Before you come to Jesus the devil isn't interested in you because he already has you. It is once you come to Jesus that his effort in your life intensifies. When you stand up and say, "This far, devil, and no further," then the game is on.

If you are in the midst of a battle then remember Job. Satan could not touch him without God's permission. He could only go as far as God would allow him to. Once Job had stood the test he came out the other side not only stronger in his faith, but completely restored in every way. God is for you, and if He is for you, then who can be against you? Don't allow the enemy to speak his lies into your life. Stand upon the Word of God. Choose to walk by faith and not by sight. Be sure that you will overcome and you will finish strong.

Prayer

My Father God, thank You for the reassurance from Your Word that no weapon formed against me will prosper. Lord, I stand secure and safe in Your promises to me. Lord, I pray that You will lift up the standard against the enemy as You have promised You will. Lord, I walk by faith. Amen.

15 August GREATER IS HE THAT IS IN YOU

Read 1 John 4

YOU ARE OF GOD, LITTLE CHILDREN, AND HAVE OVERCOME THEM, BECAUSE
HE WHO IS IN YOU IS GREATER THAN HE WHO IS IN THE WORLD.

1 John 4:4

Do you remember David Wilkerson's book, *The Cross and the Switchblade*? It is the true story of a gang leader by the name of Nicky Cruz. He was converted through the ministry of David Wilkerson. One night Wilkerson was preaching at a meeting in a cinema. When it was time to take up the collection he asked Nicky Cruz and some of his gang members to do it. He was a brand spanking new Christian; he still had the wrapping paper on! Cruz took the bag and walked among the people collecting the money. One of Wilkerson's leaders came to him and warned him to be careful. He told him that Cruz had to go up on to the stage, behind the curtains, and then come down again to get to the other aisle. Behind the stage was a back door.

It would have been easy for Nicky Cruz to leave with the money. After all, the pull of the gang must still have been strong. Wilkerson assured his leader that this wouldn't happen. The leader wasn't so sure. They watched Cruz walk up the steps with the bag full of money. He went behind the curtains, then he came down the other side and continued to collect the money. We are tested sometimes. Certainly the devil will test you. He will say: "Have one last fling with those drugs before you pack it in." No! You cannot do it. Finish it today. If this is your choice then I want to assure you that God will give you the victory.

Our victory comes at a price, my friends. The price was Jesus' death on Calvary. He took the fall so that you and I can have the victory. Salvation is a free gift from God, but it cost Him everything He had. You cannot earn it, you cannot buy it, but you can value and appreciate it. The devil will try to belittle and demean the gift, but we know its value. We know that He who is in us is greater than he who is in the world. Walk in your victory.

Prayer

My Father, I have the victory in You. Jesus, my Saviour, died to give me freedom from sin. He rose from the grave conquering death. I do not need to walk in defeat as long as I choose to follow and obey You. Lord, fill me with Your Spirit. Give me strength, courage, and faith for this new day. Amen.

Read 1 Kings 19:1–10

> So he said, "I have been very zealous for the Lord God of hosts; for the children of Israel have forsaken Your covenant, torn down Your altars, and killed Your prophets with the sword. I alone am left; and they seek to take my life."
>
> 1 Kings 19:10

It is hard to believe that Elijah, the mighty man of God, would allow himself to be cowed and run off by a woman. Yet this is exactly what happened. When Ahab reported what Elijah had done, Jezebel sent a message to Elijah threatening to kill him. There is an important lesson to be learned here: we need to take care of ourselves. When we become overly tired and worn out, we become weak and easy prey for the enemy. We have spent quite a few days looking at what can happen in our lives after a great spiritual experience. The low after the high can often be very low indeed. Elijah simply took flight and ran for forty days.

He eventually landed up at Horeb, the mountain of God. It can be said of Elijah that even in his conflicted state he ran to God, not away from Him. He spent the night in a cave. Then the Lord came to him and asked him what he was doing there. His answer is detailed in our key Scripture. Would you say that Elijah was feeling a little sorry for himself? We can hear the echoes of self-pity ringing loud and clear. Have you ever felt like this? You have been working for God with everything you have in you. Then someone misunderstands or hurts you in some way and you feel hard done by. You become depressed and discouraged, believing that no one appreciates you or your efforts.

Elijah didn't understand that what was happening was an attack of the enemy. The devil wanted to bring him down. He wanted to turn Elijah away from God. Satan cannot stand to see God's Name being glorified, so he will do whatever he can to discredit God's people. He knows that when we fail then the world looks on, and they deride the Name of the Lord. If you find yourself in a similar place to Elijah right now, then at least follow his example and turn toward God. Have your pity party at the foot of the cross.

Prayer

My Father God, I realize that so often I am too easily influenced. I allow other people to dictate my spiritual condition. Forgive me, I pray. I turn towards You, my Lord, and I ask You to give me a clear vision of the reality of my situation. Help me to look to You, to trust You, and to be faithful to You. Amen.

Read 1 Kings 19:11–18

YET I HAVE RESERVED SEVEN THOUSAND IN ISRAEL, ALL WHOSE KNEES HAVE
NOT BOWED TO BAAL, AND EVERY MOUTH THAT HAS NOT KISSED HIM.

1 Kings 19:18

Elijah needed that time out to experience God in a new way. The miracle on top of Mount Carmel was such a spectacular event, yet, on Mount Horeb what do we see? God wasn't in the wind, the earthquake, or the fire. No; He was the still, small voice.

… And behold, the Lord passed by, and a great and strong wind tore into the mountains and broke the rocks in pieces before the Lord, but the Lord was not in the wind; and after the wind an earthquake, but the Lord was not in the earthquake; and after the earthquake a fire, but the Lord was not in the fire; and after the fire a still small voice.

1 Kings 19:11–12

Elijah learned that God doesn't always appear to us in the same way. He had to be able to recognize God's voice no matter how He chose to speak to him. God again asked Elijah what he was doing there, and again he reminded God that he was the only one left serving Him. God went on to tell Elijah that he was not alone; there were 7,000 other men in Israel who had not bowed their knee to Baal. Not only was Elijah not alone, but everything did not rest solely on him. It is true of us as well. We are not the only ones serving God. He has children throughout the land, and throughout the world. We are part of a very large family.

There is no doubt, though, that God has a special purpose and plan for each of our lives. He has a purpose that we alone are called to fulfil for Him. Like Elijah, we have to choose whether we will be used by God. Will we walk in obedience and faith? As we have said, so often you cannot separate faith and obedience. Elijah chose obedience even when it meant that he landed up in the bad books of King Ahab and his wife Jezebel. Choosing the path of obedience requires walking by faith and not by sight. Is this your choice?

Prayer
My Father God, You are the God of this world, of this universe. You are my God and my Father. I bow before You. Thank You for the example of Elijah's life. Lord, I want to serve You, I want to walk in faith with You, obeying You every step of the way. Use me, I pray. In Jesus' Name. Amen.

Read 1 Kings 19:19–21; 2 Kings 2:1–14

AND SO IT WAS, WHEN THEY HAD CROSSED OVER, THAT ELIJAH SAID TO
ELISHA, "ASK! WHAT MAY I DO FOR YOU, BEFORE I AM TAKEN AWAY FROM
YOU?" ELISHA SAID, "PLEASE LET A DOUBLE PORTION OF YOUR SPIRIT BE
UPON ME."

2 Kings 2:9

I want to ask you: do you have faith in God? How is your standing with the Lord? Is your relationship with Jesus Christ growing each day, and are you having close fellowship with Him? When everything is said and done this is all that matters, my friend. When we first encounter Elisha we find him ploughing his father's field. Elijah had identified him as his successor. Elisha left everything to go with Elijah and serve God. He realized that nothing else was more important.

It was time for Elijah to be called home. He had a long and fruitful life faithfully serving God. Elisha was about to receive the mantle or cloak: "the anointing"; "the power of God from Elijah". When Elijah asked him what he wanted, all Elisha was interested in was receiving a double portion of the anointing that Elijah had had. He wanted twice as much power. It was because he was persistent, because he kept at it, that God gave it to him.

God used Elisha to perform exactly double the number of miracles, signs, and wonders that Elijah performed. Why? Because he asked God by faith. Have you asked God for anything recently? If the reason you haven't is because you are not sure that God will answer, then clearly you are not going to receive anything. Jesus told us:

So I say to you, ask, and it will be given to you; seek, and you will find; knock, and it will be opened to you. For everyone who asks receives, and he who seeks finds, and to him who knocks it will be opened. If a son asks for bread from any father among you, will he give him a stone? Or if he asks for a fish, will he give him a serpent instead of a fish? Or if he asks for an egg, will he offer him a scorpion? If you then, being evil, know how to give good gifts to your children, how much more will your heavenly Father give the Holy Spirit to those who ask Him!

Luke 11:9–13

Prayer

My Father, I come to You in the Name of Jesus, my Saviour and Lord. Father, I ask You to fill me with Your Spirit. Lord, Your Word tells me that I must seek and I will find; I must knock and it will be opened to me. So Father, today I seek and I knock. Lord, I look to You in expectant faith. Amen.

Read 2 Kings 2:9–25

> HE ALSO TOOK UP THE MANTLE OF ELIJAH THAT HAD FALLEN FROM HIM, AND
> WENT BACK AND STOOD BY THE BANK OF THE JORDAN. THEN HE TOOK THE
> MANTLE OF ELIJAH THAT HAD FALLEN FROM HIM, AND STRUCK THE WATER,
> AND SAID, "WHERE IS THE LORD GOD OF ELIJAH?" AND WHEN HE ALSO
> HAD STRUCK THE WATER, IT WAS DIVIDED THIS WAY AND THAT; AND ELISHA
> CROSSED OVER.
>
> 2 Kings 2:13–14

If you have ever been to Israel and seen the River Jordan then you will know that it is not a stream; it is a proper river, a fast-flowing deep river. You cannot walk across it, especially in times of flood. Elisha stood on the bank of the River Jordan holding Elijah's mantle. He asked, "Where is the Lord God of Elijah?" Then he struck the water and it parted so that he could walk across to the other side. "Now when the sons of the prophets who were from Jericho saw him, they said, 'The spirit of Elijah rests on Elisha'" (verse 15a).

Where is the Lord God of Elijah? This is what people are asking today. Where is He – where is the Lord? Where are the miracles, the signs, and the wonders? The writer says that the Lord God of Elijah is waiting for the Elishas of today to call upon Him. The Bible says you have not because you ask not. I have learned this the hard way. If you don't ask, you don't receive. What is the difference between Elisha and us? There is no difference at all; we are all human beings. We have blood running through our veins; Elisha had blood running through his veins. The thing that separates us from Elisha is quite simple: the prophets of Bethel told Elisha to leave Elijah (verses 3 and 5). Elisha refused. He wasn't going anywhere until he received Elijah's mantle. He persisted; he pursued the blessing and refused to give up.

The problem is that some of us give up too easily. If we don't receive an immediate reply we throw in the towel. No, my friend, there is no difference between us and Elisha. We are the same: what separates us is we haven't asked God for anything by faith. It is no good asking God for something if you don't believe that He will do it. There's no point if you ask the Lord to bless your crop, then, when nothing happens, you say: "Oh well, I didn't expect Him to answer anyway." That isn't faith!

Prayer

Lord, I pray that You will forgive my unbelief. I realize that the only thing separating me from Elisha is my lack of perseverance and faith in You. He would not let go until You blessed him. He knew exactly what he wanted and he was determined to receive it. I want that kind of faith. Amen.

Read Matthew 7:1–14

> IF YOU THEN, BEING EVIL, KNOW HOW TO GIVE GOOD GIFTS TO YOUR
> CHILDREN, HOW MUCH MORE WILL YOUR FATHER WHO IS IN HEAVEN GIVE
> GOOD THINGS TO THOSE WHO ASK HIM!
>
> Matthew 7:11

If I walk away and don't pray for a sick person who really doesn't look good because I don't believe they will get better, what does it mean? It means I don't have faith. In the Name of Jesus of Nazareth you find out what the problem is and you address it. Then by faith you speak into the person and their situation. The reason that we don't see the Lord God of Elijah is because He is waiting for the Elishas of today to call upon Him.

Many young men come to me saying, "Uncle Angus, I want you to pray over my hands. I want to lay my hands upon the sick. I want to see the sick recover. I want to see miracles." I always reply that I won't pray for their hands, I will pray that God will break their heart, so that when they see sick people they will weep for them. You know, sometimes, not being sick yourself, you don't really understand what the person is going through.

When I had my heart attack some years ago, I literally stood at the gates of Heaven. That is how close it was. I understand the shortness of time. When someone tells me that they have heart problems or that they had a heart attack, I can understand what they went through. Does it mean that we have to get sick before we can show compassion? Not at all. What it does mean is that we need to get down there where it is happening. We need to get down into the dust, into the dirt, into the gutter, and come alongside the person we are praying for. Then we must call out to God. Why are we always asking God for power? Why are we asking God for the baptism of the Holy Spirit? What for? So we can walk around town bragging that we have arrived? No! Friends, God gives you gifts, He gives you the anointing, and He gives you the power so that you can use it to glorify His Son.

Prayer

My Father God who is in Heaven, You have promised that You will give good gifts to those who ask You. Lord, I am asking You right now to please give me the spirit of Elijah; fill me with power and use me to bless others. I pray that You will glorify Your Holy Name through me. Amen.

Read 2 Kings 2:19–25

> THEN HE WENT OUT TO THE SOURCE OF THE WATER, AND CAST IN THE SALT
> THERE, AND SAID, "THUS SAYS THE LORD: "I HAVE HEALED THIS WATER;
> FROM IT THERE SHALL BE NO MORE DEATH OR BARRENNESS.'" SO THE WATER
> REMAINS HEALED TO THIS DAY, ACCORDING TO THE WORD OF ELISHA WHICH
> HE SPOKE.

2 Kings 2:21–22

We ought to turn the question, "Where is the Lord God of Elijah?" (2 Kings 2:14) around and ask: "Where are the Elijahs of God?" I want to tell you, the God of Elijah is waiting for the Elijahs and the Elishas of this generation to stand up and be counted. God hasn't changed; He's still here and He still wants to use us. He's still waiting to shake this world with His signs, His wonders, and His miracles. But you know what? He's battling to find Elijahs and Elishas.

We have spent this year looking at mighty men of God who walked by faith and not by sight. Ordinary men like you and me, but men who were willing to stand up and be counted. Each of them had their flaws and their failures, yet nothing stopped them from serving God. Their hearts were for God. Every one of them had their own unique faith journey. They each had a specific purpose to fulfil; their own part to play in God's plan for mankind. One thing they all had in common is that they had to be willing to obey God. There was no place for doubt. Questioning, yes, but the result of the questions had to be surrender to God's will for their lives.

As a result of their faith and obedience we can read about them today in God's Word. Many of them are listed in God's Hall of Faith in Hebrews 11. Their stories are a testament of God's faithfulness to those who love Him and serve Him. As we spend the next few days looking at the way God used Elisha, ask God to speak into your life. Allow His Spirit to grow your faith and expectancy, so that you will be open to Him doing miracles in and through you. God has never let me down, my friends. I have trusted Him and He has come through time and time again in the most remarkable ways. He loves you and He will do the same for you.

Prayer

My Father in Heaven, You are a miracle-working God. You have been doing signs and wonders through Your servants for centuries; all the way from Bible times until the present day. Lord, I want to be used by You. I want to have the faith to believe You for great things. Amen.

Read 2 Kings 4:1–7

> So Elisha said to her, "What shall I do for you? Tell me, what do you have in the house?" And she said, "Your maidservant has nothing in the house but a jar of oil."
>
> 2 Kings 4:2

Elisha met up with a woman who was in desperate need. She was about to lose her two sons because she could not pay her debt. We live in an era when people face disaster in their lives all the time. For some people the situation they are in is because of bad decisions they have made. For others circumstances have conspired to put them there. Whatever the reason people, need Salvation. They need to be saved from themselves. There is only one person who can save us and that is Jesus Christ.

For the woman in 2 Kings 4 it was circumstance that had brought her to the place of desperation. There are some important lessons for us in this story. First, Elisha asked her: "What shall I do for you?" Second, he used what she had to help her. Third, the blessing was limited only by her capacity to receive it. Tomorrow we will talk more about the first lesson. For now I want to focus on the second point: the fact that Elisha used what she had available. When he asked her what she had, she said "nothing… but a jar of oil." My friends, God is not limited by what we have. He can take what we have and multiply it many times over. If we are prepared to come to Him in faith and surrender what we have to Him then He will use it.

Elisha told her to borrow vessels from wherever she could get hold of them. Once she had done that she began pouring oil into them from her one pot of oil. The more she poured the more oil there was. Eventually all the pots her sons had managed to collect were full: "she said to her son, 'Bring me another vessel.' And he said to her, 'There is not another vessel.' So the oil ceased" (verse 6). The more we open ourselves up, the more we will receive. The more we exercise our faith, the stronger our faith will become. We are limited only by our capacity to receive, accept, and experience.

Prayer

My Father, I thank You that You are a faithful God. Thank You for my Salvation, for what Jesus did for me on Calvary. Lord, I love You. Help me to surrender what I have. Then help me to open myself to Your blessing in my life. Lord, I don't want to limit You working in me in any way. Amen.

Read 2 Kings 4:8–37

> AND HE SAID TO HIM, "SAY NOW TO HER, 'LOOK, YOU HAVE BEEN
> CONCERNED FOR US WITH ALL THIS CARE. WHAT CAN I DO FOR YOU?'"
>
> 2 Kings 4:13a

We have another situation where Elisha asks a woman: "What can I do for you?" The Shunammite woman had been kind and hospitable to Elisha and his servant, Gehazi, on many occasions. She had even convinced her husband to build a room for Elisha at the top of their house, so that he would have somewhere to stay whenever he passed by. She was clearly a godly woman who recognized that Elisha was a man of God. Elisha wanted to bless her in return and so he asked her what he could do for her. She didn't need anything really; the only thing that she longed for was a child.

Elisha told her that by the following year she would have a baby. At first she didn't want to believe Elisha. You can imagine how overjoyed she was when what he had promised came about. My friends, do not be afraid to ask God for what you need. Remember we looked at the following Scripture a few days ago? "So I say to you, ask, and it will be given to you; seek, and you will find; knock, and it will be opened to you. For everyone who asks receives, and he who seeks finds, and to him who knocks it will be opened" (Luke 11:9–10). The Shunammite woman's boy grew. But one day he took ill and died. This would seem a cruel thing; God gave and He took away.

When Elisha learned what had happened he hastened to help. Once again God performed a miracle through Elisha and He gave the woman her son back. Job learned the lesson that everything he had belonged to God. Have you learned that lesson, my friends? The Shunammite woman had to learn that her son was not hers – he belonged to God. God chose to restore him to her. God calls for us to surrender all that we are and all that we have to Him. He alone is our Source and our Supplier. Ask Him and He will give you what is His good and perfect will for your life.

Prayer

My God and Father, You are my only Source and Supplier. I cannot trust anything or anyone else. Help me to be completely dependent upon You. Help me to boldly come before You and ask of You. Lord, I only want what is Your good and perfect will for my life. Fill me and use me, I pray. Amen.

Read 2 Kings 4:38–44

> BUT HIS SERVANT SAID, "WHAT? SHALL I SET THIS BEFORE ONE HUNDRED
> MEN?" HE SAID AGAIN, "GIVE IT TO THE PEOPLE, THAT THEY MAY EAT; FOR
> THUS SAYS THE LORD: 'THEY SHALL EAT AND HAVE SOME LEFT OVER.'" SO HE
> SET IT BEFORE THEM; AND THEY ATE AND HAD SOME LEFT OVER, ACCORDING
> TO THE WORD OF THE LORD.
>
> 2 Kings 4:43–44

We have read of three wonderful miracles that God performed through Elisha. Two of them related to food and God's provision for His people. The poisoned stew being purified can also relate to situations within our lives. If you find yourself facing something that is "poisonous" at the moment – it could be a relationship, maybe? – bring it to God. He has the answer. He will be able to lead you to do exactly the right thing to turn it into something that will glorify His Name.

When you read about the third miracle did it remind you of the fish and loaves miracle that Jesus performed? You will also remember that I told you the story of when God multiplied the food for us at a Mighty Men Conference. God is in the business of miracles, my friends. Then there is the story of the nineteenth-century evangelist George Müller and his orphanage. How many times did God provide for them? They would be sitting down at the table with no food in front of them; George Müller would say grace, there would be a knock at the door, and someone would give them food. God provides for and looks after His people.

When last have you trusted God for a miracle? Elisha trusted God. "But his servant said, 'What? Shall I set this before one hundred men?' (verse 43a). He didn't know God like Elisha knew God. When Elisha took on Elijah's mantle he'd asked God for a double portion of Elijah's Spirit. He wasn't scared to ask God to bless him, and God had done so. Are you facing a situation where you need God to multiply your resources? He can do it. We have read several accounts in God's Word where He did this for people. He is the same yesterday, today, and forever. He is your all-powerful Heavenly Father. But if you don't ask, you won't receive. If you don't trust you won't be able to see with the eyes of faith. Ask God to give you a vision that lifts your eyes beyond the natural.

Prayer

My Father, Your graciousness is beyond my human understanding. You have shown Your love and faithfulness to Your people throughout the ages. Lord, I am so grateful that I am Your child. Undertake for me, I pray. I bring my need before You right now and thank You for Your provision. Amen.

Read 2 Kings 5:1–6

> AND THE SYRIANS HAD GONE OUT ON RAIDS, AND HAD BROUGHT BACK
> CAPTIVE A YOUNG GIRL FROM THE LAND OF ISRAEL. SHE WAITED ON
> NAAMAN'S WIFE. THEN SHE SAID TO HER MISTRESS, "IF ONLY MY MASTER
> WERE WITH THE PROPHET WHO IS IN SAMARIA! FOR HE WOULD HEAL HIM OF
> HIS LEPROSY."
>
> 2 Kings 5:2–3

If you know Jesus then you have the light of His presence in your life. What are you doing with His light? Start shining for the Lord. In the story of Naaman we see a little girl who was not scared to share her light with other people. She loved God and she told people about Him – even her boss and his wife. People will know that you serve God through the life that you live, but this has to translate into actions and also into words when necessary.

It would have been so easy for this young girl to keep quiet, wouldn't it? She was young; she was in a strange country having being taken captive from her home in Israel. Yet, when she saw her master Naaman's need she knew that she had the answer to his problems. She couldn't remain silent so she told him where he could receive help. "You are the light of the world. A city that is set on a hill cannot be hidden. Nor do they light a lamp and put it under a basket, but on a lampstand, and it gives light to all who are in the house. Let your light so shine before men, that they may see your good works and glorify your Father in heaven" (Matthew 5:14–16).

The end result of her sharing her faith with Namaan was that he came to believe in her God, the God of Abraham, Isaac, and Jacob. "And he returned to the man of God, he and all his aides, and came and stood before him; and he said, 'Indeed, now I know that there is no God in all the earth, except in Israel…'" (2 Kings 5:15). When last have you shared the light with someone who is in need? We are Jesus' hands, His feet, and His voice. Sharing our faith should be the most natural thing in the world for us. After all it is simply telling people what Jesus has done for us, and what He can do for them, isn't it?

Prayer

My Father in Heaven, I worship You and thank You for Jesus, Who is the Light of the world. Thank You, Jesus, for Your Salvation. Help me to share what You have given me with other people who are in need. Lord, I realize that this should be as easy as breathing is for me. Amen.

Read 2 Kings 5:7–19

> AND HE RETURNED TO THE MAN OF GOD, HE AND ALL HIS AIDES, AND CAME
> AND STOOD BEFORE HIM; AND HE SAID, "INDEED, NOW I KNOW THAT THERE IS
> NO GOD IN ALL THE EARTH, EXCEPT IN ISRAEL; NOW THEREFORE, PLEASE TAKE
> A GIFT FROM YOUR SERVANT."
>
> 2 Kings 5:15

The first thing that Namaan had to do was accept what God was telling him to do through Elisha. We see that this was not easy for him to do. He was a proud man. He was used to telling people what to do. He was a brave man used to doing brave and valiant acts. He felt that being told to do something as menial as washing seven times in a dirty river was an insult to him. He probably felt that it demeaned him in the eyes of his men. "But Naaman became furious, and went away and said, 'Indeed, I said to myself, "He will surely come out to me, and stand and call on the name of the Lord his God, and wave his hand over the place, and heal the leprosy"'" (verse 11). He had his own ideas about how God should heal him. He had to come to a place of acceptance.

Then Namaan had to make a decision to obey God. "And his servants came near and spoke to him, and said, 'My father, if the prophet had told you to do something great, would you not have done it? How much more then, when he says to you, "Wash, and be clean"?'" (verse 13). His servants had greater insight and understanding than Namaan himself did. Very likely they too were Israelites who knew God and what He could do. So Namaan had to put his pride in his pocket and obey God.

Naaman was healed as he came up out of the water the seventh time. The final step for Namaan was that he believed in God. He said to the Prophet Elisha, "Indeed, now I know that there is no God in all the earth, except in Israel". My friends, God is still in the business of drawing people to Himself; He is in the business of meeting their needs and saving their souls. As His children we have a part to play in this process. We need to help people to understand that they have to accept, obey, and believe God.

Prayer

My Father God, You have called me to be Your servant. As Your servant I need to share Your message of Salvation with other people. I must help them to understand that they need to accept You, obey You, and believe in You. When we do this You are able to work in our situations and circumstances. Amen.

Read 2 Kings 6:1–7

> THEREFORE HE SAID, "PICK IT UP FOR YOURSELF." SO HE REACHED OUT HIS
> HAND AND TOOK IT.
>
> 2 Kings 6:7

God is interested in the daily routine of our lives. He is not a God who is distant and removed from His people. He knows everything that is happening in your life. He cares about what you are going through. It is so often we who distance ourselves from God. We exhaust every other avenue before we turn to Him for help. Instead, He should be our first thought when things go wrong. We should run to Him to take cover. "He shall cover you with His feathers, and under His wings you shall take refuge" (Psalm 91:4a).

God cannot operate where there is a spirit of unbelief. The young sons of the prophets believed. They were out felling trees to build a larger dwelling place for themselves. I don't know if you have ever chopped down trees. When I bought my farm many years ago it was covered in trees. We couldn't afford a chainsaw so I, along with a helper, chopped all the trees down by hand. I know what it is like to have an axe-head fly off of the handle. In today's text, when the axe-head landed in the river the men immediately turned to Elisha for help. He in turn trusted God and the axe-head floated up on to the surface of the river.

Again we see a principle in action: "Therefore he said, 'Pick it up for yourself.' So he reached out his hand and took it" (verse 7). Why? Because the young prophet had to exercise his faith. He had to acknowledge that it wasn't an illusion that he was seeing. Everyone knows that an axe-head cannot float – it sinks to the bottom. By reaching out his hand he was saying that he believed. He believed that as he reached out and grabbed the axe-head it would be real. Elisha had faith to ask God for the miracle; the young man had to have faith to take hold of the miracle and make it his. If you are needing a miracle from God today, reach out your hand and take hold of it.

Prayer

My Father in Heaven, You have said: "The effective, fervent prayer of a righteous man avails much" (James 5:16c). Help me to turn to You, to trust in You, to believe that You will answer me, and then to have the faith to stretch out my hand and take hold of my miracle. Amen.

Read 2 Kings 6:8–23

> AND ELISHA PRAYED, AND SAID, "LORD, I PRAY, OPEN HIS EYES THAT HE MAY
> SEE." THEN THE LORD OPENED THE EYES OF THE YOUNG MAN, AND HE SAW.
> AND BEHOLD, THE MOUNTAIN WAS FULL OF HORSES AND CHARIOTS OF FIRE
> ALL AROUND ELISHA.
>
> 2 Kings 6:17

The king of Syria was unhappy because Elisha was informing the king of Israel about his strategies. God gave Elisha the insight and knowledge that he shared with the king of Israel. This meant that the Syrians' attempts to wage war against the Israelites continually failed. The Syrian king decided to sort Elisha out. When Elisha's servant saw that they were surrounded his first reaction was to panic. "So he [Elisha] answered, 'Do not fear, for those who are with us are more than those who are with them'" (verse 16). This is true for us also, my friends. When you face impossible odds you can know that greater is He that is with you, than he that is with your enemies. You have heard the saying, "One man plus God is an army", haven't you?

Elisha prayed and asked God to open the eyes of his servant. What did he see? "Then the Lord opened the eyes of the young man, and he saw. And behold, the mountain was full of horses and chariots of fire all around Elisha." As you read the rest of this story you realize afresh that God's ways are not our ways. I am sure that you and I would have handled this situation very differently to the way that Elisha did. The difference might be that Elisha was listening really closely to God. His aim was not to do what he wanted, but in each situation to find out what God wanted.

The outcome of this miracle was that the Syrians did not bother Israel again. Surely a better result than Israel killing the men and the war continuing. When we are faced with a situation that requires a miracle from God, let us learn from Elisha. First, know without a shadow of a doubt that God can do the seemingly impossible. Second, turn to Him to find out His solution. Third, wait for His miracle and when He sends it have spiritual eyes that are open to receive and believe. Take hold of your miracle and praise God for it.

Prayer

My Lord and God, I am so overwhelmed when I read of Your amazing exploits in Your Word. Lord, Your ways are not the ways of man. I am so honoured and privileged to be Your child. Lord, open my eyes to Your miracles in my life. Help me to grab on to them and to trust You in every way. Amen.

Read 2 Kings 8:1–6

> And Gehazi said, "My lord, O king, this is the woman, and this is her son whom Elisha restored to life." And when the king asked the woman, she told him. So the king appointed a certain officer for her, saying, "Restore all that was hers, and all the proceeds of the field from the day that she left the land until now."
>
> 2 Kings 8:5c–6

We again meet up with the Shunammite woman whose son God healed through Elisha. A seven-year famine was coming and Elisha warned her to move away with her family. It is not an easy thing to pack up and move because somebody tells you to do so. It required faith for this woman to listen to Elisha. She believed in God. She had been the recipient of a miracle from God – not once, but twice. So when Elisha told her to move, she did not hesitate to believe and to act upon her belief. When the seven years had passed and the famine was over she returned. Her land was no longer hers and she had to appeal to the king to return it to her.

You have heard me say before that with God there are no coincidences. My friends, with God nothing is left to chance; everything happens for a reason – in His good timing. At the very moment she came to appeal for her land, Gehazi, Elisha's servant, was telling the king about the exploits of Elisha. When Gehazi saw the woman and her son, he had a living example of what he was telling the king about. The king was so impressed that he restored her land, as well as all the proceeds from the lands over the seven years of the drought. God restored to Job seven times what he had lost, because he had faith in God and he was faithful. God restored to the Shunammite woman the seven years of income she lost from her lands during the famine.

God tells us in His Word: "So I will restore to you the years that the swarming locust has eaten" (Joel 2:25a). My friends, if there are things in your life that the enemy has stolen from you, God will restore them, if you come to Him in faith. Pray to Him, believing Him for a miracle, and He will honour your prayers. Submit to God, trusting that He knows what is best for your life and He will not let you down.

Prayer

My Father, thank You that You have promised that You will restore to me the years that the locust has eaten. Lord, I trust You to give me back, according to Your will, what the enemy has taken from me. I trust You, Lord, knowing that You will always do what is best for me. Amen.

Read 2 Kings 9:30–37

> THEREFORE THEY CAME BACK AND TOLD HIM. AND HE SAID, "THIS IS THE
> WORD OF THE LORD, WHICH HE SPOKE BY HIS SERVANT ELIJAH THE TISHBITE,
> SAYING, "ON THE PLOT OF GROUND AT JEZREEL DOGS SHALL EAT THE FLESH
> OF JEZEBEL.'"
>
> 2 Kings 9:36

God honours His Word, my friends. If there is nothing else that you can set store by in this world we live in, you can set store by this: if God says it, it is as good as done. Even if you don't see the fulfilment of it, others will. Elijah, the man of God, had predicted the way that Jezebel would die (1 Kings 21:23). Elijah had long gone home to glory when Jezebel died. However, exactly as he said it would be, so she died (2 Kings 9:36). Elisha remembered the words of Elijah "and the corpse of Jezebel shall be as refuse on the surface of the field, in the plot at Jezreel, so that they shall not say, "Here lies Jezebel'" (verse 37). There would be nothing left of her – no remembrance of her.

God honours His Word and He honours His servants. Elijah was a man of God. He was a righteous man. James 5:17–18 tells us: "Elijah was a man with a nature like ours, and he prayed earnestly that it would not rain; and it did not rain on the land for three years and six months. And he prayed again, and the heaven gave rain, and the earth produced its fruit." Elijah trusted and obeyed God, therefore God honoured his prayers. My friends, it is no different with us. As James says, Elijah "was a man with a nature like ours"; he was no different to us – except that he believed and trusted God. He believed that God would do what He said He would do.

Let's be honest, when he was standing on top of Mount Carmel facing the prophets of Baal, there was no room for doubt. He either believed, or he didn't. It is the same with us. When we face the difficult things – we either believe or we don't. What will it be? God honours His Word, yes, but His people need to do their part and believe Him wholeheartedly. He honours His Word when we walk by faith and not by sight, believing Him no matter what the situation we find ourselves in looks like.

Prayer

Father, You have called me to live a life of faith. You have called me to walk by faith and not by sight. As You did with Elijah and Elisha, You will honour Your Word to me if I trust and obey You wholeheartedly. Lord, You are calling me to be an Elijah. Help me to be a man like him. Amen.

POWER EVEN IN DEATH

Read 2 Kings 13:14–21

So it was, as they were burying a man, that suddenly they spied a band of raiders; and they put the man in the tomb of Elisha; and when the man was let down and touched the bones of Elisha, he revived and stood on his feet.

2 Kings 13:21

Isn't this an amazing end to a remarkable life? Even in death God used Elisha. There was still so much power within him even after he was dead. So much power that when a corpse touched his body the person was brought back to life. Elisha died as he had lived: doing the will of God. His only request was to receive double the power that Elijah had received. As we said before, he not only received double the power, but he performed double the number of miracles that Elijah had. Elisha was the Elijah of his day. Time after time God used Elisha to show His power to Israel; to speak to them and to lead them.

What about you, my friends? You have read each day of this month how God used first Elijah and then Elisha: both of them truly remarkable men of God. Take a moment now and ask God's Holy Spirit to speak to you. Ask Him to show you what it is that the Lord wants you to take with you from the lessons of this past month. Don't simply move on and begin reading about the next lot of men of faith. We so often do this, don't we? We do our duty: read God's Word, pray, and then carry on with life as normal. There is nothing "normal" about the times in which we live. God is looking for Elijahs and Elishas in this generation who will take His message to the nations.

God has a plan and a purpose for each of our lives. He has a task only you can fulfil. You are His Elijah for that situation. Have you found your purpose, and are you living as Elijah did in it? If not, don't move forward or become distracted by other things until you find it. Once you have found your purpose be single-minded as Elisha was. Beseech God to give you a double portion of the power and then use that power to serve Him faithfully all the days that you have left on this earth.

Prayer

Jesus, I come to the Father in Your precious Name today. My Father God, Ruler of Heaven and earth, I bow in Your presence. You are a Holy and Awesome God. There is none like You. Lord, I want to be Your Elijah in my situation; empower me and fill me with Your Spirit, I pray. Amen.

NEHEMIAH, JEREMIAH, AND DANIEL

Their journeys of faith began when they put God first

1. Rebuild the walls
2. Single-minded focus
3. Take up the challenge
4. God gives Nehemiah wisdom
5. This was done by my God
6. My words in your mouth
7. No idols
8. There is none like You
9. Don't serve other gods
10. For Jesus, or against Him
11. Don't tire of waiting
12. Search me, oh God
13. A heart after God
14. Lift your eyes to the Lord
15. Your whole heart
16. A new heart
17. A heart of compassion
18. Guard your heart
19. God is in control
20. Do not worry
21. God cares for you
22. The Lord removes your troubles
23. Faith to finish strong
24. The patient farmer
25. Daniel purposed in his heart
26. Daniel honours God
27. Obedience no matter the price
28. Daniel, an excellent spirit
29. Daniel prays, as was his custom
30. Knowing God

Read Nehemiah 1:1–4

AND THEY SAID TO ME, "THE SURVIVORS WHO ARE LEFT FROM THE CAPTIVITY IN THE PROVINCE ARE THERE IN GREAT DISTRESS AND REPROACH. THE WALL OF JERUSALEM IS ALSO BROKEN DOWN, AND ITS GATES ARE BURNED WITH FIRE."

Nehemiah 1:3

Through sin, neglect, disobedience, and fear the children of Israel landed up in exile. As a result of sin, neglect, disobedience, and fear, God's people, the children of Israel, had been overcome by their enemy and taken into exile. Not only was their city in ruins, but their lives also. They seemed unable to do anything about their situation. Nehemiah was the cupbearer in the court of King Artaxerxes. Hearing what had taken place in Jerusalem he was devastated. He cried out before the Lord. He was not unmoved by the plight of his fellow Israelites. It would have been easy for him to have ignored what was going on. He had a good position in the royal household and he could have pretended that it didn't concern him.

Nehemiah was a man of faith, though, so he took up his responsibility. He went before God to find out what he should do. My friends, as you look around you there are many, many people whose lives are broken. What are you going to do? You can carry on with your own life, living with blinkers on, pretending nothing is amiss, or, like Nehemiah, you could take up the challenge. You can reach out and by faith ask God to use you to minister to others, helping them to rebuild the walls of their lives.

On the other hand, it could be that as you read this your life is in pieces around you. You don't know which way to turn, what to do. You are at your wits end. You have tried everything and failed. You don't know how you have managed to get yourself into this position. Well, if this is your situation then you are in exactly the right spot for God to begin a new work in your life. Come to Him. Surrender to Him and ask Him to take control. God can mend, restore, repair, and heal whatever is wrong in your life. He is the Healer. Submit to Him right now; ask Him to come in and cleanse, forgive, heal, and restore you.

Prayer

My Father God, You have ordained this moment in time where I can come before You, and bow at Your Feet. Lord, I need Your help. I need You to touch me and cleanse me, forgive me, heal me, and restore me. Lord, help me to reach out to other people who are hurting and share Your Good News with them. Amen.

Read Nehemiah 1:5–11

> "Now these are Your servants and Your people, whom You have
> redeemed by Your great power, and by Your strong hand. O Lord, I
> pray, please let Your ear be attentive to the prayer of Your servant,
> and to the prayer of Your servants who desire to fear Your name;
> and let Your servant prosper this day, I pray, and grant him mercy
> in the sight of this man." For I was the king's cupbearer.
>
> Nehemiah 1:10–11

Nehemiah knew and loved his covenant-keeping God. He understood what the covenant that God had made with His people meant. Nehemiah was also a man of prayer and he asked God to remember what He had promised His people. And I said: "I pray, Lord God of heaven, O great and awesome God, You who keep Your covenant and mercy with those who love You and observe Your commandments" (verse 5). He reminded God that He had promised that if Israel repented and turned to Him then He would restore them. He took it upon himself to repent before God on behalf of his people.

God had called him to go back to Jerusalem and oversee the rebuilding of the walls. Nehemiah did not become sidetracked by other things. He was single-minded in fulfilling his purpose. Are you single-minded and focused upon fulfilling the purpose to which God has called you? When you have to make decisions, do you first turn to God to find out from Him what He wants you to do next? God is never wrong, my friends. You can obey Him, even when what He is asking you to do goes against human logic. Nehemiah was a man who walked by faith and not by sight. He was a man who had a compassionate heart that beat with the desire to see God's Name glorified. The way that he could glorify God's Name was to motivate his people to rebuild the walls of the city of Jerusalem.

Sin has a way of pulling us down. God's Name is not glorified when this happens. That is what had happened in Jerusalem. The people had become discouraged and distracted, and they were no longer serving God wholeheartedly. God's purpose for us is to build us up. We are saved to walk in victory. He has given us His Spirit to empower us. Don't allow the enemy to drag you down any longer. If the walls of your life are broken, now is the time to begin the process of rebuilding and repairing them.

Prayer

My Father in Heaven, thank You that You are a covenant-keeping God. Your love and faithfulness stretches from generation to generation. Lord, help me to faithfully turn to You to find out Your will for my life. Lord, I want to rebuild my own walls and also help others to rebuild theirs. Amen.

Read Nehemiah 2:1–6

> THEN THE KING SAID TO ME, "WHAT DO YOU REQUEST?" SO I PRAYED TO
> THE GOD OF HEAVEN. AND I SAID TO THE KING, "IF IT PLEASES THE KING,
> AND IF YOUR SERVANT HAS FOUND FAVOR IN YOUR SIGHT, I ASK THAT YOU
> SEND ME TO JUDAH, TO THE CITY OF MY FATHERS' TOMBS, THAT I MAY REBUILD
> IT."
>
> Nehemiah 2:4–5

The king asked Nehemiah why he was sad. Even though Nehemiah had spent time before the Lord he was still afraid when the king spoke to him. Nehemiah gathered his courage and he told the king why he was sad. His time before the Lord in preparation paid off, because the king asked him, "What do you request?" Isn't this interesting? Nehemiah could have asked the king for many different things. But Nehemiah was only interested in what God wanted for him and from him. Did you notice that he immediately prayed and asked God what he should request? He did not depend upon his own wisdom; he realized that he needed God.

He asked the king to allow him to take a leave of absence to go home and rebuild the walls. Nehemiah's courage paid off and because the king clearly trusted Nehemiah, he gave him permission to go back. Nehemiah knew that in difficult situations he could call upon the Name of the Lord. In this instance we see how God undertook for Nehemiah, opening the way for him to obey God's instruction to go back to Jerusalem. God will never ask you to do something and then not open the way for you to do it. Our part is to trust and obey; His part is to miraculously clear the pathway ahead of us.

Follow Nehemiah's example – pray to the Lord in Heaven. He will hear you and answer you. Then when you have heard from Him obey Him. God is looking for men like Nehemiah: men who are not selfish; men who will stand up and be counted; men who will lead the way by action and example. God is looking for mighty men! What a wonderful privilege we have to live in the times that we do. I am excited, my friends, when I look around me because I see God's hand at work everywhere. We serve a God of power and might. A God who undertakes for His children. A God who is faithful. Give Him Your all – take up the challenge.

Prayer

My Father, I come before You today so very aware of my need of You. Lord, You are calling me to take up the challenge to follow You wholeheartedly. As I look at the life of Nehemiah I realize that You want men who will step out and become rebuilders. Lord, I want to be one of those men. Amen.

Read Nehemiah 2:7–20

AND I TOLD THEM OF THE HAND OF MY GOD WHICH HAD BEEN GOOD UPON
ME, AND ALSO OF THE KING'S WORDS THAT HE HAD SPOKEN TO ME. SO THEY
SAID, "LET US RISE UP AND BUILD." THEN THEY SET THEIR HANDS TO THIS
GOOD WORK.

Nehemiah 2:18

God revealed the plan for rebuilding the walls step by step to Nehemiah. Before setting out on the journey he asked the king for letters of introduction; these letters meant that the people he encountered would know that he had the support of the king. They gave him authority and guaranteed his safety. It is clear God's hand was upon Nehemiah. God had a plan and a purpose, not only for Nehemiah's life, but also for the children of Israel. In the fulfilling of His will in Nehemiah's life God also fulfilled the next stage of His plan for His people.

The walls of Jerusalem were damaged when the Babylonians attacked the Israelites. They had crumbled further through ongoing neglect. It was no small task to rebuild them. Once Nehemiah arrived in Jerusalem he inspected the walls to decide what needed to be done. After he returned from the inspection he addressed the people and informed them that they were going to rebuild the walls. The people immediately responded to Nehemiah, saying, "Let us start rebuilding." God's hand was upon Nehemiah to do the work and to rally the people to the task ahead of them. The work had a physical as well as a spiritual component to it. Nehemiah was equipped in the Spirit for the work God had called him to do.

So many times when we are doing the work of the Lord we encounter opposition from people. Sadly these people are often our fellow Christians. Nehemiah also encountered people who were unhappy about his purpose in Jerusalem. They had their own agendas and they didn't want Israel becoming strong again. We know, though, that with God nothing is impossible. We know God will make a way and His purposes can never be defeated. Nehemiah's job was to trust and obey God. Sorting out his enemies was God's job. If you are facing opposition in your life because of what God has called you to do, follow Nehemiah's example: ask God for wisdom. He who has called you is faithful; He will not let you down.

Prayer

My Father in Heaven, when You call one of Your servants to do a job, You are right there with them. I know that whatever You ask me to do, You will give me the wisdom and the victory. I do not need to fear opposition. I can boldly obey You and walk forward in faith and confidence. Amen.

Read Nehemiah 6:1–19

AND IT HAPPENED, WHEN ALL OUR ENEMIES HEARD OF IT, AND ALL
THE NATIONS AROUND US SAW THESE THINGS, THAT THEY WERE VERY
DISHEARTENED IN THEIR OWN EYES; FOR THEY PERCEIVED THAT THIS WORK
WAS DONE BY OUR GOD.

Nehemiah 6:16

Yesterday we mentioned the opposition that Nehemiah faced. As you read the Scripture today you will have seen that the people who were against Nehemiah rebuilding and repairing the walls of Jerusalem were serious about trying to stop him. They tried their level best to intimidate Nehemiah; they tried to discourage him and they tried to frighten him. He took no notice of them, though, did he? God gave Nehemiah a task to perform and he accomplished it. He didn't allow anything to stop him or put him off. He was single-minded and focused upon God's command to him.

When the wall was completed Nehemiah gave God the glory. He didn't try and take the glory for himself. His enemies were silenced because they realized that God had done this thing. There was nothing that they could do about it. God will always come through to fulfil His Word and accomplish His purposes. Down through the ages He has called men to do great exploits for Him. Has God ever asked you to do something that seems impossible on the surface of it? If He has you are not the first. Noah was asked to build a boat that God would use to save a sample of humans and animals living on the earth at that time. Moses was told he had to lead the people of Israel out of Egypt. Joshua was told to walk around the walls of the city of Jericho and they would fall down. We could go on and on. There are also many modern-day examples of people being given God-sized tasks to do.

This is what faith is about, my friends. When God led us to start the Mighty Men Conferences, it was a leap of faith. We had no idea what to expect. We certainly didn't expect the numbers of men that God would call together. We could never have imagined the logistics that would go with such an undertaking. Yet each and every time God undertakes. Each time we too can say, "This work was done by our God."

Prayer

My Father, You are God of the universe. Everything rests in the palm of Your loving hand. Lord, when You call me, You equip me. You give me everything that I need to finish the job You have given me. You are a miracle-working God. When I look around I can say, "This work was done by my God." Amen.

Read Jeremiah 1

> THEN THE LORD PUT FORTH HIS HAND AND TOUCHED MY MOUTH, AND THE
> LORD SAID TO ME: "BEHOLD, I HAVE PUT MY WORDS IN YOUR MOUTH. SEE,
> I HAVE THIS DAY SET YOU OVER THE NATIONS AND OVER THE KINGDOMS, TO
> ROOT OUT AND TO PULL DOWN, TO DESTROY AND TO THROW DOWN, TO BUILD
> AND TO PLANT."
>
> Jeremiah 1:9–10

We are now going to spend some time looking at Jeremiah's walk of faith with God. Jeremiah came from a priestly family who lived in Jerusalem. He was a young man when God called him to his role as prophet to God's people. "Then the word of the Lord came to me, saying: 'Before I formed you in the womb I knew you; before you were born I sanctified you; I ordained you a prophet to the nations'" (verses 4–5). Because of his youth he didn't believe that he could be a prophet. "Ah, Lord God! Behold, I cannot speak, for I am a youth" (verse 6). God would not take Jeremiah's youth as an excuse. "But the Lord said to me: 'Do not say, "I am a youth," for you shall go to all to whom I send you, and whatever I command you, you shall speak. Do not be afraid of their faces, for I am with you to deliver you,' says the Lord" (verses 7–8).

He served God for forty years through the reign of five kings. Jeremiah's youth did not deter him from faithfully bringing God's message of warning to His people. Jeremiah's was not an easy road. His walk of faith was a moment-by-moment, day-by-day walk. The people didn't want to listen to his message. No matter what he said, they continued on in their wicked ways. He had moments of real anguish and even depression over his failure to convince the people of Israel to turn back to God.

He had to deal with false prophets who lied to the people telling them what they wanted to hear instead of the truth of God's Word. God warned him that: "'They will fight against you, but they shall not prevail against you. For I am with you,' says the Lord, 'to deliver you'" (verse 19). Jeremiah's task was to walk in obedient faith doing what God told him to do. God's job was to look after him and protect him. It is the same for us – our job is to obey God in faith.

Prayer
Lord, thank You for Your faithful servant – Jeremiah. Lord, I pray that You will teach me the lessons You want me to learn through his life. Lord, help me to be faithful to Your call upon my life. I realize that I am not responsible for other people's reactions, only my own obedience. Amen.

Read Exodus 20:1–17

YOU SHALL HAVE NO OTHER GODS BEFORE ME. YOU SHALL NOT MAKE FOR
YOURSELF A CARVED IMAGE – ANY LIKENESS OF ANYTHING THAT IS IN HEAVEN
ABOVE, OR THAT IS IN THE EARTH BENEATH, OR THAT IS IN THE WATER UNDER
THE EARTH; YOU SHALL NOT BOW DOWN TO THEM NOR SERVE THEM.

Exodus 20:3–5a

Jeremiah was God's messenger to His people during a particularly difficult period in their history. The Israelites had wandered away from God, their hearts had become corrupted, and they had made all manner of idols that they were worshipping. "I will utter My judgments against them concerning all their wickedness, because they have forsaken Me, burned incense to other gods, and worshiped the works of their own hands" (Jeremiah 1:16). They chose to rather worship false gods instead of worshipping the One and Only Living God.

The Lord says He wants no idols in our lives. Remember, our God is a jealous God. He wants us to put Him first, to forsake all others for Him. In a marriage relationship we put our spouse first; we exclusively love and are committed to that one person. Marriage is a two-way covenant. So is the covenant you have with God: it is between you and Him – nothing and no one else. I want to say to you today, our God is a jealous God, and He categorically and clearly says, "I will have no other idols before Me." In other words, my dear friend, He doesn't want to share you with anybody else, because He loves you. He created you in His own image and He wants to have fellowship with you. So it is a good jealousy; it is not an ugly jealousy. If you believe God is not jealous, you are wrong.

If you look in the book of Exodus, you will see He says, "For I, the Lord your God, am a jealous God" (Exodus 20:5b). He loves us – that is why He is jealous of us. He is jealous because He wants us for Himself and He doesn't want us running after foreign gods. Why? I will tell you why: because they don't exist. If you love God there can be no other gods in your life, only the God of Israel, the God Jehovah. We are to serve Him wholeheartedly. Love His Son, Jesus Christ, our Saviour, and follow the guidance of His Holy Spirit.

Prayer

My Father God, You are indeed a jealous God. You have declared this for all to know. You call Your people to love, serve, and worship You and only You. Lord, I bow before You; I declare my allegiance to You alone. Keep me strong, keep me faithful, and keep me true, I pray. Amen.

Read Jeremiah 10:1–12

> INASMUCH AS THERE IS NONE LIKE YOU, O LORD (YOU ARE GREAT, AND
> YOUR NAME IS GREAT IN MIGHT), WHO WOULD NOT FEAR YOU, O KING OF
> THE NATIONS? FOR THIS IS YOUR RIGHTFUL DUE. FOR AMONG ALL THE WISE
> MEN OF THE NATIONS, AND IN ALL THEIR KINGDOMS, THERE IS NONE LIKE
> YOU.
>
> Jeremiah 10:6–7

What is the Lord saying in our reading? He is saying that people take an axe, go to the forest, cut down a tree, and fashion it into a god. Then they use silver and gold to decorate the tree. They make a platform and nail the feet of the god on to the platform so that it doesn't fall over. Then they worship the god that they have made (verses 2–5). It seems almost laughable, doesn't it? But it is not a laughing matter, folks. There are too many of us who have idols in our lives. Our idols have to go; there is no place for them.

You cannot hang a medallion around your neck and believe that it will protect your car and keep you safe as you travel. This is idol worship. There is only one God who can keep you safe, and His Name is Jesus Christ. So before you travel on the road, pray like each one of us at Shalom do, "Lord, protect this car and our journey," and then off you go. Having a fancy medallion stuck on the dashboard of your car is not going to keep you safe. It is Jesus who is going to keep your car safe. Every year in South America, people professing to be Christians have a festival. They carry statues on a stretcher down the main street, while the crowds lining the sidewalks throw flowers on to the statues and worship them. They are no different to the heathen.

Some people will even worship a building. It could even be a cathedral. God is not in a building. He is in the hearts of men. You cannot contain God. This Scripture we have read today is a hard one. But God has convinced me to share it with you. There are too many people looking to other gods. You cannot do this because God will not tolerate it. You need to get rid of any objects, images, or pictures that do not bring glory to God. They must go – there is no place for them.

Prayer

My Father in Heaven, the prophet Jeremiah dedicated his life to telling Your people that their idols had to go. He called them to worship You and only You. Lord, there is none like You. You and You alone deserve my worship and my allegiance. You and You alone can save and protect me. Amen.

Read Jeremiah 11:1–13

> THEY HAVE TURNED BACK TO THE INIQUITIES OF THEIR FOREFATHERS WHO
> REFUSED TO HEAR MY WORDS, AND THEY HAVE GONE AFTER OTHER GODS TO
> SERVE THEM; THE HOUSE OF ISRAEL AND THE HOUSE OF JUDAH HAVE BROKEN
> MY COVENANT WHICH I MADE WITH THEIR FATHERS.
>
> Jeremiah 11:10

When I first became a Christian, we went through our house and we did a spring clean. Any statue or object that didn't bring glory to God, we took it out and we burned it. Why? Because it didn't glorify God. Now I also want to say by the same token, there is no power in a statue. I am not one of those people who looks for a demon behind every bush. However, a big statue of Buddha, for instance, doesn't bring glory to Jesus Christ, so it must go. I really mean it. We do not acknowledge any power in the idol, but we need to be careful that we do not give glory to other gods – because it makes our God very unhappy.

I want to tell you another story. I know of farmers who go to a witchdoctor if their cattle are stolen. The witchdoctor takes the bones and throws them. He goes into a trance and he does not speak to Jesus; he speaks to the devil, because there is no one else. Then he looks at the bones. He tells you to drive down the road for 30 kilometres. He says you will come to some huts, you are to go behind the huts and there you will find your cattle. The farmer pays the witchdoctor R500 or R1,000 for this information. Sure as anything, when the farmer goes behind the huts he finds his cattle.

Now the farmer may think he is very clever. My friend, all he has done is open the door for every demon in hell to come on to his farm. If you have done this, you need to repent today, put it behind you and press on. Why? Because it doesn't bring glory to God. "You shall have no other idols but Me", the Lord says. God has given us clear instructions on how we are to live. In Jeremiah God accused the children of Israel: "Yet they did not obey or incline their ear, but everyone followed the dictates of his evil heart" (verse 8a).

Prayer
My Father God, You are indeed a jealous God. You have called Your people to walk in covenant with You. Lord, I don't want to break Your covenant. I want to honour it. I want to walk in obedience to You. I choose to obey You and heed Your voice. I choose to follow You and glorify You. Amen.

Read Matthew 12:22–32

> HE WHO IS NOT WITH ME IS AGAINST ME, AND HE WHO DOES NOT GATHER
> WITH ME SCATTERS ABROAD.
>
> Matthew12:30

If you read your horoscope and tarot cards, or if you visited a fortune teller before you became a Christian, you need to repent of it, if you haven't already done so. If you still do any of these, stop immediately! Jesus said: "He who is not with Me is against Me". When I was still an unbeliever I attended a New Year's Eve party with my brother. We had been partying all night, and in the early hours of the morning a gentleman invited us back to his house. When we arrived he told us we were going to play "glassy-glassy". We had no idea what that was. It turned out to be a Ouija board. He placed a piece of paper with numbers and letters of the alphabet in the centre of the table and put a glass in the middle of the paper. Then we all had to sit around the table and place our finger on the glass.

My brother and I were joking and laughing because we didn't believe in that sort of thing. We thought it was childish and nonsense. The man said that I should ask the spirit a question. So I asked it to tell me my year of birth (no one but my brother knew what it was). The glass moved to 1947. I had been drinking whiskey all evening, but I immediately sobered up. Our host said to ask another question. So we asked the spirit to tell us where we had been born. The glass immediately spelt out B-u-l-a-w-a-y-o. By that time I was finished. I had nothing left to say.

If you play with fire you will get burned, my friend. God is a jealous God. He will not share your allegiance. If you have tarot cards or anything else linked to the occult, you need to stop doing whatever it is you are doing, and get rid of it. Ask Jesus to forgive you. You cannot serve two gods. If you are not serving God you are serving the devil. If you serve the devil the Lord cannot be a part of your life.

Prayer

My Father God, I come before You and I bow in Your presence. Lord, I ask You to bring to my remembrance any form of occult practice that I may have been involved in. Lord, I want to serve You and only You. I don't want any split allegiance in my life. Lord, I want to live for You. Amen.

Read Exodus 32:1–24

> AND THE LORD SAID TO MOSES, "GO, GET DOWN! FOR YOUR PEOPLE WHOM
> YOU BROUGHT OUT OF THE LAND OF EGYPT HAVE CORRUPTED THEMSELVES.
> THEY HAVE TURNED ASIDE QUICKLY OUT OF THE WAY WHICH I COMMANDED
> THEM. THEY HAVE MADE THEMSELVES A MOLDED CALF, AND WORSHIPED
> IT AND SACRIFICED TO IT, AND SAID, 'THIS IS YOUR GOD, O ISRAEL, THAT
> BROUGHT YOU OUT OF THE LAND OF EGYPT!'"
>
> Exodus 32:7–8

The Israelites built their golden calf because they became restless when Moses took too long to come down from the mountain where he was meeting with God. My dear friends, maybe somebody reading this devotional is growing tired of waiting for God. Maybe you are growing weary of walking by faith. Maybe you don't feel it is working for you. Don't go prostituting yourself to foreign gods. If you have a problem and you've lost your cattle, ask Jesus to show you the way – not a witchdoctor. If you have a problem with your health, don't go to some person who serves foreign gods and ask them to pray over you. You are asking for trouble.

I want to say this clearly: if there is anything in your life that is more important than the Lord Jesus Christ, then it is an idol and it must go. I say this because I want you to be able to live life abundantly. I want you to enjoy the fullness of God like I do. He says, "I am the Alpha and the Omega, the Beginning and the End, the First and the Last" (Revelation 22:13).

So if your own family – now this is hard – is more important to you than Jesus Christ, they are an idol. You need to repent, put God first and your family second. If your ministry – listen to me again – is more important than Jesus Christ, you have a problem, sir, and you need to repent. That is why there is no joy in your life. I am talking to myself as much as I am to you. I have a passion for preaching. Those who know me will tell you that the only time Angus is happy is when he is telling people about Jesus. But if my ministry is bigger than Jesus I have a problem. Anything in your life, whether it be your occupation or your sport, if it's more important than God, it is an idol. You serve a jealous God and He will not take second place in your life.

Prayer

My Father God, forgive me that sometimes I grow weary of waiting for You to act. It is at times like these that I am tempted to turn to "others" for help. Forgive me, I pray. Keep me faithful and keep me true. You and You alone are my God and my Source. There is no "Other" but You. Amen.

Read Psalm 139

SEARCH ME, O GOD, AND KNOW MY HEART; TRY ME, AND KNOW MY
ANXIETIES; AND SEE IF THERE IS ANY WICKED WAY IN ME, AND LEAD ME IN THE
WAY EVERLASTING.

Psalm 139:23–24

If the Holy Spirit has convicted you regarding any of the things we have been discussing over the past few days, you can choose to be free right now. Below is a prayer for you to pray. Pray it out loud in faith and God will set you free. Choose to put Jesus Christ first in your life, and you will have freedom. An idol in your life means you are a slave to that idol. Jesus died to set you free from slavery to sin. You have to choose to serve Him, though. You are saved by grace. Jesus Christ did the work on Calvary. Your Salvation depends on one thing: faith in God – "Have faith in God" (Mark 11:22). Not in idols; not in your money; not in your family; not in your career, but in God and only God. There is liberty only in Him.

Here is a prayer that you can pray to ask God to set you free from your idol.

*Heavenly Father, I come into Your presence today. Lord, Holy Spirit, will
You bring to my mind right now any area in my life that I have made an idol
of. Lord, I bring my past and my present before You."Search me, O God, and
know my heart... and see if there is any wicked way in me".*

*[Allow the Holy Spirit to show you what you need to repent of. As the things
come to your mind, speak them out.]*

*Lord, I repent of x. I break this in Jesus' Name. Forgive me, Lord. I now
surrender this part of my life to Jesus.*

*[If there is more than one thing then mention each of them as the Holy Spirit
brings them to mind.]*

*Thank You for freedom in Jesus' Name. Fill me with Your Holy Spirit right
now, I pray. In Jesus' Name. Amen.*

God tells us in His Word: "If we confess our sins, He is faithful and just to forgive us our sins and to cleanse us from all unrighteousness" (1 John 1:9). From now on, live in the freedom that is yours in Jesus' Name, my friend.

Prayer
My Father God, I thank You for freedom in Jesus' Name. Lord, I thank You that I have Salvation, full and free. I know that I can never earn it. All I have to do is walk in the fullness and the freedom of it. Lord, help me to live bringing glory to Your name each and every day of my life. Amen.

Read Hebrews 8:7–13

> FOR THIS IS THE COVENANT THAT I WILL MAKE WITH THE HOUSE OF ISRAEL
> AFTER THOSE DAYS, SAYS THE LORD: I WILL PUT MY LAWS IN THEIR MIND AND
> WRITE THEM ON THEIR HEARTS; AND I WILL BE THEIR GOD, AND THEY SHALL
> BE MY PEOPLE.
>
> Hebrews 8:10

Any professional hunter will tell you, especially when hunting big game – whether it be elephant or buffalo – that they will always aim for a heart shot. It is a heart shot that brings an animal down, not a head shot. I am not a hunter and I have no desire to be one, but this is what they tell me. You aim for the heart. The Lord wants to speak to you about your heart, my friend. Is your heart growing cold? You might say to me, "You know, Angus, when I first came to know the Lord Jesus Christ I was on fire for Him." Well that fire should continue to burn. If the fire in your heart goes out then it is over. You know what you become? You become a historian. There are some theologians who haven't met Jesus Christ personally. They know the Bible better than anyone. They can quote it from cover to cover. But they don't have a personal relationship with Jesus Christ.

I am talking about an intimate relationship with a Man, Jesus Christ, who was born in Bethlehem and grew up in Nazareth. He was a carpenter's son. His earthly father's name was Joseph. He spent thirty years doing carpentry, then the Holy Spirit came upon Him and He was launched into ministry. He only ministered for three years, but He changed the world. It has never been the same since.

Who were the men who followed Him? They were men who had hearts after God. They were not intellectuals. They were not men with particularly high IQs, but they were men with big hearts. You know, when I go into battle, folks, I don't want clever men with me. I want men with big hearts. Men who will say, "Let's go for it!" Jesus' disciples were men with big hearts, weren't they? They were fishermen, publicans; one was even a terrorist. They had a heart change and Jesus Christ became so important to them everything else simply faded into insignificance. Are you a man with a heart after God?

Prayer

My Father God, You are God and I declare that there is none like You. You are looking for men today who have hearts that are Yours and Yours alone. Lord, I want to be a man like this. I want to be a man whose heart belongs solely to You. Lord, take me and fill me with Your Spirit, I pray. Amen.

Read Philippians 1:12–30

FOR TO ME, TO LIVE IS CHRIST, AND TO DIE IS GAIN.

Philippians 1:21

Remember the old song, "Turn your eyes upon Jesus/Look full in His wonderful face/And the things of earth will grow strangely dim/In the light of His glory and grace." The Lord wants to change your heart, my friend. You see, if you walk by sight and not by faith your heart will fail you. What is the opposite of fear? It is faith! So if you are despairing today, if you are a fear-filled person, ask God to change your heart. After Paul had a change of heart, he said: "For to me, to live is Christ, and to die is gain." How can you frighten a Christian with Heaven? It's impossible. So what do we have to fear? If we live, we live for Jesus. If we die we are going to be with Him forever. We win either way!

I want to encourage you, my friend: place your heart in the forefront. You probably know the film titled *Braveheart*. William Wallace, a Scotsman, followed his heart not his head. He was for the people. It took a commoner to rally the Scottish people and lead them. In the thirteenth century, instead of their continuing to fight each other, he led them to fight for their independence and they defeated the English. They went right into northern England – as far south as Newcastle – until the lords of the clans pulled their people back and the whole campaign fell apart.

I am telling you, if ever there was a time in the history of this world that people are looking for something to believe in, it is now. Especially young people. Wherever I go, whether to the cities or the rural areas, people are looking for something in which to put their heart. Most of the letters I receive from young people finishing university say that they want to serve God. They want to serve God and they want a challenge because their hearts are on fire. Where do you find yourself right now? Has your fire died, or is your heart still beating strong for God? Turn your eyes back to Jesus today.

Prayer

My Father in Heaven, I come to You in the precious Name of Jesus, my Saviour. Lord, I love You. Lord Jesus, I lift my eyes to You; I look into Your wonderful face once again. Lord, everything around me fades and becomes as nothing as I gaze upon Your wonder, grace, and beauty. Amen.

Read Jeremiah 24

THEN I WILL GIVE THEM A HEART TO KNOW ME, THAT I AM THE LORD; AND
THEY SHALL BE MY PEOPLE, AND I WILL BE THEIR GOD, FOR THEY SHALL
RETURN TO ME WITH THEIR WHOLE HEART.

Jeremiah 24:7

Who is the One who ignites our hearts with fire for God and His purposes? Only the
Holy Spirit. If you are one of the people whose heart used to be on fire for the Lord, I
am encouraging you to ask God to give you a new heart. We have been experiencing
a revival in South Africa for several years now. I know some of the church men will
not agree with me. But I have seen hundreds of thousands of men at the Mighty Men
Conferences over the years seeking the face of God.

This was a heart thing, not an intellectual exercise. I have seen men weeping all
over the place. I know men; they are tough, and they are taught not to cry. Men are
raised to have a stiff upper lip. These same men were broken and crying because
the Holy Spirit met with them. He said, "Listen, you are wasting your life. It is time
you put your energy into something that is real and will last for eternity." Each man
represents a family, a business, a company, a sports institute, a university, a school, a
farming concern. We are talking revival.

What about you, today? Jeremiah, the prophet, spoke a lot about the condition of
man's heart and his need for a new one. In our reading he shares God's Word to His
people: "and I will be their God, for they shall return to Me with their whole heart." I
have told you many times about how on 18 February 1979 my life changed completely.
I was a man whose heart was failing him because of fear. Perhaps you've seen the film
Faith Like Potatoes, so you know what I was like. God broke away the exterior; He gave
me a new heart and changed me forever. He wants to do the same for you. He wants
to change you. He wants to light a fire in your heart. He wants your whole heart. If
you haven't done so already, will you give it to Him right now?

Prayer
*My Father God, You have been calling Your people to Yourself down through the ages. Those
who are truly Your people are the ones whose hearts are wholly Yours. Lord, I want to be one
of Your people. I want to live 100 per cent sold out to You. I want to live with fire in my heart.
Amen.*

Read Ezekiel 36:16–38

> I WILL GIVE YOU A NEW HEART AND PUT A NEW SPIRIT WITHIN YOU; I WILL
> TAKE THE HEART OF STONE OUT OF YOUR FLESH AND GIVE YOU A HEART OF
> FLESH.
>
> Ezekiel 36:26

You are never too old or too young to receive a new heart. Attending church will not give you a new heart. Some time ago, at a rally we held in Upington, South Africa, there was a couple there who were in their eighties and who gave their hearts to Jesus for the first time. Jesus met them, touched their hearts, broke their hearts, and gave them new hearts. They left the stadium like a young couple who were starting all over again. Another time a man came to a Mighty Men Conference. He was a cocaine addict and an alcoholic. He'd lost his family's car, their home, and he'd lost his job. He was a blasphemer who, instead of spending time with his wife and little children, was always with a bunch of other drunkards. He came to the conference and in one weekend God gave him a new heart and a brand new life.

He returned home and his wife wrote to tell us she couldn't believe the transformation. The first thing he did on the Monday morning was to buy himself a Bible. He began the process of putting his life and his family back together. What happened? God gave him a new heart. When God gives us a new heart He also promises us: "Then I will sprinkle clean water on you, and you shall be clean; I will cleanse you from all your filthiness and from all your idols" (verse 25). God goes a step further and He says that with the new heart and the cleansing: "I will put My Spirit within you and cause you to walk in My statutes, and you will keep My judgments and do them" (verse 27).

It is only once we have been cleansed by the shed blood of Jesus, received a new heart that beats solely for God, and have God's Holy Spirit dwelling inside of us that we can know new life. God promises us this new life, but we have to take hold of it. We have to want it and we have to come to Him to claim it.

Prayer
My Father God, thank You once again for Your Word to me. Lord, I thank You that You call me, You cleanse me, You give me a new heart, and You fill me with Your Holy Spirit. I come to You and I ask You to give me all that You want to give me. I open myself up to You, my Lord. Amen.

Read John 11:17–44

THEREFORE, WHEN JESUS SAW HER WEEPING, AND THE JEWS WHO CAME WITH HER WEEPING, HE GROANED IN THE SPIRIT AND WAS TROUBLED. AND HE SAID, "WHERE HAVE YOU LAID HIM?" THEY SAID TO HIM, "LORD, COME AND SEE." JESUS WEPT. THEN THE JEWS SAID, "SEE HOW HE LOVED HIM!"

John 11:33–36

Charles Finney was one of America's greatest evangelists. It is said that something like 85 per cent of his converts stuck to the commitments they had made till their dying day. Finney, who was studying to become a lawyer, was touched by God in 1821. He said that one night, as he lay praying in a forest, a shaft of love pierced his heart. He cried out, "Lord, if You don't stop You are going to kill me with the love." From then on he preached the gospel of Jesus. Finney believed that where there was no "Amen" and where there were no "wet eyes" there was no revival.

Our God is an emotional God. Oh yes, He is, my friends! I have read some accounts where historians write that Jesus wept more than He laughed. You know I love that account where Jesus was laughing, and He was happy as He played with the children. That is fine and He definitely had those moments. But He also weeps. For the man who has tragically lost his family. For the man whose business is on the verge of going bankrupt. Jesus weeps with the couple who have lost their baby.

When one of Jesus' best friends, Lazarus, died, He wept. I am sure He would have wanted to rush there immediately. But He waited, because the Father told Him to. Jesus knew Lazarus was coming out the tomb. So why did He weep? Because He had compassion for the people. Folks, if you want to minister to people you need to minister to them through your heart, not your head. People don't need knowledge; they can find that on the internet. They want personal contact. They want to feel a connection. I am telling you Jesus Christ loves you. He loves you so much that He died for you. "Greater love has no one than this, than to lay down one's life for his friends" (John 15:13). The only way for you to reach out to people and minister to them is with a heart filled with the love of Jesus.

Prayer

Father God, I thank You for Your great love for me. Thank You that You loved me enough to send Your Son, Jesus Christ, to die for me. Lord, I want to have Your love for other people. Lord, touch my heart like You did Finney's. Make me a servant of Yours who loves others with the love of Jesus. Amen.

Read Proverbs 4:10–27

> ABOVE ALL ELSE, GUARD YOUR HEART, FOR EVERYTHING YOU DO FLOWS FROM
> IT.
>
> Proverbs 4:23 (NIV)

Guard your heart, my friend. Guard your heart. "Keep your heart with all diligence, for out of it spring the issues of life" (Proverbs 4:23, NKJV). Luke 6:45 puts it this way: "A good man out of the good treasure of his heart brings forth good; and an evil man out of the evil treasure of his heart brings forth evil. For out of the abundance of the heart his mouth speaks." What is in your heart will come out – in the way you speak and the way you behave. It is what is in a man's heart that dictates the kind of person he is. God has been longing to give His people a new heart since He created humans.

This is what He sent the prophet Jeremiah to tell His people Israel. He wanted them to turn from their idols and worship of foreign gods to serve Him. He, the One and Only true God, wanted to give them new hearts. He wanted to place His Spirit within them. He will do the same for you and for me. God wants to give us a heart of flesh. The only way that you can minister effectively for God is if you have a heart that is filled with compassion and love. If you have a heart of stone then what you say to people will go in one ear, and out the other.

You can tell people that you love them, but actions speak louder than words – certainly louder than any sermon. That is why Mother Teresa's ministry was so successful. She didn't talk about love; she practised love. "For the love of Christ compels us, because we judge thus: that if One died for all, then all died; and He died for all, that those who live should live no longer for themselves, but for Him who died for them and rose again" (2 Corinthians 5:14–15). So, my friend, guard your heart. Don't allow any sin to come in and rob you of your blessing. God has blessed you so that you can bless others.

Prayer

My Father God, I bow before You. Lord, I bring my heart to You. I lay it at Your feet. Take it. Keep it. Lord, I want to live all out for You. I want to be able to be used by You. I desire that people should be able to see into my heart, and what they see must line up with what I say and do. Amen.

Read Jeremiah 14

> REMEMBER, DO NOT BREAK YOUR COVENANT WITH US. ARE THERE ANY
> AMONG THE IDOLS OF THE NATIONS THAT CAN CAUSE RAIN? OR CAN THE
> HEAVENS GIVE SHOWERS? ARE YOU NOT HE, O LORD OUR GOD? THEREFORE
> WE WILL WAIT FOR YOU, SINCE YOU HAVE MADE ALL THESE.
>
> Jeremiah 14:21c–22

The world experienced a recession over the past few years. The South African economy has not been spared, and there are many people who are battling. There are farmers I know who are going through difficult times. Some of our friends are struggling financially, others are struggling with their health; for many people things are simply not going well. The good news is that the Lord is ultimately in control.

The children of Israel were complaining to God: "Have You utterly rejected Judah? Has Your soul loathed Zion? Why have You stricken us so that there is no healing for us?" (verse 19a). There are many of us who are complaining to God, "Lord, have You forgotten me?"; "Lord, my child is not being healed"; "Lord, I still don't have a job"; "Lord, I am about to use the last of my money. After this I have nothing left." Jeremiah cries out on behalf of the children of Israel: "We looked for peace, but there was no good; and for the time of healing, and there was trouble. We acknowledge, O Lord, our wickedness and the iniquity of our fathers… Do not abhor us, for Your name's sake; do not disgrace the throne of Your glory" (verses 19b–21a). Jeremiah asks, "Lord, have You forgotten us? There is no rain, no food, the people are struggling Lord." Then he affirms, "Lord, You are actually the only One who can bring rain. You are the only One who can bring hope, joy and gladness to our hearts."

Jeremiah understood that God and God alone was his Source. He spent his life trying to bring the children of Israel back to God. He tirelessly told them that there was no hope to be found in their idols or in running after foreign gods. The God of Abraham, Isaac, and Jacob was their Help and their Strength. It is the same for us, my friends. Where are you turning for help? To God your Father or to man? God is the One who is in control. He is the only One who can help you.

Prayer

My Father in Heaven, You and You alone are in control. Forgive me that like the children of Israel You are often my last port of call, instead of my first. I know that You are the One who not only made me, but made the world. You hold everything in the palm of Your hand. Lord, I look to You. Amen.

Read Matthew 6:28–34

FOR YOUR HEAVENLY FATHER KNOWS THAT YOU NEED ALL THESE THINGS.

Matthew 6:32b

If I could take you to my pasture I would show you my horse. He is out there eating grass. Nothing concerns him. He knows that tomorrow morning he will wake up and there will be more grass for him to eat. He knows that I will look after him because I love him. Now I want to tell you that God loves you a lot more than I love my horse. So, why would the Lord neglect you? Why would He forget you? Jeremiah understood this. There is no reason for God to turn His back on you. What we need to do is to put our trust in the Lord Jesus Christ. We need to start to look to Him and then all of a sudden the sun will begin to shine again.

Every Wednesday morning I pray with two dear friends. The other day we were saying to each other that if we didn't have God, if we didn't have the Lord Jesus Christ to look up to, we would be in a sorry state. If all that we had to hope for was the end of the week and the next rugby game, or soccer match, wouldn't life be ever so boring? But you know something? Our hope is in God. We are looking forward to "home time". You and I are sojourners in a foreign land, my friends. This is not our home. We are not staying here – we are passing through.

It is time that we start to count our blessings. Here is a verse and the chorus from an old hymn:

So, amid the conflict whether great or small,
Do not be disheartened, God is over all;
Count your many blessings, angels will attend,
Help and comfort give you to your journey's end.

Count your blessings, name them one by one,
Count your blessings; see what God hath done!
Count your blessings, name them one by one,
And it will surprise you what the Lord hath done.

"For your heavenly Father knows that you need all these things." Do not worry!

Prayer
My Father God, thank You for the reminder that You know everything of which I have need. Lord, I choose to count my blessings. Lord, I name them one by one. There are so many. You are faithful and true. Thank You for Your goodness, faithfulness, and love toward me that never ends. Amen.

Read 1 Peter 5:1–11

THEREFORE HUMBLE YOURSELVES UNDER THE MIGHTY HAND OF GOD, THAT
HE MAY EXALT YOU IN DUE TIME, CASTING ALL YOUR CARE UPON HIM, FOR
HE CARES FOR YOU.

1 Peter 5:6–7

We have five children who are all grown up. They are all married and we have been blessed with wonderful grandchildren. I will never forget, when my second oldest daughter was about three or four years old, we were walking down the farm road together. We were going to check the maize crop. She was holding on to my little finger and toddling along beside me. At the time I was in my mid-thirties. I will never forget as we walked along, I silently called out to the Lord: "Lord, what is going to happen to this little girl if I crack up and have a nervous breakdown? If I cannot go on any more? What is going to happen to her? Who is going to look after her?" I will never forget that day, being so stressed out and crying out to the Lord.

I want to tell you that little girl is now in her thirties and she is a mother. She is married to a fine young farmer, who is a forester, and they have their own farm. She is content. She is a school teacher, and she is very involved in our school as well as our children's home on the farm. The main thing is that she loves the Lord. Yet all those years back I was concerned about how she was going to grow up.

I want to say something to dads reading this devotional. Do your best and leave the rest to God. Why are we always stressing; worrying about something that is never going to happen? "What if, what if, what if…" No! Instead let's affirm: "Lord, You are my Provider. Lord Jesus when I gave my life to You, I said I am casting all my cares upon You, for You care for me." It is a choice that we make, my friends. Choosing to trust God, because we know that He cares for us. There is no excuse for a child of God to worry. You are a man of faith so walk by faith and not by sight.

Prayer
My Father, I am so encouraged as I read Your Word. Thank You for reaffirming to me that You care for me. You know and understand every detail of my life. Lord, I cast my cares upon You. I choose to walk by faith and not by sight. I choose to lift up my head and look to You only. Amen.

THE LORD REMOVES YOUR TROUBLES

Read John 14:1–4, 19–31

> PEACE I LEAVE WITH YOU, MY PEACE I GIVE TO YOU; NOT AS THE WORLD
> GIVES DO I GIVE TO YOU. LET NOT YOUR HEART BE TROUBLED, NEITHER LET IT
> BE AFRAID.
>
> John 14:27

People will be drawn to Christ when they see the peace and the tranquillity that you have in your heart. This is not to say that we, as Christians, are exempt from hardship or tribulation. Not at all. In fact, it is when we are enduring hardship and tribulation that the world sits up and wonders, "Now how are they going to handle that?" When they see that in the midst of difficulties we have the peace of Jesus, it is a strong testimony. Jesus promised us in His Word: "Peace I leave with you, My peace I give to you".

We need to really start looking to God for our provision. When people see you depending upon the Lord it will draw them to Christ. People more than anything today are looking for something that they can believe in; every person has a hankering for something that is bigger than they are. So when your neighbour or your colleague at work sees the peace of God in your life; when they see you actively trusting God to provide for you and your family, they will be drawn to what you have.

So where do you stand? Are you going to start trusting God? Yes, you have to be responsible. Of course you have to get up in the morning and go to work. The Bible says that a lazy man doesn't deserve to eat (2 Thessalonians 3:10b). But your trust is not in your job, and it is not in your finances; your trust is in God alone. Peace is not a philosophy or a plan of action. Peace is a Person: Jesus Christ.

"Let not your heart be troubled; you believe in God, believe also in Me. In My Father's house are many mansions; if it were not so, I would have told you. I go to prepare a place for you. And if I go and prepare a place for you, I will come again and receive you to Myself; that where I am, there you may be also. And where I go you know, and the way you know" (John 14:1–4).

Prayer

Father, I thank You that when people all around are faint-hearted with panic, I am strong and secure in You. Thank You for Your peace. A peace that is not dependent upon circumstances. Lord, thank You that my heart does not need to be troubled because You are in control and You provide for me. Amen.

Read 2 Timothy 4:1–8

> I HAVE FOUGHT THE GOOD FIGHT, I HAVE FINISHED THE RACE, I HAVE KEPT
> THE FAITH.
>
> 2 Timothy 4:7

So how are we going to finish our race, you and I? Will we finish our race with joy, hope, and a positive attitude? Some of you are so weary. You are reading this and you say, "Angus, my children still have another ten years of schooling left. Your little daughter is grown up, but my children have many years to go before they will be independent. How do we do it? When I wake up in the morning I am tired before the day has even begun."

If you are feeling as if you cannot go any further, read today's Scripture again. How did Paul do it? How does anyone do it? One obedient step of faith at a time. An ancient proverb goes: "You cover the distance of a thousand miles by taking the first step." This is how Paul lived his life, which, as you know, was not an easy one. Each day he did what God was telling him to do that day. He walked by faith, he lived by faith, and he died by faith. This is why he could say to Timothy, "I have fought the good fight, I have finished the race, I have kept the faith." This is how Jesus lived when He walked on this earth one step at a time, one day at a time, in obedience to His Father.

Paul knew he was not alone, Jesus knew He was not alone, and we are not alone either:

> *Therefore we also, since we are surrounded by so great a cloud of witnesses,*
> *let us lay aside every weight, and the sin which so easily ensnares us, and*
> *let us run with endurance the race that is set before us, looking unto Jesus,*
> *the author and finisher of our faith, who for the joy that was set before Him*
> *endured the cross, despising the shame, and has sat down at the right hand of*
> *the throne of God.*
>
> Hebrews 12:1–3

This is why you can finish strong, my friends. You will do it: one day at a time.

Prayer

My Father God, I thank You for Your Words of encouragement and exhortation to me. Lord, You know how difficult it is sometimes. I become overwhelmed by all I see around me. Yet, You are telling me to look to You. It is in You that I will find the strength to finish my race strong and faithful. Amen.

Read James 5:1–12

THEREFORE BE PATIENT, BRETHREN, UNTIL THE COMING OF THE LORD. SEE
HOW THE FARMER WAITS FOR THE PRECIOUS FRUIT OF THE EARTH, WAITING
PATIENTLY FOR IT UNTIL IT RECEIVES THE EARLY AND LATTER RAIN. YOU ALSO
BE PATIENT. ESTABLISH YOUR HEARTS, FOR THE COMING OF THE LORD IS AT
HAND.

James 5:7–8

If a farmer had to sit down and think of all the things he has to do in just one season
he would probably give up or else he would end up in a mental institution. Too much!
Too much work and too much responsibility. So how does he do it? He does it one step
at a time. How do you prepare a crop? You take the plough out of the shed, and you
hitch it up to the tractor. You start ploughing the field. You plough properly and you
do it to the best of your ability. When you are finished you take your disc and you level
the ground. You make sure there is no wheat, nothing left. (No sin in your life – see?)
Then what do you do? You bring out your next machine and you start to sow good
seed. (The Word of God.) And you do it faithfully.

You don't keep looking at the weather. You don't keep saying, "Oh well, I hope it
rains this year, because if it doesn't I am finished." If you start talking like that you
will make yourself sick. First mentally, then spiritually, and finally physically. That is
right. Folks, we have to live this life by faith. Remember Jeremiah said the idols cannot
bring rain. Man cannot do it. Sacrifices cannot do it. Only God can do it. When you
start living by faith then you will not only live for a long time, but you will succeed as
well. Rome was not built in a day, my friend.

Some young men who had recently begun preaching said to me, "Angus, we
wish we could do what you do." I asked them, "Are you prepared to pay the price?"
Remember that what is happening now in my ministry didn't take place within six
months, folks. It took thirty years of blood, sweat, and tears. That is how it works;
there are no quick fixes. It is a day-by-day walk of faith with God. Learning, growing,
trusting Him to provide and undertake in all things.

Prayer

*My Father, thank You for the lesson You have taught me as we have looked at the farmer. You
are calling me to live with the same thoroughness, perseverance, and patience. Lord, help me to
stay faithful. Help me to live in hope: hope in You and in Your goodness and kindness to me.
Amen.*

Read Daniel 1

> But Daniel purposed in his heart that he would not defile himself with the portion of the king's delicacies... Now God had brought Daniel into the favor and goodwill of the chief of the eunuchs.
>
> Daniel 1:8a and 9

Daniel was a young man taken from his home and his country to a strange land with heathen customs. His parents raised him to be a godly young man. The king commanded that he wanted – "young men in whom there was no blemish, but good-looking, gifted in all wisdom, possessing knowledge and quick to understand, who had ability to serve in the king's palace, and whom they might teach the language and literature of the Chaldeans" (verse 4). Daniel was a fine specimen of a young man, and he was chosen along with three of his friends – Shadrach, Meshach, and Abed-Nego.

The idea was to indoctrinate these young men and turn them away from the God of Israel to the god of the Chaldeans. They were even given new names: "To them the chief of the eunuchs gave names: he gave Daniel the name Belteshazzar; to Hananiah, Shadrach; to Mishael, Meshach; and to Azariah, Abed-Nego" (verse 7). God, however, had a different purpose for Daniel's life: one that would honour Him and bring glory to His Name. Daniel immediately realized that he could not eat the food from the king's table. As our key says, he refused to defile himself. He told the eunuchs who served the king that he would not eat the food. They were scared to disobey the king, but our Scripture tells us that God gave Daniel favour with them. So they allowed him and his friends to eat vegetables and drink water.

As you know, at the end of the ten days the young men were healthier and looked better than those who had eaten the king's rich food. This step of faith and choice to obey God irrespective of the personal cost was a signature of Daniel's entire life. We have often said that obedience and faith are interlinked with each other. Never is this more evident than in Daniel's life. It began with Daniel purposing "in his heart that he would not defile himself". What about you, my friend: what have you purposed in your heart? Will you, like Daniel, choose to walk by faith and not by sight?

Prayer

My Father in Heaven, I am so inspired by the life of Daniel, a real man of faith. Lord, You called him and he responded wholeheartedly to Your purposes for his life. I too want to be a man of faith. A man who purposes in his heart to serve You before and above all else. I love You, Lord. Amen.

Read Daniel 2:1–6, 10–13, 19, 24–28, 46–49

> DANIEL ANSWERED IN THE PRESENCE OF THE KING, AND SAID, "THE SECRET
> WHICH THE KING HAS DEMANDED, THE WISE MEN, THE ASTROLOGERS, THE
> MAGICIANS, AND THE SOOTHSAYERS CANNOT DECLARE TO THE KING. BUT
> THERE IS A GOD IN HEAVEN WHO REVEALS SECRETS, AND HE HAS MADE
> KNOWN TO KING NEBUCHADNEZZAR WHAT WILL BE IN THE LATTER DAYS."
>
> Daniel 2:27–28a

We serve an amazing God. He is God of this universe. There is no one like our God, or Jesus Christ our Saviour. God has exalted His Son. Paul tells us in Philippians 2:9–11: "Therefore God also has highly exalted Him and given Him the name which is above every name, that at the name of Jesus every knee should bow, of those in heaven, and of those on earth, and of those under the earth, and that every tongue should confess that Jesus Christ is Lord, to the glory of God the Father." King Nebuchadnezzar looked to his advisers to give him the answer to the meaning of his dream. When they couldn't he became angry and threatened to put them to death. Daniel and his friends were in danger of being put to death with the rest of the wise men.

Daniel realized that God could provide the answer because the dream came from God in the first place. Daniel and his friends sought the Lord and He gave Daniel the interpretation of the dream. What was Daniel's first reaction? He praised God: "Blessed be the name of God forever and ever, for wisdom and might are His" (Daniel 2:20). Daniel knew that he and his friends were totally dependent upon God. He shared the dream with the king and made sure that the king understood Who had given the understanding and the wisdom regarding the dream: "But there is a God in heaven who reveals secrets…"

How did the king respond? "The king answered Daniel, and said, 'Truly your God is the God of gods, the Lord of kings, and a revealer of secrets, since you could reveal this secret'" (verse 47). The result was that the king promoted Daniel and his friends (verses 48–49). It was a wonderful testimony that the heathen king recognized God's work in and through those young men. They faithfully served the king without ever compromising their faith in any way. What a wonderful example this is to us. Ask God by His Spirit to strengthen and increase your resolve to serve Him faithfully.

Prayer

My Father God, there is no one like You. You are the Mighty God. You alone are worthy of praise, glory, and honour. Lord, I lift my voice in praise to Your Holy Name. I worship You, Jesus, my Saviour and Lord. I bow my knee to You and declare You are Lord, Saviour, and King. Amen.

Read Daniel 3:8–30

> Nebuchadnezzar spoke, saying, "Blessed be the God of Shadrach, Meshach, and Abed-Nego, who sent His Angel and delivered His servants who trusted in Him, and they have frustrated the king's word, and yielded their bodies, that they should not serve nor worship any god except their own God!"
>
> Daniel 3:28

If you want to walk in faith and obedience to God be careful of the company that you keep, no matter what your age. One of the things that stands out in the book of Daniel is how he and his friends were all obedient to what they believed. It must have been a source of encouragement being in a strange land with heathen customs to know that there were other people who supported you and believed as you did. These young men were not scared to stand up for what they believed in.

Theirs was not a wishy-washy faith, my friends. When Shadrach, Meshach, and Abed-Nego faced the choice of bowing down to King Nebuchadnezzar or being thrown into the furnace, they chose the furnace. Why? Because they knew in Whom they believed. They were prepared to die rather than denounce God. Their commitment was complete and absolute. It is an amazing story. We see Jesus appear with them in the fire. Not a hair on their heads was singed. We see the king overcome with amazement and he couldn't help himself – he had to give praise to their God.

Down through the ages people have chosen death rather than disobedience to God. Sometimes we see God miraculously intervening and saving them. Other times they have died martyrs' deaths. The dying or the living is not important – is it? We know that dead or alive we are with the Lord. God intervened in this instance because He had a higher purpose to fulfil. He wanted to show the king and the people that He was God – there was none greater than He. In our key verse we read that Nebuchadnezzar received this message loud and clear. God was glorified through their redemption. We spoke a lot about worshipping idols a few days ago. Here we see young men who refused to worship a graven image. My friend, do you too refuse to worship any god except your own God, and His Son Jesus Christ? Each day in many different ways we are faced with this same choice.

Prayer

My Father, You have called me to serve You and to serve You alone. Help me, I pray, to make the choice to obey You no matter what the personal consequences. I want to be faithful to You above all else. Lord, give me strength, courage, and the commitment to walk faithfully with You. Amen.

Read Daniel 6:1–9

> THEN THIS DANIEL DISTINGUISHED HIMSELF ABOVE THE GOVERNORS AND
> SATRAPS, BECAUSE AN EXCELLENT SPIRIT WAS IN HIM; AND THE KING GAVE
> THOUGHT TO SETTING HIM OVER THE WHOLE REALM.
>
> Daniel 6:3

Now Babylon in those days was a mighty kingdom. Nebuchadnezzar was probably the greatest ruler since the time of Pharaoh. The young boy from Israel was a captive, but because he had an excellent spirit, the foreign king, who didn't even worship Daniel's God, was prepared to put Daniel in charge of everything. Why? Because he had an excellent spirit. Daniel knew his God. Everything that he did was based upon his belief and knowledge of his God: "but the people who know their God shall be strong, and carry out great exploits" (Daniel 11:32b). Daniel could write this because he lived it.

Today we live in a time where more than ever before the world needs to witness Christians who have excellent spirits. They need to see followers of Jesus who know their God and who do great exploits as a result of knowing Him. We are not talking about a superficial knowledge here, my friends, we are talking about a deep experiential knowledge that reaches to every part and area of our lives. The people who lived around Daniel might not have liked him – they might have been jealous of him and his success – but one thing they couldn't do was point a finger at him. So they had to resort to lying about him to the king.

What about you? How do the people you work with view you? Do they recognize that you are a man with an excellent spirit? People do not judge us by what we say, they judge us by how we behave. We cannot expect to be sharing in the dirty jokes around the water cooler one minute, and then witnessing to people about Jesus the next – it doesn't work like that. Daniel and his friends clearly chose how they would live and every day they lived in that way. God blessed them and prospered them because of their obedience, their faith, and their faithfulness. They were men who had an excellent spirit. God is looking for men like this today – men who will do great exploits for Him.

Prayer

My Father God, You are a God above all gods. You rule this universe. Father, You love Your children. You are looking today, as You have done throughout history, for men who have excellent spirits. Lord, I want to be such a man. I want to know You deeply and experientially. Lord, I bow before You. Amen.

Read Daniel 6:10–28

> NOW WHEN DANIEL KNEW THAT THE WRITING WAS SIGNED, HE WENT HOME.
> AND IN HIS UPPER ROOM, WITH HIS WINDOWS OPEN TOWARD JERUSALEM, HE
> KNELT DOWN ON HIS KNEES THREE TIMES THAT DAY, AND PRAYED AND GAVE
> THANKS BEFORE HIS GOD, AS WAS HIS CUSTOM SINCE EARLY DAYS.
>
> Daniel 6:10

Daniel was a man of power – why? Because he was a man of prayer. Don't you love it? "[H]e knelt down on his knees three times that day, and prayed and gave thanks before his God, as was his custom since early days." There you have it, my friends. If you don't have power, if you feel that things are not going right in your life, examine your prayer life. The people who hated Daniel believed that they had found a way to bring him down. They knew that he would disobey the king in order to obey his God. Isn't it wonderful that they knew Daniel to be a man of prayer – who obeyed God above man?

King Nebuchadnezzar was dead and King Darius was reigning in his place. Daniel served him well and the king liked Daniel. When the evil men came to him with the suggestion about the decree, he did not realize what they were trying to do. When he realized, he was very upset and he tried everything to save Daniel, but he could not go back on a decree, even though he was the king. King Darius was not a believer, but he had witnessed Daniel serving his God. He said to Daniel; "Your God, whom you serve continually, He will deliver you" (verse 16b). Isn't that an amazing testimony to Daniel's faithfulness to his God? Even the heathen king recognized the power of Daniel's God.

Daniel fearlessly went into the den of lions. Like his friends who went into the fiery furnace he knew that whether he lived or died, he was with God. At first light the king rushed to the lions' den – there was Daniel, safe and sound. The king sent out a new decree that everyone should worship Daniel's God: "For He is the living God, and steadfast forever; His kingdom is the one which shall not be destroyed, and His dominion shall endure to the end. He delivers and rescues, and He works signs and wonders in heaven and on earth, who has delivered Daniel from the power of the lions" (verses 26b–27).

Prayer

My Father in Heaven, You are the same God who rescued Daniel from the lions' den. You are a God of power and of might. Lord, You show Yourself strong on behalf of Your children. Father, I come before You and I bow in Your presence. I worship You and I adore You, my Lord and my Saviour. Amen.

Read Jeremiah 9:23–24

> THUS SAYS THE LORD: "LET NOT THE WISE MAN GLORY IN HIS WISDOM,
> LET NOT THE MIGHTY MAN GLORY IN HIS MIGHT, NOR LET THE RICH MAN
> GLORY IN HIS RICHES; BUT LET HIM WHO GLORIES GLORY IN THIS, THAT
> HE UNDERSTANDS AND KNOWS ME, THAT I AM THE LORD, EXERCISING
> LOVINGKINDNESS, JUDGMENT, AND RIGHTEOUSNESS IN THE EARTH. FOR IN
> THESE I DELIGHT," SAYS THE LORD.
>
> Jeremiah 9:23–24

We have spent this month learning from three of God's faithful servants: Nehemiah, Jeremiah, and Daniel. Each of them had their own unique walk of faith with God. Each of them lived in different times and accomplished different things for God. Yet there are common threads that bind them together. These same threads bind all men of faith, no matter in which age or culture they live. There is the thread of putting God first in their lives. For these three we saw in each instance how they chose God's will above their own. Fulfilling their destiny was their primary purpose. They were 100 per cent sold out for God.

Each one of these men knew God. Nehemiah left his comfortable position to go back to Jerusalem. He knew his God and he wanted to honour Him by rebuilding the walls of the holy city. He faithfully carried out his assignment. He encouraged God's people to once again lift their heads and hearts in worship before their God. Jeremiah, a young man, who was bashful and would have preferred to remain in the background, stepped out in faith. He knew his God, and because he did he was able to fulfil a very difficult assignment to God's people. Daniel, another young man, taken from his home and his people. Yet, because he knew his God he was able to fulfil his purpose. He was able to say; "… but the people who know their God shall be strong, and carry out great exploits" (Daniel 11:32b).

These men knew their God, and because they did they were able to entrust their lives to Him. They had faith and they lived out that faith. One of the ways they lived it out was by obeying God. Each one experienced situations where obeying God meant putting themselves in harm's way. In each instance God was with them, He led, guided, and protected. My friends, a man of God knows his God, trusts his God, believes in his God, and obeys his God. He is a man who walks by faith and not by sight.

Prayer

My Father in Heaven, thank You that I can be Your man. I love You, Lord. I am thankful for the men of faith who have gone before me. I choose to walk with You, know You, trust You, believe in You, and obey You. I will walk by faith and not by sight. I want to glorify You through my life. Amen.

THE DISCIPLES' JOURNEY WITH JESUS

Their journeys of faith began when they said "Yes" to Jesus

1. Forsaking all to follow Jesus
2. Friend of sinners
3. Inviting others to follow Jesus
4. The calling
5. Lord, teach us to pray
6. Further instruction on prayer
7. Learning not to worry
8. Lesson on forgiveness
9. Take up your cross and follow Him
10. No greater love
11. Called to ministry
12. Lessons in faith
13. Stepping out in faith
14. The faith to suffer
15. Never alone
16. Called to serve, not be served
17. Listen, hear, and obey
18. Sanctified by the Word of Truth
19. Go and make disciples
20. Peter's denial of Jesus
21. The Lord's Supper
22. Judas's betrayal
23. John, the beloved
24. The disciples' unbelief
25. Breakfast at Galilee
26. Peter restored; Judas lost
27. Peter's restoration
28. Jesus' ascension
29. The Holy Spirit comes
30. They had been with Jesus
31. Peter ministers to the "unclean"

Read Luke 5:1–11

> So WHEN THEY HAD BROUGHT THEIR BOATS TO LAND, THEY FORSOOK ALL
> AND FOLLOWED HIM.
>
> Luke 5:11

Following Jesus has always been an all-or-nothing choice, as Matthew 4:18–22 tells us:

> *And Jesus, walking by the Sea of Galilee, saw two brothers, Simon called Peter,*
> *and Andrew his brother, casting a net into the sea; for they were fishermen.*
> *Then He said to them, "Follow Me, and I will make you fishers of men."*
> *They immediately left their nets and followed Him. Going on from there, He*
> *saw two other brothers, James the son of Zebedee, and John his brother, in*
> *the boat with Zebedee their father, mending their nets. He called them, and*
> *immediately they left the boat and their father, and followed Him.*

Jesus watched Simon Peter working with the nets as he and his brother fished for the day's catch. He spoke to Simon Peter in language that he understood. He invited him to come and catch men. Simon Peter and his brother left their nets and they followed Jesus. We see that this was not a half-hearted decision that they made. Our key verse tells us: "they forsook all and followed Him". Nothing has changed, my friends. Jesus is still calling men to follow Him. He is still in the business of calling disciples. He is looking for men who will forsake all and follow Him.

This does not mean that He is going to expect you to abandon your family – of course not – but it does mean that He asks you to live a different sort of life. One where you put Him first. One where you are sold out to Him. One where you love Him with all your heart, mind, and soul. This is the only way to follow Jesus. You will never be disappointed; you will never regret it. It is a journey that will take you all the way to Heaven. The disciples' journey with Jesus began the day they said "yes" to Him. Has your journey with Him begun? Is it an "I forsook all and followed Him" journey? Jesus is still looking for men today who will walk by faith and not by sight.

Prayer

My Father in Heaven, thank You for Jesus. Lord, You are calling me to follow You wholeheartedly. You are telling me in Your Word that this is the only way to walk with You. I want to have this kind of a relationship with You. I want to be Your man, fulfilling Your purposes and plans. Amen.

Read Mark 2:13–17

> WHEN JESUS HEARD IT, HE SAID TO THEM, "THOSE WHO ARE WELL HAVE NO
> NEED OF A PHYSICIAN, BUT THOSE WHO ARE SICK. I DID NOT COME TO CALL
> THE RIGHTEOUS, BUT SINNERS, TO REPENTANCE."
>
> Mark 2:17

My friend, aren't you thankful that Jesus dined with tax collectors and sinners? Imagine where we would be if He hadn't. In Jesus' day people did not have a very high regard for those who collected the taxes. Many times they were not honest men; they were either loathed or looked down upon. The Pharisees definitely looked down upon them, and they would not be seen associating with them. Isn't it interesting that Jesus was a magnet for those whom society had shunned? He sought out the people who needed saving. When Jesus invited Matthew, whose name at that time was Levi, to follow Him, Matthew didn't need to be asked twice. He stood up, left his tax collection table and followed Jesus.

By eating in Matthew's home Jesus showed everyone that He accepted Matthew. Word spread fast and soon many other disenfranchised people gathered around Jesus. Jesus' response to the Pharisees was that He had not come for those who "were well", but for those who needed a physician. He came for those who are sick: Jesus is the Great Physician. He came to heal those who are sick: spiritually, emotionally, and physically.

Matthew took his chance to be healed of his sin, and He accepted Jesus' call upon his life. He followed Jesus. It is interesting that we are not told of the individual calling of each and every disciple. There is a particular lesson to be learned from each one that is highlighted for us. With Matthew we are introduced to Jesus, the Friend of sinners. Matthew went on to eventually write the first book of the Gospels. I am sure that on that day when he sat at his tax collection table, and he saw Jesus walk toward him, he never realized how his life was soon to change. He was about to begin the adventure of his life. Since the day that I accepted Jesus' call upon my life in that little church in Greytown, my life has never been the same again either. What about you? How has your journey been?

Prayer

My Father God, there is nothing in this world that can compare to following You. Lord, the day that I surrendered my life to You is the best day of my life. Help me to never grow cold. I never want to take what You have done for me for granted. Lord, keep me fresh, and keep me following You. Amen.

Read John 1:35–51

> ONE OF THE TWO WHO HEARD JOHN SPEAK, AND FOLLOWED HIM, WAS
> ANDREW, SIMON PETER'S BROTHER. HE FIRST FOUND HIS OWN BROTHER
> SIMON, AND SAID TO HIM, "WE HAVE FOUND THE MESSIAH" (WHICH IS
> TRANSLATED, THE CHRIST). AND HE BROUGHT HIM TO JESUS.
>
> John 1:40–42a

We read of two people who found Jesus and then immediately went to tell someone else about Him. "Philip found Nathanael and said to him, 'We have found Him of whom Moses in the law, and also the prophets, wrote – Jesus of Nazareth, the son of Joseph'" (John 1:45). He first found his own brother Simon, and said to him, "We have found the Messiah". It is the most natural thing in the world to share good news. Jesus is the embodiment of the Good News of the Gospel. When Jesus' disciples met Him and accepted His invitation to follow Him, they naturally wanted to share their decision with others.

They did not keep it to themselves. They did not consider it to be private or personal. It was meant to be shared. Jesus later on had something to say about those who hide their light:

> *You are the light of the world. A city that is set on a hill cannot be hidden.*
> *Nor do they light a lamp and put it under a basket, but on a lampstand, and it*
> *gives light to all who are in the house. Let your light so shine before men, that*
> *they may see your good works and glorify your Father in heaven.*
>
> Matthew 5:14–16

Jesus' disciples were called to share the Good News of His Gospel with every one of those they came into contact with.

Being a disciple of Jesus today means that we are called to be the "light of the world"; we are to be a reflection of Jesus, "The Light". You cannot follow Jesus and keep it to yourself. I have often shared with you that my greatest joy is telling people about Jesus. I am happiest when I am sharing the gospel. Jesus set me free and I want to share that freedom with everyone. Are you sharing the Good News about Jesus with your colleagues at work, with your friends and with those you meet each day? When you love someone you want to talk about them – do you love talking about Jesus?

Prayer

My Father God, there is no one like You. There is no one like Jesus, my Saviour. Jesus, You are the Light of the world. You came to seek and to save those who were lost. Thank You for finding me. I want to share the Good News of Salvation with everyone I come into contact with. Amen.

Read Mark 3:13–19; Luke 6:12–16

THEN HE APPOINTED TWELVE, THAT THEY MIGHT BE WITH HIM AND THAT
HE MIGHT SEND THEM OUT TO PREACH, AND TO HAVE POWER TO HEAL
SICKNESSES AND TO CAST OUT DEMONS…

Mark 3:14–15

Jesus prayed before He made the decision about whom He should call. Luke 6:12: "Now it came to pass in those days that He went out to the mountain to pray, and continued all night in prayer to God." Mark 3:13: "And He went up on the mountain and called to Him those He Himself wanted. And they came to Him." He heard what His Father had to say, and He did what His Father told Him to do. There were many people following Him; they all wanted to be part of the "in-crowd", as it were. Many of them were probably better qualified, and more suited to the positions. But Jesus doesn't make His choices the way we often do.

Throughout this year we have seen that God chooses men based upon what is in their hearts, not their natural abilities or qualifications. What Jesus looks for, my friends, is a willing, dedicated heart. A man who is sold out 100 per cent to Him. You know that I have said it often before: God is not interested in your theological degree (not that there is anything wrong with having one, as long as it doesn't rob you of your faith in Jesus). He is interested in whether you are prepared to walk by faith rather than by sight. When a man is prepared to do this God can perform miracles and wonders through his life. I am a simple farmer, folks, but I love Jesus. I live to tell others about Him. I believe that my God can do wonders; He performs miracles when we, His children, trust Him.

This is the life that Jesus called His disciples to lead. When He came down off that mountain and "chose" them to be His close companions, their whole world changed – forever. As we examine their walk with Jesus over the rest of this month we will see exactly how radical that change was. Their lives were turned upside down; their mindsets were challenged and reset. They ended up doing things of which they would never have dreamed.

Prayer

My Father in Heaven, I worship You. Lord, I want to be Your man, and I want to be used by You to do Your work here on earth. Father, I realize that so often my mindset is wrong. Help me to get my thinking right. I want to see things through Your eyes. Fill me afresh with Your Holy Spirit, I pray. Amen.

LORD, TEACH US TO PRAY

Read Luke 11:1–13

> NOW IT CAME TO PASS, AS HE WAS PRAYING IN A CERTAIN PLACE, WHEN HE
> CEASED, THAT ONE OF HIS DISCIPLES SAID TO HIM, "LORD, TEACH US TO
> PRAY, AS JOHN ALSO TAUGHT HIS DISCIPLES."
>
> Luke 11:1

One of the things that the disciples quickly learned as they observed Jesus was that His power came from prayer. Jesus would spend long hours alone up the mountain, or in another quiet place talking to His Father. After He had returned from those times Jesus would then go out and minister. The disciples witnessed people's lives being radically changed on a daily basis. They too wanted to learn to pray as Jesus did. They wanted the power. So they came to Jesus and (verses 2–4):

> one of His disciples said to Him, "Lord, teach us to pray..."
> So He said to them, "When you pray, say:
> Our Father in heaven,
> Hallowed be Your name.
> Your kingdom come.
> Your will be done
> On earth as it is in heaven.
> Give us day by day our daily bread.
> And forgive us our sins,
> For we also forgive everyone who is indebted to us.
> And do not lead us into temptation,
> But deliver us from the evil one."

When I was younger I wanted action; now I want to listen. Prayer is simply communicating with God, speaking with God. Be encouraged, my dear friend. As you can see from our reading, even the disciples struggled with prayer. They didn't know how to pray. You might say to me, "Angus, prayer might well be talking to the Lord, but it seems to be a one-way street. I don't always hear God speak to me." Of course He speaks to you! You have to give Him time; you have to listen and you have to wait.

If you really want God to speak to you, you have to listen. You have to wait, you have to quiet your spirit and then He will begin speaking to you. Not audibly, no, but in many other ways; God speaks to our Spirit man. He speaks through His Word, through people, through nature, and through circumstances. God always confirms His Word to us. So, when He has spoken to you, He will back it up with confirmation of what He is saying to you.

Prayer

My Father, I come before You and I bow in Your presence. Lord, I realize that prayer is simply communicating with You, talking to You, and above all listening to You. Lord, quieten my spirit, my mind, and my heart so that I can hear You speak to me. Amen.

Read Matthew 7:7–12

ASK, AND IT WILL BE GIVEN TO YOU; SEEK, AND YOU WILL FIND; KNOCK, AND
IT WILL BE OPENED TO YOU. FOR EVERYONE WHO ASKS RECEIVES, AND HE
WHO SEEKS FINDS, AND TO HIM WHO KNOCKS IT WILL BE OPENED.

Matthew 7:7–8

Can you imagine what it must have been like to be one of Jesus' disciples, to sit with Him and listen to Him teach about the Kingdom of God? To walk with Him as they moved from place to place and hear Him speak the Truths of God? After Jesus taught His disciples the Lord's Prayer in Matthew 6, He then gave them further instruction regarding prayer. He told them that if they wanted God to do something for them they had to ask Him. They were to be persistent in prayer. Jesus said that they had to knock and they had to seek. This speaks not only of persistence, but also of faith. The faith to know that God will hear and answer.

As I am growing both older in years and in the Lord, I am continually becoming more and more aware of the importance of prayer. Prayer is not a hit-and-miss activity, my friend. It must happen regularly: spending time at the Lord's feet, not only talking to Him, but also listening to Him. In our reading Jesus was speaking about the relationship between a father and his child. A father who loves his child will only give him good gifts. A child who loves and knows his father will trust him and approach him with freedom and gratitude.

You cannot know Father God if you do not have a relationship with Him. You cannot build a relationship with Him if you do not spend time with Him. There is no magic formula for growing in faith. Faith develops one day at a time, sitting at the feet of the Father, receiving from His Word. It is hard to ask someone you do not know for something, isn't it? It is no different with God. We serve a God who is faithful, a Father God who loves to give good gifts to His children. All we have to do is ask, knock, seek, and believe: "how much more will your Father who is in heaven give good things to those who ask Him!" (verse 11b).

Prayer

My Father God, I thank You that You are my loving Heavenly Father. You love to give good gifts to Your children. Lord, help me to make my relationship with You a priority. I want to know You more. Out of this knowledge will flow power in prayer, power to believe, and power to do Your work. Amen.

LEARNING NOT TO WORRY

Read Matthew 6:25–34

> BUT SEEK FIRST THE KINGDOM OF GOD AND HIS RIGHTEOUSNESS, AND ALL
> THESE THINGS SHALL BE ADDED TO YOU.
>
> Matthew 6:33

Jesus was teaching His disciples about what it means to trust God for their day-to-day needs. Before forsaking all to follow Him they had all been employed. Most of them were men who were used to working hard to earn their daily keep. They toiled with their hands to provide for their families. Even Matthew, who was a tax collector, worked for a living. So have you ever thought what it meant for them to drop everything and follow Jesus? Like most men they had to learn the lesson of dependence upon God for their daily needs.

Jesus and His disciples wandered the countryside, going from town to town, preaching and healing the sick. They would walk along and as they did so they would see God's creation all around them. Jesus used the examples of the birds of the air, and the lilies growing in the fields to teach them about trusting God for their daily needs. Jesus asked them to consider some important questions: "Is not life more than food and the body more than clothing?" (verse 25c); "Look at the birds of the air, for they neither sow nor reap nor gather into barns; yet your heavenly Father feeds them. Are you not of more value than they?" (verse 26); "Which of you by worrying can add one cubit to his stature?" (verse 27); "So why do you worry about clothing?" (verse 28a); "Now if God so clothes the grass of the field, which today is, and tomorrow is thrown into the oven, will He not much more clothe you, O you of little faith?" (verse 30).

Jesus gets to the crux of the matter in verse 30, doesn't He? It is all about faith. Will we walk by faith or by sight? The choice is ours to make. It cannot be both, my friends; it has to be one or the other. The disciples chose to put their faith in Jesus to provide for them. In whom are you placing your faith: in Jesus or the economy; in Jesus or your boss; in Jesus or your own ability?

Prayer

Dear Lord God, thank You that You give me work to do. You have called me to do an honest day's work. You have given me the responsibility of doing my part to look after those I love. But I know that ultimately it is You who provides for us. I need not worry nor fret, only trust in You. Amen.

Read Matthew 18:21–35

> THEN PETER CAME TO HIM AND SAID, "LORD, HOW OFTEN SHALL MY
> BROTHER SIN AGAINST ME, AND I FORGIVE HIM? UP TO SEVEN TIMES?"
>
> Matthew 18:21

For many people forgiveness is the most difficult hurdle to cross. Despite the fact that Peter had spent time with Jesus, and witnessed the results of God's forgiveness on many occasions, he still struggled with forgiveness. He had heard Jesus' teaching in Matthew 6 when He gave them the Lord's Prayer. "For if you forgive men their trespasses, your heavenly Father will also forgive you. But if you do not forgive men their trespasses, neither will your Father forgive your trespasses" (Matthew 6:14–15).

Folks, if you forgive somebody it removes a burden from your shoulders. Forgiveness is actually for your benefit, not the other person's. Do you know that many of the people for whom I pray for healing from arthritis and migraines have issues with unforgiveness (not all of them, but many of them). It is the anger in their hearts that is making them physically sick. Often the person with whom they are angry, who has hurt them, is not even aware of it. They are walking down the street healthy, living their lives. The person carrying the unforgiveness is the one suffering. That is why Jesus tells us to forgive. It is for our own sake – so go ahead and forgive them.

But you say, "Angus, my father abused me; my mother was so deceitful." So often unforgiveness has its roots in the home. "My brothers and sisters have let me down so badly." Forgive them, my friend, and let God deal with them. There is no sin that will go unpunished, I want to tell you. People always ask, "How can God allow people to do these horrible things on earth and get away with it?" They haven't gotten away with it. The game isn't over yet, believe me. The game ends in Heaven, with God the Righteous Judge, judging every one of us. So pray for those who oppress you, pray for those who persecute you, and pray for those who have hurt you; for they are going to be dealt with severely by God. Your act of faith is to forgive.

Prayer

My Father, You have forgiven me for so much. Lord, I realize that there is no alternative to forgiveness. It is a clear instruction in Your Word. You will not forgive me, if I don't forgive those who have sinned against me. Lord, I choose to walk in obedience to You. Amen.

Read Luke 9:18–27

> THEN HE SAID TO THEM ALL, "IF ANYONE DESIRES TO COME AFTER ME, LET
> HIM DENY HIMSELF, AND TAKE UP HIS CROSS DAILY, AND FOLLOW ME."
>
> Luke 9:23

The following was a fundamental principle that Jesus wanted His disciples to understand: "Most assuredly, I say to you, unless a grain of wheat falls into the ground and dies, it remains alone; but if it dies, it produces much grain" (John 12:24). They had to die in order to live. It is no different for modern-day disciples of Jesus Christ – we have to die to self. Like never before the world needs followers of Jesus who have the courage of their convictions. People who will stand up for Jesus and who will stand up for what they believe in. Believers who will deny themselves, who will take up their cross and follow Jesus.

In order to do this we will have to lose our sensitivity to what other people think of us. Our main concern will be: what does Jesus think of me? Each of Jesus' disciples learned what it meant to take up their cross and follow Him. Each of them had their opportunity to sacrifice for Jesus. They all died for Jesus in the end. Yet, for each of them, when the time came it was no sacrifice at all. It was the most natural thing in the world to give their lives for the One who gave His life for them.

Jesus displayed the greatest courage the world has ever seen when He hung and died on the Cross of Calvary. What does the world see when you face adversity? Do they see the kind of courage that has been developed through a close walk with Jesus? My friends, to know Him is to love Him. To love Him is to be sold out to Him. To be sold out to Him is to be willing to die for Him. The disciples had the courage to be different: the courage to embrace Jesus Christ and His teachings. We too need courage: to be the salt of the earth and the light of the world. This kind of courage will come through a relationship with the Son of God and a life lived by faith in Him.

Prayer

Lord God of Heaven and earth, You are a mighty King. Lord, I worship You. Jesus, You are my Lord and my Saviour. Give me the courage to take up my cross and follow You. Help me to walk closely with You each day, in fellowship and obedience. My life is Yours, Lord. There is none like You. Amen.

Read John 15:1–17

> GREATER LOVE HAS NO ONE THAN THIS, THAN TO LAY DOWN ONE'S LIFE FOR
> HIS FRIENDS.
>
> John 15:13

Jesus was speaking to His disciples trying to help them to understand the importance of abiding in Him. He knew that He would not be with them much longer. Their strength would come from His abiding presence within them. It would come from their walking daily in relationship with Him. So Jesus used the example of the vine and the branches to help them understand this principle. Then He went on to talk about His pending sacrifice on Calvary. It would not be long before He would be making the ultimate sacrifice for their sins and for ours.

Jesus' love for us is an everlasting love. In verses 12 to 14 Jesus says the following: "love one another". If you love a friend you will lay down your life for them and we are His friends if we obey Him. Then He goes on to say:

> *No longer do I call you servants, for a servant does not know what his master
> is doing; but I have called you friends, for all things that I heard from My
> Father I have made known to you. You did not choose Me, but I chose you and
> appointed you that you should go and bear fruit, and that your fruit should
> remain, that whatever you ask the Father in My name He may give you.*
>
> Verses 15–16

Jesus laid down His life for us before we even became His friends. Have you ever thought of that? Jesus called you "friend" long before you ever called Him Friend. He thought of you long before you ever thought of Him. You were in His heart the day He hung on Calvary. This is love! "Greater love has no one than this, than to lay down one's life for his friends." The disciples had to choose how they would respond to Jesus' love for them, and so do you and I. What will your response be today to Jesus' love for you? Will it be to walk by faith and not by sight – to live for Jesus every moment of every day?

Prayer
Father, I thank You for Jesus, my wonderful Saviour. Thank You, Jesus, that I was in Your heart when You died on Calvary. Thank You that You have called me friend. Jesus, I want to live for You, I want to serve You. Lord, I give my life to You. It is Yours to do with as You please. I love You, Lord. Amen.

Read Matthew 10:1–20

> BUT WHEN THEY DELIVER YOU UP, DO NOT WORRY ABOUT HOW OR WHAT
> YOU SHOULD SPEAK. FOR IT WILL BE GIVEN TO YOU IN THAT HOUR WHAT
> YOU SHOULD SPEAK; FOR IT IS NOT YOU WHO SPEAK, BUT THE SPIRIT OF YOUR
> FATHER WHO SPEAKS IN YOU.
>
> Matthew 10:19–20

The disciples had been living with Jesus and learning from Him. He had been teaching them all about the Kingdom of God, faith, and their purpose. The day came when He was ready to send them out to minister on their own. In our reading Jesus gave them final instructions on what they could expect. He prepares them for the fact that there will be those who will not accept the message that they bring.

You know that I often say, "When you become a Christian you don't have to try and be controversial. You are controversial by virtue of the fact that you are representing Jesus here on this earth." When people are faced with the gospel of Jesus Christ there are only two reactions: acceptance or rejection. Very often those who reject the gospel choose to persecute those who have brought the Good News to them. Jesus told His disciples to be prepared for this.

He also told them not to worry. When they faced persecution they would have His Spirit within them leading them and guiding them. They were not to be concerned about what they would say in answer to the accusations; the Spirit would give the words to speak. It is no different for you and me. We are Jesus' disciples – He has called us to go out and minister in faith. When we face persecution or opposition His Spirit is with us in the same way He was with the first disciples. God doesn't change, my friends; the message of Jesus doesn't change nor does the power of the Holy Spirit at work within us. Like the disciples we can go out in confidence and fulfil our calling. After all – "If God is for us, who can be against us?" (Romans 8:31b). Jesus is commissioning you and me to go out and share the Good News of His Gospel. We do not go alone – He is with us – but it still requires a step of faith on our part. Are you ready to take that step of faith today, my friend?

Prayer

Father in Heaven, You are the same yesterday, today, and forever. You are a faithful God. You have promised that You will equip those that You have called. Lord, I know that You have called me to spread the gospel of Jesus Christ. Help me to step out in faith to fulfil my calling. Amen.

Read Mark 11:20–24

> FOR ASSUREDLY, I SAY TO YOU, WHOEVER SAYS TO THIS MOUNTAIN, "BE
> REMOVED AND BE CAST INTO THE SEA," AND DOES NOT DOUBT IN HIS HEART,
> BUT BELIEVES THAT THOSE THINGS HE SAYS WILL BE DONE, HE WILL HAVE
> WHATEVER HE SAYS.
>
> Mark 11:23

James Hudson Taylor, as you may know, took Mark 11:22 to heart – "Have faith in God". He took this Scripture from the Word of God and he travelled to the other side of the world. There Hudson Taylor preached the gospel in China. As I said earlier in the year, he was the founder of the China Inland Mission and he was part of one of the greatest revivals ever seen in China. James Hudson Taylor believed in sowing the seed of the gospel. By faith he moved mountains. He lived one day at a time, telling one person at a time, faithfully fulfilling his calling. Moving mountains isn't always about a seismic event, my friends; often it is about daily obedience in faith.

Jesus taught His disciples about faith; there were many faith lessons that they learned from Him. We will look at a few of them this month. There are many more than we have days available to cover. However, the important thing for us to learn and to integrate into our lives is that we have been called to live a life of faith. It doesn't matter who you are; it doesn't matter what you do – if you love Jesus you are called to walk a faith walk. You are called to live by faith and not by sight.

Jesus never promised us an easy road. In fact, quite the opposite. We all need to persevere in tough times. Jesus promised His disciples in John 15 that they would know hardship and persecution. Anyone who tells you to come to Jesus and you will live an easy life is lying to you. Jesus told His disciples, "But all these things they will do to you for My name's sake, because they do not know Him who sent Me" (John 15:21). But, my friends, we do not walk alone; we have nothing to fear. Jesus has promised us that faith will win the day. Jesus gave His disciples this promise: "Therefore I say to you, whatever things you ask when you pray, believe that you receive them, and you will have them" (Mark 11:24).

Prayer

My Father, thank You for calling me to Yourself. Thank You for saving my soul and giving my life purpose. I know that You have called me to live a life of faith and hope in You. Jesus, You promised that I would not be left to walk this path alone. You have given me Your Holy Spirit to dwell in me. Amen.

Read Matthew 14:22–36

> AND PETER ANSWERED HIM AND SAID, "LORD, IF IT IS YOU, COMMAND ME
> TO COME TO YOU ON THE WATER." SO HE SAID, "COME." AND WHEN PETER
> HAD COME DOWN OUT OF THE BOAT, HE WALKED ON THE WATER TO GO TO
> JESUS.
>
> Matthew 14:28–29

Peter was the impulsive disciple, the one who was emotional and volatile. He was often too quick to talk, and he would jump in without thinking. However, Peter did live out his faith. You have heard me say it before, my friends: faith is a verb, not a theory. Faith is something you do, not something you theorize about. Faith requires action: you have to do something otherwise it isn't faith. "But without faith it is impossible to please Him, for he who comes to God must believe that He is, and that He is a rewarder of those who diligently seek Him" (Hebrews 11:6).

We are told in the Word that John loved Jesus, but so did Peter. His life was all about serving Jesus, even if he got himself into trouble from time to time. When Peter asked Jesus to command him to come to Him, Jesus simply said, "Come." One word. Peter immediately responded and climbed out of the boat. You might think: "So what, he sank." Yes he did, but he had the courage to get out of the boat. He had the faith to take the step. Every journey of faith begins with the first step, my friends. That is what we have been looking at throughout this year. Each man of God, starting with Noah, had to take the first step.

Maybe Jesus has been impressing upon your heart to do something. He is standing there saying to you, "Come." The question is, will you take the step? Will you climb out of the boat and begin the journey of faith that He has set out for you? I have made many mistakes in my life, but not one of them has been as a result of obeying God and doing what He has told me to do. The mistakes have usually come about when I have done things my way. The choice to walk by faith is never a wrong choice. Are you walking by faith, or are you walking by sight? God always responds to faith.

Prayer

My Father in Heaven, You have filled me with Your Spirit and with Your love. Lord, I am so grateful that I do not walk this road alone. You have called me to a journey of faith. I know that it begins by me taking the first step. Lord, I place my hand in Your strong hand, and I take the step. Amen.

Read Matthew 11:25–30

COME TO ME, ALL YOU WHO LABOUR AND ARE HEAVY LADEN, AND I WILL
GIVE YOU REST. TAKE MY YOKE UPON YOU AND LEARN FROM ME, FOR I AM
GENTLE AND LOWLY IN HEART, AND YOU WILL FIND REST FOR YOUR SOULS.
FOR MY YOKE IS EASY AND MY BURDEN IS LIGHT.

Matthew 11:28–30

Jesus spent a good deal of time preparing His disciples for the hardships and difficulties they would face when He wasn't there any more. He also did His best to prepare them for His death. When He spoke about how He would die they couldn't really understand. However, despite the talk about suffering and difficulties, Jesus also comforted them, reassuring them that no matter what happened He would be with them. He came to this world to bring comfort to mankind. He offers rest to all those who are burdened, who labour, and who are heavy laden. It is only in Jesus that true rest can be found. Look around you and observe how so many people are frantically scrambling to find peace and rest – yet they never seem to get there. Why is this?

Because there is only one place to find complete rest – and that is in Jesus. Jesus taught His disciples that all their efforts would amount to nothing if they didn't abide in Him. Power comes from the place of rest and peace. Jesus is the Source of the power, not our own ability. When people become sick and they suffer, their faith is often called into question. Suffering does not equate to lack of faith, my friends. Some of God's most precious saints endured times of great suffering. Faith and suffering often go hand in hand. When you face times of suffering Jesus says that you must come to Him.

He and He alone is your safe place: your harbour in the storm. He says, "My yoke is easy and My burden is light." He will be there with you when you suffer. His arms will be tightly wrapped around you. You will not be alone; no matter who else deserts you, Jesus never will. This is why James 1:2–4 says: "My brethren, count it all joy when you fall into various trials, knowing that the testing of your faith produces patience. But let patience have its perfect work, that you may be perfect and complete, lacking nothing."

Prayer
My Lord God, in the midst of suffering You are there. You have not promised I will never suffer, but You have promised that You will be with me and walk with me through it. No matter what happens I can find peace, rest, and a safe haven with You. Lord, I trust You and I choose to walk with You. Amen.

Read John 14:15–31

PEACE I LEAVE WITH YOU, MY PEACE I GIVE TO YOU; NOT AS THE WORLD
GIVES DO I GIVE TO YOU. LET NOT YOUR HEART BE TROUBLED, NEITHER LET IT
BE AFRAID.

John 14:27

Jesus promised His disciples that even though He had to go away they would not be left alone. They would always have His peace. Isn't this an amazing promise? As His disciples Jesus gives you and me the same promise today. We will never be alone. He is always with us. We have His Spirit living within us so we have nothing to fear. Jesus also said, "Most assuredly, I say to you, he who believes in Me, the works that I do he will do also; and greater works than these he will do, because I go to My Father" (John 14:12).

The men who walked with Jesus were able to go on and do great exploits for God after He returned to Heaven. The Word of God bears witness to what God did through them. Each and every one of them lived full-out for Jesus. They were all willing to lay down their lives for the sake of the gospel. In the midst of whatever they went through they had the abiding peace of Jesus. Their life's mission was to share that peace with other people. Peace is not a feeling – it is a Person – Jesus Christ. It is no different for you and me. Each day, no matter what we have to go through, we have the peace of Jesus.

Literally today people's hearts are failing them through fear. It seems there has never been a time when people were more stressed, anxious, angry, and afraid. Every time you turn on the television there is a story about the results of these emotions. You cannot open a newspaper without reading about the way people are living and behaving. So much of this behaviour is either generated by fear or causes fear. This is not the legacy that Jesus left us. As His followers – His disciples – our mission is to take His peace to the world. Your world begins with those closest to you, in your own home. Then to your wider circle and after that further afield. When last have you shared Jesus' peace with someone?

Prayer

My Father in Heaven, I bow before You. Lord, I am so grateful that I am not tossed about on a sea of fear and unrest. I have perfect peace because I know Jesus, the Prince of Peace. Help me to be faithful to share the peace of Jesus with every one You send my way, each and every day. Amen.

Read Mark 10:35–45

… BUT WHOEVER DESIRES TO BECOME GREAT AMONG YOU SHALL BE YOUR
SERVANT. AND WHOEVER OF YOU DESIRES TO BE FIRST SHALL BE SLAVE OF ALL.
FOR EVEN THE SON OF MAN DID NOT COME TO BE SERVED, BUT TO SERVE,
AND TO GIVE HIS LIFE A RANSOM FOR MANY.

Mark 10:43b–45

John and James, "the Sons of Thunder", as they were known (this is the name that Jesus gave them, by the way – see Mark 3:17), came to Jesus. They told Jesus that they had a request: they wanted to sit on either side of Him. At that stage they still didn't fully realize what was going to happen to Jesus. They believed that He would set up an earthly kingdom, and they wanted to be sure to secure their place. Naturally when the other disciples heard of this "they began to be greatly displeased with James and John" (verse 41b). It was then that Jesus called them together and shared the truth that we have in our key verses for today.

Several years ago I shared a story that I want to return to today; it perfectly illustrates what it means to have a servant mindset. There was a young doctor who dedicated her life to the poor and needy. All she wanted to do was to tell them about Jesus Christ. When she had finished her studies she travelled to the Congo. She was welcomed by a large crowd of people on her arrival. She was so excited because she knew that she could help the many people who were standing on the quayside. As a qualified medical doctor, she knew the Lord Jesus Christ and she was coming to do good deeds for Him.

An old missionary who was observing what was happening walked up to her as she was leaving. He said to her, "You think you're coming here to teach these people about Jesus, don't you?" "Yes!" she replied enthusiastically. "You've got it wrong, my girl. These people are going to teach you about Jesus." The disciples quickly learned that not everyone was open to the message they brought. They also ended up learning far more than they taught. Each one of them was called upon to sacrifice much for the Kingdom. However, what they gained was beyond compare. We can never out-give Jesus, my friends; He gave everything – including His life.

Prayer

My Father, I realize that so often my motives are not pure. I want to serve You but on my own conditions. You are teaching me today that there are no conditions – it is all or nothing. You are in control. Whatever You ask I will give. My calling is to serve not to be served. Lord, keep me faithful. Amen.

Read John 16:5–16

HOWEVER, WHEN HE, THE SPIRIT OF TRUTH, HAS COME, HE WILL GUIDE
YOU INTO ALL TRUTH; FOR HE WILL NOT SPEAK ON HIS OWN AUTHORITY,
BUT WHATEVER HE HEARS HE WILL SPEAK; AND HE WILL TELL YOU THINGS
TO COME. HE WILL GLORIFY ME, FOR HE WILL TAKE OF WHAT IS MINE AND
DECLARE IT TO YOU.

John 16:13–14

Jesus did not speak His own words – He spoke what the Father told Him to say. When Philip asked Jesus to show him the Father, Jesus responded: "Do you not believe that I am in the Father, and the Father in Me? The words that I speak to you I do not speak on My own authority; but the Father who dwells in Me does the works. Believe Me that I am in the Father and the Father in Me, or else believe Me for the sake of the works themselves" (John 14:10–11). In our reading today Jesus assures His disciples that the Holy Spirit whom He would send to comfort them would guide them into all truth. He would be God's Representative on earth who would speak God's Words to them after Jesus had returned to the Father.

We live in a world where it is often very difficult to discern what the truth is and what it isn't. Jesus knew this would happen; this is why He sent us the Spirit of Truth who leads us and guides us into all Truth. If you are a child of God then you have His Holy Spirit living inside of you. You have a compass that will never let you down. When the noisy voices of the world grow too loud, listen to the still small voice of God's Spirit – He will guide you into all Truth.

You don't need to rely upon conventional wisdom – You have the Spirit of Truth living within you. He is the One to whom you need to listen. He will never give you the wrong advice. We live in a time when we desperately need to hear His voice. "Your ears shall hear a word behind you, saying, "This is the way, walk in it" (Isaiah 30:21a). My friend, you will never make a mistake as long as you listen to and obey God's Spirit. Jesus said: "… for He will take of what is Mine and declare it to you." Listen, hear, and obey the voice of His Spirit.

Prayer

My Father in Heaven, You have promised that You would not leave me without a sure Guide. Thank You for Your Holy Spirit who lives within me. Lord, guide me, direct me, and teach me. Help me to shut out all other voices. I only want to listen to Your voice of Truth. I will listen, hear, and obey. Amen.

Read John 17:1–26

> SANCTIFY THEM BY YOUR TRUTH. YOUR WORD IS TRUTH. AS YOU SENT ME
> INTO THE WORLD, I ALSO HAVE SENT THEM INTO THE WORLD. AND FOR THEIR
> SAKES I SANCTIFY MYSELF, THAT THEY ALSO MAY BE SANCTIFIED BY THE
> TRUTH.
>
> John 17:17–19

Jesus, knowing that His time was short, prayed to His Father. He made three requests to His Father. **Jesus prayed for Himself.** "And now, O Father, glorify Me together with Yourself, with the glory which I had with You before the world was" (John 17:5). In John 1:1–5 we read:

> *In the beginning was the Word, and the Word was with God, and the Word*
> *was God. He was in the beginning with God. All things were made through*
> *Him, and without Him nothing was made that was made. In Him was life,*
> *and the life was the light of men. And the light shines in the darkness, and the*
> *darkness did not comprehend it.*

Jesus is the Word and He was with God in the beginning, before the world was created.

Then, **Jesus prayed for His disciples** and asked the Father: "Sanctify them by Your truth. Your word is truth." Paul says in Hebrews 10:10: "By that will we have been sanctified through the offering of the body of Jesus Christ once for all." It was the sacrifice that Jesus was about to make on the Cross of Calvary that would sanctify His disciples. Jesus is the Way, the Truth, and the Life (John 14:6) – it is through Him, the Word of God, that we are sanctified.

Finally, **Jesus prayed for all believers** – this is you and me, my friends:

> *… for You loved Me before the foundation of the world. O righteous Father!*
> *The world has not known You, but I have known You; and these have known*
> *that You sent Me. And I have declared to them Your name, and will declare it,*
> *that the love with which You loved Me may be in them, and I in them."*
>
> John 17:24c–26

Jesus knew that in order for us to be able to love God He had to die. This was the only way that we could be sanctified. The result of being sanctified is loving God. Does your life reflect Jesus the Truth, the One who sanctified you?

Prayer

My Father, Jesus my Saviour was with You before the foundation of the world. He is Your Beloved Son. Thank You, Jesus, for Your sacrifice that means I am sanctified through You. You are the Truth; You are the Word of God made flesh. You came to seek and to save me. Thank You. Amen.

GO AND MAKE DISCIPLES

Read Matthew 28:16–20

GO THEREFORE AND MAKE DISCIPLES OF ALL THE NATIONS, BAPTIZING THEM
IN THE NAME OF THE FATHER AND OF THE SON AND OF THE HOLY SPIRIT,
TEACHING THEM TO OBSERVE ALL THINGS THAT I HAVE COMMANDED YOU;
AND LO, I AM WITH YOU ALWAYS, EVEN TO THE END OF THE AGE. AMEN.

Matthew 28:19–20

The saying goes, "Actions speak louder than words". This is too true, isn't it? Too many Christians have been good at telling people what to do but what the world is looking for are people who will show them the gospel. How do we do this? By living a righteous life – not in our own righteousness, but in Jesus' righteousness. When we live like this we will not only make converts, but we will also make disciples. Jesus told His disciples that they were to go and make disciples of all the nations. They understood what this meant because for three years Jesus had been making disciples of them.

So they simply had to go out and replicate what Jesus had done with them. The author of the following quote is disputed, but it is pertinent all the same: "Preach the gospel at all costs and, if you really have to, use words." Words are probably the least effective way of preaching the gospel of the Lord Jesus. What the disciples primarily learned from Jesus was not so much what to say, but how to live. They learned from Him how to do the will of the Father, not how to talk about the will of the Father. When Jesus chose the twelve men to whom He would entrust the work of His Father here on earth, He didn't make the decision based on human wisdom. They were an unlikely bunch, but they were the people His Father had given to Him. He faithfully invested His life into them. The time had come for them to pick up the baton and take the message further.

When God chose you, my friend, it wasn't random; it wasn't the luck of the draw – it was intentional. He has called you to be His child. He has called you to be a disciple of Jesus Christ, His Son. Your commission is to take the Gospel into all the world – your world. You are to teach people through your example what Jesus means to you and what He can mean to them. A changed life is the strongest testimony that there is.

Prayer

My Father, thank You that You have called me. You saved me and You have redeemed my life. Lord Jesus, I want to be a faithful disciple of Yours. I want to share the Good News. I want to go into my world and make disciples. Lord, fill me with Your Spirit, I pray. Give me power. Amen.

Read Luke 22:24–34

> AND THE LORD SAID, "SIMON, SIMON! INDEED, SATAN HAS ASKED FOR YOU, THAT HE MAY SIFT YOU AS WHEAT. BUT I HAVE PRAYED FOR YOU, THAT YOUR FAITH SHOULD NOT FAIL; AND WHEN YOU HAVE RETURNED TO ME, STRENGTHEN YOUR BRETHREN."
>
> Luke 22:31–32

Jesus was nearing the end of His earthly ministry and He was aware of what was to come. The Lord was warning Peter that there lay a difficult time ahead for him. However, true to form, Peter didn't want to hear anything about the fact that he could possibly deny Jesus. Yet Jesus said to Peter, "Satan has asked for you, that he may sift you as wheat." In order for Peter to fulfil his future purpose, his faith needed to be tested. Peter had to learn to depend upon Jesus and Jesus alone. He needed to come to the place where he understood that it was not he, Peter, but Jesus who would do the miracles through him.

There are several things that we can take comfort from as we think about what Jesus said to Peter. First of all, just as with Job, Satan had to ask permission before he could sift Peter. He did not have free reign in Peter's life; God was in control even during the sifting. Then Jesus promised that He would pray for Peter, while he was going through the sifting, so that his faith would not fail. Jesus would not leave him, nor forsake him – even if Peter forsook Jesus. "If we are faithless, He remains faithful; He cannot deny Himself" (2 Timothy 2:13).

Finally, when Peter came back to Jesus, He would use Peter greatly to strengthen other Christians. "And I also say to you that you are Peter, and on this rock I will build My church, and the gates of Hades shall not prevail against it" (Matthew 16:18). We all have to go through times of testing. We cannot avoid them, but we can know that we are not alone. Faith is not faith unless it has been tested. Even Jesus went through His time of testing in the wilderness. Throughout the ages Christians have been tried and tested. Very often the people that God has used the most are the ones who have been through the greatest testing. When we are under pressure, who we are emerges.

Prayer

My Father, in the midst of the crisis You are there. You never leave me and You never forsake me. I know that no matter what comes my way You will be there. Lord, when the testing comes help me to stand firm in You. Lord, I love You and I want to be faithful to You. Amen.

Read John 13:1–20

> THEN HE CAME TO SIMON PETER. AND PETER SAID TO HIM, "LORD, ARE
> YOU WASHING MY FEET?" JESUS ANSWERED AND SAID TO HIM, "WHAT I AM
> DOING YOU DO NOT UNDERSTAND NOW, BUT YOU WILL KNOW AFTER THIS."
> PETER SAID TO HIM, "YOU SHALL NEVER WASH MY FEET!" JESUS ANSWERED
> HIM, "IF I DO NOT WASH YOU, YOU HAVE NO PART WITH ME." SIMON PETER
> SAID TO HIM, "LORD, NOT MY FEET ONLY, BUT ALSO MY HANDS AND MY
> HEAD!"
>
> John 13:6–9

Simon Peter, the impetuous one, was given to exaggeration and over-enthusiasm, but what we can see from Peter's response is that he didn't want to miss out on any of the blessings that Jesus was imparting. When he realized what Jesus was saying to him, he wanted it all. The Last Supper that Jesus had with His disciples was bittersweet: He would soon be leaving the men that He had handpicked, whom He had shared His life and heart with for three years. The hour was coming. Have you ever wondered how Judas felt as Jesus knelt before him and washed his feet? Jesus went to each one of the twelve and lovingly ministered to them. This was the last time that they were alone together as a group.

When Jesus had finished washing their feet He said to them: "Most assuredly, I say to you, a servant is not greater than his master; nor is he who is sent greater than he who sent him. If you know these things, blessed are you if you do them" (verses 16–17). In other words, Jesus is saying: "Do as I do: follow My example." Jesus was the ultimate Servant Leader. How is your walk with the Lord? Have you become jaded and possibly even disillusioned? Maybe you should take a leaf out of Peter's book. Despite all his flaws Peter loved Jesus. From the first moment he met Him until the day Peter was crucified upside down, he never stopped loving Jesus.

Jesus saw something in Peter that no doubt no one else ever had. Peter responded to that with absolute devotion. If you have become tired and worn down then take some time to examine your walk with the Lord, ask Him to touch you anew with His Spirit. Regain your first love and come to Jesus so that He can wash you – not only your feet, but your hands and your head as well. In other words: "Jesus, I want it all – I want all that You have for me, so that I can love You with all of my being!"

Prayer

My Father God, You have called me to live a life of dedication to Jesus. Jesus, so often I allow myself to become beaten down and lukewarm. Forgive me, I pray. I pray that You will give me a fresh touch of Your Spirit; wash me in Your Living Water that I might be alive for You. Amen.

Read Luke 22:1–6, 45–53

AND WHILE HE WAS STILL SPEAKING, BEHOLD, A MULTITUDE; AND HE WHO
WAS CALLED JUDAS, ONE OF THE TWELVE, WENT BEFORE THEM AND DREW
NEAR TO JESUS TO KISS HIM. BUT JESUS SAID TO HIM, "JUDAS, ARE YOU
BETRAYING THE SON OF MAN WITH A KISS?"

Luke 22:47–48

"Then Satan entered Judas, surnamed Iscariot, who was numbered among the twelve"
(verse 3). There you have it, my friends. I would venture to say that the spirit that was
in Judas had been there all along. He was always the one slightly at odds with what
was happening. Remember his reaction in John 12 when Mary washed Jesus' feet
with the costly perfume and dried it off with her hair? Judas complained because the
money could have been put to better use. He simply never understood who Jesus was.
In the end it was money that enticed him to betray Jesus.

At the Last Supper Jesus had said this would happen. He knew from the beginning
that it would be Judas, yet He welcomed him into His inner circle. Jesus treated
Judas in exactly the same way as He treated the other eleven. When He prayed for
the disciples in John 17 Judas would have been included in the prayer. You see, my
friends, right up until the last moment Judas had a choice. His choice was to either
choose everlasting life or to choose eternal death. As we all know, he chose eternal
death. Even when Judas betrayed Him, Jesus still loved him.

When we are betrayed by those we trust and love, how do we react? Very often it
is not how Jesus did. So many Christians walk around with bitterness in their hearts
because they cannot forgive someone who has betrayed them. Forgiveness is not an
option if you are a child of God – it is a prerequisite. Jesus says that if we want to
be forgiven we must forgive. The Word of God says that vengeance belongs to God.
Spend some time today in God's presence and ask His Holy Spirit to examine your
heart. If there is bitterness in your heart toward someone who has betrayed you, ask
the Spirit to reveal it to you. Then make a choice and forgive the person; pray for them
and ask God to work in their lives. Don't carry the burden any longer – give it over
to the Lord.

Prayer

*My Father, the truth is sometimes so difficult to handle. Lord, You know the circumstances of
my life better than anyone. You know what has happened to me, Lord. I ask You to forgive me
for the bitterness that I have allowed to take root. I forgive those who have betrayed me and I
give them to You. Amen.*

Read John 19:16–30

> Now there stood by the cross of Jesus His mother, and His mother's sister, Mary the wife of Clopas, and Mary Magdalene. When Jesus therefore saw His mother, and the disciple whom He loved standing by, He said to His mother, "Woman, behold your son!" Then He said to the disciple, "Behold your mother!" And from that hour that disciple took her to his own home.
>
> John 19:25–27

John was never far from where Jesus was; if you were looking for him then you just needed to look for Jesus and you would find him. We do not read of any of the other disciples being at the cross, only John. When Jesus looked up there was John standing with the three Marys. Jesus utters those incredible words as He asks John, "the disciple whom He loved", to look after His mother. He knows that He can trust John to do this. Jesus loved all of His disciples; He chose each of them for a particular quality or qualities that they brought to the team who would carry His gospel into the world after He was gone. However, there is no doubt that there was a particularly tender relationship between Jesus and John.

John knew that Jesus loved him; he writes, "When Jesus therefore saw His mother, and the disciple whom He loved standing by…" John had the assurance of Jesus' love, and it was that love that brought him to the foot of the cross. Everyone had scattered, fearful of what the soldiers might do to them if they realized that they were Jesus' followers. Not John! Like the three Marys, nothing was going to separate him from Jesus.

My friend, do you know that Jesus loves you? His sacrifice on Calvary proves that He does; it was the ultimate gesture of love. Jesus never need do anything else to prove His love for you – His sacrifice was perfect and complete. What is your response to His love? Are you like the other disciples, keeping your distance? Or are you like John, keeping close to Jesus no matter what? There is only one response that adequately expresses the gratitude that we should feel for what Jesus did for us – that is complete surrender and dedication to Him. Jesus is looking for men like John whom He can trust to share His love, mercy, and grace with the world around them. Men who will put Him and their relationship with Him first in their lives, no matter what is going on around them.

Prayer

My Father in Heaven, You gave Your precious Son, Jesus Christ, to die for me. Lord Jesus, thank You for Your perfect and complete sacrifice on Calvary. Jesus, I want to be faithful to You no matter what. I want to be Your man whom You can use as You see fit to share the Good News of Your gospel. Amen.

Read Mark 16:1–18

SHE WENT AND TOLD THOSE WHO HAD BEEN WITH HIM, AS THEY MOURNED
AND WEPT. AND WHEN THEY HEARD THAT HE WAS ALIVE AND HAD BEEN
SEEN BY HER, THEY DID NOT BELIEVE. AFTER THAT, HE APPEARED IN
ANOTHER FORM TO TWO OF THEM AS THEY WALKED AND WENT INTO THE
COUNTRY. AND THEY WENT AND TOLD IT TO THE REST, BUT THEY DID NOT
BELIEVE THEM EITHER.

Mark 16:10–13

Again we see that it is Mary Magdalene, Mary the mother of James, and Salome who remained close to Jesus. Early on the Sunday morning they took spices to the tomb to anoint His body. When they arrived at the tomb the stone was rolled away. A young man in a long, white robe said to them, "Do not be alarmed. You seek Jesus of Nazareth, who was crucified. He is risen! He is not here. See the place where they laid Him. But go, tell His disciples – and Peter – that He is going before you into Galilee; there you will see Him, as He said to you" (verses 6–7).

They hurried back to tell the disciples who were in deep mourning over what had happened. The disciples allowed themselves to be swayed by the circumstances and what they could see with the natural eye. For the moment they forgot all that Jesus had taught them and promised them. Hebrews 11:1 tells us: "Now faith is the substance of things hoped for, the evidence of things not seen." Because they could not see they did not believe. How sad for them: instead of being comforted and filled with hope, they were hiding and afraid. "Later He appeared to the eleven as they sat at the table; and He rebuked their unbelief and hardness of heart, because they did not believe those who had seen Him after He had risen" (Mark 16:14).

Jesus then proceeded to remind them of their mission and what it was that they had been trained and called to do. We too need to be careful that when things do not go according to our plans we don't become fearful and discouraged. This is exactly what the enemy would want to have happen. We must keep focused upon Jesus and His promises to us. He is faithful and if He has promised it, then He will do it, no matter what the circumstances look like. The choice we face is: do we believe Him or the circumstances? Do we choose to walk by faith or by sight?

Prayer

My Father, thank You for Good Friday and Jesus' sacrifice on Calvary, but thank You even more for Resurrection Sunday – Jesus Christ, my Saviour, is alive! He is the Risen Lord! In Him is fullness of life. Lord, help me to believe in You, no matter what happens around me. You are faithful. Amen.

Read John 21:1–14

> JESUS SAID TO THEM, "COME AND EAT BREAKFAST." YET NONE OF THE
> DISCIPLES DARED ASK HIM, "WHO ARE YOU?" – KNOWING THAT IT WAS THE
> LORD. JESUS THEN CAME AND TOOK THE BREAD AND GAVE IT TO THEM, AND
> LIKEWISE THE FISH. THIS IS NOW THE THIRD TIME JESUS SHOWED HIMSELF TO
> HIS DISCIPLES AFTER HE WAS RAISED FROM THE DEAD.
>
> John 21:12–14

I have had the privilege of walking many times by the Sea of Galilee. It is not hard to imagine that morning when Jesus appeared to His disciples. With Jesus "gone", the disciples, who were fishermen by trade, had reverted to their former employment. They had been out all night in their boats catching fish. Jesus chose to have exactly the same encounter with them that He had when He first met them and called them to follow Him. You can read about it in Luke 5:1–11. Jesus is amazing: He was well aware that this would have an impact upon the men. It must have been particularly meaningful to Peter, who was still devastated at his betrayal of Jesus.

They obeyed Jesus and cast their nets on the right-hand side of the boat. Once again the catch was so great that they were not able to haul it in. John immediately acknowledged that it was the Lord, and said as much to Peter. When they reached shore there was Jesus with breakfast ready for them – don't you love it – our loving, caring, and practical Jesus. "Jesus said to them, 'Come and eat breakfast.'" Once again He served them, as He had done so many times before. It is hard to put into words what this encounter must have meant to the disciples. For them to realize at last that Jesus was not dead – He was alive – and He was with them.

Are you a "Peter"? Have you let Jesus down in some way? Are you hurting and unsure of what comes next in your life? You love Jesus, but your failure hangs heavily over you. Jesus is standing right in front of you today, saying: "Come and eat breakfast." In other words, turn back to Him, repent, and He will forgive you. Like He did with the disciples He will make you fruitful again. Don't allow the enemy to keep you captive. Jesus died to save you from your sin and from your failure. Forgiveness is assured if you repent and turn to Him.

Prayer

My Father, Your faithfulness is new every morning. You never change nor do You grow weary of showing Your loving kindness to Your children. Jesus, thank You for Your finished work on Calvary that means that I can be forgiven and restored. I turn to You, Lord. I trust You and I choose to love You. Amen.

Read Luke 24:1–12

> BUT PETER AROSE AND RAN TO THE TOMB; AND STOOPING DOWN, HE SAW
> THE LINEN CLOTHS LYING BY THEMSELVES; AND HE DEPARTED, MARVELING TO
> HIMSELF AT WHAT HAD HAPPENED.
>
> Luke 24:12

Peter, the big fisherman, was the leader of the pack, even before he became a disciple of Jesus. He was the spokesperson for all the fishermen. At the Sea of Galilee on that morning when Jesus appeared to the disciples who were fishing, Peter was a broken man. He had said, "Lord, I will never leave You. Lord, don't worry. I will support You, even if no one else does." After the cock crowed for the third time signalling Peter's third denial of Jesus, he wept and ran away into those narrow streets just like a rat in a sewer. He was so devastated and dejected because he had let the Lord down. Two of Jesus' disciples had betrayed Him: one had sold Him for thirty pieces of silver; the other had denied Him.

The one didn't do anything worse than the other. Judas betrayed Jesus and so did Peter. There was one major difference between Judas Iscariot and Peter, though. Peter repented, but Judas never did. Judas hung himself and he went to hell (Matthew 27:1–10). Peter broke down and asked God to forgive him; God forgave him and made him the leader of the church.

When the two Marys returned to the disciples and reported the empty tomb, the disciples did not believe them. However, Peter jumped up and ran to the tomb. Can you imagine the feelings racing through him as he ran? For the first time in several days there was hope. Peter ran to Jesus, not away from Him. He would rather take his chances with Jesus than with anyone else. He knew his Lord; he had experienced Jesus' mercy and forgiveness so many times that he knew he would be safe with Him. You can imagine his disappointment when he did not find Jesus at the tomb. Peter wanted instant forgiveness, but Jesus needed Peter to be ready to take on the responsibility that would be his moving forward. The moment of restoration would come on the shores of Galilee – back at the same point where they first met.

Prayer

My Father, Your mercies are ever new. You made it possible for me to be Your child through the sacrifice of Jesus, Your Son. Lord, I have let You down so many times. Yet each time You forgive me. Thank You, Lord. I, like Peter, want to live a restored life so that I can glorify You each and every day. Amen.

Read John 21:15–25

> HE SAID TO HIM THE THIRD TIME, "SIMON, SON OF JONAH, DO YOU LOVE
> ME?" PETER WAS GRIEVED BECAUSE HE SAID TO HIM THE THIRD TIME, "DO
> YOU LOVE ME?"
>
> John 21:17a

The NIV has today's key text as, "Peter was hurt because Jesus asked him the third time, 'Do you love me?' He said, 'Lord, you know all things; you know that I love you.'" Three times Jesus asked Peter, "Simon, son of Jonah, do you love Me?" I believe Peter must have been sorely perplexed and troubled by the third time. No doubt he was weeping, so desperate was he to have his betrayal put right and to receive Jesus' forgiveness. Peter had denied the Lord three times and three times Jesus asked him to declare his love for Him. The third time Peter answered, "Lord, You know all things; You know that I love You" (verse 17c).

Peter's life was totally transformed at that moment. Before then he was the one with the big mouth, the one who spoke before he thought: the impetuous, bombastic one. After that encounter on the shore of Galilee Peter was a changed man. Today there is a church built on the spot where it is said this incident took place. Jesus said to him, "'Most assuredly, I say to you, when you were younger, you girded yourself and walked where you wished; but when you are old, you will stretch out your hands, and another will gird you and carry you where you do not wish.' This He spoke, signifying by what death he would glorify God. And when He had spoken this, He said to him, 'Follow Me'" (verses 18–19). Once again Jesus invites Peter to follow Him.

This time it would be the mature, committed Peter who would go out and build the church of Jesus Christ. Legend tells us that Peter was eventually arrested in Rome and crucified upside down because he would not deny his Lord and Saviour. He asked to be crucified in this way because he did not believe that he was worthy to die as his Saviour had. When you meet the risen Christ you can never be the same again. Have you met Him, and if so, are you a changed man?

Prayer

My Father God, You have called me to follow Jesus. Lord Jesus, I bow in Your presence. I thank You for Your death, burial, and resurrection that enables me to know Your Salvation. Help me, Lord, to walk faithfully with You, loving You, serving You, and doing Your will day by day. Amen.

Read Acts 1:1–11

> AND BEING ASSEMBLED TOGETHER WITH THEM, HE COMMANDED THEM NOT
> TO DEPART FROM JERUSALEM, BUT TO WAIT FOR THE PROMISE OF THE FATHER,
> "WHICH," HE SAID, "YOU HAVE HEARD FROM ME; FOR JOHN TRULY BAPTIZED
> WITH WATER, BUT YOU SHALL BE BAPTIZED WITH THE HOLY SPIRIT NOT MANY
> DAYS FROM NOW."
>
> Acts 1:4–5

Even after everything that had happened up to that point, the disciples still didn't get it. "Therefore, when they had come together, they asked Him, saying, 'Lord, will You at this time restore the kingdom to Israel?' And He said to them, 'It is not for you to know times or seasons which the Father has put in His own authority'" (verses 6–7). They were still looking for an earthly kingdom to be set up. Jesus replied to them: "But you shall receive power when the Holy Spirit has come upon you; and you shall be witnesses to Me in Jerusalem, and in all Judea and Samaria, and to the end of the earth" (verse 8). Their task was to establish God's Kingdom upon this earth. They were to spread the Good News of the gospel of Jesus Christ.

Then Jesus was lifted up and He returned to His Father. The disciples immediately returned to Jerusalem, where, the Word tells us: "Peter, James, John, and Andrew; Philip and Thomas; Bartholomew and Matthew; James the son of Alphaeus and Simon the Zealot; and Judas the son of James. These all continued with one accord in prayer and supplication, with the women and Mary the mother of Jesus, and with His brothers" (verses 13b–14). They were waiting for the promised Holy Spirit. Jesus had promised them that He would not leave them orphans. He had to go away so that "Another" could come who would give them power to do the work He had called them to do.

My friends, it is no different for you and me. Jesus calls us to be His disciples on earth today. Our job is to spread the Good News of the Kingdom of God. This world is ripe for the gospel of Jesus Christ; the time is short and there is much work. What are you doing to fulfil Jesus' Great Commission? How will people know if we don't go? We don't minister in our own power – we go in the power of the Holy Spirit.

Prayer

My Father God, there is none like You. You are Mighty, Ruler of Heaven and earth. Lord Jesus, You returned to the Father to sit at His right hand. You completed your work on earth, and You promised Your Holy Spirit so that all Your disciples throughout the ages can minister in power. Amen.

Read Acts 2:1–4, 14, 36–47

WHEN THE DAY OF PENTECOST HAD FULLY COME, THEY WERE ALL WITH ONE ACCORD
IN ONE PLACE. AND SUDDENLY THERE CAME A SOUND FROM HEAVEN, AS OF A RUSHING
MIGHTY WIND, AND IT FILLED THE WHOLE HOUSE WHERE THEY WERE SITTING. THEN
THERE APPEARED TO THEM DIVIDED TONGUES, AS OF FIRE, AND ONE SAT UPON EACH OF
THEM. AND THEY WERE ALL FILLED WITH THE HOLY SPIRIT AND BEGAN TO SPEAK WITH
OTHER TONGUES, AS THE SPIRIT GAVE THEM UTTERANCE.

Acts 2:1–4

Throughout His earthly ministry Jesus had been preparing His disciples for the moment
that the Holy Spirit would come upon them. All the teaching, the illustrations, and
the stories had been leading them to that momentous occasion. The Day of Pentecost
would signal the beginning of the disciples' ministry. From that day onwards there
was no turning back, no option but for them to proclaim the gospel of Jesus Christ.
As Mark 16:15–20 tells us:

*And He said to them, "Go into all the world and preach the gospel to every creature. He
who believes and is baptized will be saved; but he who does not believe will be condemned.
And these signs will follow those who believe: In My name they will cast out demons;
they will speak with new tongues; they will take up serpents; and if they drink anything
deadly, it will by no means hurt them; they will lay hands on the sick, and they will
recover." So then, after the Lord had spoken to them, He was received up into heaven, and
sat down at the right hand of God. And they went out and preached everywhere, the Lord
working with them and confirming the word through the accompanying signs. Amen.*

No one can deny the power with which the disciples proclaimed the gospel of Jesus
Christ. They were changed men. No longer were they fearful – they were bold and
courageous. There was no holding them back. Whereas before they had always
viewed their relationship with Jesus from the perspective of what was in it for them,
now they were wholeheartedly committed. They expected nothing in return. All they
asked was the chance to share Christ's message with their world. Jesus is still looking
for men like these today. He needs men who will be sold out to Him; who will serve
Him wholeheartedly and unselfishly. What He promises is to give us power to do the
job He has called us to do. The same Holy Spirit power that flowed through the first
disciples – don't you want to be a part of this ministry?

Prayer
*My Lord and God, Your call to me is the same as it was to Your disciples thousands of years
ago. You promise the power of Your Holy Spirit to minister. You give men Your power so that
they can spread Your Word. Lord, I pray for the infilling and anointing of Your Holy Spirit
upon my life. Amen.*

Read Acts 4:1–22

> NOW WHEN THEY SAW THE BOLDNESS OF PETER AND JOHN, AND PERCEIVED
> THAT THEY WERE UNEDUCATED AND UNTRAINED MEN, THEY MARVELED. AND
> THEY REALIZED THAT THEY HAD BEEN WITH JESUS.
>
> Acts 4:13

Who would have thought that the same Peter who denied Jesus would be the one to preach the Pentecost sermon, after which 3,000 people were saved. In our reading we encounter the new, transformed Peter. He was afraid of no one; not because of the bravado that he so often exhibited in the past, but because he was filled with the power of God. Jesus takes the ordinary and transforms it into the extraordinary.

It is not a bad thing to feel inadequate in our own strength, my friend. So if you are feeling inadequate in any way that is good. God specializes in using people who are slow to speak, who do not have a healthy self-esteem. Jesus takes the nobodies and turns them into somebodies. In the same way that He took Peter's failure and turned it around, so He will do the same for us. This is why Jesus is known as the "Friend of sinners". If you page through the Bible you will find that the Lord has always used people like you and me to accomplish extraordinary things for Him.

As we look back over this year we have read about Noah, Abraham, Moses, Joshua, David, Job, and Daniel, to mention a few. All of those men had faults and failures, but it didn't stop God from using them. We have said it so many times – He looks upon the heart, not the outward appearance. God uses ordinary people to do great exploits for Him because He does not want anyone to share His glory. When people witnessed the disciples ministering, they didn't attribute their power to them; no, "they realized that they had been with Jesus." How wonderful it would be if people look at our lives and what they see makes them realize that we have been with Jesus. God is looking for men of faith who will walk with Him. He wants to use people like you and people like me to further His Kingdom here on earth. All He asks is a heart that is wholly His.

Prayer

My Father, Your Kingdom is an everlasting Kingdom. In Your infinite grace and mercy You choose to use men such as me to do Your work here on earth. Lord, this amazes me, but I thank You for it. I want to be Your man. I want to be used by You, Lord. I give You all the glory, honour, and praise. Amen.

Read Acts 10:1–23

> WHILE PETER THOUGHT ABOUT THE VISION, THE SPIRIT SAID TO HIM, "BEHOLD, THREE MEN ARE SEEKING YOU. ARISE THEREFORE, GO DOWN AND GO WITH THEM, DOUBTING NOTHING; FOR I HAVE SENT THEM." THEN PETER WENT DOWN TO THE MEN WHO HAD BEEN SENT TO HIM FROM CORNELIUS, AND SAID, "YES, I AM HE WHOM YOU SEEK. FOR WHAT REASON HAVE YOU COME?"
>
> Acts 10:19–21

One of the things that defined Jesus' ministry here on earth was that He was more interested in mixing with sinners than He was with the religious leaders of His day. He said He had come for those who recognized that they needed healing. Jesus wanted Peter to realize that there were to be no barriers regarding whom he would or wouldn't minister to. If there was a need then Peter was to meet that need. To illustrate this to him and prepare him for the visit from Cornelius's servants, the Holy Spirit gave Peter a vision. He told him that what God had cleansed Peter was not to consider unclean. For a Jewish man this was a radical concept.

When the servants came, Peter accompanied them, and we know that Cornelius as well as his household were saved and filled with the power of the Holy Spirit. This month, as we have journeyed with the disciples, we have seen over and over again how God worked with ordinary men to accomplish His purposes. The journey for the disciples began when they answered Jesus' call to follow Him. Each and every one of them left whatever they were doing and they joined Jesus. They came with all their faults and failures. Over the period of three years Jesus ministered into their lives. When He left them to return to Heaven, He sent the promised Holy Spirit to give them power to minister and be His witnesses here on earth.

You and I are modern-day disciples of Jesus Christ. His teachings are as relevant today as they were more than 2,000 years ago. The power of the Holy Spirit is as mighty as it was on the day of Pentecost when He shook the upper room. We have everything at our disposal that the disciples had. What is our response? Do we too heed the call to follow, minister, and serve, just as they did? Our journey as Jesus' disciples also begins with the first step of obedience to His call upon our lives. What will your answer be?

Prayer

My Father, I thank You for Your Word and the lessons that I have learned from Jesus' original disciples. Lord, how privileged I am to be Your disciple today. You have called me in the same way You called them. You have equipped me and empowered me just like You did them. Amen.

PAUL'S JOURNEY OF LOVE

Paul's journey of faith began when he met Jesus on the road to Damascus

1. Saul, the dedicated persecutor
2. Saul meets Jesus
3. Transformed by grace
4. John Wesley, saved by grace
5. God's grace is with me
6. Paul, the scholar
7. Paul, the tentmaker
8. Hope does not disappoint
9. For me, to live is Christ
10. Justified by faith
11. Joyfully finish the race
12. Fight the good fight
13. Tribulation cannot separate us
14. Pressing on toward the goal
15. I count all things as lost
16. Paul, chief of sinners
17. In the Holy Spirit's power
18. The way of peace
19. Peacemakers
20. Love is the greatest
21. Confess with your mouth
22. Persevering hope
23. A thorn in the flesh
24. God's grace is sufficient
25. Buffeted by Satan
26. Liberty in Christ
27. Alive together with Christ
28. The whole armour of God
29. I can do all things
30. Final prayers

SAUL, THE DEDICATED PERSECUTOR

Read Acts 7:51–60

AND THEY CAST HIM OUT OF THE CITY AND STONED HIM. AND THE WITNESSES
LAID DOWN THEIR CLOTHES AT THE FEET OF A YOUNG MAN NAMED SAUL.

Acts 7:58

This is the first time that we encounter Paul, although his name is still Saul of Tarsus at this point. He was an avid persecutor of the Christians. We see him standing on the sidelines at the stoning of Stephen. Although he didn't actually throw the stones, he was right there. The Word tells us that he looked after the coats of the men who stoned Stephen. "Now Saul was consenting to his death. At that time a great persecution arose against the church which was at Jerusalem; and they were all scattered throughout the regions of Judea and Samaria, except the apostles" (Acts 8:1).

Then two verses further on, we read: "As for Saul, he made havoc of the church, entering every house, and dragging off men and women, committing them to prison" (Acts 8:3). After Stephen's death persecution broke out against the church. Saul was right there as one of the main instigators. He personally arrested the Christians, condemning them to death. Saul was a religious zealot who firmly believed that he needed to stamp out Christianity. He was learned and well educated in the theory of the Jewish law. He was a walking example of what it means to have head knowledge, but no heart knowledge. Religion is dangerous when it is practised without Jesus at the centre. It is dry, empty, and worthless without Jesus and the power of His Holy Spirit at work in a man's heart and life.

Religion cannot change us; it cannot save us and it will get us nowhere – only faith in Jesus Christ makes the difference. Saul had not learned this yet: he was firmly fixed upon his own path. There are so many stories down through history of men who were set on a particular path until the Spirit of God intercepted them. Saul was no different. God had a plan and a purpose for his life. It is the same with us. Where would we be if God had not intercepted in our lives? I don't want to even think where I would be today.

Prayer

My Father in Heaven, thank You that You did not leave me to my own devices. Thank You that You intercepted in my life. You gave me a chance to make a choice for life – life in Jesus Christ, my Saviour and my Lord. Father, help me to live each day to the full in Your service. Amen.

Read Acts 9:1–19

> As he journeyed he came near Damascus, and suddenly a light
> shone around him from heaven. Then he fell to the ground, and
> heard a voice saying to him, "Saul, Saul, why are you persecuting
> Me?" And he said, "Who are You, Lord?" Then the Lord said, "I am
> Jesus, whom you are persecuting. It is hard for you to kick against
> the goads." So he, trembling and astonished, said, "Lord, what do
> You want me to do?"
>
> Acts 9:3–6a

Saul of Tarsus was a religious fanatic, a leader in the Jewish church, a member of the Sanhedrin (the Jewish ruling Council) no less. He regularly went to the temple in Jerusalem and knew the law inside out; but he didn't know Jesus Christ. That was all about to change: Saul was on the road travelling to Damascus to find and apprehend the followers of Jesus, so that he could bring them back to Jerusalem to be punished.

Saul of Tarsus was travelling along, intent upon his mission, when suddenly a light from Heaven flashed around him and he was knocked to the ground. There he lay in the dust blinded by the light.

When Jesus asked him why he was persecuting Him, Saul asked, "Who are You, Lord?" Saul immediately recognized this was a divine encounter. Notice that there was no hesitation on Saul's part to obey the instruction given to him. It was in that moment that Saul of Tarsus became a changed man. He would never be the same again. He proceeded to Damascus and waited there.

There was a man in Damascus by the name of Ananias. God came to him in a vision, saying: "I am bringing Saul of Tarsus to Damascus, the man who hates Christians and is punishing them. You are to go to the street named Straight, where you will find him." Can you imagine Ananias saying, "Lord, please don't make me do this. I have heard of him and he will probably kill me." "But the Lord said to him, 'Go, for he is a chosen vessel of Mine to bear My name before Gentiles, kings, and the children of Israel. For I will show him how many things he must suffer for My name's sake'" (verses 15–16). Ananias prayed for Saul – he recovered his sight, was filled with the Holy Spirit, and was baptized. Paul would spend the rest of his life serving Jesus and proclaiming His Kingdom to the Gentiles. Jesus met Paul and saved him in order that he might serve Him; He has done the same for us.

Prayer

My Father, You had a plan and a purpose for Paul's life. You called him to Yourself and he came. Thank You for his example of faith. He fearlessly served You. Lord, I too want to live a life that is sold out to Jesus. I want to serve You and proclaim Your Word. Lord, help me to walk by faith. Amen.

Read Ephesians 2:1–10

> For by grace you have been saved through faith, and that not of yourselves; it is the gift of God, not of works, lest anyone should boast.
>
> Ephesians 2:8–9

Even as I share with you about Paul, I am reminded of another man by the name of John Newton. He wrote the famous hymn that goes, "Amazing grace, how sweet the sound/That saved a wretch like me./I once was lost but now am found, /was blind, but now I see." Both Saul of Tarsus and Newton were spiritually blind, but God made Saul physically blind as well. When Saul's physical sight was restored, he also received spiritual sight. Paul went out and he changed the world for Jesus. Paul was the greatest apostle that Jesus ever had. Even though he wasn't one of the original twelve, he met Jesus personally on the road to Damascus. Paul was not taught by the church; he was taught by Jesus and the Holy Spirit. He spent three years in the desert, folks (Galatians 1:17–18). He came back from that time and he changed the world as it was back then.

Paul's life was transformed by grace, Newton's life was transformed by grace, and my life was transformed by grace. I want to submit to you that your life too needs to be transformed by grace. There has to come a day when you take a stick and you draw a line in the sand, saying: "Today is the first day of the rest of my life." Heaven is real, but so is hell, my friend – and the road to hell is paved with good intentions. It is a lie of the devil that tomorrow is another day: there might not be a tomorrow. Don't put off until tomorrow what you should do today.

Seize hold of grace right here, right now. For too many people, tomorrow has never come. You say, "Tomorrow I am going to start again." No, my friend. Tomorrow will never come. Today is the day and this is the hour. "Behold, now is the accepted time; behold, now is the day of salvation" (2 Corinthians 6:2b). Take the step of faith; take Jesus' outstretched hand. His grace is a gift to you and to me.

Prayer

My Father God, there is no one like You. Your grace and mercy are new every day. Your faithfulness stretches to the Heavens. Thank You for Your grace toward me. Lord, I know that I do not deserve it, but I take hold of it and I hold on to it for dear life. Lord, I am nothing without You. Amen.

Read Romans 3:21–26

> FOR THERE IS NO DIFFERENCE; FOR ALL HAVE SINNED AND FALL SHORT OF
> THE GLORY OF GOD, BEING JUSTIFIED FREELY BY HIS GRACE THROUGH THE
> REDEMPTION THAT IS IN CHRIST JESUS…
>
> Romans 3:22c–24

The Reverend John Wesley came from a godly family. He had been to university and had a Master's degree in theology, but he had never met Jesus Christ. He was desperate to get closer to God. He thought that going to the USA to preach the gospel to the American Indians might help him find God. Not one American Indian was saved, and Wesley returned home bitter and more disillusioned than before he left.

It was while on the journey to America that Wesley encountered the deep faith of a group of Moravians – a faith that was to leave a profound impression on him. On the voyage, a terrible storm hit the ship. Wesley was petrified because he thought the ship was going to sink. As the waves broke over the deck, the small group of Moravian believers clung on to the mast, singing hymns while they waited to meet Jesus. This made a real impact on Wesley; he couldn't believe it, because he had never seen anything like it in his life. These people had a living relationship with God. They weren't afraid of death: they were ready to go Home. This established a deep respect in Wesley for the Moravians, and indeed their practices were highly influential in the Methodism that Wesley came to establish. This event, and his friendship with Moravian believers subsequently, led Wesley to become convinced that he had to be born again.

When he arrived back in England he met a man by the name of Peter Böhler, a German Moravian, at Aldersgate in London. Wesley wrote of that night:

> *In the evening, I went very unwillingly to a society in Aldersgate Street,*
> *where one was reading Luther's preface to the epistle to the Romans. About a*
> *quarter before nine, while he was describing the change which God works in*
> *the heart through faith in Christ, I felt my heart strangely warmed. I felt I did*
> *trust in Christ, Christ alone, for Salvation and an assurance was given me*
> *that He had taken away my sins, even mine, and saved me from the law of sin*
> *and death.*

Wesley preached until the day he died, aged almost ninety, 250,000 miles and 40,000 sermons later. A life radically changed by the grace of God, Wesley had to reach out in faith and take hold of God's grace before it could have an effect upon his life.

Prayer

Father, I thank You that the same grace that You extended to Paul, to John Newton, and to John Wesley, You extend to me. Your grace, Lord, never changes. It is as powerful today as it ever was. I have to, like these men did, reach out in faith and take hold of it. Help me to do this. In Jesus' Name. Amen.

Read 1 Corinthians 15:1–11

> BUT BECAUSE OF GOD'S GRACE I AM WHAT I AM. AND HIS GRACE WAS
> NOT WASTED ON ME. NO, I HAVE WORKED HARDER THAN ALL THE OTHER
> APOSTLES. BUT I DIDN'T DO THE WORK. GOD'S GRACE WAS WITH ME.
>
> 1 Corinthians 15:10 (NIRV)

I doubt that there has been a man who has understood the grace of God better than the apostle Paul did. After his Damascus road experience his whole life was about sharing God's grace with others. He was the one God chose to take the Good News to the Gentiles. Paul had persecuted the Christians on behalf of the Jews before he became a follower of Jesus; after his conversion he was persecuted by the Jews, as well as the Romans. In Acts 9:15–16 Jesus told Ananias, "Go, for he is a chosen vessel of Mine to bear My name before Gentiles, kings, and the children of Israel. For I will show him how many things he must suffer for My name's sake."

Paul gladly suffered for Jesus and for his fellow Christians. Nothing held him back from spreading the Good News of Jesus Christ. He travelled constantly, sharing the gospel. He planted new churches and taught the believers. When he was away from the churches he wrote letters to them, instructing them regarding their faith and the practicalities of living out their faith in Jesus. Truly God's grace "was not wasted" on Paul. From the day that he came to know Jesus he lived a life that was characterized by faith. Each day was a day lived to the full by the grace of God.

Paul also understood that his past sins were covered by the blood of Jesus. He was saved through grace and he lived each day by grace. It is no different for you and me, my friends. I don't know what happened in your past – it doesn't matter. If you are a child of God it is covered by the blood of Jesus. What matters is how you are living now: Are you living a life reflecting the grace that God has extended to you? Can you say with Paul: "But because of God's grace I am what I am. And his grace was not wasted on me… But I didn't do the work. God's grace was with me"?

Prayer

My gracious, loving Heavenly Father, I cannot thank You enough for the grace You have extended to me. Lord, I am so grateful to You. Lord, I want to live the rest of my life expressing my gratitude to You. Lord, I want to serve You and share Your grace. Amen.

Read Galatians 1:11–24

AND I ADVANCED IN JUDAISM BEYOND MANY OF MY CONTEMPORARIES IN MY OWN NATION, BEING MORE EXCEEDINGLY ZEALOUS FOR THE TRADITIONS OF MY FATHERS.

Galatians 1:14

The apostle Paul was the most educated of all the apostles. He was a learned person who had received a good education. He says, "I am indeed a Jew, born in Tarsus of Cilicia, but brought up in this city at the feet of Gamaliel, taught according to the strictness of our fathers' law, and was zealous toward God as you all are today" (Acts 22:3). Gamaliel was one of the top teachers of that time, with some of the brightest scholars of the day under his tutelage. Despite all his knowledge Paul didn't know Jesus until the day that he met Him on the road to Damascus. Then Paul realized that all his learning could not save him. Only Jesus could save him. However, this didn't mean that God didn't use Paul's abilities for the furtherance of His Kingdom.

Paul wrote most of the books of the New Testament. We can see that his intellect and intelligence were put to good use in the letters that he wrote. He was able to understand and impart doctrine to the churches. Paul didn't only preach the gospel but he also taught the believers so that they were established in their faith. God uses our natural abilities for His purposes. Nothing that you have learned is wasted, my friends.

Galatians explains how Paul's true education took place. He spent years being taught by Jesus. When Paul returned from that time and began his ministry among the churches we see the power of God at work in him. Paul knew without a shadow of a doubt where his power came from. He knew it was all of God and nothing of himself. He simply committed all that he was to the Lord to use for His glory. God asks the same of you and me. He can take whatever we have, no matter how much or how little, and use it for His glory. The important thing is that we submit ourselves to God and His will for our lives. The rest is up to Him; He will accomplish His plans and purposes through us if we are yielded to Him.

Prayer

My Father God, thank You for Your goodness toward me. Lord, You reached down and plucked me from the mess that was my life. In You I have found forgiveness and grace beyond measure. Lord, take my life and use me to help build Your Kingdom here on earth. Amen.

Read Acts 18:1–17

> So, because he was of the same trade, he stayed with them and worked; for by occupation they were tentmakers. And he reasoned in the synagogue every Sabbath, and persuaded both Jews and Greeks.
>
> Acts 18:3–4

Most Jewish boys were taught a trade while they were growing up. Even the well-educated ones knew how to work with their hands. Paul was no different: his trade was tentmaking. So when he arrived in Corinth and he met up with Aquila and his wife Priscilla, who were also tentmakers, it seemed only natural that Paul should join them. Paul stayed with them and he worked alongside them at his trade. Then on the Sabbath Paul would go to the synagogue and there he would preach the gospel. Paul was not scared to use his hands and work for a living. He was never a burden to any of the churches with which he worked. He knew that God was his ultimate source of provision: "And my God shall supply all your need according to His riches in glory by Christ Jesus" (Philippians 4:19).

It is not only those who are in so-called "full-time" work who are used by God. Not at all, my friends: each and every one of us are called to minister the gospel. Each day as you go to your workplace, wherever that might be, you are working in your particular mission field. God uses all of His children to do His work. We are all equally responsible for building His Kingdom here on earth. I have a camera crew who work with me to do the filming of our *Grassroots* television programmes. These young men, even though no one ever sees them, are instrumental in the spreading of the gospel. So don't think for a moment that it is only the people who stand upfront who are ministers of the gospel.

Paul had those times when he was upfront preaching, but most of his teaching was done as he went about his daily work. I am sure that as customers and other people dropped by he would engage them in discussions about Jesus. He would share his testimony and he would challenge the person regarding their relationship with Jesus. So follow Paul's example and faithfully share your faith.

Prayer
My Father, You have called me to faithfully follow Jesus, my Saviour. Lord, every day You provide opportunities for me to share my faith with other people. Help me to be a faithful minister of Your gospel. I want to share what You have done for me with others. I want to share Your love. Amen.

Read Romans 5:1–11

> AND NOT ONLY THAT, BUT WE ALSO GLORY IN TRIBULATIONS, KNOWING THAT
> TRIBULATION PRODUCES PERSEVERANCE; AND PERSEVERANCE, CHARACTER;
> AND CHARACTER, HOPE. NOW HOPE DOES NOT DISAPPOINT, BECAUSE THE
> LOVE OF GOD HAS BEEN POURED OUT IN OUR HEARTS BY THE HOLY SPIRIT
> WHO WAS GIVEN TO US.
>
> Romans 5:3–5

Looking back, the times that we remember best in our lives are the hard times, aren't they? The time when your business nearly went bankrupt and then at the last moment, when you cried out to God, He undertook for you and you were able to continue. The time when your little girl was sick and you pleaded, "Lord, please heal her" and God came through for you. You don't forget times like these. You also remember the pain you went through when you lost a loved one. Everyone goes through this, because all of us are going to die some day, unless the Lord returns first.

So, my friends, the winters of our lives are very important. You cannot be an encourager if you haven't been through a fiery trial. That is an indisputable fact, folks. You know there are some people who have never been through hard times? They went to Bible college and graduated; but they have not been through the university of hard knocks; they have never experienced a time of testing. It is very hard for them to empathize and have compassion for someone who has lost a loved one. How can they understand what a man who has lost his farm because of the drought, or whatever other reason, is going through? Whatever they have to offer is based on theory and does not come from the practical outworking of their experience. People don't want theory: what they want is for you to put your arms around them and weep with them. But you cannot do this unless you have walked that road yourself.

This is why we rejoice in our tribulation, as Paul has said: "knowing that tribulation produces perseverance; and perseverance, character; and character, hope. Now hope does not disappoint". The only way to develop character is through the hard times; it isn't developed in the good times. I don't wish pain and suffering on anyone, believe me; I certainly don't want any more suffering either. But you know something, folks? There are no short cuts in the Kingdom of God.

Prayer
My Father in Heaven, thank You for Your Holy Spirit Who is my Guide and Comforter. Lord, no matter what I go through You are always right there beside me. My hope is in You, Lord. It is so true that hope does not disappoint. Lord, help me to give comfort as I have received comfort from You. Amen.

Read Philippians 1:19-30

> FOR TO ME, TO LIVE IS CHRIST, AND TO DIE IS GAIN.
>
> Philippians 1:21

I have a mielie pip (kernel of corn) in front of me. This mielie pip has to be planted in the ground, it has to die; in fact it actually has to rot. When that happens a new plant is birthed and grows from it. The problem with many of us is we are not prepared to die to our self. They say that if you kick a dead dog, it feels nothing – it doesn't even move. On the other hand, if you kick a live dog it will turn around and bite you. How many of us are really dead to the flesh? If you have died to the flesh then why are you concerned about what people think of you? Why do you become so uptight when somebody says something about you that is not true? You might say, "Oh, but I have my rights." No you don't, sir. When you are in Christ Jesus you give up your rights.

The apostle Paul understood this. It is why he wrote in Philippians, "according to my earnest expectation and hope that in nothing I shall be ashamed, but with all boldness, as always, so now also Christ will be magnified in my body, whether by life or by death. For to me, to live is Christ, and to die is gain" (verses 20–21). You couldn't frighten Paul with Heaven, and you know that I have said it many times: you cannot frighten me with Heaven either.

You cannot continue trying to do it your way, my friend; it will never work. You have to stop struggling and do it God's way. Paul had further words of wisdom for the Philippians: "Only let your conduct be worthy of the gospel of Christ... stand fast in one spirit, with one mind striving together for the faith of the gospel" (verse 27). Paul was all about Jesus – for him, there was nothing else. He lived to glorify God. For him his life only had value in relation to its usefulness to Jesus. How are you living, my friend: for Jesus or for yourself?

Prayer

My Father, I come to You in the Name of Jesus Christ, my Saviour. Lord, it is a principle within Your Word that someone has to die before they can live. I realize that so often I am all about what I perceive to be best for me. Help me to live for You, and only You, my Lord. For me to live is Christ. Amen.

Read Romans 1:17; 3:19–26

> FOR IN IT THE RIGHTEOUSNESS OF GOD IS REVEALED FROM FAITH TO FAITH; AS IT IS WRITTEN, "THE JUST SHALL LIVE BY FAITH."
>
> Romans 1:17

This was the crux of Paul's message – Jesus had called him to share with the Gentiles the message that Salvation is not through works, but through faith in Jesus Christ. So many people down through the ages have tried to work their way to Heaven. It is out of this mindset that people establish rules and regulations, believing that these will sanctify them. It can never be, my friend. Martin Luther spent years trying to be a good Christian – where did it get him? Absolutely nowhere; he ended up discouraged and frustrated, until one day the Holy Spirit led him to Romans 1:17. Then his life changed forever – he inspired the Reformation.

Many centuries before Martin Luther, Paul, the apostle, understood about faith. He learned on that day – on the road to Damascus – that his works were as filthy rags. He had been zealous for God's Word, but had denied the power thereof. God's Word is nothing without Jesus Christ. He is central to everything. Without Jesus it is simply dogma and law. Paul wrote in his letter to the Romans: "Therefore by the deeds of the law no flesh will be justified in His sight, for by the law is the knowledge of sin" (Romans 3:20). The law cannot save you; it can only make you aware of your sin.

How are we justified? "… being justified freely by His grace through the redemption that is in Christ Jesus" (verse 24). Paul tells us why we all need a Saviour; "for all have sinned and fall short of the glory of God" (verse 23). God's grace is a free gift, my friend, but Paul tells us; "even the righteousness of God, through faith in Jesus Christ, to all and on *all who believe*" (verse 22a, my italics). There you have it: "all who believe". Salvation is by faith – you are justified by faith. I cannot earn my way to Heaven – it doesn't matter how hard I try. It is a gift and a gift cannot be earned, otherwise it is no longer a gift, is it?

Prayer

Father, thank You for my Salvation. Jesus, You have made it possible for me to freely enter into the presence of the Father. I am a child of God because of what You have done for me. I do not take this for granted. I thank You that as I trust and believe in You, I walk daily in Your grace and love. Amen.

Read Acts 20:17–32

> BUT NONE OF THESE THINGS MOVE ME; NOR DO I COUNT MY LIFE DEAR TO
> MYSELF, SO THAT I MAY FINISH MY RACE WITH JOY, AND THE MINISTRY WHICH
> I RECEIVED FROM THE LORD JESUS, TO TESTIFY TO THE GOSPEL OF THE GRACE
> OF GOD.
>
> Acts 20:24

Paul's life was a love story: a love story between him and Jesus. His love story of faith began the day that he met Jesus on the road to Damascus. From that day onward Paul's life was all about testifying "to the gospel of the grace of God." When did your love story with Jesus begin? You all know that my love story with Jesus began in the little church in Greytown, South Africa. My friends, Jesus is not as interested in how we got started as He is in how we finish. Paul understood this, hence his saying, "But none of these things move me; nor do I count my life dear to myself, so that I may finish my race with joy, and the ministry which I received from the Lord Jesus." Paul single-mindedly ran the race that God set out for him to run.

The key verse that we read today comes from Paul's final interactions with the elders of the church at Ephesus. He was on his way to Rome; he knew that he was going to face death. Paul used the time that he had with the elders to make sure that they would remember all the things he had taught them over the years. His legacy was to leave behind vibrant churches that would carry on the message of the gospel. He says to them: "For I have not shunned to declare to you the whole counsel of God. Therefore take heed to yourselves and to all the flock, among which the Holy Spirit has made you overseers, to shepherd the church of God which He purchased with His own blood" (verses 27–28).

Paul could confidently state that he had shared "the whole counsel of God" with them. He did not preach a half-gospel, or a watered down version of the gospel. The apostle Paul was faithful to the message that Jesus had given him to proclaim. Not only did Paul love Jesus but he also loved the church of Jesus Christ. Paul gave himself tirelessly to the building up and the equipping of the saints.

Prayer

Father, You have given me such amazing examples of faithfulness in the men of faith that I have read about during this year. Lord, I thank You for each of Your servants through the ages who have been faithful to You. Help me too, Lord, to be faithful and true to You. I want to finish well. Amen.

Read 2 Timothy 4

> For I am already being poured out as a drink offering, and the time of my departure is at hand. I have fought the good fight, I have finished the race, I have kept the faith.
>
> 2 Timothy 4:6–7

Paul wrote to his beloved son in the Lord, Timothy, telling him that his time on earth was coming to an end. "Finally, there is laid up for me the crown of righteousness, which the Lord, the righteous Judge, will give to me on that Day, and not to me only but also to all who have loved His appearing" (verse 8). He isn't fearful, he says in 2 Timothy 1:12: "For this reason I also suffer these things; nevertheless I am not ashamed, for I know whom I have believed and am persuaded that He is able to keep what I have committed to Him until that Day." What a testimony, my friends. Paul had nothing to fear from man because his sights were on Heaven.

Jesus was waiting for Paul, and he knew that he would hear the words: "Well done, good and faithful servant; you were faithful over a few things, I will make you ruler over many things. Enter into the joy of your lord" (Matthew 25:21). The Holy Spirit had prepared Paul for what was awaiting him in Rome. (You can read about it in Acts 20:21–23.) How would you feel if that were you? Would you keep going, or would you be tempted to run away? Paul said that everywhere he went there were people bringing prophetic words. There were signs telling him that when he arrived in Rome he would encounter trouble. And by the way, folks, we know the end of the story.

Paul, because he was a Roman citizen, was not allowed to be crucified like Jesus or Peter were, so he was beheaded. Yet despite everything Paul still continued on to Rome: he ran his race to the end. We too need to run our race; sometimes that means facing tribulation. The end result, though, is this: "Finally, there is laid up for me the crown of righteousness, which the Lord, the righteous Judge, will give to me on that Day, and not to me only but also to all who have loved His appearing" (2 Timothy 4:8).

Prayer

Lord God, You are mighty to save. Your power and dominion know no end. Your loving kindness stretches from generation to generation. You never abandon Your children. Lord, I thank You that I can rest in Your love and care for me. Lord, help me to finish strong for You. Amen.

TRIBULATION CANNOT SEPARATE US

Read Romans 8:28–39

> IF GOD IS FOR US, WHO CAN BE AGAINST US?... WHO SHALL SEPARATE
> US FROM THE LOVE OF CHRIST? SHALL TRIBULATION, OR DISTRESS, OR
> PERSECUTION, OR FAMINE, OR NAKEDNESS, OR PERIL, OR SWORD?
>
> Romans 8:31b and 35

Folks, Paul knew about tribulation, that was for sure. If you are going through hardships in your life right now, are you tempted to pack it in? You could be thinking that before you became a Christian things were a lot easier for you. You're quite right. Before you became a Christian, the devil wasn't interested in you because he already had you. Now that you are standing for truth and righteousness you are swimming against the current, while everyone else is going with the flow.

Paul clearly understood that being a Christian did not mean that he would not experience hardship. What he also knew was that no matter what he went through nothing could separate him from the love of Christ. He asked this question of the Roman Christians: "Who shall separate us from the love of Christ? (verse 35a). Paul answered his own question: "Yet in all these things we are more than conquerors through Him who loved us. For I am persuaded that neither death nor life, nor angels nor principalities nor powers, nor things present nor things to come, nor height nor depth, nor any other created thing, shall be able to separate us from the love of God which is in Christ Jesus our Lord" (verses 37–39).

This is the truth of it, my friends. Nothing can separate you from the love of God. You are His child; you are saved by the blood of Jesus, and sealed by His Holy Spirit. So don't think about giving up. It was never an option for Paul, no matter how bad it became, and it should never be an option for you or for me. Paul also asked the question: "If God is for us, who can be against us?" No matter how hard the enemy tries, he will not win in the end. The die is cast; the ultimate war is won. What we experience on this earth are battles. You are on the winning side – don't give up. Stand firm, because nothing can separate you from the love of God.

Prayer

My Father, I am so grateful for Your love. It is overwhelming when I realize just how much You love me. I know that I am safe in You. I can rest secure that You will always be there to lead and guide me. The tribulations and hardships of this world will pass. One day I will live with You forever. Amen.

PRESSING ON TOWARD THE GOAL

Read Philippians 3:12–21

> I PRESS TOWARD THE GOAL FOR THE PRIZE OF THE UPWARD CALL OF GOD IN CHRIST JESUS.
>
> Philippians 3:14

Life is like a journey: unfortunately it is not always enjoyable. Nowhere in the Bible has the Lord ever promised us that it will be a bed of roses. What He has promised us is that He will never leave us as orphans. We saw yesterday that nothing can separate us from His love. He will never forsake us. He has promised us that He will be with us always, even until the end of the ages. If there is one thing that farming has taught me, it is to be patient. Farming has taught me to press on toward the goal. Paul knew all about pressing on toward the goal. He says: "Not that I have already attained, or am already perfected; but I press on, that I may lay hold of *that* for which Christ Jesus has also laid hold of me" (verse 12, my italics).

What is the "that" that Jesus has laid hold of you for? What are you aiming for? Goals are not only for young people, my friends. I am asking you irrespective of your age: What is your goal? You know what they say: "If you aim at nothing you are sure to hit it". You have to be completely disciplined in aiming for your goal. My goal in life was to own my own farm. I didn't want to be a manager all my life: I wanted my own farm. So I set a goal and I went for it. That was the "that" for which I was aiming.

So again I ask you: What is your goal? What is the race you are running, and how far do you still have to go? If you don't know where the bar is, you won't know how high you have to aim in order to jump over it. So I want to encourage you to run your race. Do what God calls you to do, not what other people tell you. Follow Paul's single-minded and dedicated focus in reaching the goal that God has set before you. Press on toward the goal!

Prayer

My Father God, I come before You aware that all too often I allow myself to be sidetracked by all manner of things. Lord, You have called me to single-mindedly focus upon the goal that You have set before me. Lord, I press on and I look to You for all that I need to achieve my goal. Amen.

Read Philippians 3:1–11

> YET INDEED I ALSO COUNT ALL THINGS LOSS FOR THE EXCELLENCE OF THE
> KNOWLEDGE OF CHRIST JESUS MY LORD…
>
> Philippians 3:8a

To the eyes of the world around him, Paul's credentials were impeccable.

> *If anyone else thinks he may have confidence in the flesh, I more so:*
> *circumcised the eighth day, of the stock of Israel, of the tribe of Benjamin,*
> *a Hebrew of the Hebrews; concerning the law, a Pharisee; concerning zeal,*
> *persecuting the church; concerning the righteousness which is in the law,*
> *blameless.*
>
> Philippians 3:4b–6

In his previous life Paul was set on the road to achieving status within the Jewish religion. That all changed the day that he met Jesus. None of his previous ambitions or desires mattered any longer.

Paul learned that Salvation comes not through being zealous or through works: Salvation comes through Jesus. He fell in love with Jesus and he said, "I have suffered the loss of all things, and count them as rubbish, that I may gain Christ and be found in Him" (verses 8b–9a). Whereas before he boasted in his own righteousness, after he met Jesus, Paul said: "… not having my own righteousness, which is from the law, but that which is through faith in Christ, the righteousness which is from God by faith" (verse 9). Paul embraced the suffering that came his way, "that I may know Him and the power of His resurrection, and the fellowship of His sufferings, being conformed to His death" (verse 10).

This is why anyone who tells you that you must come to Jesus and you will be healthy and wealthy is lying to you. Yes, God loves us and He blesses us. Yes, He provides for us and He heals us. But there are times that He doesn't. Many of God's children have suffered – in fact some of the people who have had the greatest testimonies are those who have suffered the most. Certainly the apostle Paul is an example of this. The point is that when we know and love Jesus everything else takes second place to knowing Him. In the light of that knowledge suffering is viewed from an eternal perspective. It is the knowledge of Christ Jesus our Lord that counts; it is He who is all important to us.

Prayer

My Father God, I thank You for Your Word. With the apostle Paul I want to say: "Yet indeed I also count all things loss for the excellence of the knowledge of Christ Jesus my Lord". Jesus, I want to know You more; I want to live for You. I want my life to be totally and completely surrendered to You. Amen.

Read 1 Timothy 1:1–17

> THIS IS A FAITHFUL SAYING AND WORTHY OF ALL ACCEPTANCE, THAT CHRIST
> JESUS CAME INTO THE WORLD TO SAVE SINNERS, OF WHOM I AM CHIEF.
>
> 1 Timothy 1:15

The apostle Paul said he was the chief of sinners. I identify with Paul in this – so am I, my friend. Paul knew that his ministry was all of Jesus: he had nothing to offer in and of himself. I too feel like this – it is only by the grace of God that I minister. I define the word "grace" as being undeserved loving kindness and unmerited favour. Paul didn't deserve God's grace, did he? I know that I certainly don't deserve His grace. It is mine only because Jesus died on the Cross of Calvary for me. This understanding of God's undeserved, unmerited favour is what changed Paul's life, and mine.

"And the grace of our Lord was exceedingly abundant, with faith and love which are in Christ Jesus" (verse 14). God's grace changes everything: nothing is the same ever again after you have encountered His grace in your life. Maybe you find yourself in a place where you don't believe you deserve God's grace. Maybe you have messed up so badly that you think there is no hope for you. The simple truth is, "Christ Jesus came into the world to save sinners". That is you and it is me, as well as each and every person who was ever born. God's grace is not selective, my friends; He doesn't extend it to some and not to others.

The criteria for receiving God's grace is repentance: turning from your wicked ways and believing in Jesus Christ, the risen Son of God. In other words, you need to have an encounter with Jesus Christ. Jesus has always been in the business of saving sinners. So turn away from the things that hold you back from serving God and follow Jesus. Be encouraged that the Saviour of the world did not come to save the righteous. No, He came to save those who need a Physician. He is the Healer of the bruised and broken, the Friend of sinners. Come to Jesus, just as you are, He is waiting to forgive, cleanse, and restore you.

Prayer

My Father God, Your grace is so amazing! Lord, I bow in humble repentance before Your throne. Forgive me, I pray. Wash me clean and restore me. I thank You, Lord. "Now to the King eternal, immortal, invisible, to God who alone is wise, be honor and glory forever and ever. Amen" (verse 17).

IN THE HOLY SPIRIT'S POWER

> AND YOU BECAME FOLLOWERS OF US AND OF THE LORD, HAVING RECEIVED
> THE WORD IN MUCH AFFLICTION, WITH JOY OF THE HOLY SPIRIT, SO THAT YOU
> BECAME EXAMPLES TO ALL IN MACEDONIA AND ACHAIA WHO BELIEVE.
>
> 1 Thessalonians 1:6–7

Paul was sold out to the gospel and he certainly knew what it was to suffer for his faith. After his dramatic conversion he was baptized in the Holy Spirit: "And Ananias went his way and entered the house; and laying his hands on him he said, 'Brother Saul, the Lord Jesus, who appeared to you on the road as you came, has sent me that you may receive your sight and be filled with the Holy Spirit'" (Acts 9:17).

God used Paul to work miracles, signs, and wonders. People were so amazed at what God did through Paul's life. They brought the sick out into the streets, so that as he walked past they would be healed. The people brought handkerchiefs and aprons for him to pray over. Then they took them back, placed them underneath the sick person's pillow, and they would be healed. "Now God worked unusual miracles by the hands of Paul, so that even handkerchiefs or aprons were brought from his body to the sick, and the diseases left them and the evil spirits went out of them" (Acts 19:11–12).

This still happens today – oh yes, it does. Some of you may not believe it, but it does. There is no power outside the Holy Spirit, my friends. That is why Ananias prayed for Paul before he began his ministry. If we don't have the Holy Spirit then we are simply into works. It is the Holy Spirit who breathes power and life into whatever we do. That is why Paul prayed for the Romans: "Now may the God of hope fill you with all joy and peace in believing, that you may abound in hope by the power of the Holy Spirit" (Romans 15:13). We are sharing life with people: new life in Christ; we are sharing hope with people: "hope by the power of the Holy Spirit". Paul knew the dead letter of the law from his previous life. He never wanted to return to it – why would he when he knew fullness of life in Christ? Are you living in the power of the Spirit?

Prayer

My Father, thank You for fullness of life in Christ Jesus, my Saviour. Lord, I am so grateful that I no longer live in the deadness of the law. Thank You that You have redeemed me and brought me into Your Kingdom of Light and Life. Lord, I want to live in the fullness of Your Spirit. Fill me, I pray. Amen.

Read Romans 3:1–20

AND THE WAY OF PEACE THEY HAVE NOT KNOWN.

Romans 3:17

Being right with God is the only way to know lasting peace. Jesus is our Peace – He is "the way of peace". The peace that I am talking about is not dependent upon your circumstances: it is dependent upon Jesus Christ. If Christ lives in you then you will know lasting peace. You can be in a difficult marriage, but you will have peace. You can lose everything, but you will have peace. You can be in jail, but you will have peace. There is nothing that will be able to take your peace away. Even through great tribulation and suffering the apostle Paul experienced peace. Nothing and no one could remove his peace because he knew the "way of peace" – the Prince of Peace.

If you have peace then you will also know joy, for they go together. Paul put it like this: "for the kingdom of God is not eating and drinking, but righteousness and peace and joy in the Holy Spirit" (Romans 14:17). We can spend our lives looking for peace and joy in all the wrong places. If we come to God we will receive the peace of Jesus. When we have peace, the joy of the Lord will become evident in our lives. With peace and joy comes contentment and purpose for our lives. It doesn't matter who you are or what your life has been like. When you come to Christ, God gives you a whole new purpose and reason for living.

Paul knew about contentment and that it was not dependent upon his circumstances: "Not that I speak in regard to need, for I have learned in whatever state I am, to be content" (Philippians 4:11). This is peace, my friends: don't you want to live your life like this? I join Paul in praying this prayer for you: "Now may the God of hope fill you with all joy and peace in believing, that you may abound in hope by the power of the Holy Spirit" (Romans 15:13). Whatever your circumstances, come to Jesus the Prince of Peace right now.

Prayer

My Father in Heaven, You sent Your Son, Jesus Christ, to build the bridge, so that I can have peace with You. You alone are able through Jesus to give me lasting peace and joy. Jesus, You are my Prince of Peace. You give me hope, joy, and peace everlasting, irrespective of what my circumstances are. Amen.

Read Romans 12:9–21

> IF IT IS POSSIBLE, AS MUCH AS DEPENDS ON YOU, LIVE PEACEABLY WITH ALL MEN.
>
> Romans 12:18

An outworking of the peace and joy we receive from Jesus is that we will try to live peacefully with other people. Paul took his role as a peacemaker among the churches seriously and wrote a lot to the churches about living peacefully with one another. He taught the Galatians about the fruit of the Spirit. "But the fruit of the Spirit is love, joy, peace, long suffering, kindness, goodness, faithfulness, gentleness, self-control" (Galatians 5:22–23a). If you have the Holy Spirit living within you then one of the fruit of the Spirit is peace. You will have peace with God, and an outworking of that peace will be the way you treat and behave toward other people. If you remember Jesus said in the Sermon on the Mount: "Blessed are the peacemakers, for they shall be called sons of God" (Matthew 5:9).

Isn't it sad that so many of God's children live at odds with each other? Instead of being peacemakers they spend their time fostering disunity and trouble within the church. This is a very bad witness to the world, my friends. What the unbeliever needs to see is a united Body of Christ that demonstrates to the world how to live in peace with each other. Why would people be attracted to the gospel of Jesus if they see His disciples living in constant strife? Is your home environment peaceful and loving? At your place of work, are you known as a peacemaker or a troublemaker?

Paul further instructs us to "keep the unity of the Spirit in the bond of peace" (Ephesians 4:3). He always began his letters with a greeting to his audience that usually included wishing them peace. He would remind them of the peace that they had in Jesus. He also often ended his letters exhorting them to live in peace. These were some of his final words to the Corinthian church: "Finally, brethren, farewell. Become complete. Be of good comfort, be of one mind, live in peace; and the God of love and peace will be with you" (2 Corinthians 13:11).

Prayer

My Father, thank You for peace in Jesus Christ. Lord, I am so grateful that I have Your peace in my heart. Help me to be a faithful minister of Your peace to all those I come into contact with. In my home, in the church and in my place of work I want to be an example of Your peace. Amen.

Read 1 Corinthians 13

FOR NOW WE SEE IN A MIRROR, DIMLY, BUT THEN FACE TO FACE. NOW I
KNOW IN PART, BUT THEN I SHALL KNOW JUST AS I ALSO AM KNOWN. AND
NOW ABIDE FAITH, HOPE, LOVE, THESE THREE; BUT THE GREATEST OF THESE IS
LOVE.

1 Corinthians 13:12–13

I want to tell you something. If you don't have love and if you don't know the Author of the Bible, you have nothing. We need to humble ourselves and esteem others as greater than ourselves. It is the love of God that compels a man to turn to Jesus Christ. "If someone says, 'I love God,' and hates his brother, he is a liar; for he who does not love his brother whom he has seen, how can he love God whom he has not seen?" (1 John 4:20)

It doesn't matter if a person knows the Bible from Genesis to Revelation, has a string of degrees, or is a learned doctor of theology even – none of it will help them if they do not have love. As Paul states, the bottom line is: you are nothing without love. This is what he tells us in what is known as the great love chapter in the Bible:

Though I speak with the tongues of men and of angels, but have not love, I have become sounding brass or a clanging cymbal. And though I have the gift of prophecy, and understand all mysteries and all knowledge, and though I have all faith, so that I could remove mountains, but have not love, I am nothing. And though I bestow all my goods to feed the poor, and though I give my body to be burned, but have not love, it profits me nothing.

1 Corinthians 13:1–3

The world has always needed love, but never more so than now. We need the love of Christ to permeate our world. We demonstrate the love of God not so much by what we say, but rather by what we do. Mourn with those who mourn; rejoice with those who rejoice. Perfect love has feet: we need to get out there and share the gospel of love with people. Don't tell people you love them; find ways to show them that you love them. "And now abide faith, hope, love, these three; but the greatest of these is love" (verse 13).

Prayer

My Father, You have shown me Your great love in so many ways. I want to be someone who is known for their love. Love firstly for You, then for those You have given to me. I want people to recognize me by the way I love. Lord, help me to faithfully reflect You to those I come into contact with. Amen.

Read Romans 10:1–17

[T]HAT IF YOU CONFESS WITH YOUR MOUTH THE LORD JESUS AND BELIEVE IN YOUR HEART THAT GOD HAS RAISED HIM FROM THE DEAD, YOU WILL BE SAVED.

Romans 10:9

It is by faith that we are saved. "For the Scripture says, 'Whoever believes on Him will not be put to shame'" (verse 11). We cannot earn our Salvation through good works. "And though I bestow all my goods to feed the poor, and though I give my body to be burned, but have not love, it profits me nothing" (1 Corinthians 13:3). It is only once the grace of the Lord Jesus Christ is released in our hearts that we can express the love of God. We can only experience His grace once we come to Him in repentance.

We need to confess with our mouths and believe with our hearts. The result is not that we do good works, but rather that out of the fullness of the grace we have experienced we serve others. Faith must have feet: it is a "doing" word, as I always say. Faith speaks of action. When you are born again and you enter into a living relationship with the Lord Jesus Christ, your life must change. If there is no change, there is no real faith.

Remember in Acts 16, the night Paul and Silas were put in jail? The angel of the Lord shook the jail and their chains fell off, setting them free. Instead of running away, they stayed put. The jailer was so overcome that he fell upon his knees and asked them what he needed to do to be saved. That experience changed the jailer; he and his whole household accepted Christ and were baptized. When you believe in Jesus Christ and become a follower of His, your life must change. Like Paul, you will be compelled to share with others the Good News of the gospel of Jesus Christ. One of the outworkings of faith in your life will be boldness. "So then faith comes by hearing, and hearing by the word of God" (Romans 10:17). Spend time in God's Word. Allow Him to build you up and strengthen you through the power of His Spirit. The outworking of your Salvation will be an active life of faith.

Prayer

My Father in Heaven, thank You for calling me to Yourself. I am so grateful that You have touched my life. I confess with my mouth that Jesus is Lord and I truly believe in my heart, Father, that You raised Him from the dead. I pray that You will give me an active faith that will glorify You. Amen.

Read Romans 8:18–30

> FOR I CONSIDER THAT THE SUFFERINGS OF THIS PRESENT TIME ARE NOT
> WORTHY TO BE COMPARED WITH THE GLORY WHICH SHALL BE REVEALED IN US.
>
> Romans 8:18

It is difficult to observe the life of the apostle Paul without returning time and again to the theme of suffering. It was such an integral part of his life and his testimony. I become very upset when I hear people say that there must be sin in someone's life if they are suffering. Unfortunately we live in an impure world; a world that doesn't have it all together. This is why as Christians we take comfort from the fact that we are going home to Heaven. In Heaven there is no more sickness, no more disease, no more fear, and no more weeping.

> *… we ourselves groan within ourselves, eagerly waiting for the adoption, the redemption of our body. For we were saved in this hope, but hope that is seen is not hope; for why does one still hope for what he sees? But if we hope for what we do not see, we eagerly wait for it with perseverance.*

So say verses 23b–25. When we go through a time of suffering we are not without hope. On the contrary, we have all the hope in the world because our hope is in Jesus. Paul understood this so well, he knew that his earthly body was simply a vessel to be used by God.

> *But we have this treasure in earthen vessels, that the excellence of the power may be of God and not of us. We are hard-pressed on every side, yet not crushed; we are perplexed, but not in despair; persecuted, but not forsaken; struck down, but not destroyed – always carrying about in the body the dying of the Lord Jesus, that the life of Jesus also may be manifested in our body. For we who live are always delivered to death for Jesus' sake, that the life of Jesus also may be manifested in our mortal flesh. So then death is working in us, but life in you.*
>
> 2 Corinthians 4:7–12

So, my friend, if you are going through a season of suffering take heart as we share together over the next few days around the subject of suffering.

Prayer

My Father God, You know how hard it is at the moment. I run to You and I sit at Your feet. Lord, I know that You alone are my Source of comfort and refuge. There is hope nowhere else or in anyone else. Lord, You are my Hope. Lord, I look forward to the glory that You will in due time reveal to me. Amen.

Read 2 Corinthians 12:1–10

> AND LEST I SHOULD BE EXALTED ABOVE MEASURE BY THE ABUNDANCE OF THE
> REVELATIONS, A THORN IN THE FLESH WAS GIVEN TO ME, A MESSENGER OF
> SATAN TO BUFFET ME, LEST I BE EXALTED ABOVE MEASURE.
>
> 2 Corinthians 12:7

Remember Paul, the apostle, asked the Lord Jesus three times to remove the thorn from his flesh. Now we are not going to become involved in a theological discussion, because that is not what we are about. But what I do want to say is that if the Word says it, then I believe it. The Word says that Paul had a thorn in his flesh. I know that some men say it was a spiritual thing. I don't think so, because then surely he would have said, "I have a thorn in my spirit." Instead he said, "I have a thorn in my flesh." I know if you go back to the Old Testament they speak of the Philistines being a thorn in the side of the Israelites. But as far as I am concerned, it was a thorn in his flesh. I am going to offer something to you and I have nothing to substantiate it (but then, neither can anyone else substantiate their theories).

When we get to Heaven one day, we can ask Paul, and he will tell us. I believe his "thorn" was his sight – his eyesight was impaired. Having pleaded for the thorn's removal three times, Paul says, "He said to me, 'My grace is sufficient for you, for My strength is made perfect in weakness'" (verse 9a). We can learn a lot from Paul's response: "Therefore most gladly I will rather boast in my infirmities, that the power of Christ may rest upon me. Therefore I take pleasure in infirmities, in reproaches, in needs, in persecutions, in distresses, for Christ's sake. For when I am weak, then I am strong" (verses 9b–10).

As in every other area of his life, Paul submitted to God. His commitment to serving God was not based upon God giving him what he wanted. It was based upon Paul loving Jesus and nothing being too much for him when it came to living in obedience to God. My friend, if you are going through a season of suffering, what is your attitude? How are you coping?

Prayer

Lord, thank You for Your servant Paul, who is such a fine example to me. He was truly a man who lived by faith and not by sight. He followed You faithfully and obediently. Lord, I too want to be a man like him. Give me grace to accept Your will in my life. Help me to glorify You even during this time. Amen.

Read 2 Corinthians 12:1–10

AND HE SAID TO ME, "MY GRACE IS SUFFICIENT FOR YOU, FOR MY STRENGTH
IS MADE PERFECT IN WEAKNESS." THEREFORE MOST GLADLY I WILL RATHER
BOAST IN MY INFIRMITIES, THAT THE POWER OF CHRIST MAY REST UPON ME.

2 Corinthians 12:9

You see, my dear friend, God's grace is sufficient for us. I really mean this. You know
I would rather be physically impaired but spiritually healthy than to be spiritually
sick and physically healthy. Yet, there are many people for whom the latter is true. I
believe in physical fitness – as you may know, I run almost every morning. I ride my
horse and I enjoy being physically involved on the farm. But physical fitness is not my
main objective in life: it is a means to an end. My main objective is to keep my soul and
spirit-man healthy for when God calls me home to Heaven.

Paul said: "And lest I should be exalted above measure by the abundance of the
revelations" (verse 7a). You see, God gave Paul revelations: he saw things that the
other disciples hadn't seen. God took Paul into another dimension.

*I know a man in Christ who fourteen years ago – whether in the body I do not
know, or whether out of the body I do not know, God knows – such a one was
caught up to the third heaven. And I know such a man… how he was caught
up into Paradise and heard inexpressible words, which it is not lawful for a
man to utter.*

2 Corinthians 12:2–4

So Paul could have become puffed up and filled with pride. Paul believed that that
was the reason he was given the thorn in the flesh.

As I said a couple of days ago, suffering is not always as a result of sin. God is
sovereign, my friends, and He is in control of our lives. So, if I am His child then I
have to trust Him with every area of my life. I cannot say, "OK, God, You can have this
part of my life, but not that part. You can control this part of my life, but I am keeping
control of that part." It doesn't work like that – it is all or nothing. Paul understood
this. So many of his writings address the subject of suffering and God's grace being
sufficient no matter what we are going through.

Prayer
*My Father in Heaven, thank You that no matter what I am going through or will go through
You are in control. Like Job and Peter, nothing can touch my life that doesn't first pass through
You. Lord, if You allow it then You can and will help me to live through it victoriously. I trust
in You. Amen.*

Read 2 Corinthians 12:1–10

> AND LEST I SHOULD BE EXALTED ABOVE MEASURE BY THE ABUNDANCE OF THE
> REVELATIONS, A THORN IN THE FLESH WAS GIVEN TO ME, A MESSENGER OF
> SATAN TO BUFFET ME, LEST I BE EXALTED ABOVE MEASURE.
>
> 2 Corinthians 12:7

To be buffeted is to be beaten down. There is nothing that will bring you down quicker than continual physical pain. If I get a stone in my shoe when I am running it isn't long before the stone drives me to stop and remove it. The guys who play rugby know exactly what I am talking about. There is nothing like physical pain to subdue your spirit, and I think this is what Paul is talking about. Sometimes we have to be physically handicapped in order to listen to God. It is said that the early Israelite shepherds broke the front leg of a rebel lamb that insisted on running away from the flock. Once the leg had been broken the lamb stayed close to the shepherd and never again wandered off. The shepherd didn't do this to be cruel, but because he was a good shepherd. He didn't want the lamb to be taken out by a wolf or a lion, or to fall over the edge of a cliff because it refused to listen.

An Irish girl by the name of Amy Carmichael, a mighty woman of God, preached the gospel in India in the early twentieth century. She rescued little children who were sold into prostitution by their poor families, taking many of them into her own home. Amy took ill and for the last twenty years of her life she ran the mission station from her bed, sometimes flat on her back. She wrote poetry and numerous books over the twenty years. God used her powerfully. Folks, hear me: if God has given you a thorn in the flesh, I am not suggesting for a minute that He will not heal you. I pray for the sick all the time, you know this. However, sometimes God allows us to have a thorn in our flesh for whatever reason.

In Paul's case, he says it was to keep him humble. But God reassured Paul: "My grace is sufficient for you, for My strength is made perfect in weakness" (verse 9a). Paul said: "For when I am weak, then I am strong" (verse 10c).

Prayer

My Father, I thank You for Your encouragement to me today. Lord, the bottom line is that no matter what happens in my life, as long as I stick close to You I will be fine. I can safely entrust my well-being into Your hands. You will always only do what is best for me. Thank You, Lord. Amen.

Read Galatians 5:1, 16–26

STAND FAST THEREFORE IN THE LIBERTY BY WHICH CHRIST HAS MADE US FREE,
AND DO NOT BE ENTANGLED AGAIN WITH A YOKE OF BONDAGE.

Galatians 5:1

For the last few days of our journey with Paul we will look at some of the most well-known portions of Scripture written by him. Paul is responsible for writing two-thirds of the New Testament. His journey of faith began the day he met Jesus on the road to Damascus. From that day on, he walked by faith in the Spirit. Paul knew what it meant to live in the grace of God. He was keen for the Galatians to live in the freedom that Jesus had died to give them. He didn't want them falling back into slavery to sin and the law.

Paul believed that the antidote to falling into sin was walking in the Spirit.

*I say then: "Walk in the Spirit, and you shall not fulfill the lust of the flesh.
For the flesh lusts against the Spirit, and the Spirit against the flesh; and these
are contrary to one another, so that you do not do the things that you wish.
But if you are led by the Spirit, you are not under the law."*

Galatians 5:16–18

The law and grace do not mix: they are like water and oil. Knowing the truth is what will keep us from "fulfilling the lust of the flesh". I have told you the story before of how people are trained to be able to detect forged bank notes: they are only allowed to touch and work with authentic notes, for then, when the moment comes that they hold a forged note in their hands, they can immediately tell it is a fake.

When we walk by the Spirit we will be able to discern the things of the Spirit. We will not be fooled into falling for Satan's tricks. Walk by the Spirit and the fruit of the Spirit will be evident in your life. "But the fruit of the Spirit is love, joy, peace, longsuffering, kindness, goodness, faithfulness, gentleness, self-control. Against such there is no law. And those who are Christ's have crucified the flesh with its passions and desires. If we live in the Spirit, let us also walk in the Spirit" (verses 22–25).

Prayer

My Father, I thank You that I have been set free from slavery to sin. I am so grateful that I am no longer under the law, but that I live in the freedom of Your grace and mercy. Lord, thank You for Your Spirit. I pray that You will fill me afresh and help me to walk each day in the Spirit. Amen.

Read Ephesians 2:1–10

> BUT GOD, WHO IS RICH IN MERCY, BECAUSE OF HIS GREAT LOVE WITH WHICH
> HE LOVED US, EVEN WHEN WE WERE DEAD IN TRESPASSES, MADE US ALIVE
> TOGETHER WITH CHRIST (BY GRACE YOU HAVE BEEN SAVED)…
>
> Ephesians 2:4–5

Paul was explaining to the Ephesians that they have been saved for a reason. My friends, you and I have also been saved for a reason. God had you in mind when Jesus hung on Calvary; He had me in mind. It was His great love for us that motivated His only begotten, much-loved Son to come down to this earth and die on a cross. God's plan of Salvation is the greatest act of love this world has ever seen. It is by grace that you have been saved. Paul understood all about this grace. If you remember, he said: "But by the grace of God I am what I am, and His grace toward me was not in vain; but I labored more abundantly than they all, yet not I, but the grace of God which was with me" (1 Corinthians 15:10).

If ever there was someone who did not squander the grace of God it was Paul. His whole life was motivated by his response to God's grace toward him. Paul came truly alive the day he met Jesus. This is how he describes what God did for us in Ephesians:

> *[A]nd raised us up together, and made us sit together in the heavenly places*
> *in Christ Jesus, that in the ages to come He might show the exceeding riches*
> *of His grace in His kindness toward us in Christ Jesus. For by grace you have*
> *been saved through faith, and that not of yourselves; it is the gift of God, not*
> *of works, lest anyone should boast. For we are His workmanship, created in*
> *Christ Jesus for good works, which God prepared beforehand that we should*
> *walk in them.*
>
> Ephesians 2:6–10

Have you spent any time lately considering what Jesus did for you on Calvary and what your response is to His sacrifice? We have been on a journey together this year, learning to walk by faith and not by sight. One of the aspects of this is living in the fullness of God's grace, fulfilling His purposes in your life, thereby bringing glory to Him.

Prayer
My Father God, thank You for Your love, thank You for Your grace, thank You for Your mercies that are new every morning. Lord, I cannot get over Your great love for me. I didn't deserve it in the past and I don't deserve it now, but I am so grateful that I am alive together with Christ Jesus. Amen.

Read Ephesians 6:10–20

> FINALLY, MY BRETHREN, BE STRONG IN THE LORD AND IN THE POWER OF
> HIS MIGHT. PUT ON THE WHOLE ARMOR OF GOD, THAT YOU MAY BE ABLE TO
> STAND AGAINST THE WILES OF THE DEVIL.
>
> Ephesians 6:10–11

Satan is a defeated foe: he is trapped like an animal in a corner. We all know, though, that a trapped animal can be dangerous. This is why Paul says that we are to be strong in the power of God's might. He says we need the whole armour of God so that we can withstand the onslaught of the devil. Peter, Paul's fellow apostle, put it like this:

> *Be sober, be vigilant; because your adversary the devil walks about like a roaring lion, seeking whom he may devour. Resist him, steadfast in the faith, knowing that the same sufferings are experienced by your brotherhood in the world. But may the God of all grace, who called us to His eternal glory by Christ Jesus, after you have suffered a while, perfect, establish, strengthen, and settle you. To Him be the glory and the dominion forever and ever. Amen.*
>
> 1 Peter 5:8–11

We do not have to face the enemy alone. God has thought of protection for every part of our spiritual body. Around our waist we have the truth: Jesus is the Way, the Truth, and the Life. Then we have a breastplate of righteousness: Jesus is our Righteousness. Our feet are covered with the preparation of the gospel of peace: Jesus is central to the gospel and He is our Peace. We have the shield of faith: our faith is in Jesus Christ, our Lord and Saviour who overcame the enemy. There is a helmet of Salvation that protects our minds: Salvation comes through Jesus. Finally, there is the sword of the Spirit: Jesus promised that He would not leave us alone – we have the power of His Spirit at work in our lives.

Paul says that a vital component of warfare that you must not forget about is prayer: "praying always with all prayer and supplication in the Spirit, being watchful to this end with all perseverance and supplication for all the saints" (Ephesians 6:18). When you have the whole armour of God on, you can confidently walk by faith and not by sight.

Prayer

My Father God, You have dominion over all things. There is nothing that is higher or greater than You, my God. All created beings are subject to You. Lord, how grateful I am that I am Your much-loved child. Lord, thank You for the protective armour You have given me. Help me to faithfully wear it. Amen.

Read Philippians 4:8–20

> FINALLY, BRETHREN, WHATEVER THINGS ARE TRUE, WHATEVER THINGS ARE
> NOBLE, WHATEVER THINGS ARE JUST, WHATEVER THINGS ARE PURE, WHATEVER
> THINGS ARE LOVELY, WHATEVER THINGS ARE OF GOOD REPORT, IF THERE IS
> ANY VIRTUE AND IF THERE IS ANYTHING PRAISEWORTHY — MEDITATE ON THESE
> THINGS.
>
> Philippians 4:8

What an amazing testimony Paul had that he could confidently say to the Philippians: "The things which you learned and received and heard and saw in me, these do, and the God of peace will be with you" (verse 9). Paul had faithfully carried out his mandate from God. He said: "Yes, and if I am being poured out as a drink offering on the sacrifice and service of your faith, I am glad and rejoice with you all" (Philippians 2:17). He gave himself 100 per cent to the fulfilment of the ministry that God had entrusted to him. Paul walked his talk.

In this passage of Scripture Paul shares some of the faith lessons that he has learned with the Philippian church. He says that he has learned contentment: "Not that I speak in regard to need, for I have learned in whatever state I am, to be content" (verse 11). How many of us can honestly say this and really mean it? The reason for Paul's contentment is Jesus Christ: "I can do all things through Christ who strengthens me" (verse 13). The Living Bible puts it this way: "for I can do everything God asks me to with the help of Christ who gives me the strength and power." Isn't that beautiful? Paul could endure all the suffering that he had been through since becoming a Christian because he had Jesus. Paul knew he wasn't alone; he knew that whatever God asked of him, he would be able to do it with the help of Jesus.

Are you struggling today? Do you feel that it is all too much? Take comfort from Paul's words, my friend. Paul's Jesus is your Jesus: He is with you each step of the way.

Paul finished off his letter to the Philippians with these words: "And my God shall supply all your need according to His riches in glory by Christ Jesus. Now to our God and Father be glory forever and ever. Amen" (verse 19–20). These words from God's Word are as true for you as they were for Paul.

Prayer

My Father, there is none like You! Thank You that You fill me with Your Holy Spirit power each and every day. Lord, I can do whatever You ask me to do because I have Jesus Christ, my Lord and Saviour living within me. I praise You, Lord, I have need of nothing because You so bountifully supply all my needs. Amen.

Read Ephesians 1:15–23; 3:14–21

[T]HAT HE WOULD GRANT YOU, ACCORDING TO THE RICHES OF HIS GLORY,
TO BE STRENGTHENED WITH MIGHT THROUGH HIS SPIRIT IN THE INNER MAN,
THAT CHRIST MAY DWELL IN YOUR HEARTS THROUGH FAITH…

Ephesians 3:16–17a

We see from these two readings that God needs us to walk in spiritual wisdom; there is a real need for spiritual growth in you and me. Here they are in full:

Therefore I also, after I heard of your faith in the Lord Jesus and your love for all the saints, do not cease to give thanks for you, making mention of you in my prayers: that the God of our Lord Jesus Christ, the Father of glory, may give to you the spirit of wisdom and revelation in the knowledge of Him, the eyes of your understanding being enlightened; that you may know what is the hope of His calling, what are the riches of the glory of His inheritance in the saints, and what is the exceeding greatness of His power toward us who believe, according to the working of His mighty power which He worked in Christ when He raised Him from the dead and seated Him at His right hand in the heavenly places, far above all principality and power and might and dominion, and every name that is named, not only in this age but also in that which is to come. And He put all things under His feet, and gave Him to be head over all things to the church, which is His body, the fullness of Him who fills all in all.

Ephesians 1:15–23

For this reason I bow my knees to the Father of our Lord Jesus Christ, from whom the whole family in heaven and earth is named, that He would grant you, according to the riches of His glory, to be strengthened with might through His Spirit in the inner man, that Christ may dwell in your hearts through faith; that you, being rooted and grounded in love, may be able to comprehend with all the saints what is the width and length and depth and height – to know the love of Christ which passes knowledge; that you may be filled with all the fullness of God. Now to Him who is able to do exceedingly abundantly above all that we ask or think, according to the power that works in us, to Him be glory in the church by Christ Jesus to all generations, forever and ever. Amen.

Ephesians 3:14–21

Prayer

Father God, as I come to the end of this month I can only bow in Your presence. Lord, Your grace and mercy overwhelm me. You have once again shown me how much You love me. Lord, my response to You is that I want to love You in return. I want to walk by faith and not by sight, glorifying You. Amen.

JESUS' JOURNEY OF SALVATION

Jesus' journey of faith had no beginning and has no end

1. Jesus, the Word
2. Jesus, the Christ Child
3. The names of Jesus
4. Jesus, Friend of sinners
5. Jesus, the Shepherd
6. Jesus, the True Vine
7. Jesus, the True Bread from Heaven
8. Jesus, the Light of the world
9. Jesus, the Teacher
10. Jesus, the Healer
11. Jesus, the Friend
12. Jesus, the Righteous Judge
13. Jesus, the model of the Father
14. Jesus, the Prayer Warrior 1
15. Jesus, the Prayer Warrior 2
16. Jesus, the Heir of all things
17. Jesus, the Living Water
18. Jesus, the Way
19. Jesus, the Truth
20. Jesus, the Life
21. Jesus, the High Priest
22. Jesus, the Beloved, Only Begotten Son
23. Jesus, the "Calmer" of storms
24. Jesus, the Peacegiver
25. Jesus, the Prince of Peace
26. Jesus, the Obedient Son
27. Jesus, Giver of Righteousness
28. Jesus, the King
29. Jesus, the Soon-coming King
30. Jesus, the Commissioner
31. Continue walking by faith

Read John 1:1–18

> IN THE BEGINNING WAS THE WORD, AND THE WORD WAS WITH GOD, AND
> THE WORD WAS GOD. HE WAS IN THE BEGINNING WITH GOD. ALL THINGS
> WERE MADE THROUGH HIM, AND WITHOUT HIM NOTHING WAS MADE THAT
> WAS MADE.
>
> John 1:1–3

Our Scripture tells us that He, Jesus Christ, is the Word and that He was with God from the beginning. Jesus had no beginning and He has no end. As Walter Chalmers Smith's great hymn puts it: "Immortal, invisible, God only wise, / in light inaccessible hid from our eyes, / most blessed, most glorious, the Ancient of Days, / Almighty, victorious, Thy great name we praise." Genesis 1:1–3 says: "In the beginning God created the heavens and the earth. The earth was without form, and void; and darkness was on the face of the deep. And the Spirit of God was hovering over the face of the waters. Then God said, 'Let there be light'; and there was light."

God spoke, and by the power of His Word the world was created. John tells us: "He was in the world, and the world was made through Him, and the world did not know Him" (verse 10). Jesus came to this world to reveal the Father. He came to reconcile mankind to God. Jesus came to save the world and to redeem man from his sin; He was the Word made flesh.

People rejected Jesus back when He walked on this earth and there are those who still choose to reject Him today: "and the world did not know Him." It is your responsibility and my responsibility to tell people about Jesus. We need to spread His Word throughout this land and throughout this world. If we don't do it, who will, my friends? We have to share with people that Jesus is the Word made flesh, and that there is Salvation in no one else but Him. Jesus is coming back to this world again. John the Baptist prepared the way for Jesus' first coming. He spread the Word and called people to repent and make sure they were ready. In the same way we need to be preparing the way for Jesus' second coming. We need to be faithful witnesses to the world that the Word, who is God, is coming back to this world soon.

Prayer

My Father, thank You that You sent Jesus, Your Son, the Word of God to this world. Jesus, You came to seek and to save. Lord, thank You that You have redeemed my life, cleansing and healing me from sin. I will be Your mouthpiece spreading the Word of Your gospel to those around me. Amen.

Read Luke 2:1–20

> THEN THE ANGEL SAID TO THEM, "DO NOT BE AFRAID, FOR BEHOLD, I BRING
> YOU GOOD TIDINGS OF GREAT JOY WHICH WILL BE TO ALL PEOPLE. FOR THERE
> IS BORN TO YOU THIS DAY IN THE CITY OF DAVID A SAVIOR, WHO IS CHRIST
> THE LORD."   Luke 2:10–11

Jesus is God and He came to this earth to reveal the Father to mankind. Back in the garden of Eden when Adam and Eve chose to eat the fruit from the tree, the die was cast. Man was lost and therefore had to be redeemed. Jesus Christ fulfilled more than 300 prophecies, ten of which were directly related to His birth.

1. Jesus will come from the line of Abraham. Prophecy: Genesis 12:2–3. Fulfilled in Matthew 1:1.

2. Jesus' mother will be a virgin. Prophecy: Isaiah 7:14. Fulfilled in Matthew 1:18–23.

3. Jesus will be a descendent of Isaac and Jacob. Prophecy: Genesis 17:19 and Numbers 24:17. Fulfilled in Matthew 1:1–2.

4. Jesus will be born in the town of Bethlehem. Prophecy: Micah 5:2. Fulfilled in Luke 2:1–7.

5. Jesus will be called out of Egypt. Prophecy: Hosea 11:1. Fulfilled in Matthew 2:13–15.

6. Jesus will be a member of the tribe of Judah. Prophecy: Genesis 49:10. Fulfilled in Luke 3:33.

7. Jesus will enter the temple. This is important because the temple was destroyed in AD 70 and was never rebuilt. Prophecy: Malachi 3:1. Fulfilled in Luke 2:25–27.

8. Jesus will be from the lineage of King David. Prophecy: Jeremiah 23:5. Fulfilled in Matthew 1:6.

9. Jesus' birth will be accompanied with great suffering and sorrow. Prophecy: Jeremiah 31:15, 17–18. Fulfilled in Matthew 2:16.

10. Jesus will live a perfect life, die by crucifixion, be resurrected from death, ascend into Heaven, and sit at the right hand of God. Prophecies: Psalm 22:16; Psalm 16:10; Isaiah 53:10–11; Psalm 68:18; Psalm 110:1. Fulfilled in 1 Peter 2:21–22; Luke 23:33; Acts 2:25–32; Acts 1:9; Hebrews 1:3.

Indeed the birth of Jesus was good tidings of great joy for all mankind. Jesus, who came as the Christ Child, is the Saviour of the world. Without His birth in a humble stable in Bethlehem you and I would not be able to claim eternal life. God sent His Son as a defenceless baby in order to reconcile the world to Himself. There was no other way: God had to make the ultimate sacrifice.

Prayer

My Father God, You love me so much. You sent Your Beloved Son, Jesus, to this world as a defenceless baby, so that I could be saved. Thank You, Lord, I don't have words enough to express my gratitude to You. Lord, I love You and I want to serve You for the rest of my life. Amen.

Read Isaiah 9:1–7

> FOR UNTO US A CHILD IS BORN, UNTO US A SON IS GIVEN; AND THE GOVERNMENT WILL BE UPON HIS SHOULDER. AND HIS NAME WILL BE CALLED WONDERFUL, COUNSELOR, MIGHTY GOD, EVERLASTING FATHER, PRINCE OF PEACE.
>
> Isaiah 9:6

My friends, did you know that Jesus has over 200 different names by which He is referred to in the Word of God? In our reading in Isaiah today, Jesus' birth is foretold and He is referred to by a number of different names. I love going through His titles: Jesus is the King of kings and the Lord of lords. He is the One who saved me and pulled me out of a bottomless pit, setting my feet upon Himself, the Rock. Jesus is my Saviour and Redeemer, the Captain of my Salvation, the One who gave me a second chance. He is the Redeemer of the world, who died for sinners, the One who is the Soon-coming King.

Jesus is the Lily of the Valley. Have you ever seen a lily, a white arum lily? There is nothing more beautiful and pure. Yet Jesus Christ, our Lord, is more beautiful even than the lily of the valley. King Solomon wrote of Jesus: "I am the rose of Sharon, and the lily of the valleys" (Song of Solomon 2:1).

He is the "Bright and Morning Star" (Revelation 22:16b). He is the "Lion of Judah" and the "Root of David" (Revelation 5:5b). Have you ever seen a male lion with his massive mane when he stands up, opens his mouth and roars? It is as if all of creation comes to attention because the king has woken up. Well, Jesus is the Lion of Judah. He is my King, and He is your King, if you love Him. Jesus is the Lamb of God. "The next day John saw Jesus coming toward him, and said, "Behold! The Lamb of God who takes away the sin of the world!" (John 1:29). Take some time right now to bow in Jesus' presence and give thanks and praise for all that He is to you. After all, where would you be today without Him?

Prayer

My Father of all creation – I bow before Your throne. I worship You, my Lord and Saviour. You are everything to me. I would be nothing without You. Lord, You are all that I want and desire. I worship You, I praise You, I exalt You. You are my King, my Mighty God, my Strong Tower. Amen.

Read Luke 19:1–10

> AND JESUS SAID TO HIM, "TODAY SALVATION HAS COME TO THIS HOUSE,
> BECAUSE HE ALSO IS A SON OF ABRAHAM; FOR THE SON OF MAN HAS COME
> TO SEEK AND TO SAVE THAT WHICH WAS LOST."
>
> Luke 19:9–10

Zacchaeus was a chief tax collector and a wealthy man. A tax collector in biblical times fitted into the same category as the mafia does today. I tell you, folks, the people of Jericho hated Zacchaeus because he worked for the Roman oppressors. He collected money from his own poor Jewish brothers who had no money and paid it over to the Romans. You may be asking yourself, "Did Jesus really associate and mix with people like that?" Yes, sir, He associated with prostitutes, terrorists, and thieves. You see, Jesus is for the people. It wasn't the "people" who crucified Jesus, it was the church of the day that crucified Him. We need to be careful that we do not keep Jesus away from the people. If the Lord Jesus Christ lived on the earth today we'd be shocked at where He would spend most of His time.

Zacchaeus heard that this Healer, this Miracle Worker, was coming to town. He was a short man so he couldn't see over the crowd of people lining the road. But he was clever and determined so Zacchaeus climbed a tree from where he had a good view down on to the road. When Jesus passed by He stopped, looked up into the tree, and spoke to Zacchaeus. Two miracles happened. First, Jesus knew his name – how could this be? Because Jesus is God and He knows everything. Second, Jesus chose to stay at Zacchaeus's house. There were many more important and deserving people with whom Jesus could have stayed – but He chose Zacchaeus – chief tax collector and chief of sinners.

Folks, the most important thing to remember is that Christ died for sinners like us and like Zacchaeus. Some of us wonder why people don't want to become Christians. It's because they look at us and they don't see the joy of the Lord in our lives – they don't see evidence of the new beginnings that the gospel speaks about. Zacchaeus had a new beginning on the day that he met Jesus. Are you living in the joy of your new beginning?

Prayer

My Father God, Jesus came to bring a new beginning for each and every person who turns to You. Lord Jesus, thank You for my new beginning. Help me to live in the joy of my Salvation. I want to be a positive influence to bring people to You so that they too can know the joy of a new beginning. Amen.

Read John 10:1–30

> I AM THE GOOD SHEPHERD; AND I KNOW MY SHEEP, AND AM KNOWN BY MY OWN. AS THE FATHER KNOWS ME, EVEN SO I KNOW THE FATHER; AND I LAY DOWN MY LIFE FOR THE SHEEP.
>
> John 10:14–15

Jesus is the Shepherd of the sheep. Have you ever seen a Good Shepherd of the sheep? Oh, folks, I want to tell you: He is tall, strong, handsome, gentle, and powerful. There are no predators, there are no wolves, and there are no wild animals that will come near the Good Shepherd's sheep because He is prepared to lay down His life for them. He doesn't close the gate at night when He puts His sheep in the pen – He *is* the Gate. The Good Shepherd keeps watch throughout the night and any animal that wants to touch His sheep has to go through Him.

This is why I feel totally secure as I share with you. I have nothing to worry about because I have a Good Shepherd, Jesus Christ, my Lord and Saviour. The same security that I have is yours if you know Jesus Christ. It doesn't matter what is going on in our country, or the world for that matter, our Good Shepherd is guarding us. As we trust in Him we can know that He has our lives safely and securely under His control. Our reading says that the Good Shepherd knows His sheep – this means that each one of us is precious to Him.

> *My sheep hear My voice, and I know them, and they follow Me. And I give them eternal life, and they shall never perish; neither shall anyone snatch them out of My hand. My Father, who has given them to Me, is greater than all; and no one is able to snatch them out of My Father's hand. I and My Father are one.*
>
> John 10:27–30

There you have it in Jesus' own words – "snatch them out of My Father's hand." These words spoken by Jesus are the greatest security that you can and will ever have in your life. Anything and everything that happens in our life on earth can be handled because we know that ultimately our home is in Heaven with our Good Shepherd.

Prayer

My Father in Heaven, I thank You, Jesus, that You are my Good Shepherd. You are strong and mighty to save and protect me. I rest in the knowledge that You have my life safely and securely under Your control. I am totally secure as Your child. I love You, my Lord and Saviour. Amen.

Read John 15:1–17

> I AM THE TRUE VINE, AND MY FATHER IS THE VINEDRESSER. I AM THE VINE,
> YOU ARE THE BRANCHES. HE WHO ABIDES IN ME, AND I IN HIM, BEARS MUCH
> FRUIT; FOR WITHOUT ME YOU CAN DO NOTHING.
>
> John 15:1, 5

Jesus says that He is the True Vine – this implies that there are false vines. We have to be careful that we are grafted into the True Vine. Once separated from the vine the branch is nothing – it can no longer go on living. We abide in Jesus and as long as we do we bear fruit. In order to bear good fruit the Vinedresser has to prune the branches on the vine. Jesus tells us that His Father is a Vinedresser. A good vinedresser prunes the vine right back. Sometimes pruning is sad and very painful, but all the new shoots have to be pruned off. Why? Because the Vinedresser wants you to produce good fruit.

The pruning is not done to punish us – oh no – it is done so that we can enjoy the fulfilment of Jesus' promise that we will bear much fruit. Jesus also tells us that we are to abide in His love. "As the Father loved Me, I also have loved you; abide in My love. If you keep My commandments, you will abide in My love, just as I have kept My Father's commandments and abide in His love" (verses 9–10). Abiding in Him means obeying Him and walking in faith each day. We have said so many times that love, obedience, and faith go hand in hand.

Are you filled with joy right now? Too many Christians are miserable and unhappy. How can this be when Jesus clearly says: "These things I have spoken to you, that My joy may remain in you, and that your joy may be full" (verse 11). Here is the secret to happiness and contentment, my friends: abide in Jesus and you will bear much fruit; obey Jesus' commandments and you will abide in His love; remain in Him so that your joy will be full and complete. Jesus is all and everything we need. It is His love for us that brings true meaning to our lives – without it we are lost and will end up like branches that have been discarded from the vine.

Prayer

My Father the Vinedresser, Jesus the True Vine, I come to You and I bow in Your presence. I want to constantly abide in You. I want to abide in Your love and I want to obey Your commandments. Lord, make me strong, fruitful, and useful to You. Lord, I thank You for Your love for me. Amen.

Read John 6:22–40

> THEN JESUS SAID TO THEM, "MOST ASSUREDLY, I SAY TO YOU, MOSES DID
> NOT GIVE YOU THE BREAD FROM HEAVEN, BUT MY FATHER GIVES YOU THE
> TRUE BREAD FROM HEAVEN. FOR THE BREAD OF GOD IS HE WHO COMES
> DOWN FROM HEAVEN AND GIVES LIFE TO THE WORLD."… AND JESUS SAID TO
> THEM, "I AM THE BREAD OF LIFE."

John 6:32–33, 35a

Directly after He fed the 5,000, Jesus said, "I am the bread of life. He who comes to Me shall never hunger, and he who believes in Me shall never thirst" (verse 35). This was such an amazing miracle that people were clamouring for more. Jesus didn't want people to believe only because of the signs and wonders. Jesus said to the nobleman in John 4:48, "Unless you people see signs and wonders, you will by no means believe." He wanted people to believe because they understood that He was the True Bread from Heaven and that complete satisfaction comes only through Him.

There are people who seek their whole lives to find satisfaction and never do. Some accumulate great wealth and amass many material possessions. There are others who bury themselves in their work. Then there are those who seek thrills and danger in order to find fulfilment and satisfaction. It is all futile, my friends; none of it works, none of it can provide lasting satisfaction. Jesus gave us the answer. He said: "He who comes to Me shall never hunger." Jesus, the True Bread from Heaven, nourishes and feeds us spiritually. We know that if we eat of Him we will never be hungry again.

Once your spiritual hunger is satisfied then you will know true satisfaction. If you think of the lengths people go to in order to try and find satisfaction when the Bread of Life, Jesus Christ, is offered to those who believe freely. "I am the living bread which came down from heaven. If anyone eats of this bread, he will live forever; and the bread that I shall give is My flesh, which I shall give for the life of the world" (John 6:51). Every person has a hole inside of them that longs to be filled by God. Psalm 107:9 tells us: "For He satisfies the longing soul, and fills the hungry soul with goodness." My friend, are you satisfied today? Has the longing in your soul been filled with Jesus, the True Bread from Heaven?

Prayer

My Father in Heaven, thank You that You sent the True Bread from Heaven down to earth to satisfy the hunger in the souls of men. Jesus, there is satisfaction in You and only You. Lord, thank You that You fill every area of my life to overflowing. Lord, I have all that I need in You. Thank You, Lord. Amen.

Read John 1:1–13

IN HIM WAS LIFE, AND THE LIFE WAS THE LIGHT OF MEN. AND THE LIGHT
SHINES IN THE DARKNESS, AND THE DARKNESS DID NOT COMPREHEND IT.

John 1:4–5

Life cannot be sustained without light; without it all living things will die. If you take a seedling and place it in a dark cupboard it will shrivel up and die. In order for a crop to grow it needs the sunlight. Children cannot grow strong and healthy if they do not get regular doses of vitamin D, which comes from the sunlight. In Genesis 1:2–3 we read: "The earth was without form, and void; and darkness was on the face of the deep. And the Spirit of God was hovering over the face of the waters. Then God said, "Let there be light"; and there was light." Before God created anything else, He created the light, in order to sustain life.

The apostle John writes that John the Baptist came to bear witness to Jesus. He came ahead of Jesus preparing the way and calling people to repentance. John's job was to tell people about the coming Messiah. "In Him was life, and the life was the light of men. And the light shines in the darkness, and the darkness did not comprehend it. We know that, just as there are today, in those days also there were people who "did not comprehend". Like John the Baptist, we too are called to share Jesus, the Light of the world, with people.

"Then Jesus spoke to them again, saying, 'I am the light of the world. He who follows Me shall not walk in darkness, but have the light of life'" (John 8:12). We have to make sure that we give people the opportunity to move from Satan's kingdom of darkness into God's Kingdom of Light. It is either Light or darkness, my friends. The darkness leads to eternal death, whereas the Light leads to eternal life. Faithfully share Jesus with those you come into contact with. God promises us: "Arise, shine; for your light has come! And the glory of the Lord is risen upon you" (Isaiah 60:1). Heed the call to faithfully share the gospel of Jesus Christ, the Light of the world.

Prayer

My Father, like John the Baptist, I too want to be a faithful witness for Jesus, the Light of the world. Lord, there is nothing outside of You. You have saved me and rescued me from the kingdom of darkness. I want to share the Good News of Your marvellous Light with everyone that I come upon. Amen.

Read Matthew 23:1–14

DO NOT CALL ANYONE ON EARTH YOUR FATHER; FOR ONE IS YOUR FATHER, HE WHO IS IN HEAVEN. AND DO NOT BE CALLED TEACHERS; FOR ONE IS YOUR TEACHER, THE CHRIST. BUT HE WHO IS GREATEST AMONG YOU SHALL BE YOUR SERVANT. AND WHOEVER EXALTS HIMSELF WILL BE HUMBLED, AND HE WHO HUMBLES HIMSELF WILL BE EXALTED.

Matthew 23:9–12

Jesus reserved His harshest criticism for the church of His day. In Matthew 23 He had some very uncomplimentary things to say about the religious leaders of that time. The Scribes and the Pharisees were supposed to be the ones who led the people into truth. They were supposed to help them understand the law and draw closer to God. Yet all that they did was lead the people further into bondage. Religion, my friends, will never lead you to freedom – only Jesus can do that. Obeying a set of rules and dogma will only make you religious; it won't make you righteous.

Jesus said that there was no other true teacher but Himself. He said to the people, "for One is your Teacher, the Christ." Jesus came to earth to reveal the Father; He came to share the will of the Father with mankind. The people didn't need a list of rules to follow; they needed Jesus. Down through the ages people have always more easily gravitated toward following a list of rules and regulations than they have to living in freedom. Jesus came to seek and save; He came to teach mankind about the love that the Father has for each one of us. You would have expected people to jump at the opportunity to make right with God. Yet, the religious leaders and those who followed them chose to remain in their bondage to the law.

Jesus is still our Teacher today: He gave us His Holy Spirit who is living inside of us. His Spirit teaches us the things of God, revealing to us the will of our Father in Heaven. If you have the Holy Spirit living inside of you then you have a built-in Instructor. He will lead you every step of the way through your life. You can trust your Teacher, the Christ who is the One and Only Teacher. Do not be like the religious people of Jesus' day who chose the dryness of religion rather than the freshness of life. Walk humbly with your Teacher today.

Prayer

My Father in Heaven, You are the One Father. Jesus, my Lord and Saviour, You are the One Teacher, the Christ. Lord, help me to walk humbly before You. Teach me and lead me into all truth that I may glorify You through my life. Lord, I want to be a true witness for You, sharing Your life with others. Amen.

Read Matthew 8:1–17

THEN JESUS SAID TO THE CENTURION, "GO YOUR WAY; AND AS YOU HAVE
BELIEVED, SO LET IT BE DONE FOR YOU." AND HIS SERVANT WAS HEALED THAT
SAME HOUR.

Matthew 8:13

The Gospels are filled with examples of Jesus, the Healer. John says that the world is not large enough to hold all the books containing stories of the works done by Jesus when He walked on this earth (John 21:25). But we have enough of them recorded to know that Jesus is indeed the Healer. He is the physical Healer, He is the spiritual Healer, and He is the emotional Healer. My friend, there is nothing and no one that Jesus Christ cannot heal. We also read that Jesus rewards those who believe. We have evidence of this in our reading; Jesus commended the centurion for his faith – "Assuredly, I say to you, I have not found such great faith, not even in Israel!" (verse 10b).

Do you need a healing touch from Jesus right now? I want to exhort you to believe in miracles; to trust in the Name of Jesus Christ, because the power is in His Name. I firmly believe that in these last days the Lord Jesus Christ is going to manifest Himself through signs, wonders, and miracles in a way we've not seen before. In Mark 16:17–18 we read: "And these signs will follow those who believe: In My name they will cast out demons; they will speak with new tongues; they will take up serpents; and if they drink anything deadly, it will by no means hurt them; they will lay hands on the sick, and they will recover."

Jesus is real. Jesus is alive! There is no other god who can bring healing. Only the Name that is above every other name can heal the broken-hearted and set the captives free. Remember, the power and the healing is in the Lord's Name. Jesus Christ is looking for men who will trust Him. Are you choosing to walk by faith or by sight at this moment? Come to Jesus, your Healer, and ask Him in faith for whatever it is that you have need of. He will do for you what He has done for millions and millions who have believed and asked in His Name.

Prayer

My Loving Heavenly Father, You are indeed a God of love and mercy. Your goodness is new to me every morning. Lord, I come to You in faith today, trusting in Jesus, my Healer. Lord, I ask You to touch me and heal me. Thank You, Lord, that You honour the prayer of faith. In Your loving Name. Amen.

Read John 15:1–17

GREATER LOVE HAS NO ONE THAN THIS, THAN TO LAY DOWN ONE'S LIFE FOR HIS FRIENDS. YOU ARE MY FRIENDS IF YOU DO WHATEVER I COMMAND YOU.

John 15:13–14

Joseph M. Scriven wrote the beautiful hymn way back in 1855: "What a friend we have in Jesus, all our sins and griefs to bear!" Proverbs 18:24b tells us: "But there is a friend who sticks closer than a brother." Jesus came to this world to befriend sinners – you and me, my friends. The religious leaders of His day condemned Him because He hung out with "undesirable characters". "For John came neither eating nor drinking, and they say, 'He has a demon.' The Son of Man came eating and drinking, and they say, 'Look, a glutton and a winebibber, a friend of tax collectors and sinners!' But wisdom is justified by her children" (Matthew 11:18–19).

You have a Friend whom you know will stand by you no matter what happens – who will be there in the good times as well as the bad times – His Name is Jesus. Apart from being your Lord and Saviour, your Master, your King, your Healer, and your Deliverer, He is also your true Friend. Jesus never leaves us and He never forsakes us, even if we wander from Him at times. Paul says: "If we are faithless, He remains faithful; He cannot deny Himself" (2 Timothy 2:13). Jesus' love for us is unconditional: we cannot earn it or deserve it. His love is a free gift that is accepted by faith.

He came to this world to reconcile sinful man to God, the Father. Jesus Himself said that there is no greater love than laying down your life for your friends. This is exactly what He did: He laid down His life for His friends. His friends are each and every person who accepts Him as their Lord and Saviour. Our love response to Jesus, for the sacrifice that He made on our behalf, is that we will obey His commandments. Jesus says that you are His friend if you obey His commandments. He invites us to walk a faith walk with Him that will lead us all the way to Heaven. Won't you join your Best Friend, Jesus, on this walk?

Prayer

My Father God in Heaven, You sent Your Son to reconcile man to Yourself. Lord Jesus, You are my Best Friend. There is no one else like You. Jesus, I can depend upon You no matter what happens, no matter how hard things become. Lord Jesus, I want to walk in Your commandments doing Your will. Amen.

JESUS, THE RIGHTEOUS JUDGE

Read John 5:24–30

> FOR AS THE FATHER HAS LIFE IN HIMSELF, SO HE HAS GRANTED THE SON
> TO HAVE LIFE IN HIMSELF, AND HAS GIVEN HIM AUTHORITY TO EXECUTE
> JUDGMENT ALSO, BECAUSE HE IS THE SON OF MAN.
>
> John 5:26–27

In the story that took place just before our reading today, Jesus healed the sick man next to the pool in Bethesda. After this incident the religious leaders once again took issue with Jesus. There were several things they were unhappy about, but primarily His claim that God was His Father. Furthermore He claimed that He was on earth to do the work of His Father. They did not understand that Jesus Christ was God's Righteousness revealed on earth. He came to seek and to save the lost. "As it is written: 'There is none righteous, no, not one'" (Romans 3:10). Man's righteousness is as filthy rags – we cannot save ourselves.

Jesus came to do the will of His Father. He listened to and did only what the Father told Him to do: "I can of Myself do nothing. As I hear, I judge; and My judgment is righteous, because I do not seek My own will but the will of the Father who sent Me" (John 5:30). John 3:17–21 tells us:

> For God did not send His Son into the world to condemn the world, but
> that the world through Him might be saved. He who believes in Him is not
> condemned; but he who does not believe is condemned already, because he
> has not believed in the name of the only begotten Son of God. And this is the
> condemnation, that the light has come into the world, and men loved darkness
> rather than light, because their deeds were evil. For everyone practicing evil
> hates the light and does not come to the light, lest his deeds should be exposed.
> But he who does the truth comes to the light, that his deeds may be clearly
> seen, that they have been done in God.

Be sure, my friend, that when Jesus returns to this earth one day He will come as the Righteous Judge. "Now I saw heaven opened, and behold, a white horse. And He who sat on him was called Faithful and True, and in righteousness He judges and makes war" (Revelation 19:11).

Prayer

My Father God, You are the Righteous Judge. You sent Jesus, Your only begotten Son, to this world to seek and to save sinners, like me. Lord, You have called me to repentance and Salvation. Thank You, Lord. I stand not in my own righteousness, but in the righteousness of my Righteous Judge. Amen.

Read John 5:16–23

> THEN JESUS ANSWERED AND SAID TO THEM, "MOST ASSUREDLY, I SAY
> TO YOU, THE SON CAN DO NOTHING OF HIMSELF, BUT WHAT HE SEES
> THE FATHER DO; FOR WHATEVER HE DOES, THE SON ALSO DOES IN LIKE
> MANNER."

John 5:19

Jesus modelled many things for His disciples when He walked on this earth, one of which was obedience to the Father. Jesus' whole life was about doing the will of His Father who sent Him. Throughout the Gospels we see Jesus in tune with the heart of the Father. Jesus didn't do anything without it being a direct order from God, His Father. We know that Jesus received His instructions from God during His times of prayer when He withdrew to be alone with His Father. Being obedient to the Father eventually led Jesus to Calvary. There He paid the ultimate price to secure our Salvation.

If there is one thing I have learned over the years it is that whenever things go wrong for me it is usually because I have tried to do things my way. Instead of waiting on the Lord I have gone my own way. The older I become in the Lord, the more I desire nothing other than to be in the very centre of His will, living in obedience to Him. There is no satisfaction or joy any place else, my friend. Every other path leads to heartache and failure. Jesus taught obedience to the Father to His disciples back then and He is still teaching it to us, His modern-day disciples.

We have often said that obedience is better than sacrifice. God is more interested in your day-to-day obedience than He is in any grand gesture you might seek to make: "what He sees the Father do; for whatever He does, the Son also does in like manner." So if you want to please the Father then follow the example of Jesus, His Son. Commit yourself to live a life of faith and obedience to Him. Then you will begin to see God at work in your life. It is at this point that He will be able to begin using you in ministry to do His work here on earth. If Jesus could do nothing outside of the Father, how can we ever think that we could?

Prayer

My Heavenly Father, there is no other road for me to walk except the road of faith and obedience. Lord, I have no desire for anything outside of Your will. Take my life and make it Yours. Fill me with Your Spirit's power. Lord, I submit to You and I choose to walk each day in obedience to You. Amen.

Read Matthew 6:5–13

But you, when you pray, go into your room, and when you have shut your door, pray to your Father who is in the secret place; and your Father who sees in secret will reward you openly. And when you pray, do not use vain repetitions as the heathen do. For they think that they will be heard for their many words.

Matthew 6:6–7

Our Father in heaven,
Hallowed be Your name.

My friend, we need to treat God with respect because Jesus did. We pray to the Father, through the Son, by the power of the Holy Spirit.

Your kingdom come.
Your will be done
On earth as it is in heaven.

God's will be done, not my will; and certainly not anyone else's will.

Give us this day our daily bread.

This is not about coming to God with your shopping list – give me, give me, give me. Jesus says, "Give us this day our daily bread", meaning give us enough – just enough. God gave the Israelites in the wilderness enough for each day. If they became greedy and tried to pick up more manna than they could eat it went rotten. It is the constant desire for more that causes much of the heartache in our society. You don't need to store up riches on earth when you have untold riches in Heaven.

Let not your heart be troubled; you believe in God, believe also in Me. In My
Father's house are many mansions; if it were not so, I would have told you.
I go to prepare a place for you. And if I go and prepare a place for you, I will
come again and receive you to Myself; that where I am, there you may be also.
And where I go you know, and the way you know.

John 14:1–4

This is faith, my friends: choosing to walk one day at a time by faith and not by sight.

Prayer

My Father, I come to You in the precious Name of Jesus Christ, Your Son and my Saviour. Jesus, thank You that You are the Mighty Prayer Warrior. When You were on this earth You modelled what it means to live a powerful life of prayer. You taught me in so many ways how to pray to the Father. Amen.

Read Matthew 6:5–13

IN THIS MANNER, THEREFORE, PRAY: OUR FATHER IN HEAVEN, HALLOWED BE YOUR NAME. YOUR KINGDOM COME. YOUR WILL BE DONE ON EARTH AS IT IS IN HEAVEN. GIVE US THIS DAY OUR DAILY BREAD.

Matthew 6:9–11

And forgive us our debts,
As we forgive our debtors.

This can be a hard one: if you have an issue with someone in your family you need to forgive them. You might say, "Angus, I have forgiven them but they won't forgive me." There is nothing you can do about that apart from pray. But you cannot hold anything against your family member or your loved one and expect God to forgive you. Jesus was a mighty Prayer Warrior and His disciples asked Him to teach them to pray after observing His prayer life. "Now it came to pass, as He was praying in a certain place, when He ceased, that one of His disciples said to Him, 'Lord, teach us to pray…'" (Luke 11:1)

Jesus taught His disciples to pray this prayer. Why? Because maybe some of them were in that same situation.

And do not lead us into temptation,
But deliver us from the evil one.

My dear friend, I have never seen as much temptation as I am observing in the world today. It is so easily available on cell phones, computers, tablets, and iPads. I want to tell you it is dangerous. Please, please, when you pray this prayer, mean it from the bottom of your heart. "And do not lead us into temptation." You see, being tempted is not the sin; it is succumbing to the temptation that is the sin. So if the temptation is not there then you will not be tempted. Don't go where you know danger lurks waiting to trip you up. If you have a drinking problem don't go into a pub. If you have a lust problem don't look at pornography on the Internet or television. If you are a drug addict avoid hanging out with people who can provide you with drugs. Avoid the temptation at all costs. Spend time in the Word, and in prayer: "But deliver us from the evil one." Living a holy life is a day-by-day choice to follow Jesus.

Prayer

Father God, You are my loving Father who constantly draws me through Your Spirit to Yourself. When You walked on this earth, Jesus, You taught Your disciples so many things: lessons that help me to live for You today. Thank You for Your Holy Spirit, who is within me, guiding and directing me. Amen.

Read Matthew 6:8–21

DO NOT LAY UP FOR YOURSELVES TREASURES ON EARTH, WHERE MOTH
AND RUST DESTROY AND WHERE THIEVES BREAK IN AND STEAL; BUT LAY UP
FOR YOURSELVES TREASURES IN HEAVEN, WHERE NEITHER MOTH NOR RUST
DESTROYS AND WHERE THIEVES DO NOT BREAK IN AND STEAL. FOR WHERE
YOUR TREASURE IS, THERE YOUR HEART WILL BE ALSO.

Matthew 6:19–21

For Yours is the kingdom and the power and the glory forever. Amen.

There is nothing more temporal than the time we have on this earth. Psalm 103:15–18 tells us:

As for man, his days are like grass; as a flower of the field, so he flourishes. For the wind passes over it, and it is gone, and its place remembers it no more. But the mercy of the Lord is from everlasting to everlasting on those who fear Him, and His righteousness to children's children, to such as keep His covenant, and to those who remember His commandments to do them.

Our ultimate destination is Heaven if we are a child of God. This is why Jesus told us not to store up our treasure here on earth. We should be living our lives building God's Kingdom while we are on earth.

Jesus, the Heir of all things, came from Heaven to earth to show us how to live. "I came forth from the Father and have come into the world. Again, I leave the world and go to the Father" (John 16:28).

Jesus, the Heir of all things, never had a permanent home while He was on earth. He never owned a farm, a fishing boat, or a house. He said, "Foxes have holes and birds of the air have nests, but the Son of Man has nowhere to lay His head" (Matthew 8:20).

I am, of course, not implying that it is wrong to own a home or a farm, or anything else for that matter. Of course I am not; God has blessed me and my family with these things. What I am saying is that they are not to be our focus. They are not to consume all our energy; they are not to be our first priority. God and His Kingdom is to be our first and main priority. We are to trust Jesus, the Heir of all things, with our daily needs. We are to walk in faith as He walked in faith on this earth, relying upon the Father.

Prayer

My Father, thank You that You supply all my needs according to Your riches in Christ Jesus, my Saviour and Redeemer. Lord, You have called me to live a life that is not focused solely upon the here and now. My ultimate home is in Heaven with You. My calling is to establish Your Kingdom for Your glory on this earth. Amen.

Read John 7:37–52

> ON THE LAST DAY, THAT GREAT DAY OF THE FEAST, JESUS STOOD AND CRIED OUT, SAYING, "IF ANYONE THIRSTS, LET HIM COME TO ME AND DRINK. HE WHO BELIEVES IN ME, AS THE SCRIPTURE HAS SAID, OUT OF HIS HEART WILL FLOW RIVERS OF LIVING WATER." BUT THIS HE SPOKE CONCERNING THE SPIRIT, WHOM THOSE BELIEVING IN HIM WOULD RECEIVE; FOR THE HOLY SPIRIT WAS NOT YET GIVEN, BECAUSE JESUS WAS NOT YET GLORIFIED.
>
> John 7:37–39

Everything in the Christian life is dependent upon faith; upon believing. I love the way the King James Version puts our key verse: "He that *believeth* on me, as the scripture hath said, out of his belly shall flow rivers of living water" (verse 38, KJV, my italics). Folks, I ask you today: do you believe? If you answer yes, then my next question is in whom do you believe? Notice I am not asking you what you believe. Too many Christians become caught up in dogma and doctrine. I have no problem with this as long as it doesn't take the place of what is important.

In whom do we believe? We are to believe in Jesus Christ; we are to have faith in Jesus, the Son of God – the Living Water. We do not have faith in faith. We have faith in a Person. How do we receive faith? Romans 10:17 tells us: "So then faith comes by hearing, and hearing by the word of God." This is how we receive faith: by hearing. I believe with John that Jesus Christ is the Word. He says: "In the beginning was the Word, and the Word was with God, and the Word was God" (John 1:1). You will remember we discussed Jesus, the Word, on the first day of this month. I am a fundamentalist and I believe in the literal Word of God. I believe it from cover to cover. I believe the Bible is the inspired Word of God.

Jesus came to this earth so that we could see the Word made flesh. He walked this earth, and He taught His disciples, giving them – and us, His future disciples – a clear vision of what it means to be His followers. Are you drinking daily from His Living Waters? Are you filled with His Spirit? As Jesus' followers we should be the conduit to share His Living Water with the thirsty world around us. You have what people need, my friend, so share it. Tell others about Jesus, the Living Water, who is the only One who can satisfy their thirst.

Prayer

My Father, I thank You for Jesus, the Living Water, who is the clear manifestation of Your grace and mercy. Lord, You have invited me to come and drink. I thank You that I can come time and again to receive Your Living Water. Lord, You constantly refresh me. I believe in Jesus Christ the Word made flesh. Amen.

Read John 14:1–11

> JESUS SAID TO HIM, "I AM THE WAY, THE TRUTH, AND THE LIFE. NO ONE
> COMES TO THE FATHER EXCEPT THROUGH ME."
>
> John 14:6

God instructs us to love people – we are to show the world God's love. This does not mean, though, that we are to condone sin or compromise the truth. I think sometimes we are confused on this issue. Too many Christians are reluctant to stand up for the truth. At work, do you shrink back when you see something that is blatantly wrong? God has called us to be salt and light to the world around us.

How many of us are prepared to stand up for the gospel when there is a discussion and the general consensus is that all roads lead to Heaven? God has clearly told us in His Word that there is only one way to Heaven and that is through Jesus Christ, His Son. "Enter by the narrow gate; for wide is the gate and broad is the way that leads to destruction, and there are many who go in by it. Because narrow is the gate and difficult is the way which leads to life, and there are few who find it" (Matthew 7:13–14). We have been entrusted with the task of sharing the Good News of the gospel.

How will people know that Jesus is the Way to a relationship with God, the Father, if we don't tell them? My friends, I love Jesus more than life itself. I have a burning desire to share His love and forgiveness with people. Jesus loves sinners: He loves me and He loves you. He loves your next-door neighbour and the person who sits at the desk next to you at work. The Word tells us that faith comes by hearing, and without faith it is impossible to please God. So it is up to us to share the gospel so that people have the opportunity to hear the Word. They need to be given the chance to accept that Jesus is the Way to the Father, and believe in Him as their personal Saviour. Are you going to step out in faith and share with them so that they can have what you have?

Prayer

My Father, I thank You for Jesus who is the Way to eternal life and Heaven. Lord, I want to be a faithful witness and share the gospel with those with whom I come into contact. Help me not to compromise, but to stand up for what I believe. Help me to be a witness not only by what I say, but also through what I do. Amen.

Read John 8:31–36

> THEN JESUS SAID TO THOSE JEWS WHO BELIEVED HIM, "IF YOU ABIDE IN MY
> WORD, YOU ARE MY DISCIPLES INDEED. AND YOU SHALL KNOW THE TRUTH,
> AND THE TRUTH SHALL MAKE YOU FREE."
>
> John 8:31–32

As we move toward the end of another year, I want to ask you: How is your relationship with Jesus, the Truth? I have to tell you that I am more in love with Jesus than ever before. I still have a fire burning within me that compels me to proclaim His truth to the world. You see, my friends, we do not preach an empty dogma. No, we preach Jesus the Living Word. He promises us "If you abide in My word, you are My disciples indeed. And you shall know the truth, and the truth shall make you free." How can you not want to share this freedom that you have found in Jesus with other people?

So I ask you: Do you have the same fire burning in you now as you did when you first came to know Jesus?" Do you feel compelled to shout from the rooftops, "Jesus is the only answer to the challenges faced by our world today. Jesus is the Way, the Truth and the Life!"? Folks, you don't need a theological degree to preach the gospel. That's not what preaching is about. Preaching is about sharing Jesus, the Truth; it is about speaking the Word of God simply, so that people can understand it.

It is the Lord Himself who will kindle a fire in your heart so that it will burst forth within you compelling you to proclaim His Name. Step out in faith and share with others what Jesus has done for you. Tell your story about His grace, love, and mercy in your life. Then invite them to come and be introduced to Jesus, who is the only Truth, the only Way, and the only Life. There is no greater or more precious gift: He is the best thing you can ever do for anyone. When the disciples were introduced to Jesus they couldn't stop themselves: they immediately introduced their friends and relatives to Jesus. How can you, as His beloved child, do anything less than introduce those that you love to Jesus, the Truth?

Prayer

My Father God, there is none like You. I love You, my Father. Thank You today for Jesus, who is the Truth. You have placed a fire within me that grows stronger and stronger as time goes by. Lord, I have one desire and that is to share You with the world around me. I want everyone to know You. Amen.

Read 1 John 5:1–13

AND THIS IS THE TESTIMONY: THAT GOD HAS GIVEN US ETERNAL LIFE, AND THIS LIFE IS IN HIS SON. HE WHO HAS THE SON HAS LIFE; HE WHO DOES NOT HAVE THE SON OF GOD DOES NOT HAVE LIFE.

1 John 5:11–12

John 14:6 says: "Jesus said to him, 'I am the way, the truth, and the life. No one comes to the Father except through Me.'" In our key verse John puts it like this: "God has given us eternal life, and this life is in His Son. He who has the Son has life". The Word of God is clear about this, my friend: all roads do not lead to God or to Heaven. God, the Father, wants us to know that there is life, eternal life, only in His Son – Jesus is the Life.

I have shared with you many times about the mess my life was in when I was younger. It reached a point where I didn't know which way to turn or what I should do next. I wonder if you can identify with this. Maybe you are also at the point where you don't know if there is hope for you. I understand how you feel and I invite you to do what I did: cry out to God. He will do for you what He did for me: He will reveal His Son, Jesus Christ, to you. Jesus stands before you and He says: "but whoever drinks of the water that I shall give him will never thirst. But the water that I shall give him will become in him a fountain of water springing up into everlasting life" (John 4:14).

When I met Jesus and received everlasting life my whole life instantly changed. Not only did my life have purpose, but I had hope for the present as well as for the future. It is close on forty years now and, as I said yesterday, I love Jesus more today than I did back then – if that is possible. It doesn't matter what is happening in the world around me: He is my Life. My friend, if Jesus Christ is the Lord of your life you have nothing to fear. Jesus, the Life, will transform you, you will become a new creation in Him and He will give you eternal life.

Prayer

Lord God in Heaven, I bow in Your presence, my God and Father. Thank You for loving me. Thank You for Jesus, the Life. I am so grateful that You reached down and lifted me out of the miry pit. Thank You for putting my feet upon a sure and steady path. I have eternal life and I live for You. Amen.

Read Hebrews 4

> Seeing then that we have a great High Priest who has passed through the heavens, Jesus the Son of God, let us hold fast our confession. For we do not have a High Priest who cannot sympathize with our weaknesses, but was in all points tempted as we are, yet without sin. Let us therefore come boldly to the throne of grace that we may obtain mercy and find grace to help in time of need.
>
> Hebrews 4:14–16

Whatever you are going through in your life right now, you can take courage because Jesus your Redeemer and your High Priest is with you. Turn to Him, not away from Him, with your troubles and problems. All it takes is for you to trust Him, to place your faith wholeheartedly in Him. The greatest sin in the Bible is the sin of unbelief. We need to start believing the Word of God; we need to take God at His Word. The other day I said to you that if the Bible says it, I believe it. I have no time for people dissecting God's Word and intellectualizing it.

You either believe God's Word or you don't. Remember, Jesus could perform very few miracles in Nazareth because of the people's unbelief. Jesus is our High Priest: He died, rose from the grave and ascended to Heaven, where He sits at the right hand of the Father.

So always remember:

> For such a High Priest was fitting for us, who is holy, harmless, undefiled, separate from sinners, and has become higher than the heavens; who does not need daily, as those high priests, to offer up sacrifices, first for His own sins and then for the people's, for this He did once for all when He offered up Himself.
>
> Hebrews 7:26–27

Jesus' sacrifice was a once-and-for-all sacrifice. He made it possible for us to enter into the Father's presence freely without any fear. Jesus, our High Priest, has gone before us; He has prepared the way. Don't hang back. Approach the throne of grace with confidence, knowing that Jesus is there waiting to receive you and mediate on your behalf.

Prayer

Dear Lord God, thank You that I have a Mediator who is present in Heaven to intercede on my behalf. Lord, thank You that Your Holy Spirit within me helps me to pray. You know that sometimes it is so hard, but thank You, Jesus, that You are my High Priest who knows everything. Amen.

Read Matthew 3:13–17

> AND SUDDENLY A VOICE CAME FROM HEAVEN, SAYING, "THIS IS MY BELOVED
> SON, IN WHOM I AM WELL PLEASED."
>
> Matthew 3:17

Saving us from our sins cost God, the Father, dearly. The day that John the Baptist baptized Jesus we see God reaching down from Heaven and telling us just how much He loves Jesus Christ, His Son. John put it like this: "For God so loved the world that He gave His only begotten Son, that whoever believes in Him should not perish but have everlasting life" (John 3:16). God understands the love that a parent has for a child. The wonderful thing, my friends, is that through Jesus' sacrifice you and I have also become God's much-loved children.

Jesus, the Lamb of God, made the sacrifice for our sins so that we can be reconciled to the Father. "The next day John saw Jesus coming toward him, and said, 'Behold! The Lamb of God who takes away the sin of the world!'" (John 1:29).

Through His sacrifice on Calvary Jesus became the Saviour of the world. The *Collins Dictionary* says the word "salvation" means "the state of being preserved from harm". Isn't that amazing? It is a natural human desire to want to be safe; to be preserved from harm. No normal person purposefully puts themselves in harm's way. Security is one of the main needs that people have. You need protection, you need love, you need security, you need a reason for living, and you need hope for the future. This is where Salvation comes in. Salvation is a state of being preserved from harm. I will ask you straight out: "Are you born again, my dear friend?" Remember I am just a farmer, but I love you desperately and that is the reason I am compelled to proclaim the gospel. I would be quite happy just farming if it wasn't that Jesus wants me to tell you the truth in love. As Jesus said: "Most assuredly, I say to you, unless one is born again, he cannot see the kingdom of God" (John 3:3). As we approach the day when we celebrate Jesus' birth, let us also remember the sacrifice He made in order to secure our future.

Prayer

My Father, God in Heaven, thank You that You sent Your Beloved Son to this world as a helpless babe in a manger. He grew and ultimately died on the cross so that I can know You and be called Your child. Lord, thank You for the security, the love, and safe haven I have in You. Amen.

Read Mark 4:35–41

> THEN HE AROSE AND REBUKED THE WIND, AND SAID TO THE SEA, "PEACE, BE STILL!" AND THE WIND CEASED AND THERE WAS A GREAT CALM.
>
> Mark 4:39

Countless people are walking around in South Africa at the moment – indeed in countries throughout the world – stressed and depressed. People are overwhelmed by the economic situation, the crime rate, and many other issues that stem from modern-day living. I know exactly how it feels to be stressed and to feel that you cannot cope – I've been there. Before I came to know the Lord Jesus Christ, I was a farmer who had five children to feed, clothe, and educate. Jill was a diligent, hardworking housewife and she did a lot to help me. But I used to become so stressed out that I couldn't sleep at night.

Some of you will understand what I am talking about: it is called insomnia. You lie in bed and you go into a cold sweat because you know that tomorrow you have to do a full day's work and you just don't have the strength. That's stress; as it builds up your heart begins pumping and it races like you are running a 100-metre dash. In the meantime you are lying in your bed in a pool of perspiration becoming weaker and weaker. It is at this point that the molehill becomes Mount Everest in your life.

You don't even want to get up in the morning. You eventually fall asleep at 3 a.m. and the alarm clock goes off at 4 a.m. Outwardly you look fine and there is nothing wrong with you physically. People tell you to pull yourself together, read the Word of God, and pray then He will undertake. But it is not as easy as that, is it? This is why I have a heart for anyone who suffers from depression or anxiety. Jesus understands what you are going through. He is able to bring about peace and calm in the midst of whatever storm you are going through. You don't have to pretend with Him; come to Him as you are – tell Him all that is going on and He will walk with you through the storm. Don't let go of Him: trust Him and not your circumstances.

Prayer

My Father God, I come to You today in the Name of Jesus, who can calm the storm that is raging in my life at the moment. Lord Jesus, thank You that You understand what I am going through. I can rest in You, I can relax in You, knowing that You love and accept me as I am. I choose to trust You. Amen.

Read Isaiah 26:1–12

> YOU WILL KEEP HIM IN PERFECT PEACE, WHOSE MIND IS STAYED ON YOU,
> BECAUSE HE TRUSTS IN YOU. TRUST IN THE LORD FOREVER, FOR IN YAH, THE
> LORD, IS EVERLASTING STRENGTH.
>
> Isaiah 26:3–4

When I came to Christ I literally handed my burdens over to Him. When I gave Jesus Christ my life, I also gave Him the responsibility I felt for my wife, my children, and the farm. Later on, once the ministry began growing, I also gave that over to Jesus – after all it is His not mine – and I continue doing this today still. It is the only reason that I can sleep well at night; it is the only reason I don't become stressed out. I couldn't cope before I was saved, so what happened? I am still the same person, with the same limitations, and the same character. I will tell you what happened: I took my burdens and gave them to Jesus. I took my responsibilities and I gave them to Jesus. Are you doing this?

You see, folks, stress is often brought upon us by the pressure of the world. Isaiah knew the remedy for stress: "You will keep him in perfect peace, whose mind is stayed on You, because he trusts in You."

The Bible clearly says: "The Lord is my helper; I will not fear. What can man do to me?" (Hebrews 13:6). If Jesus Christ is the Lord of your life, and if you are spending time with Him every day, you should not become stressed.

The opposite of fear is faith. "For God has not given us a spirit of fear, but of power and of love and of a sound mind" (2 Timothy 1:7). This is a promise from God. The Bible does not tell lies, friends. I have tested God's Word countless times over the years. I am telling you that every word in the Bible is true. I invite you to begin testing it for yourself today. Don't allow the enemy to rob you of what is yours in Jesus. He came to this world so that you and I can experience God's peace on a daily basis. So follow Isaiah's advice and "trust in the LORD forever, for in YAH, the Lord, is everlasting strength."

Prayer

My Father God, I come to You, Lord, and I bow at Your feet. I place my burdens at the foot of the cross. Lord God, I choose today to keep my mind firmly stayed upon You. Lord, I will trust You and only You. I know that only in You is there everlasting strength, peace, and security. Thank You, Lord. Amen.

Read Luke 2:8–20

> GLORY TO GOD IN THE HIGHEST, AND ON EARTH PEACE, GOODWILL TOWARD MEN!
>
> Luke 2:14

These are the words of the hymn of praise sung by the angels to the shepherds in the fields as they heralded Jesus' birth. Centuries prior to this event the prophet Isaiah wrote: "For unto us a Child is born, unto us a Son is given; and the government will be upon His shoulder. And His name will be called Wonderful, Counselor, Mighty God, Everlasting Father, Prince of Peace" (Isaiah 9:6). As we mentioned at the beginning of this month, Jesus is known by 200 different names in the Bible, Prince of Peace being one of them. One of the benefits of Salvation is that we receive Peace. We have said it so many times, but it is the truth: Peace is not a state of mind or a feeling; it is a Person, Jesus Christ.

Peace comes as a result of having our sins forgiven. "And He said to her, 'Daughter, your faith has made you well. Go in peace, and be healed of your affliction'" (Mark 5:34). Notice that Jesus tells the woman that her faith has made her well, and then He tells her to go in peace, and be healed. So, my friend, if you have a need today, come to Jesus the Prince of Peace in faith; trust Him to meet your need and then go in peace as you continue to walk by faith.

Jesus, the Prince of Peace, even has control of the elements. "Then He arose and rebuked the wind, and said to the sea, 'Peace, be still!' And the wind ceased and there was a great calm" (Mark 4:39).

No matter what you are going through at the moment you can know complete peace in the midst of the storm, if you know Jesus. As a Christian your peace is not dependent upon your circumstances.

"Peace I leave with you, My peace I give to you; not as the world gives do I give to you. Let not your heart be troubled, neither let it be afraid" (John 14:27). "These things I have spoken to you, that in Me you may have peace" (John 16:33a).

Prayer

My Father in Heaven, I am so grateful that You sent Jesus, the Prince of Peace to this world to save me. Lord, I can now live a victorious life because I do not walk alone. My life is hidden in You. I rest and hide in Your love and peace. I can face all things as I walk each day trusting You to undertake for me. Amen.

JESUS, THE OBEDIENT SON

Read Luke 22:39–46

> ... AND HE KNELT DOWN AND PRAYED, SAYING, "FATHER, IF IT IS YOUR WILL, TAKE THIS CUP AWAY FROM ME; NEVERTHELESS NOT MY WILL, BUT YOURS, BE DONE." THEN AN ANGEL APPEARED TO HIM FROM HEAVEN, STRENGTHENING HIM.
>
> Luke 22:41b–43

The devil is trying to kill us with his lies. If you have heard me preach and speak then you will know that I don't give the devil any glory. But we have to be honest about one thing and that is that he does exist. We know this because Jesus spoke about him. When we are under stress and pressure we must apply the same principles that Jesus did when He was under pressure. When Jesus was in the garden of Gethsemane He was so stressed that He began sweating great drops of blood. I have read medical accounts that say it is possible for a person to actually sweat blood when they are under extreme pressure.

Now Jesus was God, but remember: He was also a man who was tempted in every way, just like you and I are tempted. Jesus warned His disciples in the garden: "When He rose up from prayer, and had come to His disciples, He found them sleeping from sorrow. Then He said to them, 'Why do you sleep? Rise and pray, lest you enter into temptation'" (verses 45–46). Isn't it interesting – when Jesus was under stress He turned to His Father and prayed. When the disciples were under pressure they fell asleep. "He found them sleeping from sorrow." How do you react to stress?

What Jesus faced was far greater than anything we could ever face. He faced separation from His Father and the knowledge that He had to die on the cross. So how did Jesus overcome the stress factor? He conquered it on His knees in the garden of Gethsemane. All His trusted men were sound asleep and He was on His own – only He wasn't on His own, was He? No, God sent angels to strengthen Him. Jesus found ultimate peace in submission to the will of His Father for Him – "... not My will, but Yours, be done." We will find peace and strength in the same way, by following Jesus' example and submitting to the will of the Father for our lives.

Prayer

My Father, You are good and loving. Your kindness stretches from generation to generation. Father, Your will for my life is perfect and good. Lord, I follow Jesus' example and submit to Your will. Help me to rest in it; strengthen me as You did Jesus. Lord, I want to walk in obedience and submission to You. Amen.

Read Colossians 3:1–11

> FOR YOU DIED, AND YOUR LIFE IS HIDDEN WITH CHRIST IN GOD. WHEN
> CHRIST WHO IS OUR LIFE APPEARS, THEN YOU ALSO WILL APPEAR WITH HIM
> IN GLORY.
>
> Colossians 3:3–4

As a child of God, "your life is hidden with Christ in God." One day soon Jesus is coming back to receive you for Himself. He is coming to fetch us, so that we can be with Him in God's Kingdom. Paul urges the Colossians to put away anything that will prevent them from being ready for Christ appearing (verses 5–9). He says we are to "put on the new man who is renewed in knowledge according to the image of Him who created him" (verse 10). How are you doing when it comes to putting off the old man, my friend? The only way you can live a righteous life is if your life is hidden in Jesus.

It is His righteousness that needs to cover you. Romans 3:10 tells us: "As it is written: 'There is none righteous, no, not one'" – the reason being, "For He made Him who knew no sin to be sin for us, that we might become the righteousness of God in Him" (2 Corinthians 5:21). The time is short, my friends. Jesus is coming to fetch those who are faithful – will that be you? Don't allow the trials and stresses of this life to cause you to let go of the baton this late in the race.

The blessed assurance that you have as a believer is that you are hidden with Christ. He is all and everything you will ever need. It doesn't matter what you go through here on earth, your home is in Heaven with Jesus. You are only passing through this world on your way to your eternal home.

> *Do not lay up for yourselves treasures on earth, where moth and rust destroy*
> *and where thieves break in and steal; but lay up for yourselves treasures in*
> *heaven, where neither moth nor rust destroys and where thieves do not break*
> *in and steal. For where your treasure is, there your heart will be also.*
>
> Matthew 6:19–21

Travel lightly and make sure that your heart does not become mired in the mud of the cares and stresses of this world.

Prayer

My Father, I lift my voice to You in praise and worship. I bring You the praises of a grateful heart today. Thank You that this is not my home. My treasure is laid up in Heaven with You. Jesus, I am hidden in You; I stand in Your righteousness alone. Lord, I look to You and long to see You. Amen.

Read John 18:33–38

> PILATE THEREFORE SAID TO HIM, "ARE YOU A KING THEN?" JESUS
> ANSWERED, "YOU SAY RIGHTLY THAT I AM A KING. FOR THIS CAUSE I WAS
> BORN, AND FOR THIS CAUSE I HAVE COME INTO THE WORLD, THAT I SHOULD
> BEAR WITNESS TO THE TRUTH. EVERYONE WHO IS OF THE TRUTH HEARS MY
> VOICE."
>
> John 18:37

The Jewish people of Jesus' day lived under Roman oppression. They wanted a king who would establish an earthly kingdom and set them free. Jesus spent a lot of time explaining to the people that He had not come to overthrow the government of the day. Even His disciples, right up to the last, hoped that He would establish an earthly kingdom. Eventually they understood that the Kingdom Jesus came to establish was a Heavenly one. As a result of Jesus' death we have moved from the kingdom of this world to become citizens of His Heavenly Kingdom.

Jesus rode into Jerusalem on the back of a donkey at the last Passover before His crucifixion. He was the Servant-King. He wore a towel around His waist and washed His disciples' dirty feet. He suffered death on the cross. When Jesus returns the second time, the book of Revelation tells us He is coming on the clouds, and every eye will see Him. He returns as the King of kings and the Lord of lords. Jesus returns as the Judge, the Commander of all the armies of Heaven. He has the keys of hell and death and he is coming on the back of a white charger. He is coming to do battle once and for all with the devil. In righteousness He will judge and make war. It will be a great and terrible day. The Day of Judgment where every knee shall bow, every tongue will confess He is Lord.

John says in Revelation 1:5: "and from Jesus Christ, the faithful witness, the firstborn from the dead, and the ruler over the kings of the earth. To Him who loved us and washed us from our sins in His own blood". Our allegiance is to Jesus who is your King and my King. We don't live according to this world's rules, but according to the rules of God's Kingdom. As you move toward the end of this year take some time to pay homage to King Jesus. Give Him the praise, honour, and worship that is due His Name.

Prayer

My Father God, I pay homage at Your throne of Grace. Lord Jesus, my King and my Saviour, I kneel before You to give You the gratitude of a humble servant. Lord, thank You that I am a citizen of Your eternal Kingdom that knows no end. I give You praise, glory, and honour due to Your Holy Name. Amen.

Read Revelation 19:11–16

> NOW I SAW HEAVEN OPENED, AND BEHOLD, A WHITE HORSE. AND HE WHO
> SAT ON HIM WAS CALLED FAITHFUL AND TRUE, AND IN RIGHTEOUSNESS HE
> JUDGES AND MAKES WAR… AND HE HAS ON HIS ROBE AND ON HIS THIGH A
> NAME WRITTEN: KING OF KINGS AND LORD OF LORDS.
>
> Revelation 19:11, 16

Before Jesus left this earth He made us a promise:

> *Let not your heart be troubled; you believe in God, believe also in Me. In My Father's*
> *house are many mansions; if it were not so, I would have told you. I go to prepare a place*
> *for you. And if I go and prepare a place for you, I will come again and receive you to*
> *Myself; that where I am, there you may be also.*
>
> John 14:1–3

Revelation says He is called "Faithful and True" – Jesus keeps His promises, my friend.
When Jesus came the first time He came as a helpless babe in a manger. As we said
yesterday, when Jesus returns He will be riding a white horse – He will return as the
Righteous Judge; He

> *judges and makes war. His eyes were like a flame of fire, and on His head were many*
> *crowns… He was clothed with a robe dipped in blood, and His name is called The Word*
> *of God… Now out of His mouth goes a sharp sword, that with it He should strike the*
> *nations. And He Himself will rule them with a rod of iron.*
>
> Revelation 19:11c–12a, 13, 15a

Over the years I have become a cloud watcher. I am looking skyward, watching and
waiting for my King Jesus' return – the day is fast approaching, folks. Where are you
looking today? Are you caught up with the cares of this world or are you looking
to the clouds waiting in anticipation for the Bridegroom to return? Where do you
stand right now: is your life in order with the Lord? We need to be ready to go home
at a moment's notice. If God comes knocking at your door now, will He find you
ready? "No, Angus, I am not ready. I haven't packed my bags yet; I have unfinished
business." If this is your answer, then, my friend, make haste to get ready. King Jesus
is coming soon and you need to be ready to meet Him; to welcome Him as your "King
of kings and Lord of lords".

Prayer
Almighty God, Ruler of Heaven and earth, I bow before You. I lift my hands in surrender to
Your Holy Name. I look to Jesus, my Soon-coming King. I declare You to be "King of kings and
Lord of lords". I am watching and waiting. I am ready, Lord, and looking forward to spending
eternity with You. Amen.

Read Matthew 28:9–20

> AND JESUS CAME AND SPOKE TO THEM, SAYING, "ALL AUTHORITY HAS
> BEEN GIVEN TO ME IN HEAVEN AND ON EARTH. GO THEREFORE AND MAKE
> DISCIPLES OF ALL THE NATIONS, BAPTIZING THEM IN THE NAME OF THE
> FATHER AND OF THE SON AND OF THE HOLY SPIRIT, TEACHING THEM TO
> OBSERVE ALL THINGS THAT I HAVE COMMANDED YOU; AND LO, I AM WITH
> YOU ALWAYS, EVEN TO THE END OF THE AGE." AMEN.
>
> Matthew 28:18–20

It is an amazing thought that Jesus wants us to be with Him forever. He loves us so much that He was willing to die for us. Jesus believed that sinners like you and me were worth everything that He had to go through. Oh how great is His love for us! Before He left this earth, Jesus entrusted His disciples (and this includes you and me) to take the message of His love for the world to people everywhere. As Christians we've been given the Great Commission: to preach the gospel. There are many different ways of fulfilling this Commission.

Some of us are called to be preachers and we fulfil our calling by preaching His Word. Not all of us are called to be evangelists, but we are all called to let our lights shine. We are all called to serve Him by spreading love and truth in unique and special ways. For you, it might mean living your normal everyday life in a way that glorifies God: sharing your story of what Jesus has done for you with the person on the bus, at work, or on the sports field. The most effective people I know are men who are shining in the area where they work. I know of farmers who have put huge crosses up on their farms so that when the sun goes down the cross lights up.

If you are fearful of sharing your faith, remember that the disciples were also terrified after Jesus went back to Heaven. It was only after they were filled with the Holy Spirit and they received power from on high that they became bold. Jesus promised them: "But you shall receive power when the Holy Spirit has come upon you" (Acts 1:8a). Then they went out and took the world for Jesus. They turned this world upside down. Your life and my life will never be the same because the disciples were faithful to their calling. We can only do God's work through His power. Ask Jesus to fill you with the power of His Holy Spirit.

Prayer

My Father God, I come to You realizing that I can accomplish nothing without the power of Your Holy Spirit working through me. Lord, I pray that You will fill me afresh with Your Spirit. Lord, give me Your power so that I can faithfully obey the command of Jesus, my Saviour, to share the Good News. Amen.

Read 2 Corinthians 5

FOR WE WALK BY FAITH, NOT BY SIGHT.

2 Corinthians 5:7

Over the past year we've looked at the lives of the great men of faith in the Bible. Today I want us to be reminded of some of the faith lessons we have explored together. If you want to be a mighty man of God, you have to walk by faith. It is the road of faith that will lead you to fulfil your destiny and purpose. Every person called by God to accomplish a great task for Him has had an encounter with God.

Abraham, the father of the faith, waited for twenty-five years for God to fulfil His promise to him. He stayed faithful to God. Noah obeyed God's command to build an ark despite the ridicule of those around him. God established His covenant with Noah because of his faith and obedience. One of the greatest lessons to be learned from the life of Joseph is forgiveness. He believed through faith that God could take the things people did to harm him and use them for good. Moses' walk with God began reluctantly, but after his encounter with Him he became a great man of faith. Joshua, Samuel, and Job had different purposes, yet their lives were characterized by obedience and faith in God.

David was chosen by God for his faith and trust. Elijah and Elisha were men who knew what it was to move in the power of God's Spirit. Nehemiah, Jeremiah, and Daniel were men who, because of their belief in God, were used mightily by God to accomplish His purposes in their generations. Jesus chose the most unlikely men to be His disciples. He saw the potential in them that would turn the world upside down. Paul's life was radically interrupted by Jesus. Lastly we looked at our Lord and Saviour, Jesus Christ, God's only begotten Son.

Take some time to think about these men and what God has been saying to you throughout this year. As you go forward into the new year make a covenant with God that you will be a man who walks by faith and not by sight.

Prayer

The Lord says to you: "Wait on the Lord; be of good courage, and He shall strengthen your heart; wait, I say, on the Lord!" (Psalm 27:14). Father God, I come to You in the Name of Jesus, my Saviour. Lord, I choose to step into this new year as a man who will walk by faith and not by sight. Amen.